THE REEDUCATION OF RACE

Stanford Studies in
　　　COMPARATIVE RACE AND ETHNICITY

THE REEDUCATION OF RACE

*Jewishness and the Politics of Antiracism
in Postcolonial Thought*

Sonali Thakkar

STANFORD UNIVERSITY PRESS
Stanford, California

Stanford University Press
Stanford, California

© 2024 by Sonali Thakkar. All rights reserved.

No part of this book may be reproduced or transmitted in any form or by any means, electronic or mechanical, including photocopying and recording, or in any information storage or retrieval system, without the prior written permission of Stanford University Press.

Printed in the United States of America on acid-free, archival-quality paper

Library of Congress Cataloging-in-Publication Data

Names: Thakkar, Sonali, author.
Title: The reeducation of race : Jewishness and the politics of antiracism in postcolonial thought / Sonali Thakkar.
Other titles: Stanford studies in comparative race and ethnicity.
Description: Stanford, California : Stanford University Press, 2024. | Series: Stanford studies in comparative race and ethnicity | Includes bibliographical references and index.
Identifiers: LCCN 2023005177 (print) | LCCN 2023005178 (ebook) | ISBN 9781503636446 (cloth) | ISBN 9781503637337 (paperback) | ISBN 9781503637344 (ebook)
Subjects: LCSH: Race in literature. | Jews in literature. | Literature and race—History—20th century. | Anti-racism—History—20th century. | Holocaust, Jewish (1939–1945)—Influence. | Postcolonialism in literature. | Unesco—Influence.
Classification: LCC PN56.R16 T43 2024 (print) | LCC PN56.R16 (ebook) | DDC 305.892/400904—dc23/eng/20230523
LC record available at https://lccn.loc.gov/2023005177
LC ebook record available at https://lccn.loc.gov/2023005178

Cover design: Jason Anscomb

For Zach

CONTENTS

	Acknowledgments	ix
	Introduction: The Reeducation of Race	1
1	Rupture and Renewal	41
2	The Racial Residuum	64
3	Culture and Conversion	96
4	Reeducation as Repair	137
	Coda: The Waning Consensus	191
	Notes	197
	Bibliography	243
	Index	261

ACKNOWLEDGMENTS

This book was written over many years, in two cities and three institutions, but the most meaningful parts of the process happened in Chicago, and only thanks to the intellectual and moral support of a community of friends. Adrienne Brown, Harris Feinsod, and Nasser Mufti have read more of this project, in more stages and phases, than almost anyone else, and their enthusiasm and acuity have given me the confidence to go on at difficult moments and afforded me the pleasure of finding my ideal readers. Leah Feldman and Rachel Galvin have directed their warmth my way and I am so grateful for their unstinting friendship. Na'ama Rokem, Itamar Francez, and their children Alma and Reed made Chicago feel like home for almost a decade; Na'ama and Itamar have also been tireless interlocutors. Much love to Pete Coviello, Julie Orlemanski, Corey Byrnes, Tristram Wolff, Emily Licht, Andy Ferguson, Daniel Borzutzky, Kim O'Neil, Chris Taylor, Sarah Pierce Taylor, David Simon, and Gerard Passannante for inspiration, all-day hangs, and the joy of their company. Ben McKay welcomed me to Chicago and Kate Broitman helped me make important connections in the city. Other friends enriched my life in Chicago with their camaraderie, especially Alexis Chema, Hoda El Shakry, Edgar Garcia, Adom Getachew, Tim Harrison, Florian Klinger, Liz McCabe, Natacha Nsabimana, Kaneesha Parsard, Justin Steinberg, and SJ Zhang. I'm grateful to Richard Jean So and Andrew Leong for bringing some of us together early on.

The University of Chicago was perhaps the only place where I could have conceived this book, not least because of the Regenstein Library's extraordinary resources; I am grateful to the library's staff. Colleagues in the English Department, including Elaine Hadley, Frances Ferguson, Deborah Nelson,

Sianne Ngai, Leela Gandhi, and Jim Chandler, took a kind interest in this book and offered their institutional savvy. The late Lauren Berlant was singularly welcoming and their generosity over many years taught me so much. The Pozen Center for Human Rights and the Center for the Study of Gender and Sexuality were vibrant and collegial spaces where I found important, sustaining intellectual community. At the Pozen Center, I am especially grateful to Mark Bradley, Tara Zahra, and Ben Laurence; at CSGS, to Linda Zerilli, Leora Auslander, Daisy Delogu, Lucy Pick, and Kristen Schilt. Ingrid Gould in the Provost's Office offered crucial support. It was a joy to learn alongside my students, especially Rebecca Oh, Upasana Dutta, Tim DeMay, Hadji Bakara, Nell Pach, Darrel Chia, and Tristan Bates.

This book was completed in the supportive environment of NYU's English Department, and I'm so grateful to the colleagues and staff who have made me feel welcome and eased the transition. Elizabeth McHenry, Jini Kim Watson, and Crystal Parikh have offered excellent guidance. Many thanks also to John Archer, Toral Gajarawala, Lenora Hanson, Wendy Anne Lee, Sonya Posmentier, and Robert J. C. Young. Alyssa Leál, Mary Mezzano, Lissette Florez, and Jaysen Henderson-Greenbey have patiently answered my many questions.

It was one of the great good fortunes of my life to do my doctoral work at Columbia and learn from Marianne Hirsch, Joseph Slaughter, Brent Edwards, and Andreas Huyssen. Their transformative scholarship and teaching have profoundly shaped my thinking. Even as my project has shifted and changed, I have rediscovered their influence in my work over and over again, each time with great pleasure. That they were also the kindest of mentors is that much luckier for me, and I thank them for sticking with me through my doctoral studies and supporting me well beyond. Marianne Hirsch has poured so much care into me and my work for well over a decade and has taught me so much about building intellectual community. She and Joey have been there since the beginning, and I thank them both with much love.

The kind encouragement and enjoyable distractions friends offered through the years made this long process more bearable and much more fun. I'm grateful to Sherally Munshi, Kate Stanley, Jenny James, Saskia Cornes, Lisa Kerr, Jonah Westermann, Lindsay Caplan, Lauren Hall, and Nathaneal Brotherhood. Ioana Bala and Leslie Barnes have been dear and constant friends for so many years and they have my love and admiration.

ACKNOWLEDGMENTS

The National Endowment for the Humanities supported the crucial year of research leave in which I reconceived this project. Fellowships from the Pierre Elliott Trudeau Foundation, the Social Sciences and Humanities Research Council of Canada, the Mellon Foundation, and the Imgard Coninx Stiftung supported early stages of this work. Staff at the UNESCO archives in Paris facilitated my access to materials and made my time there productive and pleasant. Librarians at the London School of Economics kindly provided me with documents from Morris Ginsberg's papers. The arguments in this book were improved by the thoughtful engagement of audiences at University of Illinois Chicago, Northwestern University, Columbia University, and Illinois State University. The conference "Anticolonialism as Theory" at Berkeley in the final stages of this book helped me write toward my audience, and I'm grateful to Poulomi Saha and Yogita Goyal for creating this space for postcolonial studies, and to Yogita for sage advice. An earlier version of chapter 1 was published as "The Reeducation of Race: From UNESCO's 1950 Statement on Race to the Postcolonial Critique of Plasticity," in *Social Text* 143, vol. 32, no. 2 (2020). I thank Duke University Press for permission to use this material here. I thank Molly Robinson for her early and enthusiastic research assistance; Samriddhi Agrawal and Ryan Healey provided expert assistance in the final stages of manuscript preparation.

It is a pleasure to be publishing this book with Stanford University Press. My editor Dylan Kyung-lim White made the publishing process sane, humane, and meaningful, and Sarah Rodriguez offered kind assistance. Tim Roberts patiently guided the manuscript through production and Barbara Armentrout copyedited it with care. I'm grateful to Kate Wahl for her early encouragement. I could not have asked for more astute, engaged, or generous readers' reports, and I thank the Press's two readers for helping me to better identify this book's story and how to tell it.

My family has supported me through this process in countless ways, stretching all the way back to my own beginnings. My parents, Villoo and Nidhi Thakkar, have offered inexhaustible love, patience, and care. Even when they have not understood the paths my interests have taken, their commitments, aspirations for me, and confidence in my capacities have made it possible for me to write this book. Zubin Thakkar has been the best of brothers and the best of friends. His belief that I could do this, and other things besides, have been an important source of strength. My late uncle Rasesh Thakkar was an inspiration to me; as a child, he showed me what an academic and intellectual life looked like and how exciting it could be. His love and support meant a great deal to me and this book would have meant a lot to him; I wish he were here to see its publication. My family has been expanded and enlivened by my wonderful in-laws and nephews: Tushara Thakkar, Kian and Kaleo Thakkar, Alan Samalin and the late Joan Shulman, Danielle Samalin, Max Fripp, and Xavier and Kai Fripp.

Niloufer Yashi Samalin was born when there was still quite a road ahead of me on this project. Along with all the usual baggage of an expectant mother, the suitcase I took to the hospital contained an article assuring me that, psychoanalytically speaking, birthing a child was in fact an excellent way to facilitate the completion of a book.[1] I think this may be true, for Niloufer has certainly taught me about creation and finitude (not least, the limits of time) and about all the aspects of life that make books important but not exclusively so. But she is so much more than the object within, and my greatest joy during the completion of this project has been watching her write her own story.

Lorel Greene's efforts, intelligence, and care have seen me through so many years and finally to the end of this process. Lorel, I hope you know this book would not exist without you.

It has sometimes been very difficult to find the words to write this book, but it is almost as hard to capture the depth and breadth of my gratitude to Zach Samalin. For more than a decade, Zach has listened to my ideas at every stage and has taught me to trust my intuitions. Our discussions have helped me not only refine my ideas but articulate them in the first place, and the creativity he brings to the work of thinking and teaching helps me remember why I want to do this work. But he has done so much more than this, keeping me and this book going through jobs, moves, crises, pandemics, and parenting with his inexhaustible optimism, belief, and steadiness, and with the material labor of his love. This book is for him.

THE REEDUCATION OF RACE

INTRODUCTION

THE REEDUCATION OF RACE

In a short 1943 communication titled "How to Combat Racial Philosophy" published in the British anthropological journal *Man*, the Czech-Jewish physician Ignaz Zollschan decried anthropology's role in the elevation of Nordic racial superiority from a "philosophy" to a "faith" that in turn had "formed an important part of the ideas which have led to the present world conflict."[1] Individual anthropologists, or those who claimed the name, may have irresponsibly propagated this baleful ideology, but it was now clearly too late—five years into a cataclysmic global race war—for even the most effective and best-willed scientists singly to undo the damage: "Anthropological pronouncements by individual scholars alone are not sufficient to prevent the further growth of this faith; science as a whole must undertake the task."[2]

Zollschan's communiqué—a summary of remarks delivered at a meeting of the Royal Anthropological Institute—appears modestly among a series of such proceedings. Yet it has a certain pathos, for in the mid-1930s, Zollschan had urgently pursued exactly such an effort to impel "science" to speak as one and issue a decisive, wholesale refutation of Aryan racial theories and Nazi race science. In 1934, after the Nazis came to power in Germany, Zollschan left Czechoslovakia for England to carry on what Elazar Barkan calls his "personal campaign to combat Nazi anti-Semitism" as well as to find supporters for his more ambitious plan to launch an "international inquiry into the question of race."[3] Zollschan was not the only one thinking along these lines, and efforts to organize systematic investigations of the race concept as an antidote to Nazi propaganda were pursued by others, including the anthropologist Franz Boas on the other side of the Atlantic.[4] What distinguished Zollschan's initiative, however, is that he routed it not just through professional scientific organizations such as the Royal Anthropological Institute but also through the League of Nations and its International Institute of Intellectual Cooperation (IIIC) in Paris. The IIIC was a direct predecessor of UNESCO, the United Nations Educational, Scientific and Cultural Organization, which on its founding in 1946 absorbed the remnants of the IIIC. Zollschan thus sought sponsorship for his proposed inquiry from an organization whose focus anticipated, in embryonic form, UNESCO's postwar mandate, "that since wars begin in the minds of men, it is in the minds of men that the defences of peace must be constructed."[5]

In his 1943 communication to *Man*, Zollschan's focus was fixed on this postwar moment still to come, and his thoughts were turned to the problem of education. His own efforts of the 1930s had collapsed amidst the outbreak of war in 1939. In issuing his wartime call to action, Zollschan was under no illusions that a scientific reappraisal would alter Germany's pursuit of racial war and extermination. Instead, he was thinking ahead to the yet undefined and unknowable period after war's end, urging his readers to begin preparing a concerted program for the reformation of racial ideologies that he was convinced would be required in war's aftermath. Even the defeat and destruction of Nazi Germany would not guarantee the disappearance of its racial "superstition or pseudo-religion," Zollschan warned his readers, unless its opponents had "prepared in good time" the instruments necessary "to make the peoples concerned desire re-education."[6]

In fact, the early postwar era produced something very much like the program of racial reeducation Zollschan called for in 1943. World War II produced a fundamental shift in modern racial discourse, and in the late 1940s, UNESCO initiated a project on the race question that sought to fulfill the unfinished efforts of the interwar period. Publicly inaugurated in 1950 with UNESCO's epochal Statement on Race, the project's chief purpose was to develop a global antiracist educational campaign anchored by a rigorous scientific interrogation of the race concept. As such, it once again attempted to make "science as a whole" (in Zollschan's words) an instrument of antiracism, now closely allied with the new human rights regime formulated at the UN in the same period. This postwar project of reeducation is the starting point for this book's story.

The 1950 Statement on Race is at the heart of both my story and UNESCO's race project. The statement was crafted by leading figures in the midcentury biological and especially social sciences, including the anthropologists Ashley Montagu and Claude Lévi-Strauss and the sociologist E. Franklin Frazier. UNESCO's ambitions for the statement were grand: the statement was to definitively establish, once and for all, the scientific facts about race and so transform the public's relationship to the idea of race. In UNESCO's vision, the statement would be a powerful instrument for the correction of racial prejudices and the reeducation of the pervasive race thinking that had saturated political life and driven the world to war. While UNESCO certainly did not achieve these aims, the 1950 statement and its 1951 revision, Statement on the Nature of Race and Race Differences, remade the race concept. Over the next decade, UNESCO published a series of supplementary educational booklets by prominent scientists associated with the project, which were designed to further educate a global public about race relations and various elements of the race and culture concepts. Although the project continued beyond the 1950s, these years represented the height of its influence. Alongside these statements and investigations, the project was also ideologically and practically entangled with UNESCO's efforts in third world development during this era, particularly in the field of education. UNESCO's race project was an extraordinary intervention into the making of antiracism and, in my view, the single most important site for the canonization of the liberal antiracism that continues to profoundly shape our racial present.

My central claim in *The Reeducation of Race* is that anticolonial thought and postcolonial literature deeply registered and critically recast the liberal scientific antiracism formulated at UNESCO in the late 1940s and 1950s. I recover the evidence of this engagement by reading seminal anticolonial and postcolonial works—Frantz Fanon's *Black Skin, White Masks* (1952), Aimé Césaire's *Discourse on Colonialism* (1950, rev. ed. 1955), Ama Ata Aidoo's novel *Our Sister Killjoy* (1977), and Caryl Phillips's essays and his novel *The Nature of Blood* (1997)—in contrapuntal dialogue with the rich archive and sprawling intellectual network of UNESCO's race project, which has thus far received no sustained scholarly attention in postcolonial literary studies.

The crux of this engagement emerges from the ambivalence of UNESCO's antiracism. UNESCO's refashioning of the race concept was driven by an antiracist pedagogical imperative: the task was to produce a constitutively antiracist definition of race. This was science in the service of human rights. However, this imperative generated ideological frictions that the 1950 statement sought to address by advancing concepts that could resolve these tensions. Specifically, UNESCO had to somehow reconcile antiracism with the perpetuation of a colonial world order that the United Nations and its member states were in no hurry to dismantle. I argue that these conceptual and political contradictions are not just the race project's context. Instead, the 1950 statement directly sought to manage and ameliorate them by defining race as plastic and changeable. Racial plasticity is a biopolitical and managerial concept at odds with a politics of antiracism that understood race and racism as questions of power and exploitation, embedded in colonial histories and relations. In the statement's conception of race, it was easier to imagine an end to race than an end to racism.

My authors register UNESCO's race project in various ways. In some cases, these engagements are explicit, such as in the 1955 edition of Aimé Césaire's *Discourse on Colonialism*, which addresses UNESCO's race project at a critical juncture in its argument. Indeed, the most significant changes Césaire made between the 1950 and 1955 editions of this essay were in response to public debates about the race project in postwar intellectual culture. In a striking way, then, Césaire was hailed by UNESCO's antiracist pedagogy, even as he responded with what I describe as a counterpedagogical critique of UNESCO's agenda of racial repair. While Césaire's engagement with UNESCO is readily visible in *Discourse on Colonialism*'s footnotes and elsewhere in his writings, its implications have not been robustly remarked, nor have such encounters been emplotted as part of a larger story, as I do here. In other cases, these connections have gone unnoticed and require historical reconstruction and close reading; I reread Frantz Fanon's 1952 *Black Skin, White Masks* in order to demonstrate how closely his work interrogates the ideas of racial plasticity, educability, and natality that were central to UNESCO's renovated race concept.

UNESCO's midcentury remaking of the race concept and anticolonialism's radical antiracist humanisms are historically and conceptually intertwined in ways that expand how we understand anticolonialism's engagement with the institutions of postwar worldmaking. In my telling, there are two antagonistic but overlapping scenes: the new institutions of a liberal global order, where real anguish about the political and spiritual dangers of racism coexisted with the colonial status quo, and insurgent anticolonialisms from below, which identified in the midcentury crisis of race an opportunity to further the fight for colonial self-determination and challenge racial inequality on a global scale. The book connects these scenes by adopting a contrapuntal method. As Edward Said theorizes it in *Culture and Imperialism*, contrapuntal reading describes a postcolonial interpretive method that draws together what might appear to be "experiences that are discrepant, each with its particular agenda and pace of development." For Said, reading contrapuntally entails identifying the elisions, asymmetries, and even suppression that metropolitan or colonial discourse imposes on the reality and representation of the "other setting"—that is, the colonial setting.[7] In turning to contrapuntal reading as a methodological frame for the kind of readings I pursue in this book, I am drawing less on Said's characterization of contrapuntality as a mode of reading that restores to visibility experiences, perspectives, and voices that were "once forcibly excluded" and rather more on his exhortation to seek out the "knotted," "overlapping," and "interconnected" elements of apparently discrepant discourses and experiences.[8] Insofar as the historical connection of postcolonial thought with these postwar institutions is still insufficiently explored in the field of postcolonial studies, this book reads across what are too often still treated as separate scenes.

However, there is more to this story: I triangulate these discourses with the prewar history and postwar afterlife of the Jewish question. UNESCO's race project and the race concept it canonized in the 1950s were constitutively shaped by the Holocaust, as well as by long-standing debates in social scientific thought and Jewish politics about race, difference, and assimilation. Indeed, there are multiple and sometimes competing Jewish questions at stake in the midcentury reeducation of race, and these require some careful mapping.

At the broadest level, Nazism's racial persecution of European Jews was a central element of the postwar crisis of race that compelled UNESCO's race project and drove the ascension of liberal antiracism in the 1940s and 1950s. UNESCO's race project would not have looked the same without this recent history; indeed, to my mind the project is inconceivable apart from it. The catastrophic consequences of European antisemitism functioned as the moral and rhetorical frame for the 1950 statement. An annotated edition of the statement for educators and students by the American anthropologist Ashley Montagu, the drafting committee's rapporteur, opens with Montagu's grave observation that "in the decade just passed more than six million human beings lost their lives because it was alleged they belonged to an inferior race." It was this "barbarism," he explained, that had galvanized "an agency of the United Nations" to convene a group of scientists to "clarify the whole concept of race." Montagu notes that UNESCO's offices were housed in the very building German military had taken as its headquarters during the occupation of Paris, and he movingly reflects that "except only if our deliberations had taken place at Auschwitz or Dachau, there could have been no more fitting environment to impress upon the Committee members the immense significance of their work."[9] Writing in the shadow of Jewish persecution, then, these scientists were fully aware of the urgency of formalizing antiracism as a moral universal.

More specifically, Jewish scientists and activists whose own lives had been deformed by antisemitism or who had addressed questions of Jewish identity and belonging in their work profoundly shaped UNESCO's race project and especially the 1950 Statement on Race. Of the eight social scientists who drafted the statement, three were of Jewish background. These three members of the drafting committee—the anthropologists Ashley Montagu and Claude Lévi-Strauss, and the sociologist Morris Ginsberg—played especially decisive roles in the statement's formulation. They had complicated relationships to their own Jewishness as well as dramatically different intellectual positions on debates in Jewish social science; their identity tells us very little in and of itself about their politics, as is also true for E. Franklin Frazier, the Black American sociologist who chaired the drafting committee. UNESCO's race statement was by no means a politically radical document, and its limitations on the question of colonial racism are very much the focus of this book. Moreover, each of the statement's authors was individually implicated in various projects of colonial ethnography and neocolonial modernization at UNESCO and beyond.[10] Yet for all of this, the statement is nonetheless a document of damaged life, written in the main by authors whose involvement in this antiracist endeavor was shaped by their own experiences as minoritized subjects.

While these individuals' biographies are less important than the concepts I will go on to describe, they help to situate the statement intellectually and historically, and we will encounter these figures again at multiple points throughout the book. The best-known member of the committee from our contemporary perspective, the French anthropologist Claude Lévi-Strauss, would relate in his 1955 work of memoir and ethnography, *Tristes Tropiques*, how he had fled France in 1941 after its capitulation to Germany, recognizing himself "to be potential fodder for the concentration camp."[11] Biographers and critics have noted the relatively minor role that Judaism or Jewish identity appear to have played in Lévi-Strauss's formation, despite the fact that his grandfather, in whose home he was partly raised, was the rabbi of Versailles.[12] Lévi-Strauss himself rather brusquely dispenses with the question when, in *Tristes Tropiques*, he declares that his attitude of unbelief dates to his early childhood and describes his grandfather's home (which was attached to his synagogue) as a place "lacking precisely in the human warmth that was a necessary precondition to its being experienced as sacred," with "worship within the family circle . . . no less arid."[13] Yet as David Damrosch has nicely observed, Lévi-Strauss nonetheless makes Judaism the "frame-tale" for *Tristes Tropiques*: "inverting chronology, [he] uses his flight from Nazi genocide to introduce his earlier transatlantic voyages, when he pursued his ethnographic research in Brazil. . . . Lévi-Strauss thus marks his Jewish background at the opening of his book."[14] Scholars have debated the question of what influence Lévi-Strauss's Jewish background did or did not have on his political commitments or his anthropological work, but it materially shaped the circumstances that led to his involvement with UNESCO's race project; his forced exile in the United States, from which he had only recently returned to France in 1947, brought him into close contact with scholars, including Boas and the French anthropologist Alfred Métraux, who in different ways would contribute to the transatlantic study of race and racism.[15]

Also on the committee was the English sociologist Morris Ginsberg. Born in Lithuania in 1889, he emigrated to England and began his studies at University College London in 1910, despite knowing little English.[16] A professor of sociology at the London School of Economics from 1929 to 1954, he is best known for extending the work of his teacher L. T. Hobhouse. In his 1935 Hobhouse Memorial Trust Lecture, titled "The Unity of Mankind," Ginsberg observed that his mentor's faith in humanity's achievement of self-realization and the self-conscious development of civilization would be sorely tested by "recent events," including "the glorification of race" and "the bitter attacks on the central ideas of humanitarian ethics."[17] The principles he goes on to elaborate in the lecture about the biological and moral unity of mankind echo other popular works of interwar liberalism, such as *We Europeans: A Survey of "Racial" Problems*, co-authored by the biologist and future first director-general of UNESCO Julian Huxley and the ethnologist A. C. Haddon.[18] However, Ginsberg also brought sociological methods to Jewish studies, contributing to the sociological study of antisemitism and founding the *Jewish Journal of Sociology* in 1958; Pierre Birnbaum observes that he had "two parallel careers, one devoted to general sociology, the other to research on Judaism."[19]

Montagu, who did more than anyone else to determine the final text of the 1950 statement, was born Israel Ehrenberg in London in 1905 to working-class Jewish immigrants. He experienced antisemitism as a child in London's East End and as a student at University College London in the 1920s, prompting his name change. He immigrated to America in the late 1920s, and by 1934 he was a doctoral student in the anthropology program at Columbia University under Ruth Benedict and Franz Boas. Antiracism was the focus of Montagu's long and celebrated but often controversial career. His 1942 book *Man's Most Dangerous Myth: The Fallacy of Race* (today in its sixth edition) cemented his reputation as a powerful public voice on race and antiracism. As the drafting committee's rapporteur, animated by a strong vision of the principles UNESCO ought to affirm, Montagu did much to shape some of the most characteristic but also subsequently controversial elements of the 1950 statement, such as its rousing but questionable declaration that "biological studies lend support to the ethic of universal brotherhood."[20] Montagu's efforts on the 1950 statement were both lauded and resented at UNESCO and especially in the broader scientific community, where the resistance to the 1950 statement among some physical anthropologists, biologists, and geneticists compelled UNESCO to publish a revised 1951 statement that represented these perspectives more fully. Montagu's political activism eventually led to the loss of his faculty position at Rutgers University during the McCarthyism of the 1950s, and professionally, he was attacked by "white scholars who wished to 'out' him as a Jew, presumably with the goal of revealing Montagu as a duplicitous activist who cloaked his fight against 'race' and racism in academic rigor."[21] Montagu's biographer Susan Sperling has noted that "it is perhaps ironic that one who fought prejudice so heroically should have felt the need to efface his ethnic identity," and while this may be true, the more interesting point is that Montagu (along with Huxley) was central to putting the category of the "ethnic group" into wide circulation as an alternative concept to race in, for instance, *Man's Most Dangerous Myth*, where he interrogated ethnicity's relevance to Jewishness.[22]

For all that these individuals' biographies were shaped by antisemitism and the Holocaust, they do not on their own tell us much about how either the Nazi genocide or debates about Jewish difference and assimilation inflect the statement or UNESCO's antiracist ethos. While the horrors of Nazi antisemitism rhetorically framed the project, the statement had little to say about Jews beyond averring that, like Catholics, Protestants, and Muslims, they were not a race. Instead, we can identify these connections at the conceptual level, since the concepts the statement advanced in service of its refashioning of race were drawn from early twentieth-century Jewish social science, by which I mean, following Mitchell Hart, "Jewish knowledge about contemporary Jewish [social] conditions."[23]

The chief concept in question is racial plasticity, which was influentially theorized by the German Jewish, later American anthropologist Franz Boas. In the first decade of the twentieth century, Boas famously demonstrated the apparent plasticity of racial form among Jewish, Central European, and Southern European immigrants to the United States. Boas's relationship to his own Jewishness was ambivalent. Antisemitism prompted his decision to emigrate to the United States, where it continued to limit his prospects. While he was a radical assimilationist, with little interest in the preservation of Jewish culture or community, he devoted great effort during the 1910s–1930s to combatting antisemitism and in the 1930s especially was the public face of anti-Nazi activism in the US and transatlantic scientific communities.[24] His manifestly political research on plasticity was in service of these assimilationist positions, yet this work was shaped by the influence of close colleagues like the physician and ethnologist Maurice Fishberg, who sought to preserve Jewish specificity while emphasizing the importance of Jewish assimilability in the diaspora.

As I argue in this book, racial plasticity was the organizing concept of UNESCO's 1950 race statement, and the statement's most profound intervention was to redefine race as plastic. For Boas and others, plasticity was a capacity common to all humankind but was also paradigmatically Jewish. Its installation at the heart of UNESCO's antiracism represents racial plasticity's elevation to the status of an unmarked universal. Despite its formal universalization, plasticity was differentially distributed; not all peoples were equally subject to the imperative to be racially plastic. At the same time, Boas's account of plasticity and UNESCO's antiracism both suggested that some of the racial differences most urgently in need of transformation and amelioration, Blackness in particular, were insufficiently plastic and even resistant to plasticity. Moreover, in UNESCO's discourse, plasticity was indissolubly linked to another quality the statement called "educability." Plasticity thus came to recapitulate enduring patterns of colonial educability in a new register. This was true despite a changing dispensation that made racial reeducation an urgent priority in Europe, which had demonstrated its racial savagery and so figuratively changed places with the native subject. The consequences of this conjuncture are the subject of this book.

The anti- and postcolonial writers I examine critically engaged plasticity's new centrality as a racial norm, as well as the broader project of racial reeducation in which it was embedded. I argue that their common preoccupation with Jewish difference and the history of the Jewish genocide emerges from this encounter, offering us a new frame for theorizing the relationship between Jewishness and postcolonial thought. Important recent literary and cultural scholarship has examined this interface, often with a focus on memory. I shift the focus from memory to race and propose that the concepts central to the new moral economy of liberal antiracism functioned as the very medium for this engagement.

COLONIALISM AND CRISIS

UNESCO's race project must be understood as a response to a midcentury crisis of race. This crisis had two overlapping aspects, both of which were urgently registered at UNESCO in its early years. The crisis was in part epistemological. Most obviously, it took the form of despairing wonderment at how much devastation had been wrought in the name of racial philosophies that scientists, liberals, and some educated laypeople had long confidently decried as myth, error, and pseudoscience. "Looking back now, moderns are horrified at all the blood that was shed for centuries in religious conflicts," noted the American anthropologists Ruth Benedict and Gene Weltfish in a 1943 educational booklet, *The Races of Mankind*. "The twenty-first century may well look back on our generation and be just as horrified. . . . Our era will seem a nightmare from which they have awakened."[25] One of UNESCO's chief tasks was to bring about that awakening. In the words of its constitution, "the great and terrible war which has now ended was a war made possible by the denial of the democratic principles of the dignity, equality and mutual respect of men, and by the propagation, in their place, through ignorance and prejudice, of the doctrine of the inequality of men and races." Only the "unrestricted pursuit of objective truth" and its free and wide dissemination could correct what ignorance and prejudice had wrought.[26]

But there was more at stake than just reeducating the misled masses or debunking concepts that had little scientific currency but much popular purchase, such as the racial categories Aryan and Semite. A tectonic shift was also underway in the very status of race as an object of scientific knowledge production. There was a new sensitization to the place of scientific credos and pursuits that while not going unchallenged, nevertheless had still fallen comfortably within the bounds of legitimate scientific inquiry. Long-standing convictions about the racial determinants of individual intellectual ability, the differential cultural capacities of racial groups, the social and biological harm of race mixing, and the implacable hereditary transmission of racial forms and mentalities were met with heightened public skepticism as well as intensified scrutiny within the scientific establishment by biologists, geneticists, and anthropologists. While the statement sought nothing less than the enlightenment of a global public, it was also a highly controversial attempt to stabilize the race concept at a time when the protocols of scientific investigation into race—who could speak for and about race and what could be said—were in disarray and the very legitimacy of such endeavors was in question. As such, the statement was a project in the making of race's ontology.[27]

This remaking of the race concept can be understood only in the context of the second dimension of that crisis of race, which was political. In the aftermath of World War II, racism was situated for the first time at the center of international political life. At the most general level, there was a widespread sense that race thinking had shattered the old political organization of the world and presented a grave threat to the new one being established in its place, so long as political conflicts continued to be naturalized as racial antagonisms.[28]

As the meaning of race and the morality of racism were challenged with new intensity, so too was the status of race as a technology for the organization and management of social and political relations, including imperial international relations constitutively structured, in Adom Getachew's words, by "unequal integration and racial hierarchy."[29]

The consequences—and contradictions—of these developments were nowhere more apparent than in the colonial question, as race's status as a justification for colonial rule was challenged as never before. With the end of World War II and the birth of the new international institutions of liberal governance, a peculiar double vision set in. In the international setting of the United Nations, the pressure to formally renounce and reject racism was especially strong. At the same time, the UN Charter made generous provision for undisturbed continued imperial domination in Asia, Africa, the Caribbean, and the Pacific, thanks to the UN's trusteeship system and its stringent policy of noninterference in the sovereign affairs of member nation-states. Enthusiasm for the colonial status quo was woven into the organization's fabric, as W. E. B. Du Bois noted in his reflections on the UN's founding, which he described as a "plan for world government designed especially to curb aggression, but also to preserve imperial power and even extend and fortify it."[30] So too was racism, and Du Bois scornfully noted the "twisted contradiction" of Jan Smuts, architect of South African apartheid, standing "before the assembled peoples of the world and plead[ing] for an article on 'human rights' in the United Nations Charter."[31]

Although it would be some years before the ranks of UN member nations swelled with newly sovereign African and Asian nations and longer still till the right of self-determination articulated by these postcolonial states was established in international law, antiracist and anticolonial activists did not wait to make use of these new institutions to further their cause. Instead, they seized on the glaring contradiction between the avowal of human rights, antifascism, and antiracism on the one hand and the perpetuation of imperialism and racism on the other. Such public reckonings, which included Du Bois's and the NAACP's *Appeal to the World* and the Civil Rights Congress's declaration *We Charge Genocide*, depended for their impact on new kinds of political shame about the presence of racism in international life.[32] Shame converged with the calculations of realpolitik, which understood racism in the Western liberal democracies and especially the United States as a vulnerability in an emergent

Cold War context, as the Soviet Union trumpeted its antiracist and anti-imperial bona fides to anticolonial and civil rights movements worldwide.[33] While aspiration, exhaustion, and opportunism all played a role in these shifts, the indictment of racism came to reliably function as a wedge with which to pry open these questions of the global order and its injustice. Importantly, such rhetorical maneuvers also made their way into works I discuss in this book. As A. James Arnold notes of Aimé Césaire's denunciation of racism in *Discourse on Colonialism*, "Césaire understood that in 1950 the forces supporting a colonial empire were not yet sufficiently vulnerable on their own ground.... At the time the efficacious tactical maneuver was to tie colonialism so tightly to racism as to undermine the stronger position by attacking the weaker."[34] While Césaire's text was not in the first instance directed to the UN's General Assembly or the offices of its Human Rights Division, it nonetheless engaged the UN's projects on human rights, race, and racism.

The formal delegitimization of race ran ahead of any willingness actually to relinquish imperial spoils but eventually made the latter position more politically costly. Leaders of anticolonial movements in such places as India were able to press their demands for independence in light of World War II. This was not just because they had contributed to the war effort or because an exhausted Britain did not have the postwar resources to retain its unruliest colonies. It was also because of the political and rhetorical contradiction between Britain's avowed fight against fascism and racism in Europe and the prospect of brutal repression against its brown subjects of empire. This is not to imply that such counterinsurgent brutalities did not take place throughout the British and French empires during the era of decolonization[35] or that the racial hypocrisies and imperial contradictions of the British and French positions were not deeply felt by colonial subjects.[36] But a new political configuration was emerging, and even where it seemed to entail little more than new euphemisms for old arrangements, it was driven in part by the untenability of the old racial order. Whether understood in terms of a new ethos or through the particulars of historically significant struggles at the United Nations, the politics of the early postwar period were as destabilized by the recent race war as the race concept was itself.

My narrative is consonant with this account but advances a specific claim about the status of race in this moment. The intersection of the crisis of race and the conflicts of empire prompted UNESCO's race project. However, in my reading, the remaking of race at midcentury advanced concepts that not only reflected these conflicts but sought to resolve them. In the next two sections, I map the two related concepts, educability and plasticity, that enabled this work.

THE REEDUCATION OF RACE

The reeducation of race has a number of nested meanings. In the postwar milieu, reeducation is most closely associated with Allied efforts at denazification in Germany and the territories it occupied by coercion or consent, as well as with the democratization of fascist political culture in other Axis countries. As Jaimey Fisher notes, in early postwar Germany, the debates about reeducation were so pervasive that it "became a catchall term, a synecdoche for the occupation in general."[37] The singular emphasis on German reeducation flowed from the conviction that democratization was not primarily an institutional project but a spiritual one. "Free elections, democratic constitutions, independent political parties, and local self-government were simply institutional features," notes the historian James Tent in his study about American reeducation efforts in Germany; "they required an inner spirit to give them meaning."[38]

In the postwar milieu, reeducation's significance reached far beyond Germany's borders, and this spiritual sense was uppermost. UNESCO's own founding was an expression of this impetus for reeducation on a global scale. As histories of the organization narrate, UNESCO's most proximate origin was the wartime Conference of Allied Ministers of Education (CAME) in London, which officially began to meet in 1942.[39] Much of the organization's initial focus was on the educational reconstruction that would be required in fascist-occupied countries on the European continent after the war, which concerned not just rebuilding educational infrastructures (schools, higher-education programs, textbook development and publication, libraries, and so on) but also the more ineffable work of "'revictualling . . . the mind' of Europe."[40] As CAME's membership continued to grow, including representatives from the United States, the Soviet Union, and China, there was growing support for a permanent organization that would be global in scope and tied to other international institutions, including the embryonic United Nations.[41] As we will see in chapter 4, UNESCO's project of reeducation entailed both efforts at the material rehabilitation of educational institutions and resources in Europe, as well as an abiding commitment to education as part of a strategy of third world development, and these institutional-infrastructural efforts are crucially connected to the spiritual dimension of UNESCO's work. For now, let me simply stress that reeducation as it was articulated and pursued at UNESCO was oriented to the making of new kinds of subjectivities, and to what I describe in this study as "soul-making," borrowing a term from Gayatri Chakravorty Spivak.[42] In Spivak's account, soul-making describes imperialism's pedagogical project of civilizing savagery into humanity. In the wake of World War II and amidst the political and moral crisis of race, soul-making was now a global project, especially urgently required in Europe, and UNESCO was to be its agent.

However, UNESCO's race project sought to wed this educative and spiritual project to claims about the biological unity of humankind, which racisms of many varieties had rejected and denied. The 1950 statement sought to retain the biological and scientific salience of race, while also conscripting race to do antiracist work. The statement's definition of racial form as plastic subtended these operations, so that the very material nature of race ratified and indeed seemed to require the statement's particular framing of racism and antiracism. The statement drew heavily on the methods and insights of population genetics to make the case for race's fluctuating and malleable character. This field, which consolidated itself in the 1950s, was a product of the modern evolutionary synthesis that combined Darwinian evolutionary theory and Mendelian genetics. In brief, the category of *genetic population*, which the 1950 UNESCO statement expressly suggested be substituted for the term *race* in scientific and popular discourse, afforded an explanation for diversity among groups that stressed the contingent, fluctuating, and changeable quality of these differences over time. Population genetics focuses on the frequency of specific gene alleles in a given population, and variations in the proportional distribution of particular alleles help define and demarcate a population. These frequencies are not permanent but rather change over time due to evolutionary processes such as mutation, natural selection, and genetic drift. As such, the argument goes, populations themselves are relatively contingent and fluctuating. The determination of genetic frequency may ground propositions about the geographical distribution and historical development of a population, but populations, identifiable primarily at the molecular level, have no ontological fixity; they fluctuate as a result of both molecular changes, many of which are the result of random variations such as mutation, as well as historical pressures such as migration and contact, which remake populations through eminently human experiences but in non-deterministic ways.[43] The discourse of population genetics then and now insists that race is only identifiable and meaningful at scales that confound easy recognition by the untutored eye or capture by the taxonomizer's blunt distinctions; race is a molecular-level difference, and even when it is made through human history, this is on a timescale of countless generations that can be only imperfectly reconstructed through expert scientific investigation.

Population genetics at midcentury was held to be constitutively antiracist. It retains much of that luster even today,[44] though important scholarship has demonstrated both the field's midcentury imbrication with the "old" idea of race it supposedly superseded,[45] as well as the manifold political ambiguities of population genetics in the present.[46] Some of the field's most important researchers (and popularizers) were closely involved with the UNESCO statements, including the biologist Julian Huxley, who served as UNESCO's first director-general; the American geneticist L. C. Dunn, who was the rapporteur of the 1951 statement; and the geneticist and evolutionary biologist Theodosius Dobzhansky, who helped to review the first statement and draft the second. These scientists, who in some cases had been active in interwar antifascist and antiracist activism in the scientific community, were seen at UNESCO as natural allies of any antiracist program undertaken with the imprimatur of "science."[47] Population genetics thus played an especially felicitous role in UNESCO's scientific antiracism; the emergent scientific consensus displacing race with population seemed both to impel and to conform to the antiracist ethical imperative organizing UNESCO's discourse.

While this is an important source for the statement's turn to racial plasticity, it is not the only one. The historian of science Sebastián Gil-Riaño has argued that studies of the 1950 statement have overstressed the centrality of population genetics at the expense of attending to its affinities with "southern currents of racial science," which "conceptualized race through the prism of historical and socio-economic processes such as modernization, urbanization, acculturation and assimilation."[48] I am wholly in agreement with Gil-Riaño's call to resituate the UNESCO statements "within a genealogy that encompasses late colonial, post-colonial and Cold War theories of socio-economic development," and chapter 4 pays particular attention to the race project's context and afterlife in third world development discourse.[49] However, it seems to me that the concept of racial plasticity, which Gil-Riaño notes in passing as one of the characteristic emphases of these "southern conceptions of race," spans and draws together both these racial-conceptual registers.[50]

Indeed, these two registers in which the plastic might be articulated—the molecular and the environmental—are closely connected in the 1950 statement. I argue that the hinge for this connection is education and specifically something the statement calls "educability," or the capacity for directed growth, development, and learning. When we look for the statement's formulation of plasticity, we find the term *educability* indissolubly paired with it, so that reeducation is embedded in the very definition of race; in my reading, the statement's key intervention is its declaration that "the one trait which above all others has been at a premium in the evolution of men's mental characters has been educability, plasticity. This is a trait which all human beings possess. It is indeed, a species character of *homo sapiens*."[51] On its face, this is a claim about the mental makeup of human beings. However, the statement's rhetorical presentation, its historical and ideological context, and the genealogy of the concept of racial plasticity all suggest that this is equally a claim about the nature of racial form. I argue that the statement's conception of race, racism, and antiracism alike all depend on this conjoined assertion of "educability, plasticity." Let me explain what I mean.

These sentences appear midway through the statement, in a paragraph rejecting the supposition that inherited genetic differences play any major role in group-level differences of culture and cultural achievement; these differences are rather explained by the "history of the cultural experience" of a people. At its most literal, the statement's affirmation of "educability, plasticity" as the paradigmatic human quality is a claim about the priority of culture over nature in the making of human communities. Metonymically, this assertion also encodes the statement's pedagogical aspirations and its pedagogical wager. This wager was that racism—which had demonstrated an intractability rivaling that ascribed to racial form itself—was changeable and reeducable owing to the essential educability of the human. Confronted with the scientific truth about race, in a rhetorical register foregrounding the moral solidarity of humanity, people could be induced to exert their plastic natures and move beyond the racial ideologies which had miseducated them to apprehend cultural difference as racial and racial difference as unchangeable.

UNESCO's affirmations of human plasticity and racism's reeducability were exhortatory and aspirational. Despite the statement's confident assertion that these were constitutively human qualities, UNESCO's interventions on race in the 1940s and 1950s were haunted by the question, Just how plastic was the human, really? As I show in chapter 1, UNESCO's early discourse was preoccupied with the extent to which the given and the inherited limited the promise of the new, as well as reeducation's potential to reform what already existed. Among these limiting inheritances was race itself, which hardly lost its associations with permanence and intractability. As such, racial plasticity was both a promise and a hedge. Race would change thanks to its inherent mutability, but this process might itself require development and direction—that is, education. This brings us to two questions: First, what is the precise relationship between educability and plasticity, those two terms that the statement curiously described as "one trait"? And second, how does plasticity's own educability or susceptibility to management direct us to the biopolitical dimensions of the concept and so complicate plasticity's conceptual status and political associations in the present?

THE PROMISE OF PLASTICITY

Plasticity is a contemporary keyword. In recent years, scholars in cultural, social scientific, and natural scientific fields of inquiry alike have devoted critical and creative energy to demonstrating the promise of plasticity. This promise lies in plasticity's definition: a material malleability that allows for both the assumption and transformation of form. As such, plasticity describes a capacity for change that resists the fixity and especially determinism of given forms, both human and nonhuman.

In recent work by science studies scholars, feminist and queer theorists, philosophers, thing theorists, anthropologists, and some theorists of literary form, an attunement to plasticity allows us to encounter the world with a refreshed alertness to the unacknowledged capacities for change—and with it, adaptation, repair, responsiveness, and growth—of everything around us.[52] These capacities inhere in the most seemingly inert or stolid aspects of the environment (rocks and metals, for instance) as well as in forms of life, including the human body, whose malleability is well established even if its full biological, political, and ontological implications have yet to be teased out. Assertions and ascriptions of the plastic character of one or another body or thing necessarily invoke related qualities, such as changeability, malleability, moldability, adaptability, and elasticity, all of which help describe that material unfixity that defines the plastic. But alongside these qualities, we find frequent reference to a set of related values, such as resilience, dynamism, and aliveness, that signal and amplify the excitement and even optimism that attaches to plasticity in our time. Plasticity extends the promise that bodies and things may be less fixed than they seem and so simultaneously more susceptible to dynamic change and environmental influence—and thus more capable of resilience and repair—than we may have imagined.

These plastic ontologies are often molecular in scale but their implications are social, for the changeability of bodies and things naturally extends to the social relations in which they are situated. In a world whose unjust political and economic arrangements seem increasingly intractable and unchanging, plasticity promises qualities and capacities we "cannot not want," to use Spivak's phrase.[53] It is compelling to imagine that change is occurring all the time in ways we cannot determine or even always perceive but that nonetheless shape our genes, environment, and affects, especially when human efforts at radical transformation seem often to end in stasis and stagnation. Contemporary critics who engage eagerly with plasticity and its affordances insist that matter does not simply await the ascription of meaning through discursive representation and figuration; it is not "the passive background to social formations" but "an active force at work in the production of culture, identity, and agency."[54] As Catherine Malabou repeatedly remarks in her varied reflections on plasticity, the term's etymology includes the capacity to assume or take on form as well as the capacity to endow form or even annihilate it.[55] Plasticity describes matter's agency, its capacity to do, make, and mean in ways not reducible to metaphor. As a result, there is a distinct tendency to assume a politics of plasticity that flows directly from this malleability and resistance to fixity.

Such a tendency is apparent, for instance, in Malabou's own work on neuroplasticity. In the opening pages of *What Should We Do with Our Brain?*, she explains that she turns to plasticity as a concept because with it she can describe and theorize the brain's simultaneously dynamic, structural, and organizational dimensions. But even as she situates plasticity as a concept that both emerges from and offers something compelling to contemporary neuroscientific discourse, she also finds it to be a material quality of the brain itself. In her account of the brain's "developmental," "modulational," and "reparative" plasticities, it becomes clear that she is asserting its plastic ontology.[56] Correspondingly, her argument about the political horizon of the neuroplastic and its freedoms—"resistance to neuronal ideology is what our brain wants"—depends on this prior assertion of the brain's inherent plasticity.[57] In contrast, I am arguing that the politics of plasticity cannot be read off of or derived directly from the materiality of any of the plastic bodies, objects, and substances that we now seem to find everywhere around us. Rather, the power ascribed to the plastic for the undoing or remaking of social arrangements is itself a political configuration that demands our scrutiny.

In *The Reeducation of Race*, I attempt to do exactly this by attending to the historical entanglement of race and plasticity, two concepts whose contemporary meanings are unthinkable without each other.[58] Race is no footnote to the discourse on plasticity. Indeed, it is in the domain of twentieth-century racial anthropology that we find perhaps the most explicit and robust conscription of plasticity for the remaking of the individual and social body. As I have noted, in the early twentieth century, Boas and his collaborators formulated an instantly controversial and enduringly influential claim about the "plasticity of human races."[59] A German Jewish émigré, Boas settled in the United States in 1887, and his focus eventually expanded from fieldwork in indigenous communities of the Pacific Northwest to America's large cities and their growing population of immigrants, many of them from Eastern and Southern Europe. Enlisted for his anthropological expertise by the United States Immigration Commission, Boas in 1908 began a study of Eastern European Jews (and eventually other Eastern and Southern European migrants) in New York City, especially schoolchildren. Boas's object of study was "racial form": the physical characteristics of a racial group, whose constancy among individual members and invariability over generations together defined the racial type and its permanence. Boas's data, which included measurements of the cephalic index of schoolchildren, instead appeared to demonstrate that racial form could be altered within a single generation by the influence of environment. "We must speak," he concluded, "of a plasticity (as opposed to permanence) of types."[60]

Boas furnished the concept of racial plasticity as part of a sociopolitical intervention into a social problem. The United States Immigration Commission commissioned Boas's study in order to determine whether the growing numbers of migrants to the United States from Central, Eastern, and Southern Europe were socially and racially assimilable in light of the difference in their racial stock from that of US citizens of Western European and Nordic descent. For Boas, the resolution of this social question depended on the character and behavior of the human body, and it was the surprising plasticity of racial form—which demonstrated the unexpected responsiveness and malleability of the raced body to its environment—that promised to secure a solution to the problem of assimilation. In Boas's influential account, the plasticity of matter could not but lead to the remaking of social arrangements. The discovery of racial plasticity promised the assimilability of raced bodies that were apparently more malleable than anyone had imagined, and it demonstrated the assimilative capacities of a society whose environment exerted powerful influence on these responsive bodies.

There are three things to note at this juncture. The first is that the theorization or "discovery" of racial plasticity had a social purpose and even a telos.[61] Plasticity not only promised to solve a social problem but also to function as a technology of inclusion, assimilation, and social management. We see this in the interface between the malleable racial plasticity of immigrant bodies and the dynamic plasticity of a society that could both absorb and remake them with what Boas called its "marvelous powers of amalgamation."[62] The second thing to note is that this brings us squarely back to the question of educability. Boas was circumspect about which aspects of the American environment specifically brought about such rapid and marked changes in racial form: "I find myself unable to give an explanation of the phenomena," he wrote in response to his detractors in 1912. "All I try to do is to prove that certain explanations are impossible."[63] But his insistence that physical plasticity guaranteed the mental plasticity necessary for cultural and political assimilation suggested that it was not only physical or infrastructural aspects of the American environment that were plausibly spurring these changes (climate and air, nutritional changes, housing arrangements) but also the nation's social and institutional life. This was nowhere more so the case than in schools, where Boas conducted his study and where one finds that exemplarily plastic creature, the child.[64] The assertion of plasticity in the context of the social management of race problems and the implication that plasticity itself required management in the form of education, or directed cultivation and development, together suggest the biopolitical dimension of racial plasticity. Crucially, plasticity does not mean infinite malleability but instead malleability within limits. The cultivation and management of plasticity—or what I am describing as the role of education in actualizing, augmenting, and directing the purported plasticity of matter—is one means of determining the shape and expanding the scope of those limits.

It is worth pausing a moment to observe that colonial history frequently prefigures the Boasian logic I have been describing. As I discuss in chapters 2 and 4 through readings of Fanon, Césaire, and Aidoo, colonial and postcolonial subjects did not view racial plasticity as a liberatory promise of change but rather as a recognizable reiteration of a long-standing colonial imperative. Deepika Bahri, writing from the perspective of postcolonial studies, has argued that "colonial investment in racial border patrol based in ideas of deterministic difference was complicated by imperial designs on impressionable, *plastic* body-minds at the level of ideology as well as the micromanagement of the subject's bio-physiology."[65] In other words, it is not enough to disrupt the familiar story of colonial racism premised on irremediable racial difference with a by-now also familiar account of mimicry and hybridity as ambivalently assimilative cultural practices. "The invitation to colonial mimicry," Bahri argues, depended on an "as-yet scientifically unverified but implicit belief in human bioplasticity and aesthetic reformation" and conscripted the colonized's malleable biological being.[66]

The legitimacy of Boas's formulation of racial plasticity as a potential theory of racial form depended on its demonstration as a scientific fact; his work in the first decade of the twentieth century thus constitutes one important moment in the apparent verification of the intuitive investment in human plasticity that Bahri identifies at work in colonial governmentality. What makes the mid-century moment so consequential, however, is that plasticity at this juncture is itself remade: no longer just a strategy of assimilation, plasticity emerges as a principle of antiracism. This brings me to the third thing I want us to note about Boas's intervention. Boas was contending with not one but two social problems. His explicit focus in the 1908–1910 study for the US Immigration Commission was the racial plasticity of the immigrant, but humming away unmistakably in the background here—and moving to the foreground in the 1910s and 1920s—was Boas's concern with the malleability of race prejudice, or racism. "Race antagonism may be considered from two points of view," he observed in his 1921 essay "The Problem of the American Negro." "It may be asked how much truth there is in the assumption of superiority of one race over another. . . . Or the sources of race antagonism, aside from the question of actual race differences, may be subjected to investigation."[67] How much did any scientific insights about race matter if prejudices were intractable and fixed, beyond the reach of modification by newer, better facts? In other words, how plastic was racism? As we will see in chapter 1, this question would similarly trouble the scientists who drafted UNESCO's Statement on Race in late 1949. Boas's answer in 1921 had been that racism was not very plastic at all:

Mankind has travelled a long road from the time when every stranger was an enemy. According to our modern theoretical standards, we maintain that justice should be given to the individual, that it should not be meted out to him as to a representative of his class. And still, how very far removed are we from the realization of this ideal! The natural habit of protecting ourselves against a supposedly hostile foreign group determines our life in great matters as well as in small details, and the life of nations as well as the life of the individual and of the family. For this reason there is no great hope that the negro problem will find even a half-way satisfactory solution in our day.[68]

Boas was writing in the shadow of World War I, which he described as having "called forth" and taken to new heights this "spirit that prevents us from recognizing individuals and compels us to see only representatives of a class endowed with imaginary qualities that we ascribe to the group as a whole."[69] He was also writing in the wake of the tremendous violence and racial reprisals directed at Black WWI veterans and others during the Red Summer of 1919 and beyond, which he did not mention but which lend historical urgency to his framing questions about the intransigence of racism and its insusceptibility to reason. His conclusion, striking in its political pessimism and even defeatism, was that racism is less malleable than race. In a "population that is so deeply saturated with class consciousness as our own," every kind of education was bound to fail, even "the education of the young," in whom it might be hoped racial prejudice had not yet fully calcified. No reeducation of racism, then, at least not on the Negro problem. Instead, Boas proposed that the remaking of racial form was the only plausible strategy for racism's amelioration: "The greatest hope for the immediate future lies in a lessening of the contrast between negroes and whites which will bring about a lessening of class consciousness"—that is, race mixture or miscegenation, deliberately pursued as a strategy of amalgamation and assimilation.[70] In the face of racism's intransigence, race's changeability was both a promise of an escape from race and an imperative that this responsibility be borne by the racialized themselves.

I want to map the consequential implications of this repeating structure I have been describing both in Boas's work as well as in the midcentury remaking of race influenced in no small part by Boas's ideas. First, questions about the fixity and inertness or, conversely, the changeability and responsiveness of matter are always racially situated and implicated. No axis of character or quality is more central to race thinking than that of fixity/changeability, whether in discourses of eugenic perfectibility, racial degeneration, hereditary transmission, climatic influence and adaptation, or racial-social assimilation. Nor are the racial dimensions of these qualities limited to the matter of human flesh, as Mel Chen has shown.[71] Plasticity is a racial quality and quantity; at times it is by its excess and at other times by its absence that the racial body is identified, marked, and managed. For instance, in her reading of (neo)slave narratives, Zakiyyah Iman Jackson has argued that American chattel slavery depended on plasticity, demanding of enslaved Blacks a "seemingly infinite malleability" that precluded the "determinacy or resistance" of form and produced instead "coerced formlessness."[72] In contrast, in my reading of racial plasticity at midcentury—for instance as refracted in Frantz Fanon's work—Blackness is both the target of plasticity's imperative and that which frustrates and resists it, never plastic enough.[73] In both cases, however, we see that plasticity, when read through the history of racial violence, represents not pure potential but rather the way that changeability of form, in Jackson's words, "can be turned against itself by bonds of power."[74]

By the same token, antiracist discourse that relies on the plasticity of racial form as the solution to racism is necessarily a position that has already assumed and naturalized the prevailing terms of race thinking. "Biology is a metaphor for the destiny imposed on the other," observed Albert Memmi.[75] Colonialism justifies itself, he means to suggest, through the imposition of racial taxonomies and hierarchies. But his aphorism might also serve as a rejoinder to the *antiracist* tradition I have been describing, which sought to promulgate plasticity as part of an emancipatory project that nonetheless insisted on the educability of race. Moreover, amidst what at times feels like an interdisciplinary romance with plasticity in our own contemporary critical moment, it is worth holding on to the recognition that plasticity is itself made plastic, put to work for political projects that draw recursively on its power. Plasticity has no inherent meaning, liberatory or otherwise, but it can nonetheless do political work.

Second, the itinerary of racial plasticity, from Boas's early twentieth-century formulations to its midcentury redeployment in the 1950 Statement on Race, has some striking features. It is not news that Boas advanced the concept of racial plasticity, nor has it gone unremarked that UNESCO's race project and its statements on race, particularly the 1950 statement, bore his influence and were shaped by scholars close to him.[76] However, Boas explicitly articulated plasticity as a theory of racial form in the context of a racial (or physical) anthropology.[77] In contrast, the 1950 statement invokes plasticity not in reference to racial form but as a characteristic of mental character, as I have noted. Let us refresh our memory of the exact wording: "The one trait which above all others has been at a premium in the evolution of men's mental characters has been educability, plasticity. This is a trait which all human beings possess. It is indeed, a species character of *homo sapiens*." There is something seemingly counterintuitive about a document that specifically defines race as changeable and that even enshrines plasticity as the exemplary capacity of the species yet withholds mention of racial plasticity per se.

However, this circumvention of racial plasticity and its transposition into a related register tells us a great deal. What occurs here is a transit whereby plasticity is shorn of its explicit relation to race and recast as the universal property of the human: "This is a trait which all human beings possess," the statement reads. Plasticity becomes the deracialized universal that anchors the new racial regime erected in what Eric Porter has aptly called "the first postracial moment."[78] Of course, plasticity does not lose its associations with race nor, rhetorically, is it meant to. A reader unfamiliar with Boas's racial plasticity will still register the metonymy of the statement's assertion of race as changeable and its avowal of the human as plastic. It is this simultaneous silencing and reverberation of plasticity's racial dimension that suggests its utility for a postracial politics. There is compelling textual evidence for my suggestion that plasticity is put to work as a universal norm; as I show in chapter 1 through a close reading of early drafts of the statement, the statement's authors initially intended to make a forceful statement about the fact of human equality. Unable ultimately to commit themselves to such a claim, they replaced equality with "educability, plasticity"—an aspirational equality to come, contingent on the formation and reformation of some human beings.

This brings me to the third implication of plasticity as a strategy for managing both race and racism. Plasticity at midcentury may have emerged as a deracinated universal but the historical and contemporary life of racial plasticity demonstrates that its distribution is uneven in dramatic and consequential ways. Kyla Schuller and Jules Gill-Peterson, who similarly note the differential distribution of "the capacity of corporeal malleability," have observed that "plasticity is equated with potential itself and assigned to whiteness." They are careful to note that this plastic endowment "need not be restricted to groups socially or politically recognized as white" but is rather best defined by the fact that it is "routinely denied to the racialized."[79] However, I would complicate Schuller and Gill-Peterson's account by suggesting that plasticity's racial history is more varied and less stable than an equation with whiteness can capture. As I have noted, and as chapter 2 describes in detail, plasticity was theorized in the early twentieth century through Jewishness, but not in a way that made Jewishness reducible to or synonymous with whiteness. At the same time, the association between Jewishness and plasticity is not essential, exclusive, or fixed; plasticity's ascription is historically variable and politically situated. In an illuminating recent analysis that examines postwar Asian American and transpacific racial formation in an era of environmental degradation and oceanic pollution, Michelle N. Huang has described plasticity as "an Asian American 'racial form.'"[80] The contemporary stereotype of the plastic as an Asian and especially Chinese material solidifies the association between plasticity's material qualities and Asian American ethnicity, so that "without a unique essence, plastic can be read as exhibiting the 'weak ethnicity' attributed to Asian Americans as a race."[81] It is the very weakness of this plastic racial form, Huang argues, that reveals the ambivalence of assimilation: "Plastic is the model minority substance: its superficial pliability and lack of resistance serve as both characteristic and function," even as the "molecular recalcitrance to being digested" demonstrated by the long life of the plastics in our environment "suggests the ultimate failure of any superficial logic of assimilation."[82] When read alongside the historical associations of plasticity with Jewishness that I track in this book, Huang's argument about postwar Asian Americanness helps demonstrate both the variability of plasticity's racial distribution and the constancy of its racial associations. While one or another group may seem to represent or exemplify the racially plastic in a given conjuncture, it remains an assimilatory logic, much as in Boas's early formulation. Moreover, while it seems to promise the changeability of form, this is always malleability within limits; as we will see, the characterization of Jews as paradigmatically plastic produced a series of questions and remainders about how then to conceive of or even acknowledge the specificity and survival of Jewish difference as an identity whose meaning was distributed across the overlapping domains of the cultural, national, religious, ethnic, and sometimes racial registers in liberal antiracist, antisemitic, and Jewish discourses alike.

CONTRIBUTIONS AND CONNECTIONS

This project contributes to scholarly conversations in postcolonial studies, human rights, race and ethnic studies, and Jewish studies/Holocaust studies. Here, I map the book's interventions and trace the cross-cutting connections I see between these fields, which are too often still treated in relative isolation from one another.

The Reeducation of Race speaks first and foremost to postcolonial studies by demonstrating that UNESCO's work on race exerted a consequential but understudied influence on the development of anticolonial thought, shaping the ways that anticolonial and postcolonial theory addressed key moments and concepts in the history of race-making. As such, it is aligned with an impetus in the field to systematically recover the extent to which midcentury anticolonial thinkers deeply engaged the new institutions of the postwar liberal order. As Gary Wilder notes, there has long been a tendency to read the postwar history of decolonization "as a series of dyadic encounters between imperial states and colonized peoples" in which the horizon of struggle was the achievement of a postcolonial nation-state. In this reading, anticolonialism's engagement with an international order was largely limited to the aspiration of joining the "system of formally equivalent nation-states around which the postwar order was organized." This "methodological nationalism," Wilder observes, obscures a fuller recognition of decolonization as "an epochal process of global restructuring that unfolded on a vast political terrain inhabited by diverse actors and agencies."[83] These projects necessarily entailed efforts to make the new institutions of the liberal global order, especially the UN, a site for the articulation and achievement of anticolonial aspirations.

In many existing accounts of these historical entanglements, the emphasis falls around 1960, when a newly independent cohort of postcolonial nation-states set about "refashion[ing] the United Nations as the international forum for decolonization."[84] According to such accounts, only once "decolonization [had] virtually remade the UN, between the late 1950s and mid-1970s," can we justifiably deem the institution a significant site for the pursuit of anticolonial and postcolonial politics.[85] In this historical narrative, the 1960 passage of the Declaration on the Granting of Independence to Colonial Countries and Peoples, which enshrined self-determination as a right, represents a historical inflection point when the United Nations was finally made to reflect the political demands of the decolonizing world.[86] Undoubtedly, the belated inclusion of African, Caribbean, Asian, and Arab peoples means that anticolonial involvement in the UN in the 1940s and early 1950s was often a tale of insurgent efforts and alternative institution building. However, such exclusions make it all the more important to consider indirect cultural influence alongside official institutional history.

By beginning my story around 1950, I demonstrate that such engagements existed all along in places scholars have not yet robustly examined, such as UNESCO, and are visible when we look to cultural production and literary history. This is not a version of what Joseph Slaughter has described as the myth of the "multicultural making of human rights law," in which we retrospectively look back to the documents of the 1940s to find evidence of cultural diversity in the formulation of these texts.[87] Instead, as I have noted, the method is contrapuntal, and the authors I examine have a constitutively critical relationship to UNESCO's race project, even as they are sometimes interpellated as its pedagogical subjects. Exclusion, intervention, and entanglement, then, all describe the dynamics at work. Postcolonial studies is especially attuned to such questions, and important works in the field have assessed how these new institutions mediated anticolonial imaginaries and generated new kinds of cultural politics.[88] Yet while this work has produced fine-grained accounts of the cultural resonance of key human rights concepts, such as personhood and dignity, and has traced the imaginative and intertextual influence of human rights documents from the midcentury to the present, there has been strikingly little sustained attention to UNESCO.[89] UNESCO may be relatively uninteresting to scholars of culture precisely because it is perceived as the kind of bloated bureaucracy where culture goes to die. Indeed, Sarah Brouillette's recent book on UNESCO's enduring efforts to arbitrate literary value in the postwar global literary economy, which is an important exception to the general inattention to UNESCO, highlights how UNESCO's work may be most important for the ideologically and aesthetically constraining role that it has played over time.[90]

In this book, I suggest UNESCO's rich but largely unassessed significance for the historical development of anticolonialism and the contemporary rereading of its archives. There are three points in particular I want to highlight. First, UNESCO is a key domain in which to examine how the international institutions of the postwar liberal order both transformed and retained the problem of colonial educability that has been such a central question for postcolonial literary studies.[91] The midcentury reeducation of race, I argue, entailed a new global distribution of the problem of the native child's plasticity and educability yet also recapitulated familiar colonial patterns in a new register. Second, this book sheds new light on another abiding preoccupation of postcolonial theory: the critique of anthropology and its role in the creation of imperial hierarchies and the legitimation of imperial rule. UNESCO's race project focuses our attention on the historical conjuncture in which anthropology becomes the key discourse in the making of liberal antiracism, improbably resituating a discipline of colonial knowledge production at the antiracist vanguard.[92] This disciplinary reorientation provokes a sustained dialogue between the new anthropology and anticolonial thought, as I show in my readings of Fanon and Césaire, for instance, by demonstrating their critiques of anthropology's midcentury aspiration to anchor a new regime of racial repair.

Third, in focusing on UNESCO and anticolonial thought, this book aims to intervene in questions about racial periodization and the making of liberal antiracism that are more often addressed in an American studies context.[93] Liberal antiracism has not just been a globally influential discourse but has been influentially (though of course not solely) formulated in the precincts of the postwar global institutions. This does not mean that the US racial context is not important. Indeed, concepts formulated in a US context, such as Boas's racial plasticity, with which he sought to manage not just Jewish difference but also that of Black Americans, were internationalized and universalized. What I hope to show in this book is that the relay of these concepts through the new international institutions of the UN meant that anticolonial thinkers—whose conceptions of race and racism were certainly influenced by the United States but hardly determined by it—encountered them in newly inflected forms. Such international transpositions and transmissions suggest the artificiality of a strict division between postcolonial objects and methods and the questions of US race and ethnic studies. Moreover, in light of the centrality of Jewishness and the Jewish question to these debates, they also create an opening to think comparatively across these fields and Jewish studies.

This project intersects with urgent questions in Jewish studies and Holocaust studies in several respects. I aim to contribute to the growing body of work that seeks to establish connections between the Holocaust, colonial history, and postcolonial politics. Race, rather than memory, is my key term, and my questions concern both the "relational" or comparative dimensions of racialization, as well as the periodization of racial regimes.[94] Part of the existing scholarship on postcolonial studies and Jewish studies/Holocaust studies—pursued in particular by historians as well as scholars of comparative genocide—has closely examined the claim that the genocidal logics and techniques practiced against Jews and other minority or stigmatized populations in Europe were in fact developed in the context of colonial genocide and imperial racism, particularly in Africa.[95] Cumulatively, this work makes the case that the Holocaust was not an event sui generis, or without precedent, but rather needs to be understood as part of a longer history of racial and colonial modernity.

Another part of these efforts in which literary and cultural critics have had an especially strong hand focuses on memory. Literary scholars have shown how the representation and commemoration of the Holocaust as an event only emerged alongside the recollection or forgetting of colonial histories. These historical imbrications have been most influentially captured by Michael Rothberg's formulation of "multidirectional memory." Rothberg demonstrates that the postwar formation of Holocaust memory and the decolonization of former European colonies in the same era produced a long under-recognized "history of cross-referencing," as intellectuals and writers who were critically engaged with France's war with Algeria or with the legacies of Atlantic slavery drew comparative historical insight from Jewish experiences during and after the Holocaust in ways that reframed the parameters of group identities and expanded the limits of solidarity.[96] In collective conversation organized around the field of cultural memory studies, other scholars have proposed complementary terms and approaches that contribute to the recovery and theorization of the political and aesthetic entanglement between Holocaust and postcolonial (or, more broadly, global) memory and history.[97] Such historical excavations and literary readings have convincingly demonstrated just how thoroughgoing and also diverse these intersections are, assembling an archive of aesthetically distinct and politically dissensual works that raise questions of complicity, solidarity, and representation from Algeria to the Black Atlantic to the Indian Ocean.[98]

I initially articulated my own interest in these intersecting fields in terms of cultural memory yet became increasingly aware that it was easier for me to engage the question of racism than to analytically stabilize the operative concepts of race at work. While work in memory studies focuses on the shared experience of racial violence and the unfinished reckoning with racism's traumas as the basis for its comparative or multidirectional approach, its central focus has not been on the concepts of race that subtended these experiences. But race itself has a history; as Stuart Hall writes, race, "because it is relational, and not essential, can never be finally fixed, but is subject to the constant process of redefinition and appropriation: to the losing of old meanings, and appropriation and collection and contracting of new ones."[99] As I considered this question, I was led backward to the midcentury period as a key moment in the accrual and divestment of racial meanings and so also in the formation of new racial regimes. Of course, this is also a key period in which early postwar theories about the relationship between antisemitism and imperialism crystallized in the work of thinkers like Hannah Arendt, Césaire, and Fanon, all of whom I discuss in this book. But the analytically incisive connections these thinkers established, I argue, were mediated by the new international institutions. Moreover, by focusing on UNESCO in particular, I show how the formation of what we might read as cultural memory was first and foremost a question about education and educability.

Indeed, memory does not suffice as a lens for this study because—despite everything I have said about the irreducible connection between UNESCO's race project and Nazi antisemitism—the reeducation of race was neither a robust engagement with the Jewish genocide nor a project of Holocaust memory. Remarks such as Montagu's solemn invocation of Auschwitz and Dachau (the latter of which despite imprisoning tens of thousands of Jewish inmates over its twelve-year existence was first a camp for political prisoners), of course do not tell us very much. Important historical scholarship has long argued that the Jewish genocide was neither fully acknowledged nor meaningfully commemorated in the early postwar period, much less that it occasioned a moral outrage that birthed the Universal Declaration of Human Rights (UDHR) and a new era of human rights.[100] Such revisionist histories have had an important corrective and demystifying effect, even as new scholarship has characterized the resulting narrative as a monolithic "myth of silence" itself in need of revision and complication.[101]

What UNESCO's race project demonstrates instead is the extent to which the experience of Nazi antisemitism and exterminatory violence was formative for a postwar politics of race and antiracism, even if this history had not yet consolidated itself as the Holocaust.[102] The race project foregrounded Nazi antisemitism and its catastrophic consequences; it did not seek to commemorate the Holocaust as a discrete event. This relative inchoateness of Holocaust consciousness in the project's framework meant that antisemitism was one element of what the project understood to be the broader and more multifaceted race question. Precisely by looking beyond the Holocaust memory paradigm, we can see how other kinds of questions about Jewishness—its plasticity and particularism, the periodization of antisemitism, the relationship between antisemitism and racism, and the question of who Jews were if not a race—were encysted within the programmatic formation of liberal antiracism at midcentury.

These other questions, in turn, direct us to one of the organizing issues for comparative work today at the intersection of postcolonial studies and Jewish studies, concerning Zionism and the colonization of Palestine. Despite Said's foundational status in postcolonial studies and the centrality of Palestine in his work, scholars have observed that Palestine has not always been taken up in postcolonial theory. At the same time, the settler-colonial status of Israel-Palestine is one reason that the engagement between postcolonial studies and Jewish and Holocaust studies has been deferred or intermittent, even though midcentury thinkers identified these connections early on.[103]

This book's coordinates in the late 1940s and early 1950s coincide with the founding of the Israeli state and the Palestinian Nakba. In addition, its focus on the institutions of the UN, which has been responsible for the management of Palestinian refugee populations since 1948 and a crucial site for Palestinian claims and public victories, suggest potential connections between the race project and this unfolding history.[104] While I address some of these questions in chapter 3 and the book's coda, it is important to explain here at the outset that the versions of Jewishness and the formulations of Jewish difference that proved so central to UNESCO's race project belonged squarely to what Mitchell Hart calls a "Diasporist" rather than "Zionist" strand of Jewish social scientific thought, as I discuss in chapter 2.[105] For Zionists, in contrast, paradigms of Jewish plasticity were a threat to Jewish survival and national integrity.[106]

Indeed, we might say that at UNESCO, a Diasporist conception of Jewishness as plastic quite literally prevailed over competing Zionist mobilizations of Jewishness in the service of combating antisemitism. As I noted in the opening pages of this introduction, Ignaz Zollschan's efforts were one important precursor to UNESCO's 1950 Statement on Race. But Zollschan was also an ardent Zionist who in the 1910s had sought to define Jewishness in an explicitly racial way, and his writings unabashedly called for the colonization of Palestine.[107] At the time when Boas and Zollschan were both engaged in efforts to produce a scientific statement against race on opposite sides of the Atlantic, Boas "viewed Zollschan as too extreme in his racial views to support him," and when the two met in New York, "Boas, who was moving in an anti-essentialist direction, rejected Zollschan because of his overly zealous Jewish nationalism."[108] On the occasion of the 1950 race statement's publication, the anthropologist Alfred Métraux, who was then directing the race project for UNESCO, honored Zollschan as its progenitor, observing that UNESCO had taken up after fifteen years the project Zollschan had sought to initiate with the International Institute of Intellectual Cooperation, but which the IIIC had "let drop in compliance with the policy of capitulation and fear prevailing in those strange times."[109] Yet despite this nod to Zollschan, it was Boas's quite different conception of Jewishness that is installed in the statement itself. This should in no way be taken as a triumphalist claim about the righteous victory of an antiessentialist definition of race. Instead, one argument of this book is that such a conception, despite resisting attempts to mobilize Jewish identity in exclusive terms, could nonetheless function to reinscribe racial inequality between Jews and Blacks, for instance. In the main, it is this story and these connections that this book establishes.

However, as I have noted, questions of Jewish particularism haunted the formulation of racial plasticity. The scientific antiracist discourse that crystallized at UNESCO sought to enshrine an argument about the racial diversity of Jews and followed Boas in deeming Jewishness especially plastic and susceptible to conversion, assimilation, and exogamy. At the same time, it also sought to explain, as a decidedly secondary question and with considerably less unanimity, the persistence of Jews as a people and tried to name the character of this difference. Were Jews, as Julian Huxley and A. C. Haddon suggested, a cultural remnant, held together largely by the prejudices of those around them? Were they simply practitioners of a religion called Judaism, just one religion among others, as the 1950 statement declares? Or were they a race after all, in the newly authoritative sense of a genetic population, as the population geneticist L. C. Dunn (also the rapporteur of the 1951 UNESCO Statement on the Nature of Race and Race Differences) argued in his genetic studies of isolate Jewish populations in Venice?[110] As Nadia Abu El-Haj has shown, such studies in the field of population genetics in the 1950s, directly in the aftermath of the Nazi genocide, were pursued in Israel as part of a project to establish the integrity of the Jewish people as a genetic population and so legitimize the state-building project.[111] These ambiguities suggest how this reeducation of race, for all that it centralized Jewishness, also marginalized it as a kind of remaindered difference that could not, in the end, be readily explained or managed. As Dunn's example suggests, at the edges of the race project, questions continued to lurk about who Jews were and what would become of them. While works associated with UNESCO's race project were circumspect on the question of Palestine, this sense of the perplexing persistence of Jewishness—which for all its assimilability continued to demonstrate its difference—suggests a connection to those operations that produced the

INTRODUCTION   35

figure of the minority that Aamir Mufti, for instance, has traced.[112] I touch on these questions in chapter 3 when I discuss how the redefinition of the race concept affected the fate of culture, another overdetermined term under which the equally overdetermined meanings of Jewishness come to be clustered.

Finally, this book contributes to debates in human rights, which have often paid insufficient attention to race, racism, and antiracism. As I show in chapter 1, the 1950 statement was constitutively a human rights document, even as its drafters jettisoned the key concept of equality that would have most clearly manifested this connection. There has been spirited debate about the recency of human rights as a popular movement and its relative illegibility at midcentury.[113] However, the history of the race statement's production, which saw the UN's Human Rights Division demand that UNESCO produce a constitutively antiracist account of race in the service of human rights, demonstrates the transposition of a human rights imperative to a document whose explicit connection to human rights is muted in its final form and whose historical connection to this discourse has not been centered by human rights scholars. In other words, our own purportedly postracial moment, which UNESCO's statements did much to ideologically advance and discursively formalize, is itself a refraction of a midcentury human rights paradigm.

ORGANIZATION OF THE BOOK

This project has a hub-and-spoke structure, with UNESCO's race project at its center. The book's first chapter accordingly focuses on UNESCO's early postwar efforts to make education the medium for the reconstitution of universal humanity in the aftermath of racial war. Through close readings of archival materials, such as the records of UNESCO's first general conference, I demonstrate that UNESCO's founding discourse was saturated by anxieties about the likely contamination of the new humanist subject by the implacable inheritance of both racial forms and racist miseducation. This tension carried over into the organization's race project, fundamentally determining the character of its antiracist pedagogy. Racial plasticity and educability emerged as the key elements of UNESCO's retooled race concept because they both expressed and provisionally ameliorated the anxiety that neither race nor racism would ever be sufficiently malleable for real human or social transformation.

However, this development was not inevitable. Through reconstruction of early drafts of the 1950 statement, I show that *equality* was initially intended to be the central value of the statement, only to be eventually displaced by *educability* over the course of the drafting process. I draw several conclusions from this striking substitution. The 1950 Statement on Race, I argue, should be resituated as a human rights document. The initial emphasis on equality was explicitly framed as a human rights imperative, owing to the important institutional role the UN's Human Rights Division played in the drafting process. Despite equality's erasure in the finished document, important formal and rhetorical connections to the UDHR are still evident in the statement. At the same time, the eclipse of equality by "plasticity, educability" exposes the statement's ideological investment in managing the pressures generated by anticolonial freedom struggles and insurgent antiracisms. I demonstrate this connection by reading the circumstances of the statement's production in counterpoint to W. E. B. Du Bois's and the NAACP's *Appeal to the World* to show that these were historically related developments, expressive of two very different versions of antiracism in action.

Chapters 2 and 3 each take up a key racial logic that unfurls from the midcentury remaking of race. Chapter 2 examines race's persistent association with epidermal difference in the era of racial plasticity and the tension between the relative plasticity and fixity of Blackness and Jewishness. I ask how one ought to read anticolonial thinkers who discerned that Nazi antisemitism and genocidal persecution in Europe were related to colonial racism yet nonetheless insisted that there was an unbridgeable difference between Jews, who, however persecuted, could lay claim to racial whiteness or at least unmarkedness, and Blacks, who were constricted by a seemingly irreducible epidermal difference. We find such reflections, for instance, in Fanon, whose forceful assertions that the Jew "is a white man" and the Holocaust just another squabble in a long family history I scrutinize at length. These writers grappled with their sense that while Jews and Blacks had both been racialized and subjected to racial violence, some were more properly the subjects of race than others and so were more fully the victims of an oppressive racism.[114] How do we understand Fanon's apparent naturalization of this difference?

I propose that we can read the furious force of Fanon's reflections on Black fixity and Jewish whiteness as a critical engagement with the remaking of race then underway. I read Fanon alongside UNESCO's race project and Franz Boas's early twentieth-century writings on plasticity to make this case. I argue that as race was recast as plastic and its meanings divided across the domains of the genetic population on the one hand and the ethnic group on the other, the redefinition of race also produced what I call the racial residuum: the idea that, when all was said and done, one could not gainsay the racial common sense of "the man on the street," who knew race when he saw it. Fanon perceives how Blackness is rendered residual in this way; at the same time, he engages with what Boas and later UNESCO described as the exemplary plasticity of Jews. His reflections on Jewish whiteness are thus better understood as reflections on Jewish plasticity. At the same time, Fanon is also attuned to Jewish particularism, and the chapter traces the subtle shifts in Fanon's descriptions of Jews and Jewishness across his writings, arguing that for him, Jews have a claim to genealogical continuity and the status of a nation, or people, that the Black diaspora lacks. The chapter thus rehistoricizes Fanon, situating him among these midcentury social scientific debates in order to suggest how this frees us from certain impasses in the reading of his work.

As Fanon's reflections on Jewish plasticity and particularism suggest, there are many terms at stake in light of the historical overdetermination of Jewish difference. In chapter 3, I argue that these debates converge around the question of *culture* and its varied meanings at midcentury and in the present. "In racial thought" through the early twentieth century, observes Nadia Abu El-Haj, "as we all know, there were no clear distinctions between cultural and physical elements, between social and biological heredity.... The size of one's brain, the shape of one's head, for example, all those measurements for which anthropologists became famous, did far more than classify groups. They simultaneously signified and *explained* racial-cultural distinctions."[115] One of the primary operations of the midcentury remaking of the race concept was to try to disaggregate culture from race.[116] Nonetheless, our racial present is characterized by what critics have variously called cultural racism, neo-racism, racism without races, and anthropological racism. What brings about this development in which culture seems like nature? How is the very attempt to separate race from culture implicated? And how does this apparent regression of racial ideology confound the periodizing of race and the view that race is a strictly modern formation?

Chapter 3 takes up several seemingly distinct articulations of these questions, which I show can be productively read in counterpoint. I examine works associated with UNESCO's race project to trace how culture paradoxically took on race's associations with fixity: as race was recast as a plastic difference, culture in some respects appeared not as more but now as less plastic than race. We find in UNESCO's own antiracist idiom not just a diagnosis but also a legitimization of the same philosophy of difference that undergirds the cultural racisms of the late twentieth and early twenty-first centuries. The most pressing question about the genealogy of cultural racism, however, concerns the tension between its "old" and "new" dimensions. In my analysis, I seek to pair a reading of the race-culture nexus as it is both dismantled and refashioned in UNESCO's liberal antiracism with a reading of how postcolonial thought has contended with a postwar cultural racism whose antecedents are the long traditions of European anti-Judaism and Islamophobia. These formations are often treated as cultural, religious, or sometimes national or ethnic antagonisms that nonetheless cannot be explained as racism, since they are not properly modern and neither wholly conform to ideas about the raced biological body nor depend on supposedly modern epistemologies and technologies that make race proper an object of knowledge production.

Literature, I argue, can productively complicate these questions of racial periodization and comparative racialization. I examine Caryl Phillips's 1997 novel *The Nature of Blood* and his related essays from the 1980s through the 2000s. I argue that Phillips's theorization of race shifts from an initial concern with the fixity of epidermal difference to a preoccupation with cultural fidelity and religious conversion. This shift, I suggest, should be understood against the backdrop of cultural racism's increasing centrality as a racial ideology in Britain and Europe over that same period—a development to which Phillips is attuned. I examine Phillips's interest in the unstable periodization of race across the supposed divides of the premodern and the modern and pay particular attention to the figure of conversion as an analogue of racial plasticity and a site for the unmaking or persistence of race. Consequently, I show how Jewishness once again is figured at the juncture of the plastic and the particular in a postcolonial context in which the racial binary of Black/white is complicated by both Jewishness and Islam as differences that unsettle the boundaries of race and religion.

In chapter 4, I examine reeducation as a practice of repair. At UNESCO, there was an anguished sense that the war had degraded global humanity but had especially demonstrated the spiritual and political deficits of European culture. The reeducation of race was a project of global scope, yes, but it appeared to be required nowhere more urgently than in Europe. I argue that this reversal should be understood as a variation and extension of the return to Europe of its own colonial violence that Césaire theorized as a *choc en retour* (return or reverse shock) and Arendt as a boomerang effect. I show that we can find in the writing associated with UNESCO's race project an early description of this same dynamic, understood now as a pedagogical problem with profound political consequences for Europe and the colonial world. In UNESCO's view, the appropriate response to this return was not just soul-making in Europe but a reparative ethos that sought to ameliorate the harms Europe had historically inflicted in the colonies through a new commitment to third world development. These projects of development, technical assistance, and "equalization" threatened to reprise colonial relations, now in a neocolonial register.

In response, we find in the writings of Césaire and the Ghanian writer Ama Ata Aidoo critical counterpedagogies that challenge the developmental dimensions of the reeducation of race and resist repair. In their work, I argue, these critiques are not only staged on the terrain of education, they also emerge specifically through Césaire's and Aidoo's engagement with a postwar liberal antiracism that purports to teach lessons about European antisemitism and the history of the Jewish genocide. In Césaire's consequential engagements with both UNESCO's race project and its development work, we find the most striking and explicit instance of this book's claim that anticolonial and postcolonial thought critically register and recast UNESCO's race project and the versions of antiracism it sought to elevate to the status of liberal common sense. In Aidoo's 1977 novel *Our Sister Killjoy*, meanwhile, her polemical representation of the lures of migration, the threat of deracination, and the dangers of diasporic life in Europe suggests a resemblance between her figure of the killjoy and Arendt's figure of the Jewish pariah: in both cases, the threat of racial shame and the seduction of assimilation and upward mobility are to be resisted in favor of a communal but nonetheless critical solidarity with one's people.

In the coda, I reflect on this book's method and on the significance of the midcentury reeducation of race from the perspective of our present moment, when the liberal antiracist consensus it helped formalize appears to be waning. Amidst the resurgence of right-wing antisemitism and ongoing debates about the definition of antisemitism in the context of Palestinian activism and solidarity movements, I consider the lessons the authors I examine offer—and that they themselves learned—about the connection between antisemitism and racism.

CHAPTER 1

RUPTURE AND RENEWAL

"In the decade just past more than six million human beings lost their lives because it was alleged they belonged to an inferior race," wrote the anthropologist Ashley Montagu in 1951. "The horrible corollary to this barbarism," he continued, "is that it rested on a scientifically untenable premise. On this the scientists of the world are agreed. And through an agency of the United Nations a group of them have gone on record to clarify the whole concept of race."[1]

This group of scientists comprised mostly anthropologists and sociologists, among them Claude Lévi-Strauss, E. Franklin Frazier, Juan Comas, Morris Ginsberg, and Montagu himself. They gathered in Paris in December 1949 at UNESCO's behest to offer their expertise on what UNESCO termed "the race question." Over the course of three days of discussion, they drafted a document whose purpose was to establish authoritatively the scientific facts about what race was and was not. This document circulated for comment among other members of the scientific community who had been active against Nazism or who had liberal and antiracist sympathies, including the geneticists Gunnar Dahlberg, Theodosius Dobzhansky, and L. C. Dunn; the biologist Julian Huxley; and the sociologist Gunnar Myrdal. In its final form, it was published and widely disseminated as UNESCO's 1950 Statement on Race—the first mainstream, global antiracist document.

UNESCO convened these "experts on race problems" as the cornerstone of a project on race that the organization inaugurated in 1948 at the request of the United Nations Commission on Human Rights (UNCHR) and pursued for more than two decades. UNESCO's 1950 statement sought to remake race, but it was just as profoundly an experiment in the making of antiracism, and it was this antiracist ethos that drove the statement's racial science. This framework, however, makes apparent the tension implicit in turning to scientific facts about race—race science, that is—to challenge racism. The initial request to UNESCO for an educational campaign came from the UNCHR at the same time that the commission's drafting committee was formulating the Universal Declaration of Human Rights (UDHR), where "race" would appear at the head of the list of grounds on which it was impermissible to persecute, discriminate against, or deny equality to either individuals or groups. However, the text of the UDHR was agnostic as to race's ontological status and historical meaning. Race's biological naturalness or social constructedness, its scientific validity or vacuity were precisely the questions the authors of the statement were tasked with answering, but in the context of a self-consciously antiracist pedagogical program. This dual mandate produced tensions that are tangible in Montagu's remarks, which appear in the preface to an annotated edition of the statement produced specifically for teachers and students. His somber invocation of the six million dead and his conviction that rethinking race was an imperative task for the repair of the world sit uneasily alongside his peculiar phrasing, which seems to suggest that the murder of six million Jews was somehow more terrible because the theories justifying it were not scientifically sound. Montagu's observation points to the limited way the UNESCO statement understood the political and ideological dimensions of racism. It also indicates that even as the statement sought to mark a decisive break in race's legitimacy as a scientific term, it emphatically preserved race as a domain of scientific knowledge production.

The question of why a scientific statement about race was the preferred idiom for UNESCO's antiracist pedagogy is thus also a question about the periodization of racial imaginaries and racial regimes. It is not unusual to come across references to the 1950 and 1951 statements that describe their publication as the unambiguous end of scientific racism and the beginning of an era of unyielding mainstream consensus about race's intellectual and political illegitimacy. Even far more measured scholarly appraisals of the two statements regularly situate them as marking a break or historical discontinuity. Insofar as they self-consciously repudiated, in an official key and in the name of international scientific authority, racial theories that had wide (though not uncontested) currency as scientific facts, scholars have described the statements as "a palace coup . . . in the citadel of science" and a "revolution in the concept of race" that marked the end of an era of scientific racism inaugurated in the eighteenth century.[2] Scholars have also deemed the statements "a key event in the consolidation of the postwar liberal orthodoxy," identifying in the politics of their production a shift in the construction of race as an object of knowledge, as the social sciences claimed race—or "race," as their constructivism would sometimes have it—to fall within their disciplinary purview in light of its newly affirmed instability as a scientific category.[3] The statements' enduring status as a periodizing break underscores just how ideologically influential they have been, not least in retrospect.[4] Of course, the story is considerably messier than this, and continued contestations over the statement's political implications and scientific validity emphasize the incompleteness of any such historical closure.[5] The statement is no mere historical curiosity, for it canonized a set of claims about race that produced, if not a consensus, then certainly a conjuncture whose force is still felt. The statement's influence endures not only in accounts of race still very much indebted to its terms but also with respect to the versions of antiracism it has helped elevate to the status of the legible and even commonsensical.

Michelle Brattain has observed that the interest and provocation of UNESCO's race statements is that they "acknowledged implicitly that race had once been one thing and now it was another."[6] However, we might more precisely conceive of the 1950 statement as a project that sought not only to effect a historical shift in the definition of race but to enshrine change and transformation as race's very meaning. As I discussed in the introduction, the statement's commitment to this understanding of race as changeable and malleable culminates in its assertion that "the one trait which above all others has been at a premium in the evolution of men's mental characters has been educability, plasticity. This is a trait which all human beings possess. It is indeed, a species character of *homo sapiens*."[7] However, the statement's avowal of plasticity as the principle of racial formation and transformation is driven by an antiracist ethicopolitical aspiration. It is this ethicopolitical or, more properly, pedagogical purpose—and not any paradigmatic shift in the natural sciences—that brings about plasticity's installation as the organizing figure of UNESCO's scientific antiracism.[8]

In this chapter, I focus on UNESCO's founding moment in order to establish the cultural and political matrix out of which plasticity would emerge as both an ethicopolitical horizon and as the very definition of race. This definition's central purpose was to mediate the tensions between likeness and difference and between the given and the changeable. I argue that this problem, writ large, framed UNESCO's conceptualization of education in the early postwar period. UNESCO's race statements, like UNESCO itself, were products of the midcentury perception of a profound disruption of humanity and of the deformation of species life. The preoccupation of UNESCO's first years, I show, was the necessity and the problem of not just reestablishing but making anew, in the aftermath of the human catastrophe of the war, what this time was to be an enduring political and moral constituency: "mankind" or "humanity." This was no mere attempt to revive a pallid figure of the Enlightenment human nor even an effort to tightly suture the new human to the language of human rights that other branches of the UN family were busy formulating then. Rather, UNESCO's project sought to ground the meaning of humanity in species life and to elevate the fact of biological commonness to a governmental principle that would determine the political shape of the postwar world. We see this at work in the recurring appearance of the figure of the child in UNESCO's early discussions about the potential for reeducation in the aftermath of racial violence. I argue that this exemplarily plastic creature, the child, stages the problem that attends UNESCO's antiracist pedagogy: namely, how do the given and the inherited limit the promise of the new? Among those limiting inheritances is race, of course, and the statement's commitment to plasticity is an attempt to challenge popular and scientific convictions about the ineluctable transmission of racial form.

But this was not the only function of the figure of the child, nor was race the only limiting inheritance whose malleability UNESCO worried over. As we will see, the problem of reeducation saturated UNESCO's early postwar institutional discourse. Specifically, UNESCO was concerned with how it might promote the unlearning of racism, which seemed so prevalent and persistent as to thwart all attempts at reeducation. UNESCO conceptualized this problem via the figure of the child, a figure persistently associated with natality. Moreover, natality's implicit tension—between the anticipation of the new, on the one hand, and the circumscription of the new by the old, on the other—was at the heart of UNESCO's conception of reeducation. Both race and racism were thus organized by this tension between the given and the changeable, the inherited and the new, and both, I argue, were subjected to the mandates of education and reeducation. It is for this reason that the statement installs not just plasticity but its twinned quality, "educability," as the defining characteristic of species life.

The implications of this entanglement of plasticity and educability become apparent when we consider the wider political context of the postwar world in which UNESCO formulated its Statement on Race. Even as UNESCO sought to dispel the scientific racism it associated most closely with Nazism, the statement's privileging of plasticity not only accommodated but extended the logics of biopolitical management that had long been integral to colonial racism. The statement thus contends with race in two ways, both troubling. It tries to interrupt racism with the promise that race itself can be transformed and that changes to racial form are not only possible but inevitable. At the same time, it turns away from alternative versions of antiracism that, at the same historical moment, were being offered by anticolonial discourse; in some instances, these confrontations over the colonial ordering of the world transpired within the very institutions of the United Nations.

THE REEDUCATION OF HUMANITY

In a 1942 article for *Harper's Magazine*, Julian Huxley—biologist, eugenicist, antiracist activist, colonial apologist, and statesman, who three years later would become UNESCO's first director-general—declared that "the world's most important fact is not that we are in a war, but that we are in a revolution." He was not speaking of an insurrection against authority, he explained, but about revolution as a radical rupture in mentalities and socialities, or what he termed "a drastic and major change in the ideas and institutions which constitute the framework of human existence."[9] Germany, Japan, and Russia had recognized most fully that "the war is not merely a symptom of the world revolution; it is also one of the agencies for its accomplishment," directing those revolutionary tendencies toward maximal militarization in order to impose their political vision on the world.[10] Paired with this diagnosis, however, was a call to action. Although certain aspects of the revolution were inescapable, the point Huxley sought to impress upon his readers was that "its form and character are not."[11] The revolution had begun long before the start of armed conflict, and it was destined to continue long after its formal conclusion. The task at hand, then, was to give purposive shape to the world being birthed as well as destroyed through the current convulsions. The most urgent matter was determining a new political form for the postwar world, for there would be no going back after the war to "the old social and international system."[12] Huxley's remarks articulate and even embrace what would emerge as a central topos and ethicopolitical preoccupation of the early postwar period—namely, how to seize and cultivate newness from the ruins of the prewar world.

UNESCO, established in 1946 as the first specialized agency of the UN, was one of the institutions of "the new system" that Huxley had promised was "destined to emerge from the transformation of the old."[13] Its mission was to foster international cooperation through the production of knowledge and instill universal values derived from the domains of science, culture, and education. More profoundly, its role was the cultivation of a humanist subjectivity; per UNESCO's constitution, "since wars begin in the minds of men, it is in the minds of men that the defences of peace must be constructed."[14] In UNESCO's view, its work was thus the precondition for the task of remaking the world that confronted the new international organizations. At UNESCO's first general conference in 1946, the French socialist politician and conference president Léon Blum explained that while the United Nations had been created to bring about "the realization of peace between peoples and the achievement of human progress," it was UNESCO that was responsible for "creating the intellectual, moral, and emotional atmosphere upon which the operation of the whole system rests."[15] New political forms would not be sufficient to maintain peace without the mentalities and solidarities to go with them.

UNESCO's role was the (re)creation of humanity as a moral and political constituency with which every member of the human species would identify.[16] Only this would ensure, as one delegate put it, that "humanity [will] avoid bloody catastrophes like the one whose depths we have still to plumb." UNESCO understood this project to require interventions at the psychic and spiritual levels that would modify beliefs, values, and perceptions. "The political organs of the United Nations are engaged in the negative task of preventing acts of aggression," the Indian philosopher Sir Sarvepalli Radhakrishnan reflected. "We are assigned the positive function of building peace in the minds of men through science, education and culture." While education was the means for the cultivation of this new ethicopolitical disposition, it could not be merely remedial. What one delegate called "the intellectual rehabilitation of the human race" was widely deemed insufficient; instead, as another put it, the task was "the re-education of humanity."[17]

The emphasis on reeducation connects UNESCO's early work to the pervasive issues of repairing and remaking the world that were chief preoccupations of the entire UN organization in the postwar moment, at a time when the past was suspended somewhere between ruin and renewability. In a telegram to the delegates at the first general conference, UN Secretary-General Trygve Lie wrote: "While other organs of the United Nations set to the task of repairing material disaster, to build up the ruins, to restore the economic conditions in a devastated world, your Specialised Agency is entrusted with the noble and grave mission of helping to re-construct the educational institutions . . . [and] to re-establish favourable conditions for the spiritual life of the world." While Lie stressed UNESCO's distinctive mission, he also presumed that UNESCO and the UN's other agencies faced a common task—one that entailed the repair, restoration, and reestablishment of what had been devastated and destroyed. But in a particularly poignant dilemma for an organization devoted to the transmission of knowledge and culture, many at UNESCO wondered whether the world undone by the war ought to be recovered. Even as some grieved Nazism as "the complete negation of human dignity and culture," others observed that culture was not Nazism's victim but its source; a representative from Czechoslovakia, noting that a French politician had written to Hitler to warn that a war "would this time wipe out the whole of world culture," exclaimed at this "logical topsy-turvydom," for "how could cultural disintegration be the *result*, since it was the *cause* of the war." UNESCO sought, in Radhakrishnan's words, to build "peace in the minds of men through science, education and culture" but its delegates recognized that each of these domains had been instruments of brutality. While the war had left behind a profound sense of rupture, one of the chief problems taken up at UNESCO's first general conference was how to contend with the many ways in which the past continued to exert a baleful influence on both the present as well as on a possibly calamitous future. "We are afraid of ourselves, we are afraid of the atom bomb, we are afraid of we know not what," said Radhakrishnan. "When we look at the way in which the embittered politicians talk to each other, talk at each other, we sometimes feel that we are in 1939, and not 1946. The play goes on, only the actors change."[18] Continuity was, in many ways, as vexing as rupture. The problem, in sum, was the usability of the old for the creation of the new.

This temporal and logical structure describes precisely the problem and promise of reeducation. And indeed, it was in the realm of debates about education that these dilemmas were most palpable. For if reeducation was necessary for the repair and even remaking of the world, education was also responsible for the conflagration. The chief object lesson here was Nazism, which at UNESCO was framed first and foremost as a consequence of education—or rather, miseducation. At UNESCO's first general conference, delegates described Nazism as a perversion of both educational values and pedagogical practices. The Nicaraguan delegate's pained assertion that "representatives of a great culture and an advanced civilization belonging to the white and yellow races" were responsible for the recent catastrophe registers his distress at culture's seeming susceptibility to barbarism. But he also recognized that civilization is responsible for barbarism:

In a concentration camp in Poland where wholesale cremation was practiced, a little Jewish girl danced, full of confidence and joy, in front of the door of the crematorium. She did not know her fate, but her torturer did. He was a civilised man of the twentieth century, disciplined and educated to burn innocent children to death in a crematorium.[19]

Familiar in its invocation of the victimized and innocent child, the threat here is nonetheless posed by civilization's representative—"a civilized man of the twentieth century"—and especially by the disposition with which he goes about his atrocious task, not in a spirit of wantonness but as the conditioned expression of "discipline." The monstrousness of the transgression, then, lies not only in the torturer's acts but also in the fact of his own deformation. And the latter, the Nicaraguan delegate continued, is "the fault of the teachers, the governing classes and all men responsible for the fate of their country," for his "blind obedience ... is a striking result of the education he had received."[20] By reassigning culpability from the "man" to his teachers and elders and by invoking his youth, the delegate's remarks complicate the ready opposition between adult and child with the more troubling possibility of youthful vitality stunted, misdirected, and miseducated. Education was not just a casualty of the war or the instrument of postwar renewal, it was the medium of transmission for ideologies, chief among them racism, that were the war's very source.[21]

What kind of education, wondered UNESCO's delegates, could counteract and correct these deformations? Some delegates asked whether there might be an unimpeachable pedagogy that could instill a political disposition resistant to tyranny and "totalitarianism," producing instead what a Luxembourgian delegate described as a new "collective mentality" that would make the populace "capable of resisting ill-judged enthusiasm." But it was the values themselves as well as the forms of their transmission that were compromised, other insisted. As such, what was required was the production and generation of newness. UNESCO, Radhakrishnan declared, had to stand "not merely for a new set of adjustments but for a new way of life, a new outlook, a new philosophy which will inspire humanity."[22]

THE NATAL AND THE PLASTIC

The exemplary figure of this discourse was the child, who I will argue represented not only the promise of the new and the natal but also the challenge of reeducation and its limits. While the Nicaraguan delegate invoked the image of a "little Jewish girl danc[ing] ... in front of the door of the crematorium," the specificity of the Jewish child was also readily generalized and dissolved into a generic figure. In the view of UNESCO's delegates, the child was both victim ("the child is the most tragic victim of the last war," said one) and savior, having not yet undergone "the gradual distortion of man from childhood to maturity through the process of his education."[23] Rebekah Sheldon has identified this "slide from the child in need of saving to the child who saves" as the quintessential logic of post-catastrophic history as it struggles to imagine a future, and it was with such a sense of crisis that UNESCO urgently set about putting the child to work.[24] In UNESCO's discourse, the child was figured as a resource with which to renew and revitalize the human. Several delegates were moved to observe that if humanity had been as profoundly warped and miseducated as events indicated, its rehabilitation might need to be measured in generations rather than years. Some imagined nothing less than a generational break on the scale of the species: the task was to "form a new generation, instil in it from childhood the ideals that are its cornerstones," an Iranian delegate argued. "A generation educated in this way will know no other ideals than those of international collaboration."[25] The figure of the child thus represented the continuity of species life in the shadow of total war, as well as the consolation of rupture and discontinuity.

The child's association with newness, however, was matched by its association with the inheritance and reproduction of the given. As Claudia Castañeda has observed, the child's paradigmatic quality is that its form by definition is not fixed or final; what "makes the child so apparently available," she writes, is that it is "not only in the making, but is also malleable—and so can be made."[26] In UNESCO's discourse, the child's salvific function depended on the fact that it had not yet been educated and thus deformed. The task at hand was to make the child a bulwark against the past and its repetition. It was clear, the South African delegate observed, that UNESCO should concentrate on childhood development and particularly on "education in the nursery school stage." Extending the language of UNESCO's Constitution, which affirms that "wars begin in the minds of men," he proposed that "it is in the minds of infants that the defences of peace must be constructed."[27] The greatest challenge to these aspirations was the transmission of the given and the inherited, which threatened to circumscribe the possibility of newness. In other words, the problem of reeducation was bedeviled by the fact that the plasticity of the human and even of the child entails malleability of form within limits.[28]

At stake here is what education studies scholar Natasha Levinson, reading Hannah Arendt, has described as "the paradox of natality . . . in the midst of belatedness."[29] In Arendt's work, natality designates the capacity of human beings to bring newness into the world. In the final lines of *The Origins of Totalitarianism*, Arendt concludes her grim analysis of the horrors of the nineteenth and twentieth centuries with a reflection on the possibility that something new might nonetheless emerge: "Every end in history necessarily contains a new beginning; this beginning is the promise, the only 'message' which the end can ever produce."[30] She does not use the term *natality* in *The Origins of Totalitarianism*, nor does she do much more than hint at how this capacity for new beginnings is related to the human condition of being born, merely writing that "this beginning is guaranteed by each new birth; it is indeed every man."[31]

But in *The Human Condition*, Arendt specifies this capacity for beginnings as natality and makes its relation to the fact of birth more explicit, writing that "the new beginning inherent in birth can make itself felt in the world only because the newcomer possesses the capacity of beginning something anew."[32] Natality thus represents the possibility of a new beginning inaugurated with each new person who enters the world, each new birth.[33]

However, such newness is tempered by the world that precedes and forms us. As Levinson notes, we are "simultaneously heirs to a particular history and new to it."[34] The problem is thus one of preserving newness when it is always belated in relation to a past that has already occurred but whose force is inherited by the present, not least because, in Arendt's words, "the chances that tomorrow will be like yesterday are always overwhelming."[35] Natality risks collapsing into repetition, while its promise is not unmediated newness but rather "*re*action, response, *re*configuration."[36] Arendt declares that "the essence of education is natality," but she also cautions that education, which in her view risks being reduced to no more than received knowledge or political opinion, threatens to curtail and extinguish the child's capacity for newness by molding it to the already existing adult world, and so "strik[ing] from the newcomers' hands their own chance at the new."[37] Education is thus the paradigmatic scene of this natal paradox.[38] We might conceive of natality, I am arguing, as a figure for the possibilities and limits of reeducation's mediation of the inherited, the given, and the already transmitted. As such, the paradox of natality reveals itself to be the very problem of "educability, plasticity."

At UNESCO in 1946, the fearsome inheritance that preoccupied the delegates was the transmission of racism, which threatened to corrupt the new almost from its first appearance. The problem of how to protect the child's difference from what had come before was, more specifically, a question of antiracist education and pedagogy. "There is so much distilled racial and political and communal poison in many of the textbooks of the world that it corrupts the minds and the emotions of the young children at the very beginning of their lives," noted one delegate. In the view of the South African delegate, "fear of the consequences will deter the present generation from making war but only until prejudices and phobias are once more exacerbated to a pitch where passion outweighs reason." How ought one to preempt racism when "race prejudices are implanted at a very tender age"?[39] Behind all of these questions lurked the anxiety that the phobic character of antagonism between groups and the power of prejudice as a passion that overwhelms reason were simply a birthright—so pervasive that it was impossible to distinguish between the given and the learned. Racism as inheritance might inevitably mark the limits of the natal and the plastic.

ANTIRACISM AND THE ACCOMMODATION OF EMPIRE

What emerges is a portrait of the postwar child, to whom is owed an education that may yet separate it from a tainted inheritance and who requires an urgent intervention to redirect and retrain its instincts. This portrait resembles nothing so much as the enduring figure of the "native" child and even the native *as* child in light of the imperial utility of the nineteenth-century theory that ontogeny recapitulates phylogeny. This resonance suggests a line of continuity between the developmental hierarchies and evolutionary gradients of colonial race science and the antiracist pedagogy meant to supplant them. At stake here is what Gayatri Chakravorty Spivak has described as imperialism's practice of "soul-making," which civilizes savages into subjects and engenders the very form of the human.[40] As we will see in chapter 4, part of what makes UNESCO's work on race in the 1940s and 1950s so interesting is that it understood soul-making to be a global project, required most urgently in the heart of Europe itself, where questions about the extent of human educability, stunted development, and regression had come home to roost. In that chapter, I trace the complicated relationship between soul-making in Europe and the perpetuation of colonial empire, but for now, let us focus on how UNESCO could center the problem of racism without addressing its relationship to colonialism.

The question of racism's relationship to colonialism did not make its way into UNESCO's 1946 discussion of the problem of racial reeducation. In fact, UNESCO and the new international framework to which it belonged provided renewed imperial inspiration for some. At the first general conference, a British delegate observed that his delegation "includes representatives of the 63 millions of the Colonial Empire" as well as "some of our most competent colonial experts." Since "the task of my country is to administer vast expanses of the world," he continued, the latter had been invited "with the idea that they would carry away with them a new spirit of objectivity with which to consider the scientific education of the masses and the culture of the peoples to whom they devote their activity."[41] The readiness with which the British delegate could harmonize imperialism and internationalism and the consonance these remarks assume among colonial administration, mass education, and UNESCO's spirit of scientific humanism are telling. They underscore Mark Mazower's argument that rather than looking for the UN's origins in Wilsonianism, we should instead consider the significance of British imperial thought as a foundation for twentieth-century internationalism. "The UN's later embrace of anticolonialism," he observes, "has tended to obscure the awkward fact that like the League [of Nations] it was a product of empire and indeed, at least at the outset, regarded by those with colonies to keep as a more than adequate mechanism for [empire's] defense."[42] And of course there is no small irony in a delegate from South Africa—which would withdraw from UNESCO a few years later on the grounds that a publication of UNESCO's race project criticized apartheid and so interfered in its sovereign affairs—bemoaning the young age at which racism is instilled in children.[43] UNESCO could simultaneously centralize the problem of combating "race prejudice" while leaving largely unchallenged the continued colonial ordering of the world and the global color line.

Yet even in the 1940s, the United Nations was a site of contestation over racism and colonialism. In 1946, when South Africa introduced the Asiatic Land Tenure and Indian Representation Act, a piece of nakedly discriminatory legislation targeting its Indian population, India successfully maneuvered the UN General Assembly into considering its official complaint against South Africa.[44] But such efforts, including thousands of petitions directed at the UNCHR met with stubborn resistance and rejection.[45] In an episode with resonances for our story, in 1947 W. E. B. Du Bois and the NAACP attempted to force the UNCHR to hear their petition on the plight of African Americans in the United States, only to be refused the public hearing they demanded. Much of the fierce debate over the petition took place in the UNCHR's Sub-commission on the Prevention of Discrimination and the Protection of Minorities in late 1947.[46] At the very same time, this same subcommission determined to ask UNESCO to consider "the desirability of initiating and recommending the general adoption of a program of disseminating scientific facts with regard to race," "designed to remove what is commonly known as racial prejudice"—the request that gave rise to UNESCO's race project and the 1950 Statement on Race.[47] How do we understand the United Nations' and UNESCO's desire to think about racism alongside their refusal to reckon with an antiracist politics from below? It would be too simple to conclude that the statement was merely an ideological alibi for their inaction and resistance. Rather, a scientific statement on race functioned as a strategy for managing and ameliorating such conflicts. The statement evaded the problem of racism as a political question produced by power and interests and instead proposed that racism could be overcome because race itself could be overcome thanks to its malleability and potential for change.

At the same time, UNESCO concentrated a considerable portion of its resources in its first years on various development programs that approached the problem of civilizational differences from a managerial and biopolitical standpoint. Although I consider these interventions at length in chapter 4, they deserve some mention here. Léon Blum, reflecting at the first general conference on the organization's proposed program for its first year, noted that "two kinds of achievement are expected from UNESCO; achievements by no means incompatible. On the one hand, precise, methodical and progressive enterprises in a number of essential technical spheres; on the other hand, a general combined action affecting what I may call the spiritual condition of peoples and individuals."[48] The technical and the spiritual were to be combined in a program animated by that spirit of "scientific world humanism," but these dimensions were uneven in their geopolitical distribution. Within UNESCO's first program year, some countries of what would soon come to be called the "third world" were on the receiving end of interventions to establish "a basic minimum of education," which encompassed "hygiene," "improved agricultural methods," "community welfare" and literacy. UNESCO also dispatched field missions to "areas where science and technology are less advanced" and where it was thought contact with scientists would "help to raise the local standard of life."[49]

Julian Huxley, outlining UNESCO's vision for the postwar world, emphasized what he called one of the "fundamental principles of UNESCO's work—equalization." As Huxley outlined it in his vision for UNESCO upon assuming the position of director-general, equalization involves the targeted application of technical strategies to those "parts of the world, where the educational and scientific level is . . . low, not through their own fault or as a result of war, but through the accidents of history and geography."⁵⁰ The goal, Huxley suggests, is not to make—or perhaps not *just* to make—these zones economically productive or to alter their civilizational standing. Rather, this "equalization upwards" is a necessary precondition for the unification of humanity, premised in his view on the possibility "of a world-wide culture" in which it is impossible to participate without the minimal requirement of literacy. But if equalization constitutes the basis for an intellectual, moral, and cultural "world-wide" constituency of humanity, it is also the vehicle for a biopolitical project of "healthy living," "prosperous agriculture," and ecological interdependence that depends upon technological uniformity. The "rational applications of science" are to reach every outpost and hinterland where "undernourishment and disease" flourish, in turn precluding the acquisition of education.⁵¹ As Huxley lays out UNESCO's program, the "rehabilitation" UNESCO will undertake in Europe (soul-making) and the "habilitation" it will establish elsewhere (techniques of modernization) should eventually be integrated, as newly reconstituted souls and newly incorporated global citizens continue their evolutionary progress.

There are meaningful continuities between the nineteenth-century evolutionary theories that inflected imperial discourse about civilizational hierarchies and the postwar development discourse that colonial administrations, postcolonial governments, and experts in the applied social sciences would articulate in terms of modernization. If the watchwords of an earlier era of imperialism were civilizational development and cultural tutelage on the slow path to self-rule, the techno-optimism of such endeavors articulates itself in a different register: that of development and underdevelopment, resource management, and life indexes. Such management of human and environmental capacities is closely connected to the transformation of race into population, as we will see as we turn to the 1950 race statement. In the text of the document and the process of its production, we will track the migration of technical "equalization" into an ethicolegal discourse of "equality," and we will see how the statement's central commitment to "plasticity, educability" operates in a biopolitical register.

FROM EQUALITY TO EDUCABILITY

The statement's conception of race, I have been arguing, depends on treating human educability and biological malleability as being so closely related as to be almost interchangeable. To recall, the statement declares that "the one trait which above all others has been at a premium in the evolution of men's mental characters has been educability, plasticity. This is a trait which all human beings possess. It is indeed, a species character of *homo sapiens*."[52] Here, I track what was ideologically at stake in the crafting of the statement and in the rhetorical decision to offer "educability, plasticity" as "one trait" torn in two and promptly sutured back together.

When the scientists UNESCO had summoned met in Paris in 1949, it was not clear at the outset that their work would culminate in a statement, nor was it obvious what form such a statement should take. Instead, the first item on the agenda was to formulate a definition of race. The sociologist Robert Angell, who had taken over as interim director of the Department of Social Sciences after the sudden death of the Brazilian anthropologist Arthur Ramos, opened the meeting by observing that "Dr. Ramos had believed that the main purpose of the meeting should be to define race itself; he had hoped that the Committee would establish an 'operational' definition of race that would serve as a reference in all discussions of the race problem."[53] However, the statement's authors moved to set aside this question. As the sociologist Morris Ginsberg noted, attempts at such a definition had previously been essayed "with the co-operation of the best talent available: the efforts had invariably proved futile." The African American sociologist E. Franklin Frazier reminded the group that "knowledge about race—and the fallacies concerning it—did not prevent the existence of prejudice," so that "the idea people had about 'race' was of more practical importance than the true meaning of the term."[54] The statement's authors were quick to grasp that the antiracist telos of UNESCO's project would determine the shape of their work.

They were helped in this by a representative from the UN Secretariat's Human Rights Division, Edward Lawson, who was there to observe and remind them of the pedagogical and political import of their efforts. He informed them that "after much consultation," the Human Rights Division had already "come to the conclusion that the concept of a definition of race was scientifically illegitimate, and that there was no way of defining race in any generally acceptable sense." But he encouraged the committee to keep the matter of a definition on its agenda, "if only to arrive at the conclusion that it was not a scientifically illegitimate concept." "It had [also] been decided," in the UN's view, "that what was needed was a clear, concise statement of fact about race which could be disseminated all over the world and which would serve as a basis for eliminating false ideas about race." Lawson asked that the committee should therefore endeavor to provide such a statement, while emphasizing again that "the important point was, not to define race, but to make a clear scientific statement of facts which could not be challenged by anyone in the world."[55] This series of prompts and requests are remarkable and revealing in their sheer incoherence. From a perspective cast under the institutional name of "human rights," the definition of race is "illegitimate," indeed "scientifically" so, and moreover impossible. Let us note, however, that he allows that such a definition may yet emerge, so long as it can be retrofitted for antiracist ends.

In response, the group agreed that the statement should affirm a principle rather than define an object. The one philosopher in the group, Humayun Kabir, noted that definitions were often achieved by negatives, and this was restated so that negation became the inherent character or limit of any possible definition of race: "In trying to work out a definition, the Committee would succeed in showing what race was not, whereas it should try to arrive at a positive conception." "Human equality" quickly emerged as a key term, and Lawson proposed that "the committee might speak of human equality in a positive sense, i.e., issue a statement of fact about it saying that (1) all human beings were equal in the essential functions of human life; (2) that all individual and group differences were superficial and had no scientific significance." The scientists in attendance, particularly Claude Lévi-Strauss, took up this suggestion with enthusiasm and began to imagine a document that would echo the form of the UDHR by opening with a "preamble" to establish the document's political commitments. Specifically, Lévi-Strauss called for a preamble "proclaiming the necessity of separating the norm of equality from the fact of the non-identity of men." In phrasing the matter this way, Lévi-Strauss understood himself to be restating the sociologist Morris Ginsberg's view that "it was essential, in any declaration on the equality of races, to distinguish clearly between the moral law of the universal equality of men and a declaration of equality based on objective facts."[56] In fact, they were speaking of two quite different things, which map precisely onto the terms "educability" and "plasticity."

To see how this is so, let me turn to a draft of the preamble Ginsberg offered for the committee's consideration, comprising four "brief scientific statements" that encapsulated the document's central assertions about the facts of race and a fifth point that established a normative framework for glossing them, which read:

> All human beings of whatever race have always and everywhere shown themselves to be equally able to share in a common life, to understand the nature of mutual service and reciprocity and to respect social obligations and contracts. None of the differences that have been alleged to exist between members of different races, even if they prove well substantiated, have any relevance to problems of social and political organization, moral life and communication between human beings.[57]

In Ginsberg's formulation, the operative term is not species life or even human or biological likeness but the unassailable fact of "common life." Ginsberg's language is markedly more receptive to the possibility that "alleged" racial differences might yet prove more meaningful than the text of the published statement, but this position in fact highlights the normative assertion that drives this paragraph.

In subsequent drafts of the preamble, however, Ginsberg unfolded a second set of considerations about human equality that divided its meaning between the ethical and the empirical:

> We have now to consider the bearing of those considerations on the problem of human equality. It must be asserted with the utmost emphasis that equality as an ethical principle in no way depends on the assertion that human beings are in fact equal in endowment. Nevertheless the characteristics in which groups and individuals differ from one another are often distorted and are used as a basis for questioning the validity of equality in the ethical sense.[58]

While the earlier paragraph emphasizes that racial differences have no ethical relevance to sociality, or "problems of social and political organization," this statement renders "human equality" itself as a "problem" that demands to be read through both ethical norms and actually existing social realities. Equality appears to interrupt the very question of racial difference by insisting on the permanent subordination of racial facts to ethical norms. But its normative force is necessarily aspirational once its meaning is split between that of an "ethical principle" and the empirical matter of equality of "endowment" among human beings.

The significance of this qualification comes into view when we look to the text of the published statement. The sentence "All human beings of whatever race have always and everywhere shown themselves to be equally able to share in a common life" has been modified to read: "All normal human beings are capable of learning to share in a common life."[59] Gone is the principle with which Ginsberg began—that what unites human beings is not the shared fact of their biological life but the existence, "always and everywhere," of a life lived in common and of a world made through the pursuit of quintessentially human activities, regardless of race. Instead, this principle of commonness is now cast as an aspirational horizon which human beings can reach through their capacity for learning. It is this capacity for learning, rather than a principle of equality, that anchors the published statement's vision of what constitutes the representative characteristic of humanity and the social world humans build with one another. This capacity for learning is the "educability" that the statement affirms as the distinguishing quality of the human species. By replacing equality with educability, the statement makes the promise of a common life contingent on the formation and reformation, the education and reeducation of some human beings.

This remaking concerns not just the moral and social but also the biological life of populations, and it is for this reason that educability and plasticity are conjoined and described as a single trait. To see how this is so requires examining what I suggested was Lévi-Strauss's quite different understanding of how equality was at stake in the statement. For Lévi-Strauss, "the necessity of separating the norm of equality from the fact of the non-identity of men" concerned the "need to explain to men why they are not identical." The non-identity Lévi-Strauss had in mind was not the singular difference of the individual, or Ginsberg's problem of differential endowment, but rather visible differences or "physical non-identity" between groups. The problem, in his view, was how to reconcile the fact of racial difference as an embodied and perceptible matter of racial form with the fact of human likeness in which he grounded the "norm of equality." For the statement to be persuasive and pedagogically meaningful, it had to explain the physical non-identity of groups in a fashion that would allow it to be "dissociated in men's minds from the psychological and physiological elements of 'temperament.'"[60]

The substantive issue to which Lévi-Strauss was pointing was the necessity of unmaking a concept of race premised on the idea that inner qualities reflect or mutually constitute outer ones and that discernable differences in bodies express differences of intellect, morality, character, psychology, emotional aptitude, or spiritual condition. Rhetorically, he argued, accomplishing this aim required "a definition of race from the physical and biological points of view." This might seem to represent a surprising turn in the proceedings, in light of the committee's decision to set aside the work of defining race. In Lévi-Strauss's opinion, however, "all the experts could agree that genetics had so far provided the only sound definition of race."[61] Let us recall here that Lawson, the UN Human Rights Division's representative, allowed for the possibility that an authoritative definition of race might yet present itself—but a definition that would harmonize with the human rights imperatives of the statement's production. In decisively recasting race in the terms of population genetics, the statement's authors understood themselves to be articulating just such a definition. The question is why a genetic definition of race proved so hospitable to the statement's pedagogical aims and its version of antiracism.

The statement makes three key claims about the genetic character of race: First, differences among groups are the result of "evolutionary factors of differentiation such as isolation, the drift and random fixation of . . . genes," as well as hybridization and natural selection. Second, as a result, "the species *homo sapiens* is made up of a number of populations, each one of which differs from the others in the frequency of one or more genes," even as the vast majority of each person's genetic constitution is "common to all human beings regardless of the population to which they belong." And third, the only meaningful definition and use of the word *race* is as a designation of "a group or population characterized by some concentrations, relative as to frequency and distribution, of hereditary particles (genes) or physical characters, which appear, fluctuate, and often disappear in the course of time."[62] As such, the statement explains, this legitimate meaning of the term *race* is to be strictly distinguished from its casual and incorrect use to describe other kinds of differences that are better described as matters of culture or ethnicity.

The statement's institutional and discursive indebtedness to the UN's human rights paradigm has not been centered in the scholarship on UNESCO's race project. Certainly, the progressively diminished meaning of equality that I have tracked over the statement's drafts has helped to obscure these connections. The statement's definition of race affirms the principle that "all individual and group differences were superficial and had no scientific significance," which Lawson had proposed as one prong of the statement's hoped-for assertion of human equality.[63] While the statement's authors reduce one articulation of equality—the idea that all human beings have shown themselves equally able to share in a common life—to mere equality of opportunity[64] and replace it with the concept of educability, the emphasis on a common genetic constitution allows the statement to reframe equality as biological sameness. "Scientists have reached general agreement in recognizing that mankind is one: that all men belong to the same species, *homo sapiens*," reads the first line of the published statement.[65] Donna Haraway has observed that by beginning with "scientists" and ending with a Latin taxonomical term, this sentence establishes the statement's scientific authority, leveraged here for a political claim that "mankind is one."[66] But this sentence also oscillates between the Latin nomenclature of science, which asserts the species sameness of *Homo sapiens*, and the ethicopolitical idiom activated by the term *mankind*—also the very last word of the entire statement.[67] The colon separating *mankind* and *Homo sapiens* manifests grammatically the project—and problem—of reconciling these two idioms and their *competing* authority.[68] This ambivalence about the source of the statement's legitimacy is the rhetorical trace of the human rights imperatives that drove the project.

In the statement's narrative, race, or genetic population, emerges as a result of genetic differentiation that is contingent, nonteleological, and in an ongoing state of flux—it is plastic, that is. In keeping with UNESCO's liberal antiracism, the genetic definition of race as changeable, fluctuating, and plastic deindexed qualities of interiority and human worth from the perceptible, embodied differences so often taken to constitute the substance of race. As such, the statement's seminal intervention was to make the changeability and impermanence of race the explanation for its meaninglessness. But if this interpretation was novel and radical, it was and remains politically vacuous. In making the case that "all individual and group differences were superficial and had no scientific significance," the statement sidesteps the question of whether these differences might nonetheless have political significance. The notion that races are plastic promises that all difference is subject to change over time and that the problem of grasping the meaning of any particular difference is tempered by the fact that it, too, shall pass. Or, as Lévi-Strauss put it during the drafting of the statement, race has "a purely historical, wholly relative and extremely fluid value, since the concentration of genes never reache[s] a point of density and permanence sufficient to make the resulting character unchangeable and non-reversible."[69] Finding the possibility of freedom in the plasticity of race depends on treating the mere fact of genetic change as itself liberatory.

The authors of the statement understood themselves to be making no specific claims about how changes among populations would come about or what they would produce. But while they emphasized such factors as natural selection and genetic drift, they also noted that genetic populations emerged from and shifted through changing patterns of what they called "geographic and/or cultural isolation." That is, even as they observed that "national, religious, geographic, linguistic and cultural groups do not necessarily coincide with racial groups," they acknowledged that genetic populations are in part made through cultural and social practices.[70] This matters not just because it hints at the fault lines in the statement's strenuous attempt to oppose race and culture—a topic I take up in later chapters—but also because it raises questions about the ways in which population-level differences are identified and managed. The statement noted that populations of "varying stability and degree of differentiation ... have been classified in different ways for different purposes."[71] But how do such differences come to be understood as targets of intervention or preservation? How are particular populations or racial groups descriptively stabilized at any given moment, and what are the politics of such attempts to define and describe these differences? The statement did not offer adequate answers to these questions. The problem with the statement's position was therefore not just its apolitical celebration of biological change for its own sake but its unwillingness to consider the political and biopolitical dimensions of the genetic population.[72]

Here, it is worth considering the statement's position on what kinds of differences were not just scientifically legible but descriptively and perceptively meaningful at that historical juncture. "Now what has the scientist to say about the groups of mankind which may be recognized at the present time?" it asked.⁷³ Even as the statement stressed race's plasticity and genetic flux, it also retained and decisively reaffirmed the familiar taxonomic categories of physical anthropology and its "three major divisions" of "present-day mankind": the Negroid, the Mongoloid, and the Caucasoid.⁷⁴ Confronted with this triad of unequally marked and asymmetrically situated racial groups amidst postwar confrontations over the global color line, we must ask, To whom is this promise of racial plasticity being extended? The next chapter sets out to answer this question. As we will see, educability is racialized, while racial plasticity is subject to the mandates of reeducation. I return to this racial taxonomy and its production of what I call a racial residuum via an engagement with the work of Frantz Fanon. Blackness, I argue, emerges as intractable and resistant to plasticity's imperatives. But what we will also find, as we reconstruct the prehistory of the concept of racial plasticity in the work of the anthropologist Franz Boas and his contemporaries, is that not only are Jews figured as exemplarily plastic but also that the very concept of plasticity installed at the heart of UNESCO's version of antiracism is theorized through an account of Jewish racial origins and racial form.

CHAPTER 2

THE RACIAL RESIDUUM

Shortly after the October 2018 massacre at the Tree of Life synagogue in Pittsburgh, Pennsylvania, which occurred only days after another armed white supremacist tried to enter a Black church before shooting two African Americans at a Kroger supermarket in Jeffersontown, Kentucky, I noted several people posting to social media the following passage from Frantz Fanon's 1952 *Black Skin, White Masks*:

At first glance it might seem strange [*étonnant*] that the attitude of the anti-Semite can be equated [*s'apparente*] with that of the negrophobe. It was my philosophy teacher from the Antilles who reminded me one day: "When you hear someone insulting the Jews, pay attention; he is talking about you." And I believed at the time he was universally right, meaning that I was responsible in my body and soul for the fate reserved for my brother. Since then, I have understood that what he meant quite simply was that the anti-Semite is inevitably [*est forcément* (is necessarily)] a negrophobe.[1]

Here and elsewhere in his writings, Fanon suggests a politically appealing historical affinity between Blacks and Jews. Such solidarity flows from a shared experience of racial violence—the Jew, he writes, is his "brother in misfortune"—and from Fanon's humanist universalism, which prompts him to describe antisemitism as a violation of the rights of man.[2] For Fanon's readers, including those who turned to this passage after the racial violence in Pittsburgh and Jeffersontown, these lines are an opening to consider how antisemitism and anti-Blackness (what Fanon calls Negrophobia) are related formations, despite the asymmetry of Black and Jewish relations to whiteness.

As such, critics have eagerly cited and reiterated this passage. For instance, Paul Gilroy offers it as the epigraph to the introduction of *Against Race: Imagining Political Culture beyond the Color Line*.[3] Fanon's sentiments resonate powerfully with that work's commitment to imagining cosmopolitan solidarities that relinquish an identification with race. But rather remarkably, Gilroy does not address the many other passages in *Black Skin, White Masks* that suggest a much more vexed relationship for Fanon between Jewishness and Blackness and between antisemitism and anti-Black racism.[4] There is a desire, and not just on Gilroy's part, to highlight and even valorize this dimension of Fanon's thinking over and against other aspects of his reflections on Jewishness that are more challenging. Specifically, I have in mind Fanon's assertion that the Jew "is a white man" and his caustic observation that the persecution and even genocide of the Jews "are just minor episodes in the family history" (*ce sont là petites histoires familiales*), as well as the binary opposition he appears to establish when he writes that "the black man represents the biological danger; the Jew, the intellectual danger."[5] However, Gilroy is hardly the only theorist to highlight one dimension of Fanon's reflections on Jewishness while glossing over other aspects that are not so readily reconciled to the reading in question. Recent Afro-pessimist scholarship has sought to recruit Fanon in service of arguments about the impossibility of Black ontology and has selectively taken up his remarks on antisemitism and Jewishness, producing striking misreadings.[6] These are instances of what Henry Louis Gates Jr. long ago described as a critical pattern of "successive appropriations" of Fanon, which he noted are of "unfailing symptomatic interest." In response to this tendency, Gates called for a rehistoricization of Fanon's *Black Skin, White Masks*, which he argued would begin by situating it in respect to key works from the period, including Jean-Paul Sartre's *Reflections on the Jewish Question*. The quality in Fanon that Gates identified, of being "wide open to interpretation," has certainly inflected the wildly divergent readings of Fanon's remarks on Jews, Jewishness, and the recent Jewish genocide, which occupy a prominent place in Fanon's first book, as well as appearing more sporadically in his later writings.[7] His own positions are at times in tension, if not seemingly in contradiction with one another, and have been variously applauded and deplored by critics. But the point here is also that these critical readings press Fanon into service on behalf of very different, even incompatible, positions about the plausibility and payoffs of comparative or relational readings of Blackness and Jewishness.

In this chapter, I propose that some of Fanon's most vexing remarks on Jewishness can be productively resituated and reread in the context of what I show is his engagement with the midcentury remaking of the race concept. Jean-Paul Sartre is certainly an important and explicit interlocutor in *Black Skin, White Masks*, though I argue against the critical consensus that Fanon's ideas about Jewishness are largely derived from and dovetail with Sartre's. Instead, I suggest that we can historicize Fanon's reflections by reading him alongside less expected texts and contexts, including documents from UNESCO's race project, which circulated widely in the period, as well as the work of the anthropologist and anti-Nazi activist Franz Boas. Historicizing and contextualizing Fanon in this way allows us to explain and reconcile some of the disparate tendencies in his theorization of Jewishness. This reading suggests that Fanon's sometimes ardent and sometimes skeptical reflections on Black and Jewish solidarity were mediated by increasingly important and institutionalized discourses of liberal antiracism. It also allows us to consider his reflections on Blackness as an engagement with the changing, though in many ways also intractable regimes of race and racial meaning in the midcentury period in which he is writing, rather than as atemporal, ontological claims about Blackness, as some critics have recently been inclined to read them.

This is a story about the contestation among competing genres of antiracism. We are used to thinking of Fanon as a trenchant critic of metropolitan and colonial racism but he also critically scrutinized antiracist discourse and the ideological implications of the increasingly frequent appeals to antiracism in postwar political culture.[8] This chapter asks us to consider Fanon's thought in the context of interwar and early postwar efforts to redescribe and redefine race in general and Jewish racial difference in particular as they were formulated in the service of antiracist politics and pedagogies. As Alastair Bonnett has observed, antiracism has not received the same kind of scholarly treatment as race and racism. While it may be discussed in terms of policy and practice or prescribed as a politics, its discursive and historical complexity and the differences among various articulations and visions of antiracism are understudied.[9] Indeed, part of what I am arguing was at stake for anticolonial thinkers at midcentury was how to engage with liberal versions of antiracist discourse that were then moving to the mainstream, as antiracism became a project of global scope and new urgency.

My account of Fanon's overlapping engagements with UNESCO and with Jewishness traces two arcs in his thinking. The first two sections of the chapter make the case for Fanon's engagement with ideas of racial plasticity and specifically the plasticity of Jewishness. As we saw at the end of the previous chapter, the 1950 Statement on Race hedged its arguments about racial plasticity by conceding that while "human races can be and have been differently classified by different anthropologists . . . at the present time most anthropologists agree on classifying the greater part of the present-day mankind into three major divisions as follows: (a) the Mongoloid division; (b) the Negroid division; and (c) the Caucasoid division."[10] In making this concession, the authors sought to reconcile the claim that race was plastic with a competing and seemingly commonsense understanding of race as physical difference. While the authors were at pains to emphasize that physical differences had no ethical or evaluative significance and were only the epiphenomenal expression of differences whose material substrate (genes) elude sensory perceptions, they had to somehow account for differences in racial form that might be meaningless and mute but whose facticity could not be denied. By arguing that the term *race* should be jettisoned in favor of *genetic population*, yet nonetheless retaining physical anthropology's racial categories and purchase, the statement's authors paradoxically underscored the notion that physical differences were the expression of major differences among groups. Moreover, in reaffirming these divisions, they deepened the sense that race was self-evidently recognizable. That is, they recast physical difference as a kind of racial residuum firmly attached to the body. At the same time, they promised that "the biological processes which the classifier has here embalmed, as it were, are dynamic, not static. These divisions were not the same in the past as they are at present, and there is every reason to believe that they will change in the future."[11] The language here is revealing. The fixity of racial classification is deadening. Worse, it is an embalming, preserving something that has already expired, allowing it to outlive what should be its ongoing transformation. That transformation is not decomposition but dynamic change, or plasticity. Even as the statement makes its uneasy compromise with racial taxonomies, it tries to insist that race is in motion and not static, that it is dynamic and not dead. This attempt to put race in motion as a way out of the impasses of racial fixity is the ideological essence of plasticity. I argue that *Black Skin, White Masks* reflects on this simultaneous reinscription of racial fixity and promise of change to come, and I situate Fanon's reflections on Jewishness in light of his critical engagement with racial plasticity.

The chapter's second argument is that Fanon is equally preoccupied with the idea that Jewishness has a special claim to genealogical and historical continuity. As I show through close readings of *Black Skin, White Masks* and careful comparison of this text with Fanon's later writings, there is in his work an emphatic and increasingly pointed contrast between Jews, who have the status of a nation or people, and the Black diaspora, which in Fanon's view lacks this patrimony and can imagine it only through a formation such as *négritude*. Fanon resists the Boasian imperative to be racially plastic and resents the gap between Black intractability and Jewish plasticity—a gap made more pronounced owing to the way Jewish plasticity takes on a normative dimension. At the same time, much more so than Boas, Fanon recognizes the political significance of Jewish specificity and he recognizes the genocidal dimensions of Nazism's attack on Jewish difference. As I discuss in the chapter's conclusion, Fanon's reflections on Jewishness in fact seem to anticipate some of the recent insights of genocide scholars who have theorized genocide as natal alienation.

THE RACIAL RESIDUUM

Let us pick up our story in the 1950 statement's aftermath. A year after the 1950 Statement on Race, UNESCO published a revised statement, the 1951 Statement on the Nature of Race and Race Differences. This one was supposed to be the sober second thought, when biologists and geneticists would tamp down some of the more exuberant claims of the original. The geneticist L. C. Dunn, who led the drafting committee, wrote a preamble in which he remarks:

We were careful to avoid dogmatic definitions of race, since, as a product of evolutionary factors, it is a dynamic rather than a static concept. We were equally careful to avoid saying that, because races were all variable and many of them graded into each other, therefore races did not exist. The physical anthropologists and the man in the street both know that races exist; the former, from the scientifically recognizable and measurable congeries of traits which he uses in classifying the varieties of man; the latter from the immediate evidence of his senses when he sees an African, a European, an Asiatic and an American Indian together.¹²

Dunn offers reassurances about race's changeable character while also ratifying physical anthropology's continued claim on racial knowledge production. But the final word goes to the man on the street, who, anyway, knows what he knows about the facticity of race on the basis of a racial common sense derived from the inarguable evidence of his senses. This is an instance of what Irene Tucker has called "the moment of racial sight"—that is, "modern race's quality of immediacy and self-evidence," so that despite everything we know about race's nonnatural and contingent character, it continues to make itself known in the register of the visual "with an instantaneousness that feels precritical."¹³

Black Skin, White Masks, published in 1952, is a key text for capturing the continued authority of this racial common sense organized by visuality. In its famous fifth chapter, "The Lived Experience of the Black," Fanon vividly describes the psychic violence of the white gaze and the force with which its racial interpellation compels him to experience his body as saturated wholly by his color—as an object that both overwhelms him and from which he is alienated. That episode turns on Fanon's repeated narration of being seen and identified as Black, and it is so iconic that the phrase "Look! A Negro!" (which appears repeatedly in that chapter) is enough to invoke it. Nicole Fleetwood has dubbed it "the Fanonian moment," calling it "the inaugural moment for writings on black visual culture."¹⁴ Its condensation into a "moment," recognizable at a glance, as it were, tells us something both about its theoretical force but also its temporal and epistemological structure—that is, we know race when we see it.

Yet we can replot this moment within a different temporality—one characterized by beginnings that don't properly begin and by the circumscription of the new by the old. Here, I read "The Lived Experience of the Black" as a meditation on the failed promise of natality for the Black subject and a reflection on the imperatives of racial educability and the limits of racial plasticity. The chapter opens with Fanon's hymn to natality: "I came into this world anxious to uncover the meaning of things, my soul desirous to be at the origin of the world." But directly prefacing this avowal, and thus his entrance into the world, appear the phrases of racial (mis)recognition—"'Dirty nigger!'" (*Sale nègre!*) or simply "'Look! A Negro!'" (*Tiens, un nègre!*)—that make such a claim to newness or originality impossible.[15] The significance of these racial epithets is not just that they interpellate the Black subject or that they signify the weight of his racial visibility and the violence of the white gaze but that they anticipate and precede him.

As such, we can situate this episode in terms of the relationship between natality and plasticity that I mapped in chapter 1. Natality, in Hannah Arendt's formulation, is the promise of a new beginning inaugurated with each new person who enters the world, each new birth. Each of us has the opportunity to have a hand in remaking the world because we are shaped but not indelibly fixed by what has come before. In Fanon's narrative, however, the fixity of Blackness snatches away this natal promise. He mourns it throughout the chapter, as when he notes "I would have liked to enter our world young and sleek, a world we could build together."[16] This being impossible, he narrates his arrival a second time, now as a story of fixity that ironizes newness:

I arrive slowly in the world; sudden emergences are no longer my habit. I crawl along. The white gaze, the only valid one, is already dissecting me. I am *fixed* [*Je suis fixé*]. Once their microtomes are sharpened, the Whites objectively cut sections of my reality. I have been betrayed. I sense, I see in this white gaze that it's the arrival not of a new man, but of a new type of man, a new species [*genre*]. A Negro, in fact![17]

Fanon here describes as lived experience what Natasha Levinson, retooling Arendt, calls "the paradox of natality… in the midst of belatedness."[18] While natality for Arendt designates the human capacity to bring newness into the world, this possibility of newness is tempered by the world that precedes and forms us, and so newness always threatens to be circumscribed and stifled by the force of the inherited and the given. As I discussed in chapter 1, this natal paradox haunted UNESCO's discussions about the malleability of the human, of the child, and of race and racism alike. Indeed, the project of reeducating race is structured by this problem, for it is bedeviled by the question, Just how plastic is the human, really? And just how malleable and reeducable is racism, in fact?

Fanon's response is to show how the fixity of Blackness and the stubborn persistence of a racial common sense that falls back on race's supposed self-evidence cannot be reconciled with the promise of the new human that is meant, this time, to be properly universal. The first line of the original 1950 statement ushers in just this man: "Scientists have reached general agreement in recognizing that mankind is one: that all men belong to the same species, *homo sapiens*."[19] But the statement's classification of the "major divisions" of mankind suggests that some divisions—some genres of the human—are so significant that the unity of mankind must be interrupted to make note of them. Fanon describes precisely that quality of racial intractability that the statement both reinscribes and promises will eventually be dislodged through the mobilization of plasticity. Whereas UNESCO's universalizing antiracism looks to create humanity as a constituency by insisting on species sameness, Fanon reminds us ironically that we are marking the arrival not of a new man or universal humanity, but of a type. For the Black subject, there is no escaping the strictures of racial taxonomy, he suggests. Instead, speciation prevails, and the Black body is made an object of study, subjected this time not to the calipers that measure the cephalic index but to the microtomes that produce samples for the molecular gaze, as a new racial regime both retains old taxonomies and recasts race as genetic population.

But Fanon also points to the way that plasticity works upon Blackness in a colonial context, demanding its reformation and assimilation. He describes how Blackness is both simultaneously intractable and subjected to demands for transformation, caustically invoking experiments with racial form, such as a so-called "denegrification serum," as well as "lactification," his term for interracial sexuality as a means of racial-social transformation and mobility.[20] As such, he registers how Blackness is cast as simultaneously resistant to plasticity and that which demands to be made plastic, so that it can be improved and assimilated. In my reading, he responds critically to this midcentury racial discourse and its production of the racial residuum: the intractable racial difference that is both plasticity's remainder and its project.

Sandwiched between Fanon's iconic description of the moment of racial sight and the passage I discuss above, we find his extended reflection on the racial (un)detectability of Jews:

The Jewishness of the Jew, however, can go unnoticed [*le Juif peut être ignoré dans sa juiverie*]. He is not integrally what he is. We can but hope and wait. His acts and behavior are the determining factor. He is a white man, and apart from some debatable features, he can pass undetected. He belongs to the race that has never practiced cannibalism. What a strange idea, to eat one's father! Serves them right, they shouldn't be black. Of course the Jews have been tormented—what am I saying? They have been hunted, exterminated, and cremated, but these are just minor episodes in the family history [*ce sont là petites histoires familiales*]. The Jew is not liked as soon as he has been detected. But with me things take on a *new* face. I'm not given a second chance. I am overdetermined from the outside. I am a slave not to the "idea" others have of me, but to my appearance.[21]

This passage seems ripe to be read as an extension of his powerful insights about racial sight and epidermal difference in this same chapter. The tendency in the scholarly literature has been to read this passage in one or some mixture of the following ways: first, that Fanon makes an important point about the asymmetry of Black and Jewish relations to whiteness, even if he puts it more caustically and less carefully than we might like; second, that this is a crude comparison and an instance of competitive suffering; and, third, that Fanon is simply echoing some of Jean-Paul Sartre's formulations in *Reflections on the Jewish Question* and *Black Orpheus*.[22]

Yet how might Fanon's engagement with the question of racial plasticity allow us to reframe his remarks on Jewishness and his characterization of the Holocaust as a family quarrel? While Fanon declares that the Jew "is a white man," his more insistent emphasis in this passage is not about racial whiteness but racial undetectability, or rather, undecidability. As I will unfold, Fanon's comparison between Jewishness and Blackness is not reducible simply to an ontological contrast of white and Black. Rather, the operative difference here is better understood in terms of the emplotment of Jewishness and Blackness along an axis of changeability and fixity—that is, as a problem of plasticity. To see how this is so entails a consideration of Jewish difference and its characterizations at this historical juncture.

"WHITE HUMANITY," JEWISH PLASTICITY

The Statement on Race was the most prominent example of scientific antiracism, but it was the culmination of a larger effort on the part of scientists in the interwar and postwar periods to leverage their disciplinary knowledge for the purposes of critiquing racism and especially Nazism. The goal was to dismantle and debunk "racial myths" for the general public. Among the racial myths most urgently in need of correction, particularly once the Nazis had come to power in Germany in 1933, were those asserting the Jews' incorrigible status as a race apart and their inherently unassimilable nature. To refute this characterization, popularizing works of interwar and early postwar scientific antiracism—such as Julian Huxley and A. C. Haddon's *We Europeans: A Survey of "Racial" Problems* (1936), Ashley Montagu's *Man's Most Dangerous Myth: The Fallacy of Race* (1942), and Juan Comas's volume for UNESCO, *Racial Myths* (1951)—offered alternative accounts of Jewish origins and the nature of Jewish difference. They held in common that Jews were not a race but rather a mixed-race population with a demonstrated capacity for racial and cultural assimilation. As I describe in what follows, this account of Jewishness was first advanced by a number of both Jewish and non-Jewish social scientists, who had in common a conviction that such a theory could be mobilized against antisemitism. Among them was Franz Boas, whose concept of racial plasticity dovetailed with this account of the mixed-race origins and varied racial development of Jews. Boas would go on to rehearse and extend these arguments about Jews in his prolific interwar activism against Nazism. Later, in the postwar milieu, the Boasian concept of plasticity—now given a genetic and population-level (rather than primarily environmental) interpretation—determined the antiracist discourse of UNESCO's 1950 Statement on Race, as I established in the introduction. In what follows, I read the work of Boas and other social scientists he influenced or was in dialogue with in order to show how assertions about the exemplary racial and cultural assimilability of Jews were the context out of which racial plasticity emerged. Such a reading demonstrates that plasticity is theorized through Jewishness. But if Jews are paradigmatically plastic, a comparative reading of Boas's reflections on Blackness from the same period reveals that Blackness, in contrast, resists the imperatives of plasticity and its assimilative politics.

It is a notable quality of the Statement on Race that it was occasioned by the Jewish genocide but makes only cursory mention of Jews. But this is not so surprising when we recall that the statement sought definitively to establish what race was, while the broader scientific antiracist discourse to which it belonged was intent on demonstrating that Jews were not a race. Indeed, the statement's sole mention of Jews appears in its discussion of the many kinds of differences—"national, religious, geographic, linguistic, or cultural"—that are habitually but incorrectly described as racial in character:

> Obviously Americans are not a race, nor are Englishmen, nor Frenchmen, nor any

other national group. Catholics, Protestants, Moslems, and Jews are not races, nor are groups who speak English or any other language thereby definable as a race; people who live in Iceland or England or India are not races; nor are people who are culturally Turkish or Chinese or the like thereby describable as races.

National, religious, geographic, linguistic and cultural groups do not necessarily coincide with racial groups: and the cultural traits of such groups have no demonstrated genetic connexion with racial traits.[23]

The statement refuted the racialization of Jews by declaring them one religious group among others. The aptness of such a characterization, which treats Jewishness as a confessional difference that can be identified as "Judaism," is itself a contested question that has vexed Jewish and non-Jewish thinkers in modernity. As various critics have argued, Jewishness is not reducible to religion; Judaism, Daniel Boyarin has argued, is not a Jewish term. The effects (and often intentions) of such designations are instead regulatory. For Boyarin, among others, the Christian invention of Judaism is part of Christianity's self-consolidation in opposition to a "dark double," thus "transforming Jews from a People to an *Ekklesia*."[24] But although the recasting of Jews as the practitioners of Judaism was, until relatively recently, a strategy of external management and manufacture, in modernity, the designation of Judaism as religious practice has also been essential to Western European Jews' emancipation and assimilation, producing the category of the religious minority and the view that one's Jewishness could be a private matter, a religious persuasion with little bearing on one's conduct or progress through the public sphere.[25] Of course, racial antisemitism rejected the view that Jews were distinguished merely by religious difference that could be quarantined to the private sphere and neutralized. Gil Anidjar has observed that "in keeping with the racial discourse that had been elaborated by the nineteenth century, the Nazis thoroughly racialized and detheologized the Jew."[26] One strategy for correcting "the myth of the Jewish race," accordingly, was to reestablish—or rather, establish for the first time, since this had never yet been fully secured—Jewishness as religious persuasion. This is precisely how the Statement on Race approached the issue.

But behind the statement's seemingly simple formulation lay a more complicated discursive and conceptual operation. To decisively undo the idea that Jews were a race, it was not enough to assert the religious nature of Jewry. It was also necessary to dismantle or at least resignify the category of the Semites—a category that works against the oppositional relationship between Jewishness as race and Jewishness as religion, depending as it does on the mutual imbrication of the two.[27] The historian Maurice Olender has noted that "vague and incendiary as these terms [Aryan and Semite] were, they continued in widespread use until 1945 and the collapse of Nazism."[28] But the debunking of these concepts in the public discourse did not occur on its own or all at once in the postwar period. It depended on popularizing antiracist works, issued from positions of scientific and social scientific authority, to disseminate the notion that the racial taxonomy of Aryan and Semite was already discredited in the scholarly circles from which it had sprung. For instance, Julian Huxley and A. C. Haddon adopted this approach in their 1936 *We Europeans: A Survey of "Racial" Problems*, an important precursor to the Statement on Race and one of the best-known works of interwar scientific antiracism. Offering a capsule narrative of the development of the concepts Aryan and Semite, they schooled the reader in what they called "the trap of the linguistic fallacy which caught the nineteenth-century 'Aryan' philologists," when what had hitherto been—and in their view remained—a correct and defensible argument about language groups was extended into a theory of race.[29] Huxley and Haddon stressed the role of the philologist F. Max Müller, to whom they attribute this fatal idea but whose chief importance to their account was that he had issued a retraction, writing in 1888 that "Aryas [*sic*] are those who speak Aryan languages, whatever their colour, whatever their blood. In calling them Aryas we predicate nothing of them except that the grammar of their language is Aryan."[30] In Huxley and Haddon's telling, the myth of the Aryan and Semitic races was an accident of history, the consequence of a wrong turn in philology that, through error and opportunism, had contaminated science and politics. In a refrain that runs through these midcentury works of antiracist demystification, Huxley and Haddon insist that "the term 'Semite,' like the term 'Aryan,' should not therefore strictly speaking be employed save as a linguistic and cultural description."[31]

If there was no Semitic race then, racially speaking, who were the Jews? The position among those eager to debunk the idea of a Jewish race was that Jews were of mixed racial descent. The intellectual historian Amos Morris-Reich has reconstructed the origin and circulation of this theory in ethnographic circles, attributing it to the (non-Jewish) Austrian anthropologist Felix von Luschan, who championed it in the 1890s.[32] Von Luschan sought to discredit antisemitic ideologies of the era that insisted on the racial intractability of Jews and the permanence of the Jewish type. Among those who reiterated and extended this idea in the early twentieth century were Jewish social scientists of what Mitchell Hart has termed a "Diasporist" persuasion, who produced theories about Jewry that promoted assimilation, while remaining "committed to the idea of a viable collective Jewish life in the Diaspora," as well as radical assimilationists such as Boas.[33] This theory was also taken up and put to work in ways counter to von Luschan's intentions and was by no means as decisive a refutation of antisemitism as von Luschan and those he influenced hoped. Morris-Reich points out that, perhaps predictably, Nazi race theorists such as Hans F. K. Günther were quick to turn the argument around: the problem with Jews was not that they were an unchanging race apart, as some antisemites argued, but that they were irredeemably mongrel and a threat to the purity of other nations and races.[34] Nor was this theory warmly received by those Jewish social scientists who were ideologically invested in assertions of the homogeneous origins and racial distinctiveness of Jews.[35] The point, then, is that the emergence and embrace of this theory was not historically inevitable. Its articulation was politically implicated and ideologically contested, even as it proved central to the Boasian antiracist discourse I am tracing.

In the postwar period, however, this view of the mixed-race character of the Jewish people was vigorously advanced and enshrined. It appears without fail, for instance, in UNESCO's antiracist educational materials. In his 1951 book *Racial Myths*, Juan Comas (also the author of a Spanish-language text *¿Existe una raza judía?*) observes that Jews had been a mixed people since antiquity and in their migrations had always "interbred with the aborigines."[36] "Thus despite the view usually held," Comas explains, "the Jewish people is racially heterogeneous; its constant migrations and its relations—voluntary or otherwise—with the widest variety of nations and peoples have brought about such a degree of crossbreeding that *the so-called people of Israel can produce examples of traits typical of every people*."[37] And in his 1960 UNESCO booklet *The Jewish People: A Biological History*, the anthropologist Harry L. Shapiro, a student of Boas's, advanced at length the argument that the Jews had always been a mixed people: "The [ancient] Israelites were not isolated genetically from the rest of the population. In fact, the evidence is beyond question that the early Israelites were freely mingling with their neighbours who were in most cases closely related to them by language, culture, and racial origin. From this we are obliged to conclude that biologically they had absorbed elements from the surrounding people and that they approximated the prevailing type."[38] "They were," he concludes, "a kind of synthesis of the population elements living there at that time."[39] The elevation of this argument about the diversity of Jews to a consensus view and a kind of racial common sense was of course impelled by the knowledge of just how devastating the consequences of racial antisemitism had been. But it was also constitutively linked to other elements of the antiracist thesis that were central to this discourse, including the idea that all peoples were the product of mixture and that "there are no pure human races."[40]

It is against the backdrop of these accounts of the racial diversity of Jews that we should read the assertions about Jewish whiteness that also figured in this discourse. At a 1934 lecture titled "Aryan and Semite: With Particular Reference to Nazi Racial Dogmas," featuring the physician and ethnologist Maurice Fishberg and his colleague and friend Franz Boas, Fishberg dismissed the titular distinction as a "perennial . . . controversy" whose central terms had already been discredited.[41] Jews, he averred, like the "Nordic, Alpine or Mediterranean," belonged to "white humanity."[42] Fishberg's statement appears to affirm the idea that there exist what the statement would call different "groups of mankind" demarcated by color, and that Jews, once the fiction of the Semitic race had been dispensed with, could be readily subsumed by whiteness. But while Fishberg does accept the fact of racial types, his assessment of Jews' place in these racial taxonomies offers a more complicated picture than his refrain of "white humanity" might suggest. In his encyclopedic 1911 volume *Jews, Race, and Environment*, which sought to investigate "the racial characteristics of the modern Jews" and to determine the influence of environment and heredity on that character, Fishberg documented the diversity of Jews in order to demonstrate that the Jews were not a single type, much less a race. "The prevailing opinion [is] that the Jew's physiognomy is typical, that his cast of countenance is uniform, and that one can pick out a Jew from among a thousand non-Jews without any difficulty," he writes.[43] But his ethnographic survey of Jewish communities around the world, which drew extensively on photographs he collected, allowed him to advance a very different conclusion, which was that

Jews not only differed greatly from one another but invariably resembled the populations among which they lived. "The Jews during their migrations in various parts of the world have taken up almost everywhere new racial elements and incorporated them by fusion into the body of Judaism.... There are more differences to be seen in the anthropological type of the Jews in the Caucasus when compared with their co-religionists in Tunis than between each of these groups of Jews and the peoples around them," he wrote.[44] This diversity among Jews and commonality between Jews and their neighbors may or may not have always already existed—"viewed from this standpoint, the question of the origin of the Jewish 'race' loses its significance"—but what mattered was that it was unceasingly reaffirmed and deepened through the accession of converts to Judaism and through exogamy, the two processes that constitute what Fishberg called "fusion."[45] Thus, when Fishberg anatomizes "white Jews" or argues that "the specific difference between Jews and other white people consists mainly in the difference in religious belief," his assertion and even naturalization of Jewish whiteness among a particular segment of Jews is contingent on and secondary to his global argument about the empirical fact of Jewish diversity and what such diversity indicates about the malleability and assimilative capacity of Jews.[46]

At around the same time as Fishberg's 1911 volume, Franz Boas, Fishberg's close colleague, furnished the term—*plasticity*—that would come to encapsulate and explain the changeability of racial form in general and Jewish racial form in particular.[47] In his famous study *Changes in Bodily Form of Descendants of Immigrants*, which examined the assimilation of immigrant and especially Jewish children in New York City for the United States Immigration Commission, Boas offered his field-altering formulation about the "instability or plasticity of [racial] types."[48] Basing his claims on an examination of the cephalic index of Eastern and Southern European schoolchildren, he argued that his measurements demonstrated that this supposedly most stable of traits, much beloved by the physical anthropologist for its role in the taxonomizing of racial types, could be altered within a single generation by the influence of environment. This confirmed that the assimilation of immigrants was possible, at least "as far as the form of the body is concerned."[49] Of course, Boas's argument (implicit here, explicit elsewhere) was that immigrants were capable of not just physical but also cultural and political assimilation. However, it is notable that he routed this claim through physical anthropology; in doing so, he seemed to suggest that the transformation of racial form was not only a prerequisite of assimilation writ large but the very means for its accomplishment.[50]

In fact, these would be the very arguments that Boas would subsequently make about Jewish assimilation, not just about recent Jewish immigrants to the United States but about the entire racial history of the Jewish people. Boas believed that his findings about human plasticity had wide, even universal, applicability. However, what we find in his interwar writings on Jewishness—authored specifically as rebuttals to Nazi racial thought and largely aimed at the wider public—is an account of Jews as paradigmatically plastic. He opens a short piece from 1923, "Are the Jews a Race?," by observing that "people who concern themselves with the so-called 'Jewish question' are accustomed to considering the Jews as a homogeneous race with definite characteristics different from the European groups among whom they live." However, he cautions, "it is most important to realize that even in antiquity, while the Jews still formed an independent state, they represented a thorough mixture of divergent racial types."[51] "The dispersion of the Jews all over the world," he continues, "has tended to increase considerably the intermixture. A comparison of the Jews of North Africa with those of Western Europe . . . not to speak of those of Southern Asia shows very clearly that in every single instance we have a marked assimilation between the Jews and the people among whom they live. . . . The Jews of North Africa are, in their essential traits, North Africans. The Jews of Europe are in their essential traits, Europeans, and the black Jews of the East are in their essential traits members of a dark-pigmented race."[52] Boas would repeat versions of this formulation throughout the 1930s, including in his anti-Nazi propaganda pamphlet *Aryans and Non-Aryans*, which his student Melville Herskovits deemed his most widely read work.[53] In Boas's account, Jews, because of their history of dispersion and diaspora, are racially plastic and their history is one of various scenes of assimilation. As Amos Morris-Reich nicely puts it, drawing our attention to the contrast between Boas's perspective and other refutations of antisemitism: "Boas's first move was not to suggest that Jews could assimilate but that they are *already* assimilated. In other words, he reversed the order of the argument: Jewish assimilation is not a possibility but has already in fact occurred."[54]

In other words, Boas's view is that European and especially German anti-semitism are ideologies that do, in a sense, represent family quarrels, not because Jews are white but because they are plastic and their assimilation is everywhere secured by their malleability. Indeed, in Boas's work as well as in the work of his like-minded contemporaries, Jews exemplify this racial plasticity, demonstrating throughout the length and breadth of their ancient and modern diasporic history a singular capacity for assimilation of and to the peoples among whom they live. Multiracial in their origins, diverse in their physical expressions, and plastic in their capacity for racial assimilation, Jews in this discourse come to represent the very antithesis of race and racial fixity. "Jews have lived in many parts of the world," observes Montagu, and "wherever they have lived many of them have intermixed with members of the indigenous populations, that were often quite mixed themselves, hence the variability of Jews physically is quite probably greater than one is likely to encounter in any other population."[55] Montagu's argument is that no people is more mixed, more shaped by the experience of migration, and thus *less racial* than the Jews. But while the Jewish experience is held up as singular, it is also cast as representative of the human tendency toward migration and intermixture. Shapiro's UNESCO volume *The Jewish People: A Biological History* concludes with this reflection:

In many ways the biological fortunes of the Jews through the millennia of their existence as a people typify the complex forces that are exerted upon any, indeed all, peoples. The continuities, the changes, the adaptations to varying conditions, the interplay of cultural and historical currents affecting biological developments are to be found wherever man exists. The resultants may differ but the process is universal. The Jews, in particular, have as a consequence of their history displayed some of those forces with enough clarity to enable us to discern their course.... Through their dispersion they remained a world people, enormously expanding their geographical and racial contacts. Few other peoples in modern times have had consequently so varied a biological history. As a result they have contributed something of their genetic heritage to perhaps more different people than any other group and have, in return, absorbed an equal number of new genetic strains, enriching and diversifying themselves.[56]

In Shapiro's description, Jews are both typical and exemplary. As such, they epitomize the promise of the UNESCO statement's concept of race: all peoples are mixed, and the presumed stability of racial groups has always been and will continue to be subject to change and transformation.

This simultaneously typical and exemplary status lends a normative dimension to the Jewish experience and returns us to the question of educability. In Boas's study of immigrant racial form and in his response to critics, Boas was careful to make no categorical claims about the underlying cause of the transformations he so assiduously documented. "It will, therefore, be seen that my position is that I find myself unable to give an explanation of the phenomena," he wrote in response to his detractors in 1912, "and that all I try to do is to prove that certain explanations are impossible."[57] It is a testament to how dramatically the concept of racial plasticity departed from prevailing ideas that Boas felt little compulsion to explain what specific aspects of the American environment produced changes in the seemingly most stable traits of racial form; the point was to assert the receptiveness of racial form to transformation, rather than inventory the social or environmental factors that produced any specific change. Indeed, the very uncertainty of the particular mechanisms by which racial form was reshaped meant that Boas's argument culminated in the assertion of plasticity, lending the concept a kind of recursive plasticity of its own, as the labile ground from which other investigations and arguments might be launched. "As long, then, as we do not know the causes of the observed changes," he wrote, "we must speak of a plasticity (as opposed to permanence) of types."[58]

Despite this circumspection, there is no question that Boas understood plasticity to have a political telos. In a letter to one member of the Immigration Commission, he observed that in light of the growing number of Eastern and Southern European immigrants to the United States, "the question has been justly raised, whether this change of physical type will influence the marvelous power of amalgamation that our nation has exhibited for so long a time." An empirical determination about the plasticity of racial form would settle the question of whether these immigrants "can be assimilated by our people."[59] For Boas, assimilation was the horizon of racial plasticity. It was not enough for racial form simply to be susceptible to change; for social and political assimilation to occur, its malleability needed to be shaped and directed in such a way as to produce a concordance between bodily form and mental makeup: "If we grant the correctness of our inferences in regard to the plasticity of human types, we are necessarily led to grant also a great plasticity of the mental make-up of human types.... We must conclude that the fundamental traits of the mind, which are closely correlated with the physical condition of the body and whose development continues over many years after physical growth has ceased, are the more subject to far-reaching changes."[60] "The adaptability of the immigrant," he observes, "seems to be very much greater than we had a right to suppose."[61] The Statement on Race presents Boasian plasticity first and foremost as a capacity of mentality and intellect—"the one trait which above all others has been at a premium in the evolution of men's mental characters has been educability, plasticity"—even as plasticity functions as the organizing concept for the statement's account of racial form.[62] But as I discussed in this book's introduction, in Boas's original formulation, the order is reversed, making explicit that the malleability or educability of mentalities depends upon and is extrapolated from the transformation of racial form. It is not enough—a point Fanon will make repeatedly and at length—for the immigrant or colonized subject to have their ideas, tastes, references, and values formed through a colonial or assimilative education, so long as the form of the body remains tethered, unchanging, incorrigible.[63]

The plasticity of racial form Boas discovered in this study is not the only means of securing racial assimilation. As both Fanon and Boas affirm, though with very different political inflections, the dream of racial plasticity also depends on racial amalgamation and interracial sexuality. While Boas initially theorizes racial plasticity in the context of the changes wrought by environmental influence, he notes in *The Mind of Primitive Man* that there are two mechanisms for the modification of types, the second being "race mixture."[64] And in fact, he will ascribe great importance to what he variously calls "race mixture," "intermingling," "miscegenation" and "intermarriage" for the resolution of the political problems posed by race and racial difference. The "parallelism between the bodily form of the Jews and that of the people among whom they live" that Boas extols is achieved, he explains, through race mixture.[65] The racial history of the Jews demonstrates the axiom that "no matter how rigid prohibition laws and customs may be, races living in the same area will always intermingle."[66] Jewish plasticity offers a model trajectory that Boas will urge on others.

However, despite his views about the inevitability of racial intermixture and in contrast to his account of the established fact of Jewish assimilation,

Blackness for Boas is a difference that has not been and may yet resist being dissolved in a like manner. He takes the better part of his 1921 article "The Problem of the American Negro" (published just two years before "Are the Jews a Race?") to present exhaustive anthropological evidence that disproves racist claims about Black physical and mental inferiority. But in the final pages, he shifts focus, acknowledging that the thornier problem is the intransigence of "racial prejudice," which persists despite the flimsiness and successful refutation of its biological and psychological justifications. What perpetuates race prejudice, he argues, is the perception that individuals belong to a class whose characteristics they share. In the case of Black Americans, this "class consciousness," as he calls it, is heightened and "kept alive by the contrast presented by [the Negroes'] physical appearance with that of the whites."[67] Or, as he put it in his 1906 commencement address at the historically Black Atlanta University—which W. E. B. Du Bois, who was in the audience, would later describe as an important influence on his own thought—the question was how to create solidarity between "two peoples [that] have been brought into close contact by the force of circumstances, who are dependent upon each other economically but where social customs, ideals and—let me add—bodily form, are so distinct that the line of cleavage remains always open."[68] Boas's formulation is yet another articulation of what I have described as the racial residuum—that is, the idea that certain racial forms give rise to categorical differences within humankind that are biologically meaningless and ought to be recognized as socially irrelevant, in no way disturbing species unity or the sense that "mankind is one," even as they remain perceptually undeniable, that which we cannot not see. What makes the racial residuum residual is that this stubborn intractability is paired with the assertion of race's malleability and plasticity, so that it might yet be reeducated and remade.

It is in this spirit that Boas proceeds. The only solution he can imagine to this problem of racial class and racial consciousness is to "decrease the contrast between the extreme racial forms" via "an increase of the amount of white blood in the negro population," so that "it would seem, therefore, to be in the interest of society to permit rather than to restrain marriages between white men and negro women."[69] Boas's proposed eugenic solution to the "problem of the American Negro" is hardly unique; such racial "amalgamation schemes," to use Jared Sexton's apt phrase, are a mainstay of racial-social engineering, retooling a redemptive hybridity from the threat of mongrelization.[70] But Boas's advocacy of amalgamation is rich with implications, and his description of Blackness as a "line of cleavage" that "remains always open" is highly suggestive. A line of cleavage is commonly understood to describe something like a fault line, the natural trajectory or path along which something will split or divide with the application of pressure—for instance, in minerology.[71] But in anatomy and surgery, lines of cleavage, also known as Langer's lines or skin cleavage lines, denote where human skin is least elastic, owning to the organization and alignment of the muscles beneath the dermis. Though outdated now, the schematization of the body according to its lines of cleavage would determine the placement of surgical cuts, with cuts along the line of cleavage remaining closed, in contrast to a perpendicular cut that is pulled open as the elastic fibers of the dermis recoil. To describe Blackness as a line of cleavage, then, is to say that it lacks elasticity. Moreover, in surgery, one would cut along Langer's lines because the lack of elasticity would allow such an incision to heal nicely: the skin draws together rather than pulling apart. To describe Blackness as a line of cleavage that remains *open*—persistent and unsuturable—is to characterize it as unnatural, resistant, and even defiant. Boas thus reiterates the logic of anti-Blackness, combining the imperative that Blackness be racially assimilated with the perception that it exceeds or defies such attempts at amalgamation and amelioration.[72]

As I have suggested, the discourse of racial plasticity depends upon theories and fantasies of racial amalgamation and hybridity. While the UNESCO Statement on Race, written after the modern synthesis, premises its account of plasticity in large part on population-level accounts of genetic change, its Boasian ethos also entails an affirmation of the role of both environmental influence and racial mixture in the production and especially transformation of racial form.[73] Moreover, one of the key "racial myths" that the statement and the associated antiracist discourse sought to puncture was that racial mixture resulted in biological inferiority. Indeed, the 1951 revised statement's more muted take on the plasticity of race tracks with its agnosticism about the outcomes of racial mixture. These interventions and equivocations demonstrate, as Tavia Nyong'o has observed, that "racial mixing and hybridity are neither problems for, nor solutions to, the long history of 'race' and racism, but part of its genealogy."[74]

Boas's treatment of Blackness as a social and racial difference that can be reconciled only by the imperative of amalgamation provides an answer of sorts to the question I posed in chapter 1, apropos the statement's triad of racial categories: To whom is the promise of racial transformation being extended? But more telling is Boas's account of Blackness as that which resists and cannot be recuperated by plasticity. In Boas's account, Blackness is not just epidermal difference. "The contrast between the extreme racial forms" may be reducible to the contrast of color, white and black. But epidermal difference is itself a shorthand, a metonym for the problem of the changeability or intractability of racial form. Blackness is inelastic and impermeable in contrast to other racial forms that more readily come to resemble those that surround them. I have argued that plasticity, as it is articulated in Boas's racial anthropology and, by extension, UNESCO's scientific antiracism, is theorized via a conception of Jews as paradigmatically plastic. But paired with this is another aspect of racial plasticity's historical articulation—the implication that Blackness is inimical to plasticity.

It is against this backdrop that I think we can understand both Fanon's reflections on Jewish whiteness and his designation of their familial bond with their persecutors: Jewishness and Blackness are differently situated not simply with respect to the immediacy or irreducibility with which they are perceived (Jewish whiteness versus Black skin) but with respect to their plasticity. We are no longer simply in "the moment of racial sight" but in an elongated temporality of the changing regimes of racial meaning and racial (and thus social and sexual) assimilation.

CIRCUMCISION ENVY

While the foregoing discussion has sought to reframe Fanon's provocative remarks on Jewish whiteness and the Holocaust as a family quarrel, these are not his text's last or even most extended reflections on Jewishness. Later, Fanon writes:

> Since Jean-Paul Sartre has masterfully studied the question of anti-Semitism, let us try to see what we can find out about negrophobia. This phobia is located at an instinctual, biological level. . . . What is important to us here is to show that the *biological* cycle begins with the black man.

No anti-Semite, for example, would ever think of castrating a Jew. The Jew is killed [*On le tue*] or sterilized. The black man, however, is castrated. The penis, symbol of virility, is eliminated; in other words, it is denied. The difference between the two attitudes is apparent. The Jew is attacked in his religious identity [*sa personnalité confessionnelle*], his history, his race, and his relations with his ancestors and descendants; every time a Jew is sterilized, the bloodline is cut [*on tue la souche*]; every time a Jew is persecuted, it is the whole race that is persecuted through him.

But the black man is attacked in his corporeality. It is his tangible personality [*sa personnalité concrète*] that is lynched. It is his actual being that is dangerous. The Jewish peril is replaced by the fear of the black man's sexual power. . . . The black man represents the biological danger; the Jew, the intellectual danger.[75]

If the passage I examined in the first part of the chapter represents a Fanon that critics have received with some unease—acknowledging the force of his point while questioning the tone and character of its particulars—this passage, particularly the binary opposition with which it concludes, has been met with strenuous dismay and distaste. The charge is that at this point, Fanon is simply reiterating antisemitic stereotypes and is increasingly prone to what Bryan Cheyette calls "a contagion of rigid antitheses with regard to Jews and Blacks."[76] Again, Fanon is read as having adopted some of Sartre's descriptions, to the detriment of his analysis. Cheyette suggests that Fanon not only reiterates "Sartre's overdetermined characterization of the disembodied Jewish mind" but amplifies it such that a reader can track in *Black Skin, White Masks* an increasing characterization of antisemitism as "a mere cerebral matter" as it "lessens its importance for Fanon."[77]

In fact, a close reading reveals that the operative difference in this passage is not about the Black body and Jewish mind per se but instead turns on Fanon's ascription of national and historical continuity to Jewishness, in contrast to the profound cultural alienation and impossibility of a return to origins that he suggests characterizes Black experience under conditions of colonialism and especially diaspora. Such a claim might seem to be in tension with this chapter's first arc, which sought to establish the influence of ideas about Jewish plasticity on Fanon's remarks. How do we square that argument with the one I intend to offer about Fanon's recognition of Jewish specificity? First, Fanon is thinking across and experimenting with multiple registers in which to theorize Jewishness: we see evidence of his philosophical interlocutors (Sartre is the most explicit intertext), traces of social scientific debates, and the resonance of psychoanalytic reflections on Jewishness, as I will discuss. Fanon is receiving but also responding to multiple ideas from various sources and discourses. Second, Fanon's ideas shift not only across the text of *Black Skin, White Masks* but also over the course of his later work. As I will show, the account of Jewish particularism I find embedded in this passage deepens and comes into focus in his subsequent writing without being at odds with the idea of Jewish plasticity or even whiteness. Finally, while Fanon resists the normative dimension of Jewish plasticity as it is articulated in antiracist discourse, he is attuned to the affirmative meaning of Jewish identity. As I noted in the book's introduction, the liberal antiracist discourse formulated at and around UNESCO vigorously insisted on Jewish plasticity but was much less confident and unified in its assessments of what Jewish difference was if Jews were not a race. The unanswerable question as to whether Jewishness was religious, ethnic, national, cultural, or perhaps racial after all treated the meaning of Jewishness as another kind of vexing residual formation. In contrast, Fanon affirms the significance and integrity of Jewish cultural continuity and historical memory.

"The Jew is attacked in his religious identity, his history, his race, and his relations with his ancestors and descendants," writes Fanon. To appreciate how significantly this view differs from Sartre's, let us recall that the most enduring criticism of Sartre's *Reflections on the Jewish Question* concerns Sartre's evacuation of any affirmative meaning to Jewishness or even Judaism—a position encapsulated in his famous formulation that "it is the anti-Semite who *makes* the Jew."[78] In Sartre's view, the antisemite might derive the outline of his views from Christian anti-Judaism or from strains of nationalist thought that mobilize antisemitism, but his central argument about antisemitism is that it is not an opinion or an ideology but a passion in search of an object. While this argument captures the unreason of antisemitism and racist thought generally, it also eases the way for Sartre to fall back on the explanation of scapegoating; according to this logic, racism and antisemitism bear no particular shape in relation to their objects but are irrational passions that overflow and attach themselves to whatever is at hand. Or, as he puts it, "The Jew only serves [the anti-Semite] as a pretext; elsewhere his counterpart will make use of the Negro or the man of yellow skin."[79]

Fanon, in contrast, proposes not only that the antisemite's violence targets Jewish difference in its specificity (religion, history, descent) but also that violence against the individual Jewish body seeks to undermine the existence and perpetuation of a collective or corporate Jewish identity: "Every time a Jew is sterilized, the bloodline is cut; every time a Jew is persecuted, it is the whole race that is persecuted through him." What we see here is Fanon ascribing to Jewishness an affirmative meaning that inheres in the genealogical. By genealogy, I mean both the familial bonds of descent as well as their quasi-metaphorical extension, connecting an individual not only to his forbears and offspring but to the "ancestors and descendants" of a collective or shared identity—that is, to Jews as a *genos*, or people. As such, Fanon's apparent opposition between Jewish disembodiment and Black corporeality might be reframed; what he identifies in Jewishness is a metonymic bond that binds an individual Jew to the collective and for the antisemite means that any Jew is a synecdoche for the group. The opposition Fanon is trying to establish here is that Blackness, in his view, does not similarly refer to a collective identity; it is merely singularized fleshly difference. Indeed, these are both positions he returns to in his later writings. The term Fanon uses in *Black Skin, White Masks* to characterize this sense of collective Jewish identity, or Jewish genos, is *race*. However, in his 1955 essay "West Indians and Africans," first published in the Parisian journal *Esprit*, we see him alter and refine his language in a way that is in keeping with the sharp challenge he issues in that piece to the priority or even relevance of race for the consciousness and consolidation of shared identity and for a politics meaningfully derived from it.

At issue in this 1955 essay is the salience of the term *peuple noir* (Black people) to designate the totality and the unity of people of African descent, both in Africa and in the diaspora. Fanon argues that this appellation is meaningless because color cannot constitute a people. He asks, rhetorically, "*Que serait le 'peuple blanc'?*" That is, to which category of meaningful collective life—the possibilities he offers are "nation, people, fatherland, community" (*nation, peuple, patrie, communauté*)—does racial whiteness correspond?[80] His answer, of course, is none, and he argues by analogy that "*peuple noir*" is equally politically untethered. He explains that "the truth is that there is nothing, *a priori*, to warrant the assumption that such a thing as a Negro people [*peuple noir*] exists."[81] He momentarily allows that the two groups of the essay's title, West

Indians and Africans, can lay claim to peoplehood. But in a footnote he immediately retracts this, describing it as "fictitious" and declaring: "Philosophically and politically there is no such thing as an African people. There is an African world [*un monde africain*]. And a West Indian world [*un monde antillais*] as well. On the other hand, it can be said that there is a Jewish people; but not a Jewish race [*on peut dire qu'il existe un peuple juif; mais pas de race juive*]."[82] By rejecting the formulation "a Jewish race" in favor of "a Jewish people," Fanon not only reiterates what I am arguing is his ascription of affirmative meaning to Jewishness in *Black Skin, White Masks*, but he more carefully differentiates his terms in a way that helps us to reconcile his assertions of Jewish plasticity and Jewish particularism.

Fanon does not retract his suggestion of Jewish plasticity or racial whiteness. His insistence that there is no Jewish race leaves open the question of what relative position Jews may occupy in relation to the racial whiteness and Blackness that he argues are incongruent with meaningful political identities but are not therefore insignificant. Instead, he resituates Jewishness as his example of a people whose existence is neither reducible to nor a response to the imposition of race. In contrast, he argues, the term *peuple noir* is a signifier without a referent, because it assumes something that is absent—namely, what he calls "a principle of communion" (*un principe de communion*).[83] What is missing, we might say, is precisely the covenant that characterizes the vertical and horizontal lines of belonging that render Jews a people in Fanon's view.

With this reading in mind, let us return to the lines "No anti-Semite, for example, would ever think of castrating a Jew. The Jew is killed or sterilized. The black man, however, is castrated." Several critics have scrutinized this passage, and Daniel Boyarin, who has given it its most sustained reading, has argued that Fanon's remark "could not be more mistaken historically."[84] Boyarin offers a compelling but I think incomplete symptomatic interpretation that reads Fanon's remark in light of Freud's suggestion that antisemitism stems from the entanglement of Jewish circumcision with the castration complex. Freud first makes this provocative and consequent claim almost in passing, in a footnote to his 1909 "Analysis of a Phobia in a Five-Year-Old Boy," or the Little Hans case study:

I cannot interrupt the discussion so far as to demonstrate the typical character of the unconscious train of thought which I think there is here reason for attributing to little Hans. The castration complex is the deepest unconscious root of anti-semitism; for even in the nursery little boys hear that a Jew has something cut off his penis—a piece of his penis, they think—and this gives them a right to despise Jews. And there is no stronger unconscious root for the sense of superiority over women. Weininger (the young philosopher who, highly gifted but sexually deranged, committed suicide after producing his remarkable book, *Geschlecht und Charakter* [1903]), in a chapter that attracted much attention, treated Jews and women with equal hostility and overwhelmed them with the same insults. Being a neurotic, Weininger was completely under the sway of his infantile complexes; and from that standpoint what is common to Jews and women is their relation to the castration complex.[85]

As the text's only reference to Jewishness, this footnote is enigmatic even to the present-day reader. It would have been more so to Freud's contemporaries, since the identities of Little Hans and his father (Herbert and Max Graf) were then unknown to readers, as was the fact of their Jewishness. Freud's musings on antisemitism thus appear strangely untethered from the case at hand. Boyarin and others have argued that Freud's circumspection here is, by extension, an effort to suppress or disavow his own Jewishness: "In presenting 'Little Hans' and Weininger as if they were gentiles gazing . . . at the Jewish penis and becoming filled with fear and loathing . . . Freud is actually representing himself (or at least an aspect of himself) gazing at his own circumcised penis and being filled with fear and loathing."[86] As Boyarin and Eliza Slavet both astutely note, Freud's argument about the unconscious source of the antisemite's contempt for Jews cannot be quarantined only to gentiles; it belongs equally to the Jewish male, Freud perhaps included, who finds in the sight of his circumcised penis an embodied confirmation of his difference and inferiority.[87] For Boyarin, this experience of inferiority and lack, produced through a complex scene of gazing or looking, underscores Freud's status as a "postcolonial subject" caught in precisely the drama of dividedness that Fanon describes and, like Fanon, inclined to manage this diminishment through misogyny and homophobia.[88] Fanon's psychological portrait of the colonized is also a portrait of fin-de-siècle emancipated Jewry.

However, the crux of Boyarin's critique of Fanon is that he cannot recognize this shared experience because he remains convinced that the Jew "is a white man." Boyarin draws a straight line from Fanon's remarks on Jewish whiteness to his dismissal of the threat of Jewish castration. In this reading,

Fanon's stubborn perception of Jewish whiteness permits his studious forgetting or strategic ignorance of the pronounced and, in Freud's view, even constitutive link between antisemitism and castration. Caught in the grip of his anguished sense of racial inferiority, Fanon identifies this subject position only with his own plight, ignoring the historic and psychoanalytic evidence for this condition as a site of possible commonality rather than competition between Jewish and colonial subjects. He thus reveals, in Boyarin's words "his envy for the Jew's imaginary phallus"—that is, his envy of Jewish racial whiteness.[89]

In contrast, I am arguing that much of the pathos of Fanon's comparison of Blackness and Jewishness stems from Jewish claims to genealogical cultural continuity—that is, his envy of Jewish *difference*, not whiteness. Fanon's remark is an instance of what I am calling circumcision envy. The lack embodied in the circumcised Jewish penis, which Boyarin generalizes when he writes that "the racial other is 'he' who lacks the phallus," is in Fanon's racial economy also a gain.[90] It is the physical manifestation of the genealogical and national inheritance that affords Jews, in Fanon's view, the status of a people. As I noted earlier, Fanon implies that Blackness does not refer to a collective identity. The Black subject is atomized, merely flesh—to adopt Hortense Spillers's distinction between the body that signifies and flesh as the "zero degree of social conceptualization."[91] To attack the Black man "in his corporeality," as Fanon says, is to treat the body as in no way referential or representative of something beyond itself.[92] When Fanon insists that "the *biological* cycle begins with the Black man," he is marking a distinction between Black biology and Jewish genealogy. We can thus read Fanon's assertion that the Jew is sterilized in a different light, not as a refusal to recognize the historic association between antisemitism and castration but rather as a way to capture the idea that the violence inflicted on Jewishness targets not just the individual but the group, or the line of genealogical descent. Jewish circumcision, then, is not so much occluded in Fanon's account as it is representative of precisely that claim to cultural and genealogical continuity that sterilization terminates. Indeed, in the statement "every time a Jew is sterilized, the bloodline is cut," the word Fanon's translator, Richard Philcox, renders as "bloodline" is *la souche*, which refers both to a genealogical line (lineage) or biological strain but also to a stump or stub. Fanon's conception of the violence visited on the sterilized Jewish male—not simply the "cutting" of the bloodline but its murder ("*on tue la souche*")—figurally enfolds the circumcised penis rather than displacing it with the phantasmatic phallus of whiteness.

Numerous works in Jewish cultural studies have emphasized the centrality of circumcision to ideas about Jewish difference and its embodiment and have analyzed the prevalence of representations of circumcision in antisemitic discourse.[93] But while circumcision has thus been singled out as the marker of racial difference, it is also the vehicle of Jewish cultural memory. As Boyarin has elsewhere put it, in the practices of diasporic Jewry, circumcision symbolizes

> the genealogical moment of Judaism as the religion of a particular tribe of people. This is so both in the very physicality of the rite, grounded in the practice of the tribe and marking the male members of that tribe, but it is even more so as a marker on the organ of generation, representing the genealogical claim for concrete historical memory as constitutive of Israel.[94]

Circumcision thus functions as the site where memory is embodied and transmitted. As Jay Geller observes, if one of the central dimensions of the Jewish question in modern European thought is how to understand the persistence of Jews and Jewishness, circumcision has functioned as both the sign of such persistence and the very means of its reproduction, across generations.[95] But in the context of this chapter's interest in plasticity, it is worth noting the ambivalence of Jewish circumcision, for it has a peculiar status that suspends it somewhere between a natural or biological inheritance, on the one hand, and, on the other, a chosen mark that must be voluntarily inscribed and might yet be surrendered as a practice.[96] Symptomatically, this distinction at times seems to collapse altogether. One might think here of Freud's 1939 "Moses and Monotheism," whose first scandal is its claim that Moses was no Jew but an Egyptian. More provocatively, Freud also hazards the assertions that acquired traits may be inherited and transmitted and that such transmission of embodied memory explains the endurance of nations and peoples.[97] For Freud, the Jewish commitment to circumcision, despite "the disagreeable, uncanny impression" it provokes, is explained in part through the weight of the transmission of such a "phylogenetic origin," or "archaic heritage."[98] This quality of Jewish circumcision, whereby something chosen takes on the status of the given and the inherited, puts the plasticity of Jewish racial form into question, even crisis, since it interrupts the narrative of the body's ready assimilability.

Fanon's attentiveness to the way that antisemitic violence against an individual Jew is an attack on "his religious identity, his history, his race, and his relations with his ancestors and descendants" demonstrates his awareness that the intention of such violence is to extinguish cultural continuity and cut off a line of descent. In striking contrast to his earlier sardonic description of the Holocaust as a family quarrel—and again, in marked contrast to Sartre[99]—Fanon alludes to the specifically genocidal violence directed against European Jews since he recognizes what Joseph Slaughter calls the synecdochal logic of genocide.[100] Conceptually, Fanon's attunement to genocide as an attack on genealogy has implications for how he has been read by recent Afro-pessimist critics. I have been arguing that the operative distinction he invokes is best understood not primarily as a claim about Jewish disembodiment and Black physicality but rather as a distinction between Jewish genealogy and what he takes to be the Black subject's alienation from or loss of a collective identity, or *genos*. This condition is what Orlando Patterson has called "natal alienation," describing it as a state of "deracination" and "loss of ties of birth in both ascending and descending generations."[101] While for Patterson, natal alienation is a constitutive element of the social death that characterizes slave status, critics have recently reframed social death as the ongoing condition of Black life and have found in Fanon an account of racism "as a social relationship that is grounded in anti-blackness rather than white supremacy."[102] Frank Wilderson, calling for "a radical return to Fanon" in light of what he takes to be Fanon's refusal to acquiesce to the pieties of "a post-World War II era fixated on the Jewish Holocaust," finds in Fanon the affirmation of his own view that "Jews went into Auschwitz and came out as Jews. Africans went into the ships and came out as Blacks."[103] Wilderson uses Fanon to advance an absolute distinction between the natal alienation of slavery and the Jewish genocide. However, Fanon cannot rightly be pressed into service on behalf of this position, for while he distinguishes Black deracination from Jewish genealogy, his description of antisemitic violence highlights its focus on undoing the ties that bind the individual to "his ancestors and descendants."

A better formulation is that Fanon recognizes that genocide entails the production of natal alienation. In my view, Fanon in fact anticipates some of the recent insights of genocide scholarship, particularly the idea that cultural genocide is not a subset of the category of genocide but its paradigmatic form.

The philosopher Laurence Mordekhai Thomas has offered a careful study theorizing the differing character of the harms inflicted on Jews and Black Americans by the Holocaust and racial slavery, respectively, which in his view are (attempted) extermination and natal alienation. Thomas observes that although the genocide of the Jews sought the "eradication" of its victims while slavery did not, "how one survives makes all the difference in the world."[104] As Thomas cogently puts it, "Mass murder by itself is not a necessary condition if the survival of a group is to be systematically and perhaps irreversibly undermined. To be sure, no people can survive as a people given the deaths of all of its members. But one reasons fallaciously in supposing that in the absence of the deaths of all or nearly all of its members, a people can be said to survive as a people."[105] Thomas is right to recognize that mere physical survival does not guarantee the survival of a culture or a sense of peoplehood. His point is not that slavery is therefore worse than genocide—he is at pains to avoid such comparisons—but that "the structure of murderous extermination and that of natal alienation are most dissimilar; neither is an extension of the other."[106] But this is a counterintuitive conclusion, in light of Thomas's insight that a group can be destroyed without the infliction of physical death, which Thomas fails to note by dint of his reasoning that "the Holocaust was not natally alienating . . . because the central tenets of Judaism—the defining traditions of Judaism—endured in spite of Hitler's every intention to the contrary."[107] However, as the philosopher Claudia Card has more recently argued, this conclusion does not adequately acknowledge that genocide's violence targets not just the individual life or even the existence of a culture but more specifically the ongoing, meaningful, and lived connection between individuals and cultures. "The survival of a culture," she notes, "does not by itself tell us about the degree of alienation that is experienced by individual survivors. Knowledge of a heritage is not by itself sufficient to produce vital connections to it."[108] Such alienation is not incidental but integral to the logic of genocide; taking the Holocaust as her example, she observes that "the murders were also part of a larger plan that included the death of Judaism, not just the deaths of Jews. . . . It entailed that survivors, if there were any, should not survive as Jews."[109] In an expansive definition that depends on understanding natal alienation as an integral aspect of genocide, Card makes the powerful argument that social death is central to genocide—it is genocide's telos or purpose.

Fanon's work captures this conception of genocide as social death and natal alienation not only with respect to the Jewish genocide or racial slavery's production of Blackness but also in the context of colonial domination. In his final work, *The Wretched of the Earth* (1961), Fanon observes that "colonialism has not simply depersonalized the colonized. The very structure of society has been depersonalized on a collective level. A colonized people is thus reduced to a collection of individuals who owe their very existence to the presence of the colonizer."[110] Fanon increasingly comes to understand colonial violence as the destruction of the cultural connections that bind individuals together as a people.

Such a shift can be discerned as early as his 1956 speech at the First International Congress of Negro Writers and Artists in Paris, titled "Racism and Culture," which I discuss at length in the next chapter. For now, let me simply note that in this speech, Fanon emphasizes that racism is a technique of "systematized oppression of a people" and "shameless exploitation" and that it accomplishes its ends through "the destruction of cultural values, of ways of life." The "systems of reference [of a native population] have to be broken. Expropriation, spoliation, raids, objective murder, are matched by the sacking of cultural patterns, or at least condition such sacking. The social panorama is destructured."[111] Fanon's theorization of racism as an attack on the cultural existence and vitality of a nation or a people develops first and foremost from his experiences in Algeria from 1953 on. However, his reflections on Jewishness help prepare the ground for this analysis. We see this, tentatively and provisionally, in *Black Skin, White Masks* and then more robustly in "West Indians and Africans," in which Fanon identifies Jews as his paradigmatic example of a group whose claim to the status of a people transcends race, as any such claim must, in his view. Fanon's reflections on Jewishness thus function as a red thread running throughout his writings. Even when he focuses on epidermal difference and racial form, Jewishness complicates the immediacy or naturalness of racial vision and challenges the salience of the visual regime of black and white. Over the course of his writings, however, as his focus shifts more decisively to questions of cultural integrity and survival, the particularism and continuity that he ascribes to Jewishness come to inform his meditations on both Black deracination and colonial alienation.

CHAPTER 3

CULTURE AND CONVERSION

"Hatred or aversion springing from differences in cultural level or religious belief is more human than prejudice claiming to be based on implacable laws of heredity," wrote the Spanish-Mexican anthropologist Juan Comas in his 1951 short book for UNESCO, *Racial Myths*. After all, "the chasm between religions can be bridged," he observed, "while the biological racial barrier is impassable."[1] Comas was one of the authors of the 1950 statement, and *Racial Myths* belonged to the series of educational booklets, The Race Question in Modern Science, that UNESCO subsequently published to reinforce and extend the principles codified in the 1950 and 1951 statements.[2] Comas sought to impress upon his general readership that culture had a special and consoling porosity. Even those who had not yet absorbed the view that race was plastic could surely agree, he suggested, that culture was an independent domain, blessedly free of race's supposed inflexibility—a "bridge," not a "barrier." The French anthropologist Michel Leiris took a similar position in his 1951 contribution to the series, *Race and Culture,* as part of his argument about the historical recency and contingency of racism. Antagonisms between groups and societies may always have existed, he wrote, but historical and ethnographic research demonstrated that these conflicts were "not biological but purely cultural," and "cultures, even more than races, are fluid."[3] Comas's and Leiris's energetic defense of culture's fluidity is hardly surprising from anthropologists but it is more than just professional reflex. Their position advances an unspoken axiom of UNESCO's liberal antiracism about the mimetic relationship of prejudice to its object. According to this view, the tractability of the object determined the tractability of the prejudice. Unlike intransigent racial prejudices, which drew their strength from supposedly "implacable laws" of biology and heredity, cultural hatreds were relatively innocent—reassuringly "human" even—because they would prove as gratifyingly malleable as culture itself.

Comas and Leiris agree on more than just culture's singular fluidity. They also tell strikingly similar stories about a time before racism. "The Crusades were launched against the 'infidels,' the Inquisition persecuted heretics and Jews, and Catholics and Protestants exterminated each other, but in every case the motives alleged were religious and not racial," Leiris explains.[4] Comas is even more explicit, identifying a specific historical shift from religious or cultural hatreds to racism proper that corresponds to the premodern/modern divide: "There was no true racial prejudice before the fifteenth century," Comas writes, "since before then the division of mankind was not so much into antagonistic races as into 'Christians and infidels'—a much more humane differentiation."[5] Leiris and Comas take for granted a strict categorical separation between religion and race. They smoothly bypass the historically sticky question of whether religious markers like "Jew," "Christian," and "infidel" designated racialized differences in the premodern period and the even more obvious question, in the wake of Nazi antisemitism, of how religious intolerance molded subsequent race thinking. In their telling, there was an age of relative innocence before race—"persecution" and "extermination" notwithstanding—when these antagonisms were managed through unnamed processes presumably spanning religious toleration, syncretism, and conversion. It makes a certain kind of sense that these intellectuals, participants in a monumental effort to impose a periodizing break in the meaning of race, were ideologically invested in reading similar periodizing ruptures back into history.[6] At the same time, for all its simplifications and elisions, their position is not especially idiosyncratic; it conforms to the orthodox view (increasingly and rightly under pressure) that race is a concept legible only in modernity.[7]

We find a very different story about culture's past and present relation to race and racism in Frantz Fanon's important intervention from the same era, "Racism and Culture." Fanon delivered these remarks as a speech at the First Congress of Negro Writers and Artists in Paris in September 1956, just a few short years after UNESCO's flurry of publications and positions on race in the early 1950s. Like Leiris and Comas, Fanon also historicizes and periodizes racial regimes, but he arrives at a dramatically different analysis. Yes, he observes, the "vulgar, primitive, over-simple racism" that justified itself on the supposedly "material basis" of biology has been largely retired.[8] The history of the last thirty years—including "the memory of Nazism," widespread human wretchedness and enslavement, and "the institution of a colonial system in the very heart of Europe"—has more or less ensured it.[9] Yet there is no cause for complacency or celebration, for racism has hardly been extinguished. As if acknowledging the ways that race has been deemed plastic and set in motion, Fanon warns that racism has adjusted accordingly: "It has had to renew itself, to adapt itself, to change its appearance" (*il lui a fallu se renouveler, se nuancer, changer de physionomie*).[10]

Far from confirming the malleability of cultural prejudices or their relative innocence, Fanon instead singles out culture as the newly dominant medium of racialization. "Crude" biological claims "give way to a more refined argument," and the old racism of genotypes and phenotypes is "transformed into cultural racism."[11] Moreover, this new cultural racism fuses appeals to "Occidental values" with the enduring cultural charge of "[the struggle] 'between the cross and the crescent.'"[12] Unlike Leiris and Comas, who find in history reassuring evidence that cultural conflicts were successfully managed in the past and so can be neutralized in the present, Fanon warns that this racism is subtle and slippery, new and old at the same time. Indeed, where Comas and Leiris see periodizing breaks, Fanon discerns novelty as well as continuity: the accretion, renewal, and strategic transformation of past forms for a changing present.

Fanon's assessment of the racial present differs in almost every particular from Comas's and Leiris's accounts. How do we explain the sheer conceptual distance between these virtually coeval accounts? After three years in Algeria, in the midst of France's brutal campaign to retain control of its colony, Fanon was certainly attuned to the way that ascriptions of civilizational backwardness were used to justify the most repressive tactics of counterinsurgency. In the era of the liberation struggle, he notes, the prevailing racist characterization of the native population no longer concerns its congenital intellectual inferiority but rather its supposedly "medieval, in fact prehistoric fanaticism."[13] In other words, Fanon had directly before his eyes vivid examples of how cultural or religious differences could be racialized, even and especially as other racial idioms were cast beyond the bounds of legitimate discourse. It would be easy enough to say that Fanon was writing from a historical and experiential vantage point that roundly contradicted the pie-in-the-sky story Comas and Leiris were telling. If we regard these clashing stories through this lens, Fanon arrives in Paris to bring tidings of brutalities in the colonial periphery that refute the official antiracism that UNESCO is furiously working to elevate to a commonsense narrative in the metropole.

This is undoubtedly part of the story—and it offers us a kind of schematic contrapuntality in which events unfolding in the colonies fill in the gaps of a metropolitan narrative that has largely suppressed them—but it is not nearly all of it. First, let me note that as is well established, Fanon's remarks were most directly a rejoinder to his fellow participants in the congress. Specifically, they challenged the way that Alioune Diop, the founding editor of *Présence Africaine* and the congress's organizer, had conceptualized culture. In brief, the congress sought to affirm the cultural credentials of Black people in Africa and throughout the diaspora. While the Middle Passage, slavery, and colonialism may have broken lines of cultural continuity and transmission, new cultural patterns had emerged, and Black people the world over had as much claim to the universal human capacity for culture as any other, indeed had demonstrated their exemplary cultural vitality. Christopher Bonner, who offers an incisive account of the congress's cultural politics, observes that Fanon's speech was "the strongest internal critique of the liberal humanist spectacle of the First Congress—that is, of its depoliticization of anticolonial sentiment through a cosmopolitan discourse of rights, civility, and recognition of cultural identity."[14] Clearly, this critique gives Fanon's remarks much of their momentum and he ends on a familiar cautionary note about the allure, for the colonized native, of an exaggerated valorization of cultural originality and cultural purity.[15]

However, Fanon's remarks are also a reflection on the changing regimes of racialization as they are mediated by midcentury liberal antiracism. Fanon opens his remarks by reflecting on cultural anthropology's centrality as a site for the definition and management of culture's evolving meaning: "The unilaterally decreed normative value of certain cultures deserves our careful attention. One of the paradoxes immediately encountered is the rebound [*choc en retour*] of egocentric, sociocentric definitions." Fanon uses the same phrase, "*choc en retour*," that Césaire offers in *Discourse on Colonialism* to describe the return to Europe of its colonial violence. I discuss this term at length in the next chapter, so let me simply note that Fanon here suggests an analogous dynamic, whereby culture's definition and deployment in service of racial hierarchy produces a repercussive effect, a backlash that forces some type of reckoning. Crucially, Fanon goes on to suggest that this reckoning is registered internally to the culture concept itself. Narrating the changing scales according to which cultural value has been measured, he observes that "there is first affirmed the existence of human groups having no culture; then of a hierarchy of cultures; and finally, the concept of cultural relativity [*la notion de relativité culturelle*]. We have here the whole range from overall negation to singular and specific recognition. It is precisely this fragmented and bloody history that we must sketch on the level of cultural anthropology."[16] In Fanon's telling, these successive conceptions of culture must be situated and emplotted both in relation to the violent historical relations they have enabled and to each other; cultural relativism, he suggests, is the most recent concept that cultural anthropology has offered to contend with the normative meaning of culture and cultural difference.

Indeed, the midcentury reeducation of race sought to enshrine cultural relativism as the proper ethical and epistemological perspective from which to consider cultural difference. This ethos was powerfully expressed in the single most influential volume of UNESCO's series The Race Question in Modern Science: Claude Lévi-Strauss's 1952 *Race and History*. It strikes me as very likely that Fanon was thinking specifically of Lévi-Strauss's book, which was a bestseller as well as an object of controversy and public debate in intellectual circles after a vituperative review by the French sociologist Roger Caillois. As I discuss in chapter 4, this review, in turn, is an important site of engagement for Césaire in the 1955 edition of *Discourse on Colonialism*. Lévi-Strauss's *Race and History* was very germane to the debates on culture unfolding at UNESCO and at the First Congress of Negro Writers and Artists, and Lévi-Strauss sent a message to the congress expressing his support for the proceedings.[17] However, while Lévi-Strauss's full-throated defense of the universal capacity for culture and the normative worth of all cultures clearly harmonized with the congress's position, Fanon was considerably more skeptical of this orientation, as we have established. While Fanon begins his remarks by noting that cultural relativism appears to have carried the day in the precincts of cultural anthropology, this is just the opening gambit for his subsequent diagnosis of an emergent cultural racism, in which "the object of racism is no longer the individual man but a certain form of existing."[18] How are these two developments—a new antiracist perspective on culture and the new centrality of culture to the biopolitics of race—related in Fanon's view?

Fanon, I suggest, is not just bringing news from the Algerian front, he is directly addressing the internal contradictions and consequences of the remaking of the race and culture concepts. He presciently recognizes the emergence of cultural racism and its amalgamation of novel and familiar elements. More presciently still, he suggests that the effort to cleanse culture of its associations with race and racial hierarchy is ironically implicated in the growing centrality of cultural racism. Indeed, this is precisely one of the consequences of the midcentury remaking of the race concept, which also necessarily rewrote the culture concept. Comas and Leiris demonstrate how this discourse strenuously distinguished between race and culture in order to rescue cultural differences from erroneous associations with biology, while also ascribing to race qualities of malleability borrowed from the model of culture. However, as race is recast as malleable and plastic, the duality of the culture concept deepens: culture is both uniquely changeable but is also now the sole medium for the transmission and survival of meaningful human differences. Paradoxically, culture comes to seem both more but now also less plastic than race. These operations are one powerful source for the rise of cultural racism as a dominant racial logic of the postwar era.[19]

I examine these developments in this chapter, paying particular attention to Claude Lévi-Strauss. He offered the most celebrated account of cultural relativism as a disposition that UNESCO's antiracist pedagogy would cultivate and instill in its global public, swiftly remediating cultural prejudices. However, by the early 1970s, this solution had lost its luster, and Lévi-Strauss offered a very different theory of cultural aversion as a strategy of cultural survival. I suggest that Lévi-Strauss's evolving perspective is symptomatically related to the development of cultural racism and should be situated against its increasing centrality to the politics of postcolonial European nations in the 1970s and onward. To be clear, my claim is not that UNESCO's race project somehow single-handedly produced cultural racism or the conditions for its flourishing. Cultural racism's ascendence, observers argue, was part of a backlash to postwar immigration from the colonies and former colonies. As Etienne Balibar puts it in his classic 1988 essay "Is There a Neo-Racism?," this "new racism is a racism of the era of 'decolonization,' of the reversal of population movements between the old colonies and the old metropolises."[20]

At the same time, I do not want to understate how consequential I think these midcentury discursive operations on the race/culture concepts were. As Fanon recognizes, the transformation afoot in the style or modality of racism is partly a matter of idiom. One of the most potent interventions of UNESCO's 1950 Statement on Race was to modify the racial lexicon. The 1950 statement sought to deontologize race, proposing that the word *race* be expunged from common speech, while unraveling and redistributing its meaning across two terms: *the genetic population* and *the ethnic group*. While *the genetic population* designated race as a molecular-level difference that was scientifically meaningful but socially insignificant, the substitution of *ethnic group* for *race* involved an equally significant ideological maneuver: "National, religious, geographic, linguistic and cultural groups do not necessarily coincide with racial groups: and the cultural traits of such groups have no demonstrated genetic connexion with racial traits. Because serious errors of this kind are habitually committed when the term 'race' is used in popular parlance, it would be better when speaking of human races to drop the term 'race' altogether and speak of ethnic groups."[21] When speaking of human races, let us speak instead of ethnicity, proposes the statement. What we find here is a logic whereby ethnicity substitutes for race but is also subsumed by it; it substitutes for culture yet subsumes it.[22]

Despite the contradictions of these linguistic contortions, they were remarkably successful in some respects. As many scholars have observed, the delegitimization of racism at midcentury did in fact constrain the ways that race was talked about and indeed whether it was talked about at all. As Alana Lentin has observed, these discursive operations had the effect of making race unspeakable. Especially in Europe, she argues, race appeared to be finished business, and postwar Europe could conceive of its societies as "*non*-racial, a status displaced only by the short and regrettable years of Nazi domination."[23] This supposedly aberrational period could itself be conscripted to legitimize this narrative, as official national Holocaust commemoration and pedagogy came to be touted as evidence of Europe's liberal bona fides. In a postcolonial Europe inhabited by former colonial subjects or their descendants, what David Theo Goldberg calls the "silencing of race" has meant that they "have no words to express their negation," as Lentin puts it.[24] To Lentin's point, I would add that for migrant or postcolonial subjects, Holocaust commemoration and pedagogy—which surface race and racialization if only as cautionary tales from the past for a present that purportedly knows better—can function as important resources for understanding regimes of racialization and their historicity.[25]

This long arc of developments in the race/culture concept is the prehistory and the backdrop for the readings I offer in this chapter of the British Caribbean writer Caryl Phillips. Phillips was born in 1958, two years after Fanon's 1956 speech to the First Congress of Negro Writers and Artists, at the dying end of this extraordinary decade of racial remaking and racial ferment. He was a child of the Windrush generation, born on the island of St. Kitts and brought to England as an infant, where he grew up in the Britain of Enoch Powell and his brand of racism. Of the authors I examine in this book, Phillips is chronologically the furthest removed from the midcentury moment, and the works I discuss in this chapter appeared in the 1980s, 1990s, and early 2000s. However, this temporal lag captures something important about the status of cultural racism and the fate of liberal antiracism in the period. The 1950 statement's assertion of race's nonexistence produced an immediate rejoinder in the 1951 statement that race's existence was a matter of common sense—a perceptual fact, visible and manifest on the body, that no statement could gainsay. In contrast, the jury stayed out much longer on the question of whether cultural prejudices could be remediated as successfully as UNESCO's antiracial pedagogical program proposed. (As we will see, UNESCO's chief propagandist on this score dramatically changed his mind but took twenty years to do so.) It was only in the late 1960s that UNESCO finally registered some of the disquieting ways in which racism was not proving amenable to remediation and indeed was changing its character. In 1967, the organization published its fourth and final statement, the Statement on Race and Racial Prejudice. This was the first acknowledgment in any statement's title that the urgent question was not just the nature of race but the nature of racism. "Racism continues to haunt the world," the statement announced in its opening paragraph, and this alarming persistence was at the center of its inquiry.[26] The statement also echoed the decisive point Fanon had recognized over a decade earlier, observing that once "faced with the exposure of the falsity of its biological doctrines, racism finds ever new stratagems for justifying the inequality of groups."²⁷ Yet even as the 1967 statement adopted a newly direct and forceful attack on racism not visible in the earlier statements, it also conveyed the impression that the midcentury's epochal sense of possibility had passed and that racism was a "scourge" not likely to be defeated.²⁸

Thus, Caryl Phillips grows up in a racial milieu characterized by virulent cultural racism that euphemizes but does not expunge the violence of epidermalization, all couched in a socially sanctioned silence that Phillips characterizes as a specifically pedagogical failure, as I argue in my reading of his 1987 travelogue *The European Tribe*. In this work, he captures something of the indeterminacy and uncertainty of these shifting racial discourses, addressing the relationship between epidermalization and culture, the silencing of race, and the centrality of Holocaust pedagogy to the consolidation of an antiracist and postracial European identity. These essays also convey Phillips's encounters with the contradictions of racism and the incoherence of liberal antiracism, which formally manifest in Phillips's many representations of his confusing childhood apprehensions of racial meaning. The relevance of the Holocaust and of Jewish persecution for his own experience as a Black British Caribbean subject is at the heart of this uncertainty, and in *The European Tribe*, Phillips is stymied by that same sense Fanon expresses of the seemingly absolute gulf between Jewish whiteness and Black fixity. However, this early nonfiction work also demonstrates Phillips tentatively probing at the significance of cultural difference and especially the racial freight of religious identity.

In this chapter, I suggest that Phillips's 1997 novel *The Nature of Blood* centralizes this question of cultural difference and its fixity or plasticity. In no small part, it does so by juxtaposing multiple narratives about racial formation and racial violence across time, from medieval and early modern Europe to late twentieth-century Israel-Palestine. As I observed, Comas's and Leiris's accounts of culture's relative racial innocence depend on treating the premodern past as evidence that there was a time before racism proper, when malleable and manageable cultural prejudices were the order of the day. But let us remember, too, that their examples all concern religious difference and divisions between "Christians and infidels" and various persecutory projects—the Crusades, the Inquisition—undertaken in the name of religious purification and conquest. When Comas insists that "the chasm between religions can be bridged," what mechanisms does he have in mind and to what extent is conversion central to this practice of cultural and religious reconciliation? Phillips engages such questions through his narrative experiments with retelling the story of the 1480 Portobuffole blood libel and Shakespeare's *Othello*.

Phillips uses the affordances of literary form to theorize cultural racism and challenge racial periodization. He also questions the apparent supersession of disenchanted racial figures, such as blood, as they are corrected and replaced by a nominally sanitized genetic conception of race. Influential accounts of cultural racism have tended to insist on a sharp break between the premodern and racial modernity. Balibar, for instance, is quick to point out that what he calls neo-racism is in fact not so new: "A racism which does not have the pseudo-biological concept of race as its main driving force has always existed. . . . Its prototype is anti-Semitism."[29] Antisemitism, he goes on to say, "is supremely 'differentialist' and in many respects the whole of current differentialist racism may be considered, from the formal point of view, *as a generalized anti-Semitism*."[30] But Balibar has in mind here the "modern Anti-Semitism" of Enlightenment Europe, and he barely acknowledges the relevance of the "statist, nationalistic inflexion to theological anti-Judaism" to his analysis.[31] This is a peculiar periodizing delimitation, since it is precisely such theological accounts of the assimilable or incorrigible difference of Jewish belief that would seem to speak most directly to the question of culture.

I argue that conversion is at the heart of Phillips's inquiry. In my reading, Phillips identifies how conversion as a purported solution to the problem of cultural and religious difference is structurally analogous to the logic of "plasticity, educability," defined by that same structure of malleability within limits. However, as I show in my reading of *The Nature of Blood*, Phillips's work is characterized by blindness as well as insight. Like Fanon, Phillips's conception of Jewishness shifts from an initial preoccupation with Jewish whiteness and plasticity to Jewish particularism, productively blurring the distinction between the given and the chosen. But much more than Fanon, Phillips seems to ascribe to Jewishness a special kind of cultural fidelity that not only risks romanticization but, when viewed in relational perspective, produces its own erasures. While Phillips represents Jewish fidelity as a resistance to conversion, conversion's false promise ensnares Phillips's Othello, a Black man tragically led astray by its promise to transcend difference. Yet Phillips never considers

Othello's potential relation to Islam. As a result, despite his attunement to the racial longue durée and to questions of race and religion, he does not address the historical or contemporary relation between antisemitism and Islamophobia or the inextricable connection between the racialization of Jews and Muslims. Symptomatically, this failure to triangulate Jewishness, Blackness, and Islam speaks to the absence of Palestinians and the occupation of Palestine in Phillips's writing, which some critics have observed and sought to interpret and which I discuss in this chapter's conclusion.

CULTURE AND THE CRISIS OF ANTIRACISM

In 1952, Claude Lévi-Strauss published his contribution to UNESCO's race project, titled *Race and History*. It was the most celebrated book in the series and the most controversial, as I discuss in chapter 4. In *Race and History*, Lévi-Strauss set himself the task of solving a weighty pedagogical problem. Although UNESCO's antiracism tirelessly insisted that race had no explanatory value when it came to cultural differences, the two were indissolubly linked in popular opinion. Lévi-Strauss opened his text by directly confronting this dilemma:

It would be useless to argue the man in the street out of attaching an intellectual or moral significance to the fact of having a black or white skin, straight or frizzy hair, unless we had an answer to another question which, as experience proves he will immediately ask: if there are no innate racial aptitudes, how can we explain the fact that the white man's civilization has made the tremendous advances with which we are all familiar while the civilizations of the coloured peoples have lagged behind?[32]

What explanatory levers could the scientist-pedagogue pull in order to reeducate these stubborn misapprehensions? Lévi-Strauss's task was to articulate a persuasive, appealing, and comprehensive philosophy that would transform how people regarded not just any specific cultural difference but instead the entire question of culture diversity in general. His accomplishment was to offer a brilliant exposition of cultural relativism as a coherent worldview substantiated, in his telling, by the whole arc of human history.

In this passage, Lévi-Strauss reacquaints us with the figure of the man in the street. Yet in contrast to the inarguable epistemological certainty the geneticist L. C. Dunn affords to the racial perceptions of *his* man in the street, who knows race when he sees it, Lévi-Strauss insists that our intuitions and judgments about other cultures cannot be trusted.[33] Instead, he whisks this hypothetical man off to another vantage point, that of a passenger on a moving train, who judges the speed of passing trains relative to his own speed and direction of movement:

> To a traveller sitting at the window of a train, the speed and length of other trains vary according to whether they are moving in the same or the contrary direction. Any member of a civilization is as closely associated with it as this hypothetical traveller is with his train for, from birth onwards, a thousand conscious and unconscious influences in our environment instil into us a complex system of criteria, consisting in value judgments, motivations and centres of interest. . . . Wherever we go, we are bound to carry this system of criteria with us, and external cultural phenomena can be observed only through the distorting glass it interposes, even when it does not prevent us from seeing anything at all. To a very large extent, the distinction between "moving cultures" and "static cultures" is to be explained by a difference of position similar to that which makes our traveller think that a train, actually moving, is either travelling forward or stationary. . . . [Cultures] appear to us to be in more active development when moving in the same direction as our own, and stationary when they are following another line.[34]

As Lévi-Strauss notes, this scenario is the very "illustration used to explain the rudiments of the theory of relativity."[35] Our assessments and even perceptions of other cultures are determined by this relativity; when it comes to culture, there is no true face-to-face encounter.

Lévi-Strauss expressed great rhetorical confidence in the demystifying and corrective power of this new perspective. Every one of us, especially "when we are caught unawares," has been given to "reject out of hand the cultural institutions—ethical, religious, social or aesthetic which are furthest removed from those with which we identify ourselves. 'Barbarous habits,' 'not what we do,' 'ought not to be allowed,' etc. are all crude reactions indicative of the same [frisson], the same repugnance [*répulsion*] for ways of life, thought or belief to which we are unaccustomed."[36] Yet we needn't concern ourselves overmuch with this "naïve" and "ethnocentric attitude," he remarked, since this book and the others in the same UNESCO series decisively refute it.[37] In other words, little could stand in the way of a properly antiracist pedagogy, once it was given a hearing in the public sphere. At the same time, there is an unmistakable tension in Lévi-Strauss's account, for he describes this aversion to the other's difference as so reflexive and deep-seated as to be almost innate. If "repugnance" is liable to well up in us on contact with ways of life other than our own, then it may in fact involve strenuous effort to discipline the ethnocentrism that Lévi-Strauss implicitly seems to suggest is as natural as it is naïve. Accordingly, the persuasive power of cultural relativism as a new pedagogical dispensation is a far more tenuous proposition than Levi-Strauss's apparent confidence might suggest.

Indeed, Lévi-Strauss gave up on his views in rather spectacular public fashion. Some two decades later, in a 1971 speech titled "Race and Culture," delivered at UNESCO to mark the inauguration of the UN's International Year of Action to Combat Racism and Racial Discrimination, Lévi-Strauss offered a markedly different account of the relationship between race and culture. Race does not determine culture; this remains true and has been further confirmed by scientific study, he notes. But work in population genetics has demonstrated that culture determines race. "How could it be otherwise," he asks, arguing that culture dictates practices of separation and points of intercultural contact and determines attitudes about exogamous or endogamous marriage. "How can it be supposed that such rules which have been obeyed for generations do not make a difference to the transmission of the genetic heritage?"[38] These observations are not novel but they are striking, insofar as they reflect precisely that inversion of race and culture's relationship to plasticity and changeability that I noted was a characteristic of the midcentury rewriting of these concepts. In Lévi-Strauss's description, race (i.e., the genetic population) is changeable, subject to the forceful impress of culture, while culture is the domain that guarantees continuity and the preservation of identity.

Even more striking, in accordance with this confirmation of culture as the primary medium of difference, Lévi-Strauss transposes the whole field of racial antagonisms, conflict, and struggle to the terrain of culture and cultural coexistence. Twenty years of efforts against racial prejudice (including his own) have been surprisingly ineffective, he notes. Cultural prejudices are not malleable, and the antipathy we feel at the encounter with different ways of life is not easily educable: "Minority groups appearing in various parts of the world today, such as the hippies, are not distinguished from the bulk of the population by race, but only by their way of life, morality, hair style and dress; are the feelings of repugnance and sometimes hostility they inspire . . . substantially different from racial hatred?"[39] This is a startling and comic example—Kamala Visweswaran reports that one Chicago newspaper ran a story the next day with the headline "Hippies Feel 'Race' Bias, Says Scholar"—but what is crucial here is Lévi-Strauss's centralization of the idea of "way of life" as an insurmountable impediment to cohabitation.[40] In 1971, it now seemed to Lévi-Strauss that neither educators, ethnologists, nor even psychologists could offer much to modify what psychological research suggested was the inevitable tendency to act with bias and injustice against members of an out-group.

In my view, Lévi-Strauss does not just describe this situation, he accedes to it. The only thing that might temper prejudice, he writes, is the preservation of adequate separation among peoples in a world that is enforcing ever more proximity and convergence. A measure of distance, both physical and psychic, is the best means of securing tolerance and the recognition of the equal worth of cultures. The reflexive antipathy that Lévi-Strauss earlier argued might be disciplined through a racial reeducation in cultural relativism is now cast as a mechanism of cultural survival. We must "relearn," he argues, that cultural originality requires and justifies "a certain deafness to outside values, even to the extent of rejecting or denying them."[41] In this speech, then, Lévi-Strauss diagnoses but also legitimizes the philosophy of difference that undergirds cultural racism.

By the 1980s, social theorists on the left were subjecting this form of racism to sustained scrutiny. In his 1981 book *The New Racism: Conservatives and the Ideology of the Tribe*, the British philosopher Martin Barker describes its manifestation in Britain: the new racism is a theory of the emotional basis of cultural unity with the nation as its crucial unit. At stake is the community's "way of life." The new racism staunchly denies any link to the old, vulgar racism of judgments about the superiority and inferiority of peoples, especially based on physical type. Rather it naturalizes xenophobia as a reasonable response, rooted in instinct itself, to others who threaten one's way of life through their refusal or inability to assimilate.[42] This is a racism of incompatible and irreconcilable cultural differences. Culture, as Paul Gilroy puts it in his 1987 *There Ain't No Black in the Union Jack*, responding to the same post-Powellite political discourse as Barker, becomes "an impermeable shell, eternally dividing one 'race' or ethnic group from another"—what is more, he argues, this logic has been generalized, accepted by all sides, no longer simply the project of the right.[43] Culture, in Balibar's words, "can also function like a nature."[44] In what follows, I examine how Caryl Phillips's work engages familiar questions about the relationship between Black epidermal difference and Jewish whiteness against the backdrop of these changing racial formations.

THE RACIAL RESIDUUM REDUX

The publication of Caryl Phillips's 1987 essay collection *The European Tribe* coincides with these works from the 1980s; its title in fact seems to echo Barker's title. The tribe here is a Europe whose nations seem to share "a common and mutually inclusive, but culturally exclusive culture."[45] Although his formative experiences of unbelonging in Britain are his starting point, the work is a travelogue of his journey from Casablanca to Moscow, as he considers the question of culture and its exclusions in a comparative register. Phillips writes these essays as a youngish man in his twenties but he frequently casts himself back to childhood and adolescence, describing a school education full of puzzling silences about race. As he tells it, his abiding preoccupation with the Holocaust and his enduring sense of kinship with persecuted Jews emerge from this silence:

I was brought up in a Europe that still shudders with guilt at mention of the Holocaust. Hundreds of books have been published, many films made, television programmes produced, thousands of articles written. The Nazi persecution of the Jews is taught at school, debated in colleges, and is a part of a European education. As a child, in what seemed to me a hostile country, the Jews were the only minority group discussed with reference to exploitation and racialism, and for that reason, I naturally identified with them. At that time, I was staunchly indignant about everything from the Holocaust to the Soviet persecution of Jewry. The bloody excesses of colonialism, the pillage and rape of modern Africa, the transportation of 11 million black people to the Americas, and their subsequent bondage were not on the curriculum, and certainly not on the television screen.[46]

Critics have remarked on this passage and Phillips's many references to his childhood encounters with an increasingly ubiquitous culture of Holocaust memory.⁴⁷ While on one level, these remarks are about memory and the asymmetry of what is and isn't represented and recollected, the operative question here concerns education.⁴⁸ Yet readings of *The European Tribe* have not fully registered how thoroughly Phillips enfolds these childhood experiences into a critique of the failures of postwar antiracist pedagogy. If "racialism" is "on the curriculum" Phillips explains, it is only vis-à-vis the Holocaust, which is "taught at school, debated in colleges," part of a sanctioned "European education." In contrast, as he relates in the book's opening paragraph, "in British schools I was never offered a text that had been penned by a black person, or that concerned the lives of black people"; instead, "references to black people were confined to the playground," and the classroom was a space of racial shame at the hands of racist educators.⁴⁹

Phillips presents us with a crisis of educability. By opening his book with these educative failures that he dates specifically to 1968, "the year of Enoch Powell's 'rivers of blood' speech in Britain," he situates us in a 1960s and 1970s childhood characterized by both resurgent racism and the growing defeatism of a liberal antiracist consensus increasingly ambivalent about the reeducability of racism and its own relativist, multicultural commitments.⁵⁰ At the same time, the representation of the Holocaust as a component of official pedagogy bespeaks the postwar racial logic Goldberg and Lentin describe as the silencing of race, which amputates the available language for addressing racism, represented by a Nazi past now overcome and duly commemorated. In this context, the Holocaust functions as a bridge between Phillips's formal and informal education. Like Ama Ata Aidoo's protagonist Sissie in *Our Sister Killjoy*, whom we will encounter in the next chapter, he must supplement the incomplete lessons of a purportedly humanist pedagogy that moralizes the Holocaust with a practice of postcolonial autodidacticism that makes the connections the official curriculum will not. In the words of a West Indian calypsonian that Phillips borrows for an epigraph, "Had I been a bright student at school / I'd have learnt more and turned out to be a fool."⁵¹

While the twenty-something Phillips who writes these essays is able to identify the racial contradictions and crises of the era, he also narrates his own childhood crisis of racial signification. While he "naturally identified" with Jewish racialization and persecution, he also reports being persistently confounded by the seemingly self-evident fact of Jewish whiteness. As a fifteen-year-old watching a documentary about occupied Holland, he describes his simultaneous outrage at the roundup of Jews and his bemusement at "why, when instructed to wear the yellow Star of David on their clothes, the Jews complied. They looked just like any other white people to me, so who would know that they were different?"[52] In a Fanonian register, Phillips relates how "the many adolescent thoughts that worried my head can be reduced to one line: 'If white people could do that to white people, then what the hell would they do to me?'"[53] This impression of Jewish whiteness as mysterious—seemingly self-evident yet clearly insufficient to ward off racial persecution—reappears in the short story Phillips reports writing afterward: a young Dutch Jewish boy refuses to wear the yellow star but is told by his parents that he must; en route to the camps in the east he jumps from the train and is rescued by a kindly farmer who sees "the sunlight shining on his yellow star."[54] The function of the star in this case is a benevolent inversion of what an adolescent Phillips imagines is its function in Nazi Europe, making visible what would otherwise be invisible. Phillips is grappling with two competing intuitions: On the one hand, the same intuition that Paul Gilroy relates when he describes his childhood awareness that the suffering of Jewish friends and neighbors in postwar England was "somehow connected with the ideas of 'race' that bounded my own world with the threat of violence."[55] On the other, his sense that this "somehow" is obscure and inarticulable when the fact of Jewish whiteness and his own Blackness seems to an adolescent Phillips so definite and determinative. Notably, both of these moments involve Phillips speculating on what seems to him the self-evident ability of Jews to pass.

However, in pointedly describing this as an adolescent perspective, Phillips turns *The European Tribe* into a work of racial *Bildung*, in which his maturation entails a more refined analysis of the regimes of racial meaning-making that organize his narrative present. Phillips expresses this maturation by shifting his focus from racial passing to the question of culture and conversion. The pivotal episode of the travelogue takes place in Venice's Jewish ghetto, and this chapter opens with an epigraph from James Baldwin's controversial 1967 essay "Negroes Are Anti-Semitic Because They're Anti-White": "The Jew must see that he is part of the history of Europe, and will always be so considered by the descendant of the slave. Always, that is, unless he himself is willing to prove that this judgement is inadequate and unjust."[56] In this essay, Baldwin triangulates whiteness, class, and Christianity. Its dominant thread concerns the class differences that confer whiteness on Jews, provoking Black resentment for exploitation at the hands of Jewish landlords and shop owners and resentment, too, about the very different futures American Jews and American Blacks are able to secure for themselves and their children. But Baldwin also resituates these class dynamics in a religious idiom: "It is not the Jew who controls the American drama. It is the Christian," and Black Americans' antisemitism is the "adoption . . . of the most devastating of the Christian vices."[57] And yet despite noting antisemitism's Christian roots, Baldwin goes on to rhetorically convert Jews to Christians, writing that "the Negro is really condemning the Jew for having become an American white man—for having become, in effect, a Christian."[58] This insistence on conversion, not logically necessary to Baldwin's argument about Jewish whiteness as a class prerogative, does however amplify his point, reproduced in Phillips's epigraph, that Jews are "part of the history of Europe." Baldwin's figural conversion of Jews to Christians and his insistence on their cultural centrality to European history effectively erase both Jewish specificity and also the extent to which "Christendom," in Jonathan Boyarin's words, is "a term existing in a complex lexical and chronological relation with Europe," co-consolidated only through projects of expelling or forcefully incorporating Jews and Muslims.[59]

In elaborating on Baldwin's themes, Phillips invokes the concept of the "Judaeo-Christian" as a way to articulate his own sense that Jews are culturally interior to Europe. As he explores the ghetto, he reflects on the ghetto's sixteenth-century origins; the memorial plaque to Venetian Jews deported in the 1940s; his own identification with Shakespeare's Shylock; and the transnational racial incommensurability that organizes differing African American and Black European attitudes to Jewish persecution. Black American antisemitism is deplorable but also understandable, he muses, since American Jews cannot claim the history of European Jewish persecution and suffering. Moreover, he adds, "the tradition that is responsible for the European oppression of the Jew is a Judaeo-Christian one, the same one that continues to oppress black Americans."[60] This hyphenated formulation is meant to suggest the cultural and religious synthesis of Judaism and Christianity that purportedly characterizes the European tradition in its ecumenical aspect.[61] However, this inclusivity, projected back into history *as* tradition, necessarily obscures the violent project of establishing Europe as a Christian polity, which continues today.[62] And it produces contradictions, visible, for instance, in Phillips's own invocation of the term, which has the peculiar effect of suggesting that the *Judaeo* in *Judaeo-Christian* is the source of Jewish oppression in Europe. Indeed, what the Judaeo-Christian effectively enacts here is a similar conversion—in racial and religious terms—to the one that Baldwin more explicitly articulates. In *The European Tribe*, then, we see Phillips both wrestling with and confounded by the relationship between race, religion, and culture at the site of the ghetto's intersection of multiple temporalities and racial formations.

PERIODIZING PLASTICITY

In the preface to *The European Tribe*, Phillips suggests that the problems impelling its writing are "so urgently felt that the fictional mould seems too delicate a vessel to hold it."[63] However, the maturation of racial sensibility that *The European Tribe* narrates dictates his return to these questions in new forms, first in his 1989 novel *The Higher Ground* and then in his more experimental 1997 novel *The Nature of Blood*. In *The Nature of Blood*, Phillips implicitly revisits some of his early formulations, revising and complicating his understanding of racial differentiation.[64] The novel comprises five narrative strands that unspool along two temporal axes. Two of the five narratives are set in late medieval and early modern Venice. One focuses on the 1480 blood libel in the Venetian town of Portobuffole and narrates the murderous persecution of the town's Jewish community, and the other reworks Shakespeare's *Othello*, told now as a largely first-person confessional tale relating Othello's arrival in Venice, so as to bring us up to the play's beginning. The other three narratives are set in the twentieth century: A young German Jewish woman named Eva Stern loses her family to the Holocaust and is herself interned in first a ghetto and then a concentration camp, finally to make her way to England. An ardent Zionist named Stephen, whom we eventually learn is Eva's uncle, flees Germany for Palestine. There, he joins an armed Jewish militia intent on wresting Palestine from Britain's imperial grip and presumably from the Palestinians, whose presence the novel does not acknowledge. These narratives are each fragmented into multiple parts, each often only a few pages long, and interspersed with one another. In the final fragment of Stephen's story, Phillips introduces an

Ethiopian Jewish woman, Malka, who has been brought to Israel as part of the state's project to patriate the Beta Israel, and who takes over the narration of Stephen's story (hitherto told in the third person) in the first person. Phillips thus experiments with multiple narrative perspectives. The text's juxtaposition of these formally and especially temporally discrepant narratives demands that the reader generate some account of the connections among them, and critics have offered multiple interpretations of these connections.[65]

In this section, I discuss the way that Phillips's work confounds strict periodizing thresholds about where race begins. *The Nature of Blood*, I argue, suggests the centrality of conversion to these questions; moreover, conversion emerges as plasticity's analogue. Sensitive readings of this novel have acknowledged that its central question is the historical variability and especially persistence of race and race-making and that this inquiry motivates its interest in the relational racialization of Blacks and Jews. However, with the exception of Ashley Dawson, who provides an incisive but brief analysis of the novel's engagement with cultural racism and the racial longue durée, there is a critical tendency to observe that Phillips connects modalities of racism and historical scenes of racial terror in theoretically generative ways, without making the question of racial periodization the central focus.[66] Here, I briefly address the novel's treatment of this topic, which lays the ground for my subsequent discussion of blood and conversion as its organizing figures.

Phillips's fictionalized account of a historical blood libel against the Jewish community of the Venetian town of Portobuffole in the spring of 1480, the first fragment of which appears some fifty pages into the novel, is chronologically the earliest of the novel's multiple plots. While the other narratives allow the reader access to characters' interiority, either through first-person narration or sustained focalization, the Portobuffole narrative largely lacks such depictions of psychological depth. Instead, an unnamed narrator, intimately familiar with a sequence of events that begins with the supposed disappearance of a child and leads to an accusation of ritual murder, relates with forensic precision the eventual imprisonment, torture, and execution of several members of the town's Jewish community. As such, the Portobuffole narrative is largely a sorry catalogue of the Christian community's fears, misconceptions, and distortions of their Jewish neighbors' practices and beliefs and a chronicle of the indignities that the Christian community and the Venetian authorities visit on Portobuffole's Jews once word of the ritual murder spreads, first as rumor, then as supposed fact.

There are ambiguities in the narrator's representation of the causes of anti-Jewish violence and of the forms it takes. Portobuffole's Jews, the narrator relates, are migrants from Colonia in Germany, from whence they have been driven out by what the narrator characterizes as the "irrational[ity]" of Colonia's Christians, whose "fear of the plague" and "hysteria" eventually "manifested itself in violence."[67] The narrative seems poised to rehearse a well-established, even exhausted, story about the nature of medieval violence against minorities, violence that in its supposed irrationality and hysteria confirms a capsule description of the Middle Ages as a time of credulity, ignorance, and superstition—that is, as premodern. But this is a portrait of relatively recent origin, as the terms *hysteria* and *irrationality* suggest.[68] The narrator betrays a similarly distanced historical perspective to more jarring effect when noting that the Jews were expelled from Colonia "and then, a few years later, they were once more readmitted as though nothing had ever occurred. Such is the way of the Germans with their Jews."[69] To what extent does this laconic remark refer obliquely to the more recent history of German Jewry, and are the events of Portobuffole recounted in light of this unstated frame? The Portobuffole narrative's many references to yellow stars, Jewish bodies burned to ash, "smoke coming from the chimney," and so on certainly suggest as much and raise the question of what end these depictions serve.[70]

On one level, these are questions about what various disciplinary modes of knowing can contribute to the question of racial periodization. Zygmunt Bauman has influentially observed that diachronic narratives that treat the Holocaust as "the continuation of anti-Semitism through other means" deny the Holocaust's specifically modern character.[71] Yet Bauman's characterization of the modern relies at times on a simplified account of the premodern as its foil. David Nirenberg, meanwhile, deems such diachronic accounts bad history, arguing that historical works that "take the long view, seeking to establish a continuity between the hatreds of long ago and those of the here and now" entail a dubious practice of historians acting "as geologists, tracing the ancient processes by which collective anxieties accreted into a persecutory landscape that has changed little over the past millennium."[72] But in a work of fiction, such a "geological" approach may constitute the very literariness of the text, and the repetition and accretion of such figures certainly contribute to the accrual of meaning across Phillips's far-flung and discontinuous narrative strands. However, Michael André Bernstein makes an impassioned case against what he terms "backshadowing"—a form of narrative organization in which the representation of historical events tends inexorably toward a known historical outcome, which Bernstein argues is especially prevalent in Holocaust narratives. "When an event is so destructive for a whole people . . . as was the Shoah," he writes, "there is an almost irresistible pressure to interpret it as one would a tragedy, to regard it as the simultaneously inconceivable and yet foreordained culmination of the entire brutal history of European anti-Semitism."[73] To write and narrate thus, Bernstein argues, implies about those who perished that their lives are only a brief flash of significance in comparison to the inevitability and weightiness of their deaths.[74] This is an ethical and literary failure, owing to the "contradiction . . . between insisting on the unprecedented and singular nature of the Shoah . . . and yet still using the most lurid formal tropes and commonplace literary conventions to narrate it."[75] Phillips's approach, which at times seems to toy with the lurid teleology that Bernstein decries, thus seems aligned with bad sociology, bad history, and, most pertinently, historically and ethically irresponsible literature.

In my view, instead of treating this fifteenth-century blood libel as an example of the "signs or symptoms of a linear march toward intolerance," Phillips illuminates how purportedly premodern violence blurs the sharp distinction between the premodern and the modern, incorporating supposedly quintessentially modern elements.[76] The Portobuffole narrative gradually reveals that Portobuffole's Jews are not brutalized by irrational, hysterical mob violence but by the state, which channels and strategically preempts any such violence through a set of legal and disciplinary mechanisms that involve the various levels of the Venetian republic's government and its judiciary. In a state that "reluctantly admitted their need for the Jews," who provided "large-scale capital investment" for Venice's imperial and capitalist ambitions, such legal and political calculations are the rule and not the exception.[77] Other critics have noted the narrator's sophisticated assessment of the state's cynical alternation between tolerance and intolerance, as well as the narrator's own reiteration of the stereotypes associated with the blood libel, and so I keep my examples here brief.[78] The point is that many of our most influential accounts of race have insisted that race is a concept legible only in modernity, when purportedly characteristically modern developments such as the consolidation of the nation-state form; the global extension of empire; and scientific practices of biological systematization and classification, speculative reason, and empiricism fully take hold.[79] Even those accounts that backdate the race/modernity threshold to 1492 risk historical elision; as Jonathan Boyarin has noted, while 1492 is often taken to represent a threshold of modernity, overseas colonization was "part and parcel of the efforts to expand, rationalize, and unify Christian Europe that had been going on for centuries."[80] Phillips's retelling of the blood libel proposes that the chronology of race and the modern be reconsidered and re-emplotted.

Conversion is central to these debates, as Irene Silverblatt has shown in her account of the racial modernity of the seemingly non-modern. Silverblatt builds on Hannah Arendt's claim about the central role of imperialism in the development of race thinking. But while Arendt is myopically insistent that imperialism is a nineteenth-century phenomenon, Silverblatt argues that "it was Spain's colonial efforts, not northern Europe's, that initiated the 'civilizing' mix of bureaucracy and race thinking that Arendt found so damning."[81] The Spanish Inquisition, that "icon of premodern irrationality and cruelty," in fact introduces key modes of race-making: sophisticated bureaucracy, legal proceduralism, secular institutionalization, and a national security apparatus.[82] The Inquisitorial persecution of Jewish conversos, or New Christians, and Moriscos, Christian converts from Islam, both in Spain and in its colonies in turn shapes Spanish colonialism's racial categories. "Conquistadors brought the curse of the New Christians—the concept of stained blood (*sangre manchada*)—to the Americas," writes Silverblatt.[83] There, the perplexing questions that clustered around these converts, including whether "blood stains" were indelible and if stained blood could be cleansed through baptism or over generations, contributed to the development of categories like mulatto and mestizo, as María Elena Martínez in particular has shown.[84] Such ideas about stained blood and its transmission and/or solvency, Silverblatt argues, established religious differences as racial ones: "a racialized view of religion [was] a view born at the same time as the Inquisition itself. According to its dictates, baptized men and women of Jewish (or Muslim) descent were considered stained by ancestral heresies, regardless of conversion to Christianity or commitment to the faith."[85]

Other scholars of the period might disagree with Silverblatt's origin story, but I want to draw out from these historical debates the extent to which conversion and its limits conceptually echo the problem of plasticity.[86] Conversion seemed to hold the promise that no one was irredeemable and that even those outside the fold were coreligionists in waiting, provided they could embrace (or be induced to embrace) their own educable nature and accept the teachings of Christianity and the promise of its universalism. Yet conversion was structured by anxieties about the incorrigible and unchanging character of blood. Such beliefs and the institutions in which they were systematized and deployed for the management of populations suggest that these were projects of race-making, understood neither as the production of hierarchies of fixed racial types or the valuation of differences in color but rather as the preoccupation with the tension between the fixity and plasticity of forms. At midcentury (the twentieth century, that is), UNESCO insisted that cultural prejudices were easily remediable because cultural differences were malleable, and they pointed to conflicts between Christians, Jews, and "infidels" as evidence. But if conversion is a practice of assimilation, then the history they looked to should have offered little cause for optimism, since this key technique by which populations were forced into harmony or at least homogeneity was structured by a disbelief that differences of blood and belief were malleable enough to be truly transformed.

As we will see in what follows, *The Nature of Blood* is saturated by questions about conversion, as are Phillips's Shakespearean intertexts.[87] However, Phillips also emphasizes Jewish fidelity and its resistance to conversion. This is apparent, for instance, in the Portobuffole narrative, which concludes with the execution of some of the community's leaders upon their refusal to convert. To my mind, it also suggests an answer to the question of why Phillips engages so explicitly with *Othello* but not with *The Merchant of Venice*, when he is clearly preoccupied with Jewish difference in Venice at that time. After all, in *The European Tribe*, Phillips describes Shylock as his hero.[88] Yet where we might expect to find *The Merchant of Venice*—as the Jewish pole of the medieval–early modern Venetian axis whose other pole is *Othello*—we instead find the reconstruction of the Portobuffole blood libel of 1480. My suspicion is that this is because *The Merchant of Venice* is not about fidelity but rather about conversion and the anxieties it generates about betrayal or infidelity, as Janet Adelman has powerfully demonstrated.[89] Like Silverblatt, Adelman emphasizes that blood was the medium of such political questions about loyalty and legibility, even as blood lineage in the play determines what Adelman calls a "proto-racial distinction" among gentile and Jew.[90] As Adelman argues, there are multiple conversions in the play; while Shylock's is forced, Jessica's conversion by marriage and Lancelot's transfer of his loyalties to a Christian master are implicated as betrayals. Phillips bypasses such questions about Jewish conversion altogether; compare the end of *The Merchant of Venice* and Shylock's conversion, which is forced upon him but which he chooses over death, to the end of the Portobuffole narrative, in which Servadio and his fellow community members "rejected [a] last-minute offer of conversion, preferring to die as sinners," praying "'*Hear, O Israel, the Lord is our God, the Lord is one*' as the flames beneath them burn."[91]

Phillips runs the risk of romanticizing Jewish fidelity with dubious consequences. In the final lines of the Portobuffole narrative, the executioner sticks his shovel between the still-hot coals, "and when he pulled it out it was full of white ash ... [which] dispersed immediately."[92] Pages later, Eva Stern describes the extermination camp where she is imprisoned, including the crematorium chimney and the "ash-freckled snow" around it.[93] This is one instance of what Michael Rothberg calls Phillips's "anachronistic aesthetic," but it raises questions not unrelated to Bernstein's qualms about backshadowing.[94] In suggesting such echoes between the victims of the blood libel and the destruction of Eva Stern's assimilated, secular German Jewish family in the 1940s, the novel may gloss over the fact that, as Irving Howe puts it, most of "the Jews destroyed in the camps ... died ... not because they chose at all costs to remain Jews, but because the Nazis chose to believe that being Jewish was an unchangeable, irredeemable condition."[95] Indeed, the novel will amplify these questions about the narrative and political stakes of Jewish fidelity, and I will return to Phillips's romanticizing depiction of Jewishness in the final section. But in order to understand how the novel conceives this fidelity, we first need to consider Phillips's resignification of the novel's titular term, *blood*, in literary and historical perspective.

THE SUPERSESSION OF BLOOD

In a 1943 essay, "The Myth of Blood," reprinted in the 1945 edition of *Man's Most Dangerous Myth: The Fallacy of Race*, Ashley Montagu devotes his attention to resignifying the relation between the terms *race* and *blood*. His purpose is to staunch blood's transfusion of meaning and signification to race—for while the word *race* "has assumed a high emotional content in relatively recent times," *blood* "is a word which, from the beginning of recorded history, and long before that, has possessed a high emotional content."[96] Montagu's wager is that by resignifying blood's meaning, he can attenuate race's emotional grip on the public imagination.

The crux of the issue is the stubborn popular conviction that blood determines identity. This is a long-standing view, Montagu acknowledges, since

> from the earliest times [blood] has been regarded as that most quintessential element of the body which carries, and through which is transmitted, the hereditary qualities of the stock. Thus, all persons of the same family stock were regarded as of the same "blood." In a community which mostly consisted of family lines whose members had, over many generations, intermarried with one another, it is easy to understand how, with such a concept of "blood," the community or nation would come to regard itself as of one "blood," "distinct," *by blood*, from all other communities or nations.[97]

There are at least two kinds of transmission in question here: the "transmission of hereditary characters" from generation to generation and the seemingly unshakeable belief encoded in the enduring "cultural dynamics of Western civilization" that blood is the medium of such hereditary inheritance.[98]

As such, Montagu's task is to impose a periodizing break in the historical signification of blood. He does so by insisting that such outdated and mythical beliefs in blood transmission have been decisively superseded and corrected by a properly scientific and verifiable genetic conception of heredity:

> In the first place, let it be stated at once that blood is in no way connected with the transmission of hereditary characters. The transmitters of hereditary characters are the genes which lie in the chromosomes of the germ cells represented by the spermatozoa of the father and the ova of the mother, *and nothing else*. These genes ... are the *only* parts of the organism which transmit and determine the hereditary characters. Blood has nothing whatever to do with heredity, either biologically, sociologically,

or in any other manner whatsoever. . . . The belief that the blood of the pregnant mother is transmitted to the child in the womb, and hence becomes a part of the child, is ancient, but completely erroneous. Scientific knowledge of the processes of pregnancy have long ago made it perfectly clear that there is no actual passage of blood from mother to child. . . . This fact should forever dispose of the ancient notion, which is so characteristically found among primitive peoples, that the blood of the mother is continuous with that of the child. . . . Modern scientific investigation demonstrates that this and similar notions are quite false and thus completely disposes of the idea of a blood-tie between any two persons. . . . Hence, any claims to kinship based on the tie of blood can have no scientific foundation of any kind. Nor can claims of group consciousness based on blood be anything but fictitious, since the character of the blood of all human beings is determined, not by their membership in any group or nation, but by the fact that they are human beings.[99]

Montagu's argument is a plea for the death of a metaphor. In his account, blood is a powerful but stopgap metaphor for the workings of heredity, adopted in "a period when the nature of heredity was not understood and the existence of such things as genes was unknown."[100] Popular opinion is late to accept what science "long ago" established, but such a reeducation is now an urgent matter, since "the blood myth" has been elevated to a principle of global catastrophe by the Nazis.[101] Indeed, he notes, this myth is "almost as strongly entrenched in [the United States] as it is among the Nazis," as was demonstrated "when the Red Cross segregated the blood of Negroes for the purposes of transfusion."[102] Only this figural death, he avers, can make way "for the scientifically established universal truth that all human beings, no matter of what creed or complexion they may be, are of one and the same blood."[103]

There are several tensions in Montagu's account that I want to draw out. First, Montagu amplifies this final point about blood as a medium of universality rather than difference by turning to the New Testament and to Acts 17:26: "There are no known or demonstrable differences in the character of the blood of different peoples. In that sense the Biblical *obiter dictum* that the Lord 'hath made of one blood all nations of men to dwell on the face of the earth' is literally true."[104] Montagu's invocation of Christian universalism is striking and a little peculiar in a piece that identifies Nazism as the most vicious weaponization of the blood myth and that particularly singles out the antisemitic Nazi propagandist Alfred Rosenberg. While Montagu's central argument is that a sanitized genetic conception of heredity has decisively superseded an archaic understanding of blood community, there seems to be a second, more subtle supersession at work here. It is as though Montagu feels compelled in this piece refuting Nazi racial theories of blood to gesture, however obliquely, to the idea that Jews not only share that "popular conception of 'blood' which prevails at the present time" but indeed may be among those "primitive peoples" Montagu singles out as having endowed blood with singular power, as well as one source for the centrality of blood in the "cultural dynamics of Western civilization."[105] Second, blood unsettles the sharp distinction between race and culture so much at stake in this discourse because heredity is not a purely natural or biological category. As the historians of science Staffan Müller-Wille and Hans-Jörg Rheinberger argue, the definition of heredity as a natural law, according to which transmission "through the germ line counts as the 'first,' strictly biological, nature of a human being," itself depended on the "metaphorical transfer" from eminently cultural systems of kin classification and property distribution.[106] Even if a sanitized conception of genetic heredity dispels blood's racial resonances, blood retains symbolic importance as a medium of cultural transmission, while the gene itself is dependent on logics of cultural transmission for its legibility. Third, Montagu declares that "claims of group consciousness based on blood [cannot] be anything but fictitious." However, in saying so he sets aside the possibility that blood's significance to cultural transmission may be literal and not just metaphorical. In other words, how might blood be implicated in the very practices that constitute culture as such?

In an important study, David Biale, a scholar of Jewish history and Jewish thought, has offered a very different account of blood's centrality to the mutually constituting formation of Jewish and Christian identities. Blood is essential to both traditions' ritual practices and symbolic economies from late antiquity to the Middle Ages. Both are founded on a blood covenant (the covenantal scene of Exodus 24:8, in which Moses sprinkles blood on the people, and Christ's crucifixion, respectively), and both confront the challenge of allegorizing these covenantal scenes.[107] However, Biale points to a second "countervailing tendency" in these traditions to make the literal, material fact of blood and its management central to their ritual practice (circumcision and the prohibition on ingesting blood, and the consumption of the Eucharist, respectively).[108] The symbolic centrality and enduring persistence of such practices and prohibitions prompts Biale to propose that both Judaism and Christianity entail the formation of "blood community," which is constituted by the observance of rituals that determine, among other things, blood's proper use and correct disposal. The crux of Biale's argument is that such sanguinary practices and their observance are integral to the consolidation and perpetuation of Jewish and Christian identity. Blood does matter to what Montagu calls "group consciousness" but not in its familiar, disenchanted form as the medium for hereditary racial transmission.[109] Instead, in Biale's account, "the covenant of blood suggests that the nation was based on ritual actions at least as much as on ancestry."[110] In other words, blood makes the nation not racially but culturally. While this apparent stabilization of race and culture does not hold, not least thanks to new practices of what Nadia Abu El-Haj calls "genetic history," let me bracket this issue temporarily in order to situate Phillips alongside the discussion of Montagu's disenchantment of blood on the one hand and Biale's formulation of blood community on the other.[111]

In my reading, *The Nature of Blood* offers an extended reflection on blood community in Biale's sense, attempting to disaggregate race from culture while asking if a community constituted by ritual practice can resist the residual lure of blood as a racial metaphor. Only once in the three fragments (each approximately ten pages) that together constitute the arc of the Portobuffole narrative is there any description of Jewish ritual observance as the town's community actually practices it, rather than in the terms and figures of Christian projection and persecution. This episode depicts the community's celebration of the first night of Passover, a holiday that in the Christian imagination of the period is entangled with Easter and the abiding Christian perception of Jews as responsible for Christ's death. The narrator describes how this in turn historically lends the blood libel its dark energy: "During Holy Week it was common practice for [Jews] to re-enact this crime and kill a Christian child in order that they might draw out the fresh blood and knead some of it into the unleavened bread which they ate during their own Easter celebration, known as Passover."[112] The blood libel is also a description of blood community but precisely inverts Jewish law, accusing Jews (in Biale's words) of "what is most abhorrent to Jewish law" while projecting onto them "what Christians themselves do, namely, eat the body and blood of Christ in the form of the Eucharist."[113] However, the novel's representation of Passover in the home of Servadio, one of the community's senior members, seemingly corrects the distorted "gentile tales" of Jewish ritual sacrifice by describing the rhythms of the Passover celebration as they unfold within the seeming security and intimacy of a family home.[114] The narrator's description stresses the enduring rituals associated with Passover and suggests that the community's commitment to its observance is one measure of the extent to which Christians and Jews occupy different calendrical orders and life worlds: while the "highly spirited Christians were joyfully celebrating the Feast of the Annunciation and looking forward to the following day, Palm Sunday," Portobuffole's Jews "had gathered in the house of Servadio to begin to celebrate the night of the fourteenth day of the month of Nissan in the year 5240 since the creation of their world."[115] Implicitly rebutting the Christian myth that the coincidence of Easter and Passover confirms the latter's parodic and debauched celebration of Christ's crucifixion, the narrator's invocation of "their world" suggests that Portobuffole's Jews dwell in a different or perhaps dual temporal and spiritual world.

In the Portobuffole narrative, fidelity to a repertoire of ritual practice constitutes the meaningful basis of Jewish communal identity. This is by no means to suggest that this episode offers any sort of "thick description" or representational richness. Quite the opposite: the depiction of Passover is rife with clichés. The narrator sketches in broad strokes the elements of ritual: ridding the home of fermented food, eating unleavened "crackers" in place of bread, and "the huge tray" on which "various other objects necessary to their Jewish rituals" are placed.[116] There are sentimental women, who "left the kitchen with damp eyes and came to listen to [the] small boy who stood in front of the assembly of men," and a "proud" father, who "smiled as he recognized himself in the inquisitive young boy."[117] While this is the one instance in which Portobuffole's Jews emerge from behind the story of their victimization, they do so as hardly more than stock characters. While one might ask about the implications of such a reliance on cliché, I read this apparent representational failure as an indication that we are reading for something else—namely, an emphasis on the cyclicality and continuity of these traditions. Instead of descriptive verisimilitude or psychological depth, the narrator emphasizes historical duration: "For almost three thousand years the Jews had celebrated this holiday by reciting the same prayers, abstaining from the same foods, and reading the same stories as if reading them for the first time. This was the source of their safety, and the basis of their relative confidence and happiness."[118]

Phillips thus refuses both dimensions of Montagu's supersessionism. He challenges Montagu's supersession of blood by the gene, not because he thinks blood is the medium for the truth about race but because (like Biale) he identifies the way that cultural practices, including ones pertaining to blood and the management of its social signification, are implicated in culture and its continuity. He also refuses Montagu's Christian universalism, stressing instead cultural fidelity as the basis of the Portobuffole Jewish community's cohesion and difference. The narrator insists that the community's apartness is not just imposed by the Christians around them but is chosen. Portobuffole's Jews, the narrator asserts, "arrived as foreigners, and foreigners they remained."[119] The narrator faults Portobuffole's Jews for their continued adherence to "unseemly" modes of conduct, ranging from their clothing to their observance of the Saturday Sabbath, and largely poses the problem of assimilation as a failure of Jewish will: "Sadly, as the years passed, this mistrust did not abate. It became apparent that the Jews wished to speak only among themselves. Further, they chose not to eat or drink with the Christians, and they refused to attend to their heavy German accents."[120] "Wished," "chose," "refused": the narrator describes Jewish unassimilability in terms of stubborn particularism, rather than insoluble difference. The tension between these two characterizations is apparent in the Venetian practice of compelling Jews "to distinguish themselves by yellow stitching on their clothes."[121] There is something ironically redundant about imposing such marks on clothing when, according to the narrator, it is in part through clothing that the community sets itself apart. Yet such a practice implies that were they to cast off such external markers altogether, it might no longer be possible to distinguish them from others. This is an echo of Phillips's childhood story inspired by his youthful perplexity as to why Jews did not refuse the star and pass—a simple option, in his child's mind. Yet in *The Nature of Blood*, instead of stressing the racial undecidability of Jewishness and its ready solubility into whiteness, Phillips reconceives of Jewishness as a practice of cultural fidelity—that is, the faithful reaffirmation of a set of practices, chosen over and over again through the generations. Such fidelity, he suggests, produces an identity as socially significant as any imposed by the perception of racial fixity. This is a powerful reframing of the entanglement of blood, culture, and race that Montagu's midcentury intervention sought to rationalize.

Moreover, such a reframing not only refuses the supersessionism implicit in midcentury attempts to strictly periodize the history of racial meaning, but it also complicates the relationship between gene and culture that Lévi-Strauss articulated in 1971. Recall, in his 1971 UNESCO speech, Lévi-Strauss pointed out that while race did not determine culture, culture in fact produced race, since genetic populations were made in the first instance through cultural practices that determined a community's isolation or integration.[122] However, there is another way of reading what Lévi-Strauss treats as a causal relationship, and I turn to Abu El-Haj's resonant work on Jewish practices of genetic history in the age of DNA ancestry testing to try to elaborate this idea. Abu El-Haj examines the surge of interest in the possibility that evidence of Jewish ancestry can be found on the Y chromosome and in mitochondrial DNA. Such evidence takes the form of "noncoding genetic markers" that record mutations to which scientists ascribe little or no biological significance but which, it is thought, can be "read as 'mere' indexes of ancestry and origins"—that is, as an historical archive of sorts.[123] While "anthropological genetics" tries to distinguish itself from race science, insisting that the biological characteristics it examines have no "causal properties" with "biological and social consequences" for the organism and its place in the world, such "genetic history," Abu El-Haj argues, still "biologize[s] history."[124] Yet she notes that while the genetic markers such testing examines offer evidence of "origins, migration patterns, and descent lines (or kinship practices)," the presence of such markers in the first place depends on "the repeated act of remaining faithful to [a] religious principle" (her example is the Cohanim, which is "a scientifically legible group" only because the descendants of that lineage "have remained true to the principle of passing priestly status from fathers to sons").[125] Such fidelity necessarily precedes and produces the genetic traces that purportedly confirm identity. Or, as she puts it, "populations are visible to the molecular gaze because of a sustained and repeatedly chosen fidelity to one's traditions. And those choices, that responsibility, that fidelity is what testifies to—what produces, in fact—a *meaningful* human collectivity, a 'culture' that is."[126] Moreover, the inconclusive and contradictory genetic data is never sufficient to the historico-political work it is called upon to do; the results of such tests depend upon and require supplementation from what one scientist terms "already existing data." "That already existing data," writes Abu El-Haj, is "textual data. For its proper interpretation, genetic data depends on older, humanistic sources. The truth of Jewish origins lies elsewhere. It resides in longstanding traditions, in biblical texts, in existing 'historical' sources," as well as "in religious beliefs and practices" and "in cultural and political commitments."[127] In contrast to Lévi-Strauss, Abu El-Haj effectively argues that culture does not produce the genetic population. Culture instead produces culture, because the genetic population is itself an interpretive object, made by cultural practices that render collectivity meaningful in the first place and remade as a site of identity formation in the context of ancestry testing via interpretation and narrative resignification. Both Phillips and Abu El-Haj offer interpretations that reverse the causality and valence of the chosen versus the given. However, as Abu El-Haj shows in her examination of the work such genetic history can do to legitimize Israeli state-building and nationalist narratives that lean on accounts of the genetic integrity of Jews, these practices can be mobilized in service of claims to national exclusivity that treat blood as an authoritative discourse about the limits of belonging.[128]

At this juncture an important fissure opens up in Phillips's work. Phillips identifies how an account of Jewishness as fidelity to a set of cultural practices might not withstand other conceptions of blood. In the final strand of the novel, Phillips offers the narrative of a young Ethiopian Jewish woman named Malka, who encounters Stephen Stern in the 1990s in Israel. The very persistence of the Beta Israel, or Ethiopian Jews, as an isolated community that has held to Jewish practices seems as powerful an example of fidelity as any other, and Malka emphasizes that these practices are blood practices: "*During Passover, we kill a lamb and sprinkle its fresh red blood around the synagogue.*" But these practices are not transplantable to Israel, where "*you do not allow this.*"[129] This restriction, in turn, hints at other limitations on belonging, and Malka suggests that differences in skin, more even than the practices of the dispersed faithful, threaten to sunder her belonging to the community of Jews. The imposed conversion of practice that she gestures to is echoed by another conversion as she wonders whether "*in this new land, would our babies be born white?*"[130] Phillips has described how the creative impetus for Malka's story, which he calls the "final piece of the narrative puzzle" came in the form of a news story about Israel's practice of segregating blood donated by Ethiopian Jews, for fear of disease and contamination.[131] I think here of Montagu, who chastises the United States military in the 1940s for its continued practice of segregating the blood of Black soldiers. Indeed, the astonishment Phillips describes at reading this late twentieth-century news story is partly about the extent to which blood continues to be tainted by association with differences in color—differences that challenge the possibility of community forged on fidelity to practice. Similarly, in his review of the Israeli author Hillel Halkin's book *Across the Sabbath River: In Search of a Lost Tribe of Israel*, Phillips criticizes Halkin's eventual rejection of the supposed lost tribe he has sought to locate in India on the grounds that it is a rejection "based on blood. . . . On this point he is, of course, correct: if one uses blood and the existence of a Jewish genetic profile to determine membership of the tribe, then in all likelihood the Mizo will probably fail this test."[132] Why, he wonders, can Halkin not renounce this insistence that belonging must be adjudicated by the evidence of blood and accept that it inheres instead in practices and in narratives about the meaning of those practices?[133]

Yet even as Phillips recognizes that epidermal difference interrupts the supposed community of belief and identifies the way that blood materially and metaphorically subtends this sundering, he never acknowledges that these adjudications and consolidations of belonging shore up the distinctions not only between real and false Jews but also between Jews and Palestinians. Phillips avoids these connections not only in these essays but also in the novel; indeed, the consistency of this avoidance across the essays and fiction invites a symptomatic reading. In the next section, I show how Phillips's Othello narrative is framed in terms of betrayal rather than fidelity and suggest how this speaks to the absence of Islam in Phillips's relational thinking.

ORIENTAL APPARITIONS

Phillips represents the Portobuffole Jewish community's particularism as cultural fidelity but in his rewriting of *Othello*, Othello's willingness to betray and abandon his community to pursue personal glory at "the very centre of the empire" is the source of his undoing.[134] Othello acknowledges that he has been summoned to Venice by the state because "the republic preferred to employ the services of great foreign commanders in order that they might prevent the development of Venetian-born military dictatorships."¹³⁵ Like Portobuffole's Jews, whose usefulness makes their presence tolerable, Othello is there to fulfill a specific function, serving "only in a time of crisis."¹³⁶ Whereas the Portobuffole Jewish community is perceived as excessively and stubbornly particularist, Othello is eager to shed or suppress whatever signs of difference he can, observing that "while exterior display of a different culture was tolerated, I was learning that such stubbornness was unlikely to aid one's passage through society."¹³⁷ His marriage to Desdemona is one means of passage. As they pledge their engagement, Othello marvels at his fortune: "Was I truly the same man who had arrived lonely and unannounced? . . . The same man who had initially struggled with the language and who had, at times, wondered if he would ever settle among these strange and forbidding people? And now to be married, and to the heart of the society."¹³⁸ Like a well-executed marriage plot, Othello and Desdemona's union seems to offer the tantalizing possibility of resolving Othello's socially uncertain status. However, Othello cannot shed or suppress what he terms "my natural state," or presumptive racial difference, despite adopting Venetian ways in an effort to "subdue a portion of the ill-feeling to which [this] natural state seemed to give rise."¹³⁹ As such, Phillips's Othello is a psychological portrait of the delusion of assimilation.

The novel also makes this point in another way, by directly comparing Othello's migrant cosmopolitanism to Venice's Jews. Othello's nighttime wanderings lead him to Venice's ghetto. He explores the ghetto, observing that its sleeping inhabitants "obeyed the rhythms of day and night with a slavish adherence." In contrast to the ghetto community's obedient and harmonized cycles, Othello situates himself as a wanderer and an explorer, disturbed by the confining character of the ghetto's architecture. Startled by the juxtaposition of "well-appointed houses" and "hovels," he wonders at a mode of life in which "the rich and the destitute lived together, the denizens bound only by their faith."¹⁴⁰ He implicitly contrasts the restrictiveness of the ghetto, which he attributes to the community's desire for separateness rather than to the intolerance of Venetian society, with his sense of himself as a sovereign subject engaged in the work of self-fashioning and self-fulfillment. In my reading, Othello imagines himself as what Elizabeth Povinelli calls an "autological subject," conditioned by discourses of "individual freedom," in contrast to what he perceives as the "genealogical society" of Venice's Jews, governed by kinship and "inheritances" that lead them to limit their freedom.[141] Of course, Othello's freedom to leave his people and, in Phillips's version, to leave a wife and son will prove illusory. While Phillips's narrative breaks off at the point when Othello and Desdemona arrive in Cyprus, when Othello still dares to dream of a Venetian social order that might include him, the reader knows by dint of familiarity with the play that Othello's sense of self-sovereignty will be undermined and destroyed.

One of the freedoms Othello claims for himself in his attempt to secure his social passage is conversion, yet remarkably—in a novel preoccupied with the racial significance of religion, conversion, and the tension between fidelity and betrayal—Phillips never touches on Othello's religious identity. Othello is a convert, as he confirms to the Christian priest who performs his marriage ceremony, though he does not indicate from what faith he has converted. But this is a profound and material element of the Othello story, for Othello is the Moor of Venice, and as Daniel Vitkus notes, *Moor* could refer to "'Turk,' 'Ottomite,' 'Saracen,' 'Mahometan,' 'Egyptian,' 'Judean,' 'Indian'—all constructed and positioned in opposition to Christian faith and virtue."[142] As Jonathan Burton puts it, when we consider Othello's Moorishness we are considering "the *religious color* of his skin."[143] What becomes of Othello's "religious color" after conversion? Such a question would seem to be of great interest to a novel concerned with the racial meaning of religious belief. Moreover, in light of Othello's characterization in the novel as a traitor to himself and his community, reflection on Othello's Moorishness seems like an enticing opportunity to consider his position as an infidel and this term's many shades of meaning, which also speak to many of the tensions concerning fidelity and betrayal that structure the logic of conversion. Phillips is quite clear about who or what he thinks Othello is: "I may be in danger of stating the obvious, but I shall state it anyhow. Othello was a black man."[144] In his telling, Othello's tragedy is that he himself forgets. Compare this with Daniel Boyarin's equally forceful attempt to assert that, when we consider Othello's Moorishness, "of course, northern Africa and Islam is where we are bound to look, for Muslim is what a Moor is and North Africa where a Moor comes from."[145] The racial and religious ambiguity of *Moor* does not have to be settled; the point is precisely that the term was flexible enough to mean a host of different things and capacious enough to mean many of them at the same time.[146] Rather, the question is why, when there are seemingly many points of contact with the concerns of the novel, Phillips passes over this ambiguity and passes over the significance of Islam as a privileged referent of Moorishness, from among the latter's many meanings.

While Phillips is attuned to questions of cultural racism and to what Balibar describes as antisemitism's prototypical status in this respect, there is a striking lack of attention to the way that Islam and Islamophobia are similarly situated. Only after 9/11, 7/7, and the beginning of the War on Terror does Phillips expand his vision to consider these formations, in his 2011 essay collection *Color Me English: Reflections on Migration and Belonging*. "Color Me English" is also the title of the introduction to this collection, and like the introduction to *The European Tribe*, it opens by returning to his childhood and specifically to the formative space of the schoolyard and the schoolroom; in fact, it reads as a rewriting of the earlier work. However, this retelling, from the perspective of the 2000s, focuses on another figure, another child. Two weeks into a school year in which Phillips has girded himself to cope with familiar, grinding racism, something changes the racial calculus of his world. An "oriental apparition" named Ali shows up in the corner of the classroom, "look[ing] terrified," and his presence moves Phillips closer to the cultural center despite his color:[147]

> Although I felt some immigrant kinship with him, and had instinctively tried to help him, things between us went only so far, and no further. Although we might be enduring some of the same difficulties because of our pigmentation, there was a clear cultural difference which meant that while I was able to find a way to anxiously participate in British life, albeit in a manner that was hardly fulfilling, Ali was enduring the type of hostility that renders any thoughts of participation a distant, and decidedly unlikely, dream. My nominal acceptability to my classmates was in part related to the fact that I was bigger, stronger, and a good deal more outgoing than Ali, but it was also related to my being, at least ostensibly, an Anglican churchgoer who had the good manners not to be able to flaunt another language. Take race out of the equation and I had no place to hide from the English. . . . Ali, on the other hand, had the worlds of religion and language into which he might retreat and hide from the English which, of course, made him deeply untrustworthy.[148]

This passage and the essay as a whole narrate the crystallization of Phillips's conception of cultural racism. In this retelling of his youth in the 1970s, Phillips narrates his adolescent enlightenment about the way that culture, even more than color, might determine one's assimilability. And yet the robust articulation of this insight—which I suggested Phillips was already tentatively trying to formulate in *The European Tribe* in his commentary on Baldwin's essay and the Venetian ghetto—can only appear here, belatedly, prompted by the recollection of the "oriental apparition" who haunts but also solidifies his understanding of race's relationship to culture.

Phillips's childhood encounters with images of persecuted Jewish children had prompted him to ask, "If white people could do that to white people, then what the hell would they do to me?"[149] But Ali's presence teaches him a different lesson. Both he and Ali are "pigmented" and yet Phillips discovers that he can perhaps be colored English, as the book's title would have it. Not in the way he once imagined, when he fantasized "as a boy growing up in England . . . [that] if only they could somehow color me English—in other words, white—then nobody would know the difference," but through a broader cultural transformation that he dates to the late 1970s and attributes to the growing presence of Black Britons in cultural representation and popular culture: "I was safe in my world where I could wait for colored footballers, and musicians, and newscasters to emerge and ease my passage into the outer circle of belonging in a still defensive and racist Britain. . . . I was being colored English, as opposed to my thirteen-year-old classmate, Ali."[150] In contrast, Ali's pigmentation is not so easily resignified because it is not only skin deep: behind it lie "the worlds of religion and language in which he might retreat and hide from the English." In other words, it is the "religious color of his skin" (to use Burton's phrase once more) that determines Ali's difference and its relative insolubility. Strikingly, the passage ends with an observation that in the eyes of most Britons, these hidden depths, this interior world, make Ali seem "untrustworthy." Phillips thus returns us to the questions of conversion/assimilability and fidelity that organize *The Nature of Blood*. Can Ali be emplotted into the reflections Phillips offers there? What is his fidelity to "religion and language"? What desire does he have for "passage through society"? Of course, Phillips does not say. Ali appears in the essay only in his childhood form, "the first Muslim that I ever knew," and like so many of the childhood figures I consider in this book, he represents a certain plastic promise, his fate unknown though hardly wholly in his hands: "I often wonder what happened to Ali, and if he ever did complete the journey or if, like the three young Muslim [7/7 suicide bombers] from Leeds, the effort of trying to belong... caused him to suffer from some sort of assimilation fatigue.... I hope that Ali, unlike the three Leeds Muslims who died on 7 July, has not given up on Britain."[151] Indeed, Phillips suggests that the question of Ali's emplotment is an open but also pressing one, for 9/11 and 7/7 have revealed that the untrustworthiness Europe attributes to its Muslim migrants and citizens has consequences. This is what worries Phillips and he speaks in the cadences of liberal multiculturalism, observing that "successful integration does mean that immigrants adapt to the new country, but it also means that the new country adapts to them."[152]

This essay substantively articulates Phillips's perspective on color, culture, and conversion, but it also indicates that perspective's shortcomings, as well as the limitations of his relational analysis of Jews, Blacks, and others. On one level, we might say that Phillips's belated attunement to the racialization of Islam simply reflects the way that changing historical circumstances shape our attention and analyses. I am reminded of Emily Bartels's observation that in effect, each generation gets the Moor it deserves. That is, each generation rethinks and re-produces Othello's Moorishness in a way that fits the interpretive and political needs of the time: "In speaking of the Moor we have always had to ferret the subject out from a seemingly endless set of diverse, divergent, and sometimes overdetermined images, to decide who our Moors will be."[153] Read in this way, Phillips's portrait of Othello the Moor might look very different today. And yet, this is not quite satisfying. Unlike Fanon, for instance, who observes that postwar cultural racism grafts a new discourse of "Occidental values" onto "[the struggle] 'between the cross and the crescent,'" Phillips does not acknowledge in this essay that European Islamophobia today is related to any enduring formation of cultural history.[154] Here, he treats it as hyperbolically contemporary, periodized only according to the present.

Accordingly, "Color Me English" never situates Islamophobia in relational perspective with anti-Judaism or antisemitism, just as the glossing over of Othello's Moorishness and its variable racial-religious meanings in *The Nature of Blood* misses the opportunity to situate Jewishness and Blackness in relation to Islam. In *The European Tribe*, Phillips frequently recounts his childhood in such a way as to suggest how both the question of Jewish difference and the history of the Holocaust formed his sense of the racial coordinates of his world. In this 2011 essay, Islam is a point of cultural comparison that shifts Phillips's sense of his own relative racial standing as he considers the possibility that culture is more fixed than color. However, these various strands are not brought together. Instead, this essay treats Islam and Judaism as two analogous religious identities among others, observing that "Islam is, like Christianity and Judaism, a flexible faith."[155] More striking still, Phillips reverts to the formulation of the Judeo-Christian that he invoked in *The European Tribe*: "Europe is no longer white and never will be again. And Europe is no longer Judaeo-Christian and never will be again."[156] While this is intended as an assertion of Europe's multicultural reality, it figuratively erases those conjoined processes of the assimilation or expulsion of Muslims and Jews that Boyarin and Silverblatt, for instance, emphasize were integral to Europe's efforts to consolidate itself as a Christian (and not a Judeo-Christian) polity. Indeed, the connection between *Othello* and *The Merchant of Venice* that *The Nature of Blood* implies but also effaces enables such insights. As Gil Anidjar suggests, joint consideration of these two plays entails asking "about the community and 'fellowship' . . . of those two Venetian bodies" and thus reconsiders "the arbitrariness of the decision that separates between Moor and Jew, and historically between Muslim and Jew, between Arab and Jew."[157]

This arbitrariness of the separation between Jews and Muslims directs us to that symptomatic elision of Palestine that I noted previously. Phillips offers many representations of Israel and Zionism across his fiction, travelogues, and cultural criticism, yet there is a striking absence of Palestine and Palestinians in these works, as some literary critics have argued.[158] These readings have proposed various ways of approaching this silence, from interpreting it as a symptom of a broader inability among postcolonial writers to address settler-colonialism in Palestine, as Bart Moore-Gilbert proposes, to identifying muted allusions rather than wholesale erasure, as Rothberg and Ana Miller do.[159] Yet Ahlam Masri and Tahrir Hamdi persuasively argue that such allusions are few, fleeting, and often ambivalent, compared to the consistency with which the narratives of Eva and especially Stephen Stern naturalize the Israeli claim to Palestine and the story of the territory's availability for Jewish settlement.[160] As these readings all generally recognize, *The Nature of Blood* does engage critically with Israel's self-conception as a homeland for all Jews in the form of Malka's narrative, yet as Masri and Hamdi argue, Phillips does not connect the mistreatment of Black Jews in Israel, whose "return" is meant to validate the state project, to the dispossession of Palestinians on which the state depends.[161] However, Masri and Hamdi's reading simplifies both the sources and significance of this erasure, when they argue that the novel is "essentially a politically authorized Zionist narrative" in which the "refusal to give any space to the Palestinian narrative is a direct and intentional slighting of a whole people."[162] While Phillips's silence or indirection on the question of Palestine may indeed bespeak that hesitancy to criticize Israel even in postcolonial thought that Moore-Gilbert and Miller identify, it is equally a symptomatic absence that is connected to the broader disengagement with Islam and Islamophobia in Phillips's otherwise comparative and relational writing.

The Nature of Blood powerfully explores some of the ambiguities of the concept of culture as an aspect of a postwar racial paradigm and as a hinge in the story of race as a modern or transhistorical category. Phillips considers culture's relationship to fixity at a time when the relative plasticity and fixity of the race and culture concepts were in flux. He also develops an account of Jewishness as cultural fidelity that productively complicates the relationship between Blackness and Jewishness, as well as the relationship between the given and the chosen. Yet for all that Phillips's work makes the connections across time and difference for which he is known, his reflections on culture are still shaped by the limitation of what he assumes in both his early and later writing to be the Judeo-Christian tradition of Europe—a Europe whose exclusions he wishes to challenge, to be sure, but which he also replicates. While his lack of engagement with Palestine seems to me an extension of the romanticization of Jewish fidelity that his work at times expresses and that leads him to naturalize the idea of a Jewish national home, this elision is itself symptomatic of Islam's absence in his work, without which the story of Europe's transtemporal romance with race, or its cultural racism today, cannot properly be told.

CHAPTER 4

REEDUCATION AS REPAIR

The November 1949 issue of the *UNESCO Courier*, the organization's popular monthly periodical for a general audience, featured an essay titled "The Question of Race and the Democratic World," by the Brazilian anthropologist Arthur Ramos.[1] Originally a medical doctor specializing in psychiatry, Ramos achieved international renown in the 1930s and 1940s for his studies on Brazil's Afro-descendant communities and cultures, as well as for his vigorous promotion of Brazil's "racial democracy," an enduringly controversial term seemingly of Ramos's own coinage.[2] During the 1940s, Ramos's focus shifted from ethnographic and scholarly work to applied anthropology, specifically to anthropology's role as a resource for antiracist reeducation. In common with many of the other figures I have discussed who formed the network of intellectuals and activists associated with UNESCO's race project, Ramos's reorientation was political. It was prompted both by the racial violence of the period and by his conviction that applied anthropology in particular and the social sciences in general could contribute to the work of repair.[3] Ramos's commitments resonated at UNESCO and he was appointed the first head of the Department of Social Sciences. There, he oversaw the early stages of UNESCO's race project, including the preparatory work for UNESCO's race statements, until his sudden death in 1949, only weeks before the scholars he had assembled would meet in Paris and draft the 1950 Statement on Race.[4]

Ramos's essay was the *Courier*'s first sustained commentary on race and it set the scene for UNESCO's race project.[5] It also functioned as a hinge between UNESCO's work on race and the UN's erection of a human rights regime. The previous issue of the *Courier* had focused on publicizing and celebrating the Universal Declaration of Human Rights, and the headnote to Ramos's essay linked it to this effort: "While endeavouring to make known and understood the Universal Declaration of Human Rights, UNESCO must also encourage the creation of conditions favorable to their application. One of the important ways it can do this is by fighting against all forms of racial prejudice.... It is by seeking and assembling historical scientific data on racial questions, and in making them widely known, that UNESCO can strike a useful blow in this fight."[6] Ramos's essay was thus both self-reflexive and expansive. Its immediate task was to confront anthropology's historical responsibility for race thinking and the recent war: "No other science," he observed, "has been so deflected from its true ends. In its name, whole nations have resorted to conflict, to defend the false ideal of racial or ethnic supremacy."[7] However, its aspirations were broader than this. As he sorrowfully inventoried the material damage to humanist values and human diversity, Ramos also sought to usher in a new era of racial repair.

The inauguration of such a reparative regime depended on Europe's recognition of its own culpability. Ramos's indictment of anthropology was also an indictment of Europe, for anthropology's crime was its complicity with the enforced "Europeanization" of the world. For Ramos and others, *Europeanization* designated Europe's centuries-long, now indefensible attempt to forcibly remake the world in its image, often in the name of civilizational progress, always under the banner of imperialism.[8] Europeanization, which had once been an imperial rallying cry, was increasingly an epithet. In Ramos's essay, its use is shaded with self-implication and late-imperial melancholy, as he regards a landscape in which anthropology has contributed to extinguishing cultures rather than preserving and synthesizing them. In the first instance, then, Europe's reparation to the world would require self-reckoning and willing submission to the work of reeducation.

Such a reckoning could not be undertaken alone, nor could Europe's reeducation merely entail a solipsistic self-regard styled as the recovery of European humanist values temporarily lost to fascism and restored now to cultural primacy. Instead, Ramos suggests, Europe would have to provincialize its own humanism and subject itself to the scrutiny of the cultural other, who might rightfully cast the disgraced European subject outside the compass of the human. Accordingly, he ends his essay by challenging all who have conquered and governed in the name of Europe to confront their inhumanity:

"The Ewe of Dahomey, when speaking of a cherished friend, says *enyé amé*—'he is a man.' For their enemies, for egotistical and cruel people (including Europeans), they reserve the expression *menyé amé*—'he is not a man.'"[9] Like Aimé Césaire, who in *Discourse on Colonialism* declares that "*Europe is indefensible*," Ramos recognizes (in Césaire's words) that "today the indictment is brought against [Europe] not by the European masses alone, but on a world scale" (*sur le plan mondial*).[10] Ramos demands that the European subject, his implied reader, submit not only to the other's judgment but also to the other's description, expressed in its own idiom. It is only by enduring the moral and also epistemological humbling of such a confrontation that Europe might become party to "the new humanism we all hope will triumph in the post-war world." Moreover, this new humanism must be multilateral, erected on the correspondences among traditions; the Ewe's expressions *enyé amé* and *menyé amé*, Ramos notes, neatly correspond to the Latin *humanus* and *inhumanus*.[11]

Ramos rhetorically conscripts the Ewe as agents of what Leela Gandhi has described as anticolonialism's "reverse civilizing mission"—a "therapeutic and pedagogic" endeavor whereby colonial subjects and imperial dissenters help Europe save what is worthwhile in its culture.[12] While Ramos merely ventriloquizes the Ewe, this dynamic of reversal is central to this chapter, not least in Césaire's *Discourse on Colonialism*, which I read in counterpoint to Ramos's work and the UNESCO race project more broadly. Indeed, Gandhi notes that *Discourse on Colonialism* is an especially striking example of the reverse civilizing mission. Césaire, she observes, "presents the colonial demand for independence from Europe as an intervention by well-wishers into the solipsistic life cycle of an unendurable friend or relative and expresses as much concern for the cultural and moral flourishing of perpetrators as for the victims of colonial injustice."[13] This may be putting the point too strongly, understating Césaire's unyielding accounting of the irreparable harms Europe has inflicted and eliding his irony. But Gandhi's general description of the reverse civilizing mission as an "intervention" is exactly right. The question is, An intervention into what?

For Ramos, the reverse civilizing mission dramatizes what Gayatri Chakravorty Spivak calls soul-making: imperialism's constitutively pedagogical project of civilizing savagery into humanity proper.[14] However, Ramos prods his reader to recognize that Europe—rather than the colonized—is in direst need of this moral-pedagogical intervention. Soul-making is Spivak's resonant term for imperialism's promise to institute "civil-society-through-social-mission" by making over "the heathen into a human so that he can be treated as an end in himself."[15] She takes her cue from Kant, who observes that education is required to transform "animality into humanity" but who also (per Ben Conisbee Baer's gloss) "introduces the figure of 'savage nations' [*wilden Nationen*] . . . as a foil to illustrate the claim that to humanize the animal means to subject it to the prescriptions and discipline of reason early on lest it preserve its *Wildheit* . . . for its entire life."[16] The violence of imperial soul-making, then, is apparent in the insistent figuration of the native as recalcitrant, belated, ineducable child and in the racism that Spivak calls "the dark side of imperialism understood as social mission."[17] Writing in 1949, in his official capacity as the impresario of UNESCO's efforts to delegitimize racism once and for all, Ramos's reversal demonstrates how the postwar crisis of race reconfigured the historical terms of soul-making, as the urgency of Europe's racial reeducation was felt with humbling force.

To put it in a much more pointed way, we might say that the reversal of soul-making as civilizing mission—returning now to Europe's shores a pedagogical project practiced on the colonies—is an expression and extension of the return to Europe of its own colonial violence that Césaire and Hannah Arendt described, respectively, as the "*choc en retour*" and the "boomerang effect." As we will see, Ramos himself discerned that such a dynamic was at work, offering in "Race and the Democratic World" his version of the analysis that Césaire and Arendt would memorably advance in the 1950s—Césaire in *Discourse on Colonialism*, whose first edition appeared in 1950, and Arendt in *The Origins of Totalitarianism*, whose first edition appeared in 1951. In my reading, Ramos apprehended this *choc en retour*, or reverse shock, primarily as a kind of moral retribution. In response, he elaborated an ethos of reparation in both moral and material registers. Soul-making in Europe was one element of this reparative program and was required to morally expiate the profound cultural harms European imperialism and racism had already wrought on native populations.

However, Ramos also prescribed a more tangible component to the reparations due to the colonized world. This material reparation was to entail technical, economic, cultural, and pedagogical interventions for the purposes of techno-scientific modernization and economic uplift. In other words, this was third world development, or what at UNESCO was called "technical assistance." Such projects were integral to UNESCO's operations from the start. Over the course of the 1950s and beyond, technical assistance claimed a growing share of UNESCO's program and budget, in keeping with the growth of the postwar development regime. These efforts did not displace UNESCO's emphasis on humanist subject production but rather were deeply entangled with it.[18] Moreover, they were refracted in UNESCO's antiracist pedagogy in the 1940s and 1950s, suggesting the extent to which this reparative developmentalism emerged from the midcentury crisis of race.

My broadest argument in this chapter is that the conjuncture I have been calling the reeducation of race was a regime of racial reparation constituted by the conjoined elements of soul-making in Europe and development abroad. Let me establish at the outset some of the chief implications of this formation, which accordingly suggest why it was a site of sustained engagement for Césaire in the 1950s and subsequently for postcolonial thinkers, such as the Ghanian writer Ama Ata Aidoo, whose 1977 novel *Our Sister Killjoy* I consider in the latter part of this chapter. First, the political dispensation best suited to this reparative developmentalism, it emerged, was colonial indirect rule. As we will see, Ramos's analysis of the *choc en retour* somehow derived from this experience of historical backlash a justification for the continuance of colonial rule as ethical necessity. Such a conclusion might be deemed ironic were it not for the fact that Ramos was oblivious to historical irony. This is among the most striking differences between his account and the analyses Césaire and Arendt offered at around the same time. Irony, I suggest, functions as the rhetorical signature of a counterpedagogical position that refuses the moralizing lessons of liberal racial reeducation. As I show through readings of Césaire, Arendt, and Aidoo, this critical stance is instead characterized by a special kind of perspicacity whose combination of anticipatory political foresight and revisionist historical insight arguably describes the structure of meaningful education as such.

Second, the anticolonial and postcolonial critique of this reparative regime expose the limitations and contradictions of its moralism. UNESCO's race project consistently spoke in the cadences of what I call reparative morality.[19] According to this ethos, the purpose of antiracism was to complete the unfinished business of the racial past not only by rectifying racial irrationality with antiracist reason but also by repairing racism's civilizational ruptures through projects of cultural salvage and neocolonial cultural beneficence. This racial-colonial sentimentalism was apparent among both the liberal antiracist left and unapologetic defenders of the colonial status quo, and we find versions of it both in Ramos's thought and in the best-known contemporaneous critique of UNESCO's race project: French sociologist Roger Caillois's fervid denunciation of Claude Lévi-Strauss's 1952 UNESCO volume *Race and History*, which Césaire invokes at a critical juncture in the 1955 edition of *Discourse on Colonialism*. Indeed, Césaire offers the most explicit instance of this book's claim that anticolonial thought critically registered UNESCO's race project and assessed its import. As I show in my discussion of *Discourse on Colonialism* and Césaire's 1956 address to the First International Congress of Negro Writers and Artists in Paris, "Culture and Colonization," Césaire engaged not only UNESCO's work on race but also its broader commitment to the reparative morality I identify at work in its discourse. Among the insights such an analysis yields is a new understanding of how Césaire's reflections on the Jewish genocide and Jewish difference emerge specifically from his engagement with UNESCO's race project.

Third, this reparative moralism was entangled with what I call weak education for the colonized. Unsurprisingly, education was among the most crucial components of UNESCO's third world technical assistance program. This educative program took on an increasingly technocratic cast, rendering education a technique for social stratification that promised upward mobility to a class of native bureaucrats and teachers who would ensure their nation's successful incorporation into a global regime of economic rationality that entailed new scales of racial hierarchy. Such a conception of education was in play at UNESCO from the outset, as is apparent in the vision articulated for the organization by its first director-general, Julian Huxley, a biologist who was another important influence on the organization's race project. "Every educative program is one of 'soul-making,'" Baer has observed, so long as it conceives of education as more than merely "instilling rational and technical knowledge."[20] Yet this is precisely what UNESCO eventually prescribed for the third world. The uneven global distribution of soul-making in Europe and instrumental education in the third world thus produced a new version of colonial educability, despite the apparent reversal of the terms of the imperial civilizing mission.

However, the postwar iteration of colonial educability also conscripted the postcolonial subject as a vital resource for the global reeducation of race, as a purportedly repentant and postracial Europe renegotiated its relationship to the postcolonial world. Recall Ramos's pious characterization of the Ewe in "The Question of Race and the Democratic World": having ventriloquized the Ewe's critique of European inhumanity, he concludes that they too possess an "empirical view of human nature" and proposes that this ethnographic reversal will facilitate the reckoning required for the reclamation of Europe's humanist values.[21] There is here a touch of that condescension with which the metropole rediscovers the colony, now as a resource of cultural renewal for an exhausted Europe. This dynamic is crucial to this chapter's story, as we consider how the postcolonial subject of the 1960s and 1970s functioned as a resource for Europe's spiritual repair as well as the target of pedagogical interventions that nonetheless still celebrated the superiority of European values. The discursive conscription of the postcolonial subject for these purposes corresponds to the era's "genres of rule," which saw newly independent nations in Africa and elsewhere increasingly locked in neocolonial relations that combined extraction and exploitation with the promise of development.[22]

In the second arc of this chapter, I consider these dynamics in the Ghanaian writer Ama Ata Aidoo's novel *Our Sister Killjoy*. Published in 1977 and set a decade earlier, Aidoo's formally experimental novel offers a withering critique of the postcolonial African state in a neocolonial era. In Aidoo's portrait, the political aspirations of independence have collapsed, and a comprador class obligingly implements the technocratic schemes of a development paradigm that perpetuates Ghana's colonial subordination in a new global order of purported postcolonial sovereignty. I pay particular attention to Aidoo's representation of education's role in the formation of the postcolonial subject in this historical conjuncture, which is characterized by the competing pressures of what Yogita Goyal has called "arrested decolonization" and Joseph Slaughter has called "compulsory development."[23] The novel's educative plot is organized around the young protagonist's journey to Germany on a type of student exchange program that takes her to a youth service camp in the countryside, from whence she travels to England and then returns home to Africa. The postwar enthusiasm for student exchanges and contact among young people of different cultures, which UNESCO had a heavy hand in enabling, was a crucial component of the reeducation of race. As Aidoo's narrative richly implies, such contact was simultaneously supposed to facilitate soul-making in Europe and development in the third world. *Our Sister Killjoy* ironizes these aspirations, offering instead a postcolonial counterpedagogy that demonstrates the gap between an exhausted European humanism still seeking to replicate itself and a history of barbarism that the astute student discerns for herself.

The protagonist's encounters with traces of the Holocaust, Germany's recent fascist past, and racism both there and in England provide the potent negative energy for Aidoo's critique of the lure of migration and the text's polemical perspective on the unlivability of diasporic life in Europe. I argue that Aidoo's theorization of the postcolonial killjoy closely corresponds to Hannah Arendt's figure of the Jewish pariah: one who refuses to learn from the experience of racial shame a lesson about the necessity of racial or social assimilation and who instead turns shame and the stigma of racial difference into a badge of resistance and communal solidarity. There are thus three kinds of return at stake in this chapter: the return of Europe's violence to its own shores, which at UNESCO was taken up as a problem for postwar pedagogy and the reeducations of race; return as the promise of repair, in the form of material and moral reparations that may in fact repeat or perpetuate colonial relations; and the returns embedded in the very logic of diaspora. This chapter considers these dynamics together. It demonstrates anticolonial thought and postcolonial literature's critical engagement with the postwar reeducation of race and traces the historical and conceptual centrality of antisemitism, the Holocaust, and Jewish difference for the elaboration of this counterpedagogy.

RETURN AS REBOUND

At around the same time in late 1949 that Ramos's essay "The Question of Race and the Democratic World" appeared in the *Courier*, he published a longer version, from which the *Courier* essay was undoubtedly drawn, in UNESCO's quarterly journal, the *International Social Science Bulletin*. This more scholarly and theoretical version is also more self-critical in its assessment of European colonialism's implication in the rise of European fascism. At the heart of this essay is a fuller theorization of Europeanization and its transformation and generalization into something Ramos calls the "racial technique."

To arrive at this formulation, Ramos offers a brief history of race thinking and its relationship with Europe's gradual domination of the globe. Theories of racial inequality and superiority are a commonplace of human existence, he notes, adopted throughout history especially "when a civilization at its zenith attempted to rationalize its 'ethnocentric' feelings." But it is only with the advent of European colonialism that such relatively innocent ethnocentrism is systematized, the better to serve as colonialism's alibi, its self-interested rationalization of exploitation, extraction, and subjugation: "It was only after the non-European peoples had been discovered and exploited and the world 'Europeanised'—after, that is to say, a European outlook and culture had been imposed on every people in the world—that racial feeling began to take definite shape and base itself, by a slow process, on reasoning." From a welter of disparate "racial doctrines," each with "their defenders and their opponents," a racial principle emerges and takes on its own peculiar coherence and solidity, even as European colonization produces a racial world-system that leaves nowhere untouched.[24]

Eventually, Europeanization—which originally describes a geographically specific colonial relation between Europe and the world, particularly Africa—overruns Europe itself. Ramos inventories the destruction imposed on peoples of the Americas, Africa, and Oceania and then observes, in an echo (or rather, an anticipation) of Arendt's and Césaire's reflections:

> But the weapon of "Europeanization" was eventually turned against those who forged it. In this 20th century of ours the "racialists," in their relations with other communities, have resorted to methods characteristic of colonial policy and slavery. The cases of the Jews and Negroes are living examples of the "superiority myth" in action. This story is too well known for us to expatiate on it further.
>
> We have seen that, in human relations, the "racial" technique has led to one of the greatest states of disequilibrium that exist, namely war. The present century has just paid tribute in the shape of the European nations' Second Great War, of which there were many causes; but one cause was undoubtedly the philosophy of racial domination espoused by the racialists of our time, that is to say the Germans.
>
> We see then, in the last analysis, that racialism is a direct result of Europeanization and imperialism. . . . It is on the peoples of Europe that the results of having had to accept domination by the "master races" have borne most heavily and disastrously.[25]

Ramos's analysis operates partly in the register of moral rebound and reckoning, as Europe is made finally to pay "tribute" for its ruthless pursuit of self-interested enrichment and exploitation. Such language may seem incongruous alongside his description of racism as technique, an inhuman abstraction best assessed by the disequilibrium and destruction it generates. In fact, the moral and the technical are tightly linked. Racism's technical dimension refines Europeanization into a weapon or tool that eventually smites its maker, lending this figure its moral and retributive charge. As we will see when I eventually turn to Ramos's prescriptions for repair, he rhetorically converts the "racial technique"—which describes the special inhumanity of European racism at its apotheosis—into technical assistance, or UNESCO's version of development with a human soul.

For now, though, let us concentrate on situating Ramos's account of Nazism as the rebound of European colonialism alongside Césaire's and Arendt's related reflections from virtually the same moment. Césaire and Arendt were hardly the only ones to propose that fascism and genocidal extermination in Europe were a species of return, delivering back to Europe the consequences of imperial politics and practices of colonial violence.[26] However, their reflections have been especially generative for recent scholarship in genocide studies, memory studies, and postcolonial studies, even as scholars have had to grapple with Arendt's own racism and its implications for her analysis.[27] Césaire's and Arendt's generativity may be partly thanks to their ambiguity; neither author quite specifies which precise historical elements they think are most responsible for this dynamic of return nor stabilizes how literally or figuratively we are to understand the causality at work.[28] However, it is precisely the figurative that helps explain the joint, heightened attention they have commanded. Each offered an evocative figural condensation of this historical dynamic—Césaire's "*choc en retour*" and Arendt's "boomerang effect"—whose tangibility stands out against the elliptical quality of their accounts.[29]

In what follows, I briefly discuss how Arendt and Césaire deploy their respective figures in order to advance three arguments. First, Arendt and Césaire share with Ramos a preoccupation with the boomerang's corrosive effects on the European soul—and not just on European institutions, as Arendt's account in particular at times seems to suggest. Second, tone—rather than any particular of their historical analysis—most closely connects Arendt's and

Césaire's accounts, and I argue that the boomerang effect and the *choc en retour* crystallize the specifically ironic tonal register of both their works. While these figures may seem inherently ironic, describing a historical irony that speaks for itself, in fact this irony entirely depends on the larger rhetorical and political orientation of the two works. Tone is a tricky property to pin down, yet as Sianne Ngai observes, "so much of ideological communication is tonal."[30] Arendt and Césaire both lean heavily on the communicative power of tone to challenge an emergent liberal narrative about the midcentury as a moment of historical rupture. There is considerable difference in the timbre and temperature of their irony and an even greater difference in their political commitments. However, their irony is the rhetorical signature of an oppositional intellectual and political stance attuned to the continuities between the past and the present. Both Arendt and Césaire are intent on forcing a confrontation with the disavowed contradictions of a postwar liberal order simultaneously committed to refortifying humanism and also to perpetuating colonial history in a neocolonial key.

Third, their irony as well as their insight are closely connected to the complex temporal dimensions of their accounts. Their oppositional perspective and the insights it enabled have led critics to herald Arendt's and Césaire's especial perspicacity in identifying, early on, the links between overseas empire and European Nazism. As Michael Rothberg observes of the pair, "Whatever their shortcomings, . . . it has taken scholars half a century to catch up to these early insights."[31] This precocious or forward-looking quality of their work, however, is paired with the retrospective gaze they applied not just to history but to their own writing. Arendt and Césaire both returned to their respective texts, revising and supplementing them in order to keep up with unfolding events and to register their evolving understanding of past, present, and future. In Arendt's case, new editions of *The Origins of Totalitarianism* reflected her evolving ideas and concerns.[32] Among these updates were the new prefaces she added to each of the three sections of the book for the edition that appeared in 1968. As for Césaire, as is well known, Présence Africaine's 1955 edition of *Discourse on Colonialism* was not the essay's first appearance in print; an earlier version was published in 1950 under the Réclame imprint associated with the French Communist Party. As Daniel Delas and A. James Arnold have documented in the genetic edition of *Discourse on Colonialism*, an even earlier version of the essay appeared in 1948 under the title "L'impossible contact"—some eleven pages in the journal *Chemins du Monde* that Delas describes as the "nucleus" of the subsequent 1950 and 1955 editions.[33] While much has been made of the aesthetic and political import of the revisions Césaire made over a considerably longer period (1939–1956) to his seminal poem *Cahier d'un retour au pays natal*, the revisions to *Discourse on Colonialism* are also significant, especially for demonstrating Césaire's triangulated engagement with UNESCO's postwar projects of racial reeducation and reparative development, as well as with the Holocaust.[34] In sum, both Arendt and Césaire revised their texts not only to reflect changing historical circumstances but also their own evolving understanding of the relationship between past, present, and future. This temporal structure of early insight and necessarily belated education lends the boomerang effect and the *choc en retour*, as well as these works as a whole, their irony and acuity.

In *The Origins of Totalitarianism*, whose first edition appeared in 1951, Arendt invokes the boomerang effect only a handful of times over the nearly five hundred pages of the text, always in the context of her analysis of imperialism, a political development the book analyzes alongside antisemitism and totalitarianism. Like Ramos, who observes that racists have "resorted to methods characteristic of colonial policy and slavery," Arendt describes the disabling—though in her view not entirely unanticipated—return to Europe of the "methods and institutions" on which overseas imperial rule relied. While continental imperialism "does not allow for any geographic distance between the methods and institutions of colony and of nation, so that it did not require boomerang effects in order to make itself and all its consequences felt in Europe," the depredations of overseas empire and its novel techniques for ruling subjugated populations for a time appeared confined to those extraterritorial spaces.[35] The boomerang, which traces a path of eventual, inexorable return across a great distance, dispels this illusion and only strict efforts to maintain "a sharp line between colonial methods and normal domestic policies" could forestall this outcome. Unlike Germany, France, and other European nations, Arendt argues that Britain never allowed its national political institutions to be co-opted by the alliance between capital and mob, "thereby avoiding with considerable success the feared boomerang effect of imperialism upon the homeland."[36] It is one of the many conceptual puzzles of *The Origins of Totalitarianism* that

Arendt is concerned with the triumph of totalitarian politics in Germany yet focuses her analysis of imperialism largely on British rule in Southern Africa, even while insisting that Britain remained largely immune to fascism. The political theorist Karuna Mantena suggests that we can understand this seeming contradiction if we read Arendt to be outlining what Mantena describes as an ideological shift, rather than one pertaining to specific institutions. Arendt, Mantena argues, was tracking the "transformations in habits of mind that led to the loss of respect for the institutional foundations of the nation-state." As such, she "sought to demonstrate how the *experience* of imperial rule worked to undermine the universal validity of law and the aspirational universality of the rights of man—how it laid the grounds, morally and psychologically, for a new ideological landscape in which violent exclusion, degradation, and extermination enter the language of everyday politics."[37]

Indeed, Arendt's most powerful as well as troubling reflection on the term implies that the boomerang effect was most significant not for its effect on European institutions but for its degradation of European sensibilities once white Europeans were conditioned to think in terms of race. Arendt juxtaposes South Africa and Nazi Germany, first rejecting and then seemingly affirming the logical and possibly even causal connection between colonial racism and Nazism: "In contrast to the Nazis, to whom racism and antisemitism were major political weapons for the destruction of civilization and the setting up of a new body politic, racism and antisemitism are a matter of course and a natural consequence of the status quo in South Africa. They did not need Nazism in order to be born and they influenced Nazis only in an indirect way."[38] Nonetheless, she continues, "South Africa's race society" produced "real and immediate boomerang effects . . . on the behavior of European peoples," normalizing and generalizing a new European attitude toward non-white peoples that quickly spread beyond Africa.[39] Strikingly, the consequences manifested first not in Europe but in Asia, where transplanted Europeans experienced a change in racial subjectivity. Whereas previously, Europeans regarded the peoples of Asia as "alien and strange," they now thought and behaved in terms of "the race principle," and "for the first time," Europeans treated Asians "in almost the same way as those African savages who had frightened Europeans literally out of their wits."[40] Arendt's suggestion that European racial subjectivity was only corrupted once Europeans applied the race principle to Asians, who could rightly claim to possess culture and civilization, no matter how foreign, naturalizes European racism in Africa as an understandable reaction to the condition of culturelessness that Europeans encountered among the "savages." Objectionable as Arendt's narrative is, however, I want to stress (in keeping with Mantena's analysis) that the most sustained explanation she offers of the boomerang effect ultimately treats it as a kind of spiritual unmaking of European subjectivities, analytically distinct from and in fact prior to the damage it does to the institutions of European nation-states.

If Arendt's reflections on the boomerang effect concluded there, we would be left with an account that, ideologically speaking, would differ relatively little from Ramos's own in its combination of outrage and obliviousness. However, in the new preface to the imperialism chapters that she wrote for the 1968 edition of *The Origins of Totalitarianism*, Arendt returned to the term in her reflections on Europe's postwar colonial relinquishment. Relinquishment is really the only word to describe how Arendt characterizes the history of decolonization, which she treats as a largely one-sided affair: the British "liquidated their colonial rule voluntarily" and de Gaulle "dared to give up Algeria," seemingly of his own political volition rather than because of the pressure exerted by the Algerian struggle for independence. Arendt must accordingly provide an explanation, and she proposes that they did so not from "mere weakness or the exhaustion due to two murderous wars in one generation" but because they feared a repetition of the boomerang effect. While Arendt once again singles out Britain for its foresight, this time it is not alone; all European colonial powers except Portugal, she writes, have developed "the moral scruples and political apprehensions . . . that advised against extreme measures . . . and against a continuation of the 'government of subject races' (Lord Cromer) because of the much-feared boomerang effect upon the mother countries."[41] It would seem, then, that Arendt was of the view that postwar Europe had learned something from the experience of fascism and totalitarianism.

In fact, from the vantage point of the late 1960s, Arendt thinks little has been learned and the past threatens imminent repetition. The end of imperialism may have seemed "accomplished fact" with Britain's loss of India, but the subsequent two decades have demonstrated that imperialism is alive and well. Only its expression has changed, taking on the neocolonial inflections of the Cold War era: "No one justifies expansion any longer by 'the white man's burden' on one side and an 'enlarged tribal consciousness' to unite people of similar ethnic origin on the other; instead we hear of 'commitments' to client states, of the responsibilities of power, and of solidarity with revolutionary national liberation movements."[42] Private investment and foreign aid oil the wheels of this machinery, and this situation "turns all foreign aid into an instrument of foreign domination."[43] Arendt's analysis is a diagnosis of the neocolonial present as the return of the imperial past. Despite Europe's surrender of its colonies for fear of the boomerang effect, "in historical terms . . . we are back, on an enormously enlarged scale, where we started from, that is, in the imperialist era and on the collision course that led to World War I."[44] The question of education is the open and vexing note on which the preface concludes. Arendt warns that even searching scrutiny of the past, of the kind she offers in *The Origins of Totalitarianism*, cannot predict what will happen next: "no matter how much we may be capable of learning from the past, it will not enable us to know the future."[45]

The preface is thus an anxious and ironic query about what, if anything, a world still organized by imperial aspirations of relentless expansion can learn from the past, even when European colonial powers seem to have acted on some of its lessons. Arendt writes in the characteristically forceful yet clinical register in which she advances her often unpopular or undesired views, combining slashing certainty with moments of hesitation and equivocation, especially as she confronts an unknowable future. Lyndsey Stonebridge has argued that Arendt's irony depends on such a perspective and that "to speak double, to parrot oneself ironically, is to generate the kind of perplexity necessary to thought."[46] Here, this doubling takes the form of a temporal repetition: Arendt suggests how the return of the boomerang effect (a return of a return, in other words) demonstrates the ironic proximity of a past that the postwar dispensation has supposedly left behind, even as it seems increasingly likely to repeat itself.

Like Arendt, Césaire refuses the sentimentalism of a liberal narrative of midcentury rupture and closure. *Discourse on Colonialism* bristles with observations on the way that European culture and subjectivities have been deformed by the indulgence of colonial atrocities. The *choc en retour* is not the only figure Césaire offers to describe the dynamics at work; it appears alongside references to infection and contagion. However, it is the summation or crystallization of these developments, which is formally reflected in the phrase's first appearance at the end of a series of lines that achieve their intensity from Césaire's characteristic use of parataxis and especially anaphora:

> First we must study how colonization works to *decivilize* the colonizer, to *brutalize* him in the true sense of the word, to degrade him, to awaken him to buried instincts, to covetousness, violence, race hatred, and moral relativism; and we must show that each time a head is cut off or an eye put out in Vietnam and in France they accept the fact, each time a little girl is raped and in France they accept the fact, each time a Madagascan is tortured and in France they accept the fact, civilization acquires another dead weight, a universal regression takes place, a gangrene sets in, a center of infection begins to spread; and that at the end of all these treaties that have been violated, all these lies that have been propagated, all these punitive expeditions that have been tolerated, all these prisoners who have been tied up and "interrogated," all these patriots who have been tortured, at the end of all the racial pride that has been encouraged, all the boastfulness that has been displayed, a poison has been distilled into the veins of Europe and, slowly but surely, the continent proceeds towards *savagery*.
>
> And then one fine day the bourgeoisie is awakened by a terrific boomerang effect [*réveillée par un formidable choc en retour*]: the gestapos are busy, the prisons fill up, the torturers standing around the racks invent, refine, discuss.⁴⁷

Brent Hayes Edwards has observed that Césaire's anaphoric syntax in *Cahier d'un retour au pays natal* is best understood as an expression of ambivalence, rather than as the registration of the accumulating traumas of the past or as the evocation of primitive rhythm, as some critics have suggested.⁴⁸ However, in *Discourse on Colonialism*, anaphora seems to convey exactly such associations with trauma or primitivity but with an ironic slant: if anaphoric repetition produces the impression of primitive frenzy, it is the primitivity of Europeans decivilized into a state of savagery. Similarly, Césaire ironizes the question of trauma: by alluding to the suffering of the victims (decapitation, torture, rape), he reminds us that whatever traumatic shock Europeans experience when they wake to find Nazism at their door is the trauma of the perpetrators and not the victims.⁴⁹ When this long paragraph finally pauses and breaks, the next line—"And then one fine day the bourgeoisie is awakened by a terrific boomerang effect"—lands with the thud of a too-neat rhyme and so jangles with a kind of mockery. Indeed, the very word *awakened* (*réveillée*) is ironic in this context, for this is not the awakening of dawning enlightenment but the nonplussed awakening of people startled into wakefulness by something they are not ready to explain or understand: "They say: 'How strange! But never mind—it's Nazism, it will pass!' And they wait, and they hope; and they hide the truth from themselves . . . that it is Nazism, yes, but that before they were its victims, they were its accomplices."[50]

Césaire included the foregoing lines in the early 1948 article "L'impossible contact," retaining them with only the smallest changes in subsequent editions.[51] While the 1950 edition more than quadrupled the length of the early essay, it was only in the 1955 edition that Césaire felt compelled to return to the term, redescribing it a second time as the closing bookend of his scorching reflection on the fate of the colonizer. The litany of colonial horrors he has offered, he stresses, is evidence of the dehumanizing consequences of colonialism on the colonizer, which take place first and foremost not in the prisons, police stations, or torture chambers of the fascist state but in the soul:

They prove that colonization, I repeat, dehumanizes even the most civilized man; that colonial activity, colonial enterprise, colonial conquest, which is based on contempt for the native and justified by that contempt, inevitably tends to change him who undertakes it; that the colonizer, who in order to ease his conscience gets into the habit of seeing the other man as *an animal* accustoms himself to treating him like an animal, and tends objectively to transform *himself* into an animal. It is this result, this boomerang effect [*choc en retour*] of colonization that I wanted to point out.[52]

Césaire's repetition, which leads him pointedly to close this passage with a reiteration of the *choc en retour*'s essence as a spiritual deformation, expresses the urgency with which he wants to convey this point. A. James Arnold has observed that writers other than Césaire were making similar arguments about the decivilizing of Europeans and that Césaire's forceful style set his intervention apart and gave it its particularly shocking quality.[53] Having shocked his reader, however, Césaire seems also to want to ensure that the central lesson he wishes to convey is not lost amidst this impact.

Both Ramos and Césaire describe the return to Europe of its colonial violence as an object lesson which, if successfully absorbed, may yet lead to a different future. Having anatomized the colonizer's soul in the opening pages of the text, Césaire closes the 1955 edition by asking Europe what path it will choose to pursue in the emerging postwar international order. He seeks to warn as well as to rouse his readers. The warning cuts two ways: he first directly addresses those "dear friends" who, disgusted with Europe, may be tempted to turn to the United States as a possible liberator and economic savior—an engine of growth and development.[54] The disastrous prospect of such neocolonial dependency prompts Césaire to consider what productive role Europe might yet play. While Césaire does not address Europe directly in the second person, as he does his anticolonial comrades, it is clear the questions he poses about its future role are ones he enjoins European nations to ask themselves. As Rothberg puts it, "The encounter [Césaire] stages between genocide and colonialism ultimately serves to usher in another encounter: that of Europe with itself."[55] The prominence Césaire affords Europe in his final lines may seem peculiar, in light of the long, ferociously critical arc of the text.[56] But while Césaire declares that Europe has one final chance to redeem itself, he insists that it can do so only by joining the world, not by saving it. He perceives the paired threats of development and neocolonialism and already apprehends how these may function as carrot and stick of a postwar international order whose contours were only still emerging during the period in which he wrote (and rewrote) *Discourse on Colonialism*.[57]

In contrast, Ramos's analysis of the boomerang effect is characterized by its banality rather than its perspicacity. He and Césaire were in agreement that Europe's colonial and racial violence posed far-reaching problems of racial reeducation. But from his perch at UNESCO, he was equally certain that World War II was Europe's tribute to the racial false gods it had erected, and development the currency in which it would pay its debts to the colonized. In Ramos's account, the temporality in question was the timescale of cultural salvage. Anthropology's most pernicious contribution to race thinking, he writes, was the ultimately genocidal "idea, or rather the preconceived notion, of civilization," which permitted the erection of cultural hierarchies in which certain peoples were consigned to backwardness and subjected to "the slow destruction of a way of life and philosophy replete with unsuspected humanism, which it is now being attempted to rebuild."[58] These rebuilding attempts entail the recognition and recuperation of the cultural other's humanism that Ramos celebrates, for instance, in the Ewe of Dahomey. Yet the new role that Ramos envisions for a politically rehabilitated anthropology is suspiciously continuous with the orientation to ethnographic salvage that characterized both nineteenth-century ethnography and aspects of British imperial policy.[59] In fact, despite his calls for a break with the past, he identifies in interwar colonial policies of indirect rule an enlightened model for the present and the future:

> Objective analysis of all the results of contacts between races and civilizations has led some observers to propose certain steps for safeguarding so-called "primitive" peoples against the various attempts summarily to impose on them the methods of the ruler nations, that is to say, generally speaking, the European whites. After the First World War, British policy registered some progress by introducing "indirect rule" ("Gouvernement indirect," *indirekte Verwaltung*). Struck by the demoralization caused by the breaking up of the tribal and cultural units, the flight of the natives, the loosening of social and political ties, the loss of the characteristic marks of culture, the "disillusioned melancholy" and so forth, and also by the inevitable repercussion of this state of things on economic output, the British administrators recalled many native chiefs who had been banished from their territories and reinstated them as leaders of their former subjects.
>
> They also tried to reconstruct, so far as they could, the aboriginal cultural framework which was in process of disappearance or dissolution. This "indirect rule," i.e. rule exercised through the native chiefs, was designed to repair the serious damage previously caused to the natives' traditional civilizations. And the seal was set on this policy by the establishment of institutions which set about trying to give concrete effect to the liberal principles of applied social anthropology.[60]

Ramos at once mourns cultural losses that he acknowledges cannot be recovered, while simultaneously imagining that benevolent indirect rule might ameliorate these conditions in the name of "repair."

Alongside the invigorated pursuit of practical measures to solve longstanding anxieties about cultural survival and cultural salvage, Ramos insists that enlightened indirect rule demands both moral and technical interventions. Europe must commit itself to technical assistance, knowledge transfer, and economic development in its colonies, or what Ramos calls "technical means of securing better treatment for colonial peoples."[61] In Ramos's view, the postwar colonial relationship required a combination of the "humanitarian and scientific" that corresponded closely to UNESCO's scientific humanism.[62] Ramos's views are entirely of a piece with the UN's institutional position on the colonies in the late 1940s. The UN Charter's Declaration Regarding Non-Self-Governing Territories (Article 73) enshrined the principles of indirect rule, expressing that conjoined concern for both cultural preservation and techno-economic development that structures Ramos's program for postwar social scientific intervention in the colonies.[63]

In other words, for Ramos, neither the urgency of the reeducation of race nor the historical and moral object lesson of the boomerang effect in any way demand decolonization. Quite the opposite: indirect rule must remain in place until the (potentially ever-retreating) moment when the colonies have secured what he calls "a sufficient modicum of material culture of European origin" so as to permit their inhabitants to "enjoy the advantages [this material] can confer on them from the point of view of their making better use of the fruits of the earth."[64] Only such an approach, he wagers, can adequately address the "reawakening of . . . nationalism of a hitherto unsuspected vigour" among the colonized.[65] Not decolonization, then, but development: a new relation of colonial dependence in which the racial technique is replaced by a new technical regime where the social sciences will secure the betterment of colonial subjects, in an atmosphere free now of the racism that was necessary to justify more direct and brutal forms of rule.

Even though their prescriptions for an adequate political and pedagogical response to the lessons of the boomerang effect diverged in dramatic respects, Ramos's and Césaire's reflections emerged from a common political and historical conjuncture. Both were writing in the late 1940s, at a time when the current and future legal status of the colonies and trustee territories were in flux, when the new international legal order represented by the UN was only recently established, and when the geopolitical divisions of the Cold War were nowhere near as fixed as they would soon become.[66] They were both also writing in the midst of what Arturo Escobar has called the "invention of development," which he dates to about 1949, when US President Harry Truman laid the ideological groundwork for the development era in his second inaugural address, outlining a four-point program for global peace and prosperity that laid special emphasis on the responsibility of the United States and other industrialized nations to make the "benefits of our scientific advances and industrial progress available for the improvement and growth of underdeveloped areas."[67] Truman designated the United Nations and its agencies the essential institutional vehicle for such efforts; that same year UNESCO instituted its technical assistance program at the behest of the UN Economic and Social Council (ECOSOC), which formalized and vastly expanded the developmental ethos and apparatus already evident in the organization's first years.

As we will see in the next section, these overlapping preoccupations are not just signs of convergence but sites of engagement.

RESISTING REPAIR

In September 1956, Césaire delivered a lecture titled "Culture and Colonization" at the First International Congress of Negro Writers and Artists in Paris that was more or less a direct riposte to Ramos's and UNESCO's vision. In the opening pages of his lecture, Césaire addresses what he describes as a potential objection to the organizing framework of the congress: "If it is true . . . that culture is only national, is it not an abstraction to speak of Negro-African culture?"[68] While the congress draws together participants from seemingly disparate cultural worlds, they share a vertical solidarity, or *"a solidarity in time,"* that refers back to the original "unity of African civilization" out of which their disparate and diasporic cultures have developed and to which those cultures remain indebted.[69] Second, and more politically pressing, is the *"horizontal solidarity"* born of colonialism.[70] The historical forces that dispersed African civilizations beyond the continent have also forced them to develop in the crucible of a shared condition: a "colonial or semicolonial or paracolonial situation" that Césaire calls the "common denominator" of all those who have gathered at the congress.[71] Césaire's horizontal solidarity describes the political affinities among those contending with the same "harsh" colonial realities.[72] Chief among them, per Césaire's account, is colonialism's consequences for culture. Contra those who wonder if "a political status [can] have cultural consequences" or if the determinative element of culture is to be found elsewhere, such as in the spirit of a place, Césaire states unequivocally that a people's political situation may not birth a culture but may certainly distort and even destroy it:

> A political and social regime that suppresses the self-determination of a people thereby kills the creative power of that people.

Or, in what amounts to the same point, wherever there has been colonization, entire peoples have been emptied of their culture, emptied of all culture. . . .

The mechanism of this death of culture and of civilizations under the colonial regime is beginning to be well known. In order to flourish, any culture must have a framework, a structure. But it is certain that the elements that structure the cultural life of a colonized people disappear or are debased [*s'abâtardissent*] as a result of the colonial regime. This is first of all a matter of political organization, for it must not be forgotten that the political organization freely developed by a people is a prominent part of that people's culture, even as it also conditions that culture. . . .

One must be absolutely clear about this. When the English destroy the state organization of the Ashantis in the Gold Coast, they deal a blow to Ashanti culture. . . .

Given this limitation of the colonized civilization, this suppression or debasement of its entire structure, how can one be surprised at the suppression of one of the characteristics of any living civilization: the faculty of self-renewal [*la faculté de renouvellement*]?[73]

Césaire shares with Ramos a preoccupation with the death and potential renewal of the cultures of the colonized. Yet his portrait of profound deculturation casts doubt on Ramos's hopeful endorsement of strategies to "reinstat[e]" precolonial leaders and "reconstruct . . . the aboriginal cultural framework[s] . . . in process of disappearance or dissolution."[74] More to the point, Césaire implicitly rejects Ramos's supposition that cultural revitalization can occur under a rehabilitated regime of indirect rule devoted to what Ramos calls "repair."[75] In the absence of political self-determination, Césaire argues, there is no capacity for renewal. Moreover, Césaire critiques the delusions of cultural restoration on the one hand and techno-economic development on the other as conjoined strategies of reparative developmentalism. What he calls *la technique* ("technical methods," per Edwards's translation) is inevitably taught and transmitted in such a way as to preclude native mastery. Education takes the most impoverished forms, and all that emerges is a marginal culture that belongs to a small elite.[76] Neither the belated and arid "conservation of the native civilization" nor what he calls, following Malinowski, the "selective gift" of Europeanization redux can repair the cultural condition of colonization.[77]

Notably, Césaire's foil here is UNESCO. The organization's interventions are for him emblematic of both reparative developmentalism and its limitations. He prefaces his critique by invoking the aspiration for repair: "I know very well that for some time now it has been argued that the harms caused by Europe are not irreparable [*irréparables*]." "UNESCO," he notes, "has taken up this problem." Here, he cites the organization's then-director-general, the American political scientist Luther Evans, and his February 1956 *UNESCO Courier* article "The Human Side of Progress."[78] Evans opens his article by acknowledging that "technical assistance to the so-called underdeveloped countries"—which was deemed "'the great hope of the 20th century'"—has been recently challenged for its less beneficial effects on "the human beings and ... societies at the receiving end."[79] Evans's essay is both a reckoning with the failures and shortcomings of the program (chiefly the insufficient consideration of third world peoples' cultural integrity) and a forceful defense of the program's continued worth and necessity, albeit with some ideological and methodological improvements. Césaire scrutinizes Evans's claim that "under certain conditions technological change may be introduced in a manner to fit the prevailing culture" before dismissing this morally renovated version of colonial cultural management:[80]

All this is certainly steeped in good intentions. But one has to take a side...there is not one bad colonization that destroys indigenous civilizations and attacks the "moral health of the colonized people," and another colonization, an enlightened colonization, a colonization backed up by ethnography that could harmoniously integrate the cultural elements of the colonizer within the body of the indigenous civilizations without risk to the "moral health of the colonized people." One has to take a side: the tenses of colonization are never conjugated with the verbs of an idyll.[81]

Césaire challenges Evans's technocratic view that the postwar development regime could be optimized and humanized by a little ideological fine-tuning and some pragmatic operational updates. However, Césaire's most profound critique in these passages is of the propensity he identifies especially with UNESCO to offer development as the medium of repair for the harms of Europeanization. In counterpoint to Ramos—who called precisely for what Césaire disparages as "another colonization, an enlightened colonization, a colonization backed up by ethnography"—Césaire insists on irreparability and the non-closure of the relations of responsibility that produce the *choc en retour* and its enduring aftershocks.

In a series of interviews that took place in 2004, almost half a century after "Culture and Colonization," Césaire reiterated and elaborated his views on reparation and irreparability in conversation with the postcolonial critic Françoise Vergès. Vergès observes that calls for reparations, which have been heard more frequently in France since the 2001 national acknowledgement of slavery and the slave trade as crimes against humanity, often induce a slippage from a properly political discourse to a dubiously moralistic one focused on rigidly defined and opposed victims and perpetrators.[82] In response, Césaire insists on the "irreparable" nature of these historic harms. Glib equations for calculating damages owed on the basis of harms inflicted make it too easy and let history off the hook: "Here's your reparation. And then it would be over [*terminé*]. For me no act can put an end to it. It's irreparable. It's done. It's history. I can't do anything about it."[83] There is no return, Césaire emphasizes, no possibility of recovering or repairing the past. His position is familiar insofar as it shares with other critiques of monetary reparations an ambivalence about false closure and a distaste for the prospect of treating profound historical harms as reckonable in a financial register.[84] How could such an approach even begin to suffice for a past that he adamantly deems "utterly irreparable" (*c'est tout à fait irréperable*)?[85]

However, Césaire also draws on precisely the discourse of morality Vergès tries to bracket—"I'd like to think about it in moral terms rather than financial ones," he declares—and invokes a species of development as an alternative to reparations.[86]

> Reparation is a matter of interpretation. I know the Western world too well: "All right dear friend, how much? I'll give you half of that to pay off the slave trade. Okay? It's a deal!" Then it's over: they repaired the matter. But for me it's utterly irreparable. I don't really like the term "reparation." It implies that repairing the matter is possible. The West has to do something, it has to [help countries to develop, to be reborn] [*aider les pays à se developer, à renaître*]. It owes us this aid, but I don't believe that a simple check can pay for reparations. It's assistance, not a contract, it's purely moral. I believe it is the duty of Western countries to help us. Again, for me, it's irreparable.[87]

Césaire here distinguishes between the self-serving and self-consolidating morality he associates with reparation and an aspirational morality that provides help without pretending to dispose of a matter that does not permit settlement, that he says "will never be settled" (*ça ne sera jamais réglé*).[88] At the same time, he appears to call for development assistance in a manner that contradicts his 1956 critique of the development paradigm elaborated at UNESCO. How do we reconcile this contradiction, not least because "the very real risk of a permanent *assistanat* or state of dependency on the former colonial power is present in [Césaire's] formulation of the nature of the debt"?[89]

Césaire's resistance to reparation is not just an expression of distaste at its false closure or at the incommensurability of the harms and the recompense. As I read it, his 1956 critique of UNESCO's reparative morality rejects the imperative that the colonized gratefully refashion themselves in the image of a scientifically and technologically superior Euro-American world, which makes technical know-how the medium of reparation and consequently renders projects of supposed cultural renewal exercises in cultural salvage. This reparative morality is to be distinguished from the "purely moral" register in which Césaire in 2004 situates the problem of the irreparable past. No to reparations, he says; no to the delusion of repairing the irreparable, to false closure, to the fantasy of clean hands. But his remarks are also a challenge, for they imagine a form of assistance Europe might offer its former colonies in the service of their rebirth that does not require the reproduction of the self-same in the name of educability, equalization, and a new and properly universalist humanism.

Césaire's disparagement of reparative morality is partially illuminated by David Eng's recent effort to demonstrate that reparation must be resituated in the context of what he calls "colonial object relations."[90] In contemporary political theory and cultural criticism, reparation is a mode of doing justice to damaged or beloved objects. But Eng demonstrates that the psychoanalytic concept of reparation that Sigmund Freud and Melanie Klein, the pioneering theorist of object relations psychoanalysis, articulate in their work is inextricable from the history of European colonial violence.[91] While Klein describes the infant's efforts to repair the object it destroys in fantasy or reality, Eng observes that this reparation is in service of the infant's own survival. As such, reparation in Klein is neither an ethics nor a mode of justice nor a consequence or expression of morality.[92] Instead, it is representative of what Eng calls "colonial morality."[93] As he shows through a reading of Klein's arresting reliance on figures of colonial settlement, reparation may serve merely "to name the psychic process of responding to European colonization and genocide of indigenous peoples by repopulating the New World with images of the self-same."[94] This impulse to self-replication and self-consolidation, I am arguing, is precisely the reparative logic that Césaire identifies and disparages.

At the same time, Césaire's critique is more profound, and more historically situated, than just disputing what Eng describes as the racist denial of humanness to the colonized other. In Eng's account, the differential colonial morality of reparation—which extends repair to the self-same while leaving others "unretrieved, left to perish in the dark regions beyond the circle of love and repair"—concerns the conferral or denial of human status.[95] His question "How does affect become an object?" evokes Césaire's well-known formulation "colonization = thingification [*chosification*]," and Eng's conclusion that "the object chosen for repair is not only constituted as good and worthy of reparation but also psychically constituted as *human*" remains within the analytical axis of colonial dehumanization and rehumanization that was certainly one important element of Césaire's thought.[96] However, I am arguing that Césaire identifies incorporation, rather than dehumanization, as the most pressing danger of the postwar regime of racial reeducation and racial repair.[97] As we see in his 1956 critique of the cultural violence of UNESCO's reparative developmentalism, his preoccupation is not the colonized subject's exclusion from the colonial reproduction of the self-same but rather the colonized's conscription to it, via an acculturative and inculcative process that refuses to recognize difference even as it mourns its destruction. In other words, Césaire is not demanding humanity; he is resisting repair.[98]

CRITIQUE AND COUNTERPEDAGOGY

I now want to turn to consider another instance of Césaire's engagement with UNESCO in the 1950s, this time in the 1955 revised edition of *Discourse on Colonialism*. In an especially pertinent episode, we find Césaire engaging debates about UNESCO's race project and the 1950 Statement on Race. Among the stakes of this encounter are that it serves as an inflection point for Césaire's developing attunement to the connections between antisemitism and anti-Blackness. Superficially, this discussion may seem to exist at some remove from Césaire's remarks on UNESCO's developmental and reparative aspirations in "Culture and Colonization." Indeed, as we will see, Césaire's foil in *Discourse on Colonialism* is not UNESCO itself, but the French intellectual Roger Caillois's attack on UNESCO's race project. However, I suggest that the political questions at stake in Césaire's sharp disagreement with Caillois are closely related to "Culture and Colonization" and his 2004 remarks on reparation, as he tries to envision forms of worldmaking for racialized peoples beyond the confines of the position of beneficiaries of either colonial educability (i.e., development) or a reparative morality that forcibly produces self-sameness as the condition of recognition.

As I have noted, several versions of *Discourse on Colonialism* appeared in print. In his notes to the genetic edition of the text, which collects and compares them, Delas deems the 1950 edition the purest expression of Césaire's rhetorical powers and political critique and is unconvinced of any great qualitative import of the fifteen or so pages he added in 1955; although they maintain the text's ironic tone, they lack its stylistic flair.[99] In Delas's view, the main purpose of the 1955 additions was to update the text in order to affirm its continued relevance and timeliness. Such is Césaire's concern with remaining current that Delas notes one instance in which he refers critically to a new book that would not appear in print until several months after his own, while quoting from the author's previously published work. The point, Delas suggests, was to stay on the cutting edge of intellectual and political debate and combat.[100] As Delas notes, there are three kinds of additions, and the most substantive and lengthy, taking more than half the new pages, is the "long controversy with Roger Caillois."[101] As readers of *Discourse on Colonialism* no doubt recall, Césaire takes Caillois, a French sociologist, philosopher, and literary critic, to task for his chauvinistic assertion of European superiority in the domains of science, culture, and ethics. Césaire also assails Caillois for what he characterizes as his unselfconscious suggestion that the rights of Blacks, Jews, and indigenous peoples are best secured by colonial munificence rather than in the register of equality.

If Césaire revised the text to keep up with the times, as Delas suggests, then what was the time and timeliness of this particular conflict? As I have argued, temporality is a crucial element of meaningful education, organizing the durational structure of the gradual accrual and transformation of insight, or what Aidoo calls "knowledge gained since."[102] What educative encounter occurred for Césaire between the 1950 and 1955 editions? Michael Rothberg has noted that one important development in this period is Césaire's greater attunement to the specificity of antisemitism. Rothberg attributes this to Césaire's critical reformulation of Marxist universalism in the six years between the 1950 edition of *Discourse on Colonialism* and his 1956 *Letter to Maurice Thorez*, which announced his resignation from the French Communist Party. In the latter document, Rothberg argues, Césaire invokes both antisemitism and anti-Black racism in his critique of a Marxist universalism that refuses adequately to recognize difference or to contend with the historical and contemporary significance of racialization. As such, antisemitism importantly works to "nam[e] the problem of particularities that the party cannot subsume."[103] Rothberg also observes that *Discourse on Colonialism*'s sole mention of Jews is an addition to the 1955 edition; this emergent awareness of Jewish specificity, he proposes, is "evidence of the ongoing development of Césaire's thinking" in the early 1950s.[104]

I agree with Rothberg that "events of the 1950s were leading Césaire in the direction" of such insights but as I demonstrate, UNESCO's race project was a crucial incitement to this development in Césaire's thinking and historical consciousness. The Caillois essay to which Césaire takes such exception was published in two parts, in consecutive issues of the journal *La nouvelle nouvelle revue française* in December 1954 and January 1955.[105] At the time, Caillois was a UNESCO official and the editor of the organization's journal *Diogenes*. But far more consequential here than Caillois's direct association with UNESCO is that his essay was an inflamed and inflammatory response to Claude Lévi-Strauss's 1952 book-length essay for UNESCO's race project, *Race and History*.[106] As I discussed in chapter 3, Lévi-Strauss's *Race and History* offered a critique of the hierarchical and developmental conception of civilization. In its place, Lévi-Strauss offered an alternative account of the variable relationship between time, value, and culture and a forceful defense of cultural relativism as an intellectual and ethical stance. For him, culture presented a realm of incommensurability—of equal-because-incalculable worth. Caillois took these questions of equivalence and equality to be central but violently contested Lévi-Strauss's conclusions. He did so in part in the name of science and made mastery of the scientific method a litmus test for the measurement of how far a given culture had progressed on the path toward development and modernity.

Caillois is provoked by the same mood of self-indictment and late-imperial melancholy that Ramos, for instance, expresses in "The Question of Race and the Democratic World." For the last several decades, he argues, something like this attitude has infected a particular class of European intellectuals, none more so than those who have gravitated to ethnography. It goes deeper than self-implication and verges on self-hatred, a determination to love and exalt whatever is at odds with one's own cultural values, the better to belittle and degrade them.[107] *Race and History* is important, even epochal, he argues, because it formalizes and systematizes this perspective. In Caillois's view, however, Lévi-Strauss's cultural relativism—which comes at Europe's expense—is intellectually dishonest. Caillois experiences *Race and History* as one long exercise in Freudian kettle logic: Lévi-Strauss's perspective shifts suspiciously among the mutually incompatible claims that the question of cultural superiority is moot, that superiority doesn't prove anything anyway, and that when it exists, it is only because of chance or cultural borrowing. How can Lévi-Strauss so ardently assert that no culture can rightly be measured according to another culture's system of values and equally vigorously announce Eastern civilizations' great advancement over Western cultures in spiritual matters, to give just one example, Caillois asks. What motivates Lévi-Strauss, he argues, is the need to honor each culture with some special recognition of its particular contribution, all at the expense of denying or dismissing the contributions of the modern European culture to which he belongs.[108] But in the very formulation of such evaluations, Lévi-Strauss paradoxically reaffirms the most profound and consequential contribution of this civilization, and this civilization alone: the modern scientific method.

The best confirmation of Europe's cultural superiority, which Caillois does not scruple repeatedly to announce, is that only Europe has developed the techniques of sustained empirical observation, reasoned investigation and demonstration, and methodological coherence and rigor that characterize scientific inquiry. The scientific method, Caillois argues, is Europe's gift to the world; among its many endowments are the advantages it affords for securing prosperity through the technical mastery of the environment.[109] Moreover, ethnography is as much a product of this paradigm as the pure or physical sciences are. The best evidence for his argument, Caillois suggests, is Levi-Strauss's capacity to regard another culture systematically, to stand outside it and sympathetically observe its structure: "If I, for one, were asked to identify the principle and perhaps indisputable advantage of Western civilization,

I would unhesitatingly respond that it is finally to have produced ethnographers." For Caillois, in other words, efforts like Ramos's to insist that the non-European subject also practices ethnographic observation and formulates judgments about European culture are little more than limp special pleading: "There is no Bantu or Bororo ethnographer, or, if there is, he was educated at Cambridge or Jena," Caillois declares, in what we might describe as a clash of condescensions.[110]

Let us pause a moment to note a few things about Caillois's argument. First, per the title of his essay, "Illusions à rebours," Caillois too is concerned with reversals; here, the way in which Lévi-Strauss and others like him insist on reading against the grain, reversing the hierarchy of values, and adopting the fiction that they stand outside the culture whose intellectual beneficiaries they are, so as to now turn back on it a critical and ungrateful eye. Second, the crux of Caillois's argument concerns the relationship between science and morality. In a key passage to which Césaire pays close attention, Caillois takes Lévi-Strauss to task for his definition of fundamental Western values, which Lévi-Strauss has borrowed from the American anthropologist Leslie White: continually increasing the per capita supply of energy and extending the human lifespan. Caillois objects on the grounds that this overstates industry and longevity as ends in themselves, mechanistic pursuits of sheer increase, and understates the extent to which these pursuits are driven by admirable and ennobling commitments: on the one hand to science, whose intellectual rigor and coherence allow for technical efficiency, and on the other to ethics (*la morale*), which secures the respect for the human being that makes euthanizing the old and the infirm an abnormal and distasteful idea. Non-European primitive peoples, Caillois adds, are also concerned with maximizing energy and optimizing resources but, unconstrained by the same moral commitments, are far more likely to resort to killing off unproductive members of the community.[111]

Now, let us recall the historical situation in which Caillois is writing: in the midst of a reckoning with science's intellectual responsibility for racism and genocide and in the wake of the industrialized and highly efficient murder of millions in Europe, including the victims of National Socialism's euthanasia campaigns. The terms of Caillois's polemic closely echo the preoccupations with development and technical mastery and their relationship to morality that

I have been tracing in UNESCO's work. But while Ramos, Evans, and (as we will see) Huxley temper their prescriptions for third world development and knowledge transfer with assurances of the colonial and postcolonial world's equal and indeed perhaps superior commitment to humanism, Caillois deems the non-European neither developed nor humane, entirely missing the historical irony of his position.

In his critique of Caillois, Césaire does not explicitly lay out these historical contradictions and ironies, nor does he need to; they are available to the reader, especially one familiar with the context and import of the UNESCO project to which Caillois is responding. And certainly, these ironies make Caillois's essay especially apposite for Césaire's argument that the *choc en retour* has two dimensions: not just the techniques of violence Nazism employs but also the moral and spiritual deformation that gives lie to Europe's pretentions to the invention of humanism. However, Césaire alludes to the historical situation Caillois blithely ignores, and his most pointed allusion is his furious observation that "M. Caillois gives immediate proof of [Western] superiority by concluding that no one should be exterminated. With him the Negroes are sure that they will not be lynched; the Jews, that they will not feed new bonfires. There is just one thing: it is important for it be clearly understood that the Negroes, Jews, and Australians owe this tolerance not to their respective merits, but to the magnanimity of M. Caillois; not to the dictates of science, which can offer only ephemeral truths, but to a decree of M. Caillois's conscience."[112] As Rothberg has observed, this remark in the 1955 edition is Césaire's only explicit reference to Jews and the Jewish genocide in this text.

Importantly, Caillois's essay supplies Césaire with the context for this reference, in the form of a long footnote in part 1 of "Illusions à rebours." Here, Caillois situates Lévi-Strauss's volume as an extension of UNESCO's 1950 Statement on Race and contextualizes the statement as a response to the Holocaust. Césaire pays close attention to this footnote and draws from it his longest quotation from Caillois's essay. Here is the first part of Caillois's footnote, as quoted by Césaire:

For me, the question of the equality of races, peoples, or cultures has meaning only if we are talking about an equality in law, not an equality in fact. In the same way, men who are blind, maimed, sick, feeble-minded, ignorant, or poor (one could hardly be nicer to the non-Occidentals) are not respectively equal, in the material sense of the word, to those who are strong, clear-sighted, whole, healthy, intelligent, cultured, or rich. The latter have greater capacities which, by the way, do not give them more rights but only more duties. . . . Similarly, whether for biological or historical reasons, there exist at present differences in level, power, and value among the various cultures. These differences entail an inequality in fact. They in no way justify an inequality of rights in favor of the so-called superior peoples, as racism would have it. Rather, they confer upon them additional tasks and an increased responsibility.[113]

Césaire is quick to put his finger on Caillois's rhetorical preparation for the reassumption of the "inevitable white man's burden." What would such duties and responsibilities entail, Césaire asks, if not the "tasks of ruling the world"?[114]

However, Césaire does not just object to Caillois's suggestion of a colonial dispensation in which the colonized and the non-European are, at best, beneficiaries of Europe's enlightened rule and its monopoly on the rigors and fruits of scientific thought. His more pointed challenge here is to Caillois's assumption of a colonial morality (to use Eng's term) that guarantees the existence and survival of the cultural or racial other not in the name of equality or even an abstract universalism but rather in the name of ethics. Caillois stakes out his position in the remainder of this footnote, and he does so by ventriloquizing what he describes as a Jewish critique of UNESCO's 1950 Statement on Race. In the sentences that follow directly on the lines Césaire quotes, Caillois continues:

A few years ago, a group of scholars who had not forgotten the antisemitic persecutions of Hitler's regime agreed on a solemn proclamation affirming that nothing in the present state of scientific knowledge justified the slightest racial discrimination. Eminent Jewish figures [*personnalités israélites*] were disturbed by it. Rightly so, in my opinion. They did not concede that their fate was in any way dependent on expert opinion. They felt it would be wrong to persecute them even if science, whose verdicts are changeable, might at some point appear to justify their elimination. Indeed, this is a moral problem, and not at all a question of scientific truth or error. It is extremely dangerous to link the two domains, even if the intention—as was the case here—is to secure scientific support for the ethical. To require the support in this case of scientific findings is to allow that the strength of a position belonging to a purely moral order could be weakened if the findings in question were invalidated by the subsequent development of scientific research. It is not because science advises against it that it is condemnable to lead Jews or Blacks or anyone into the crematoria. And it is not even especially clever to add, moreover, that *today's* science doesn't permit it (which we have to acknowledge when we invoke science, since science is always changing and tomorrow's science is never the same as yesterday's).[115]

On its face, Caillois's haughty admonishment to the authors of the 1950 statement, Lévi-Strauss among them, has some validity. I think here of Ashley Montagu, who introduces the statement by declaring that "in the decade just past more than six million human beings lost their lives because it was alleged they belonged to an inferior race. The horrible corollary to this barbarism," he adds, "is that it rested on a scientifically untenable premise"—leaving himself open to the question of whether he is suggesting that a more scientifically sound campaign of murderous elimination would offer less cause for horror.[116]

However, Césaire recognizes the underlying logic at work in Caillois's remarks. If Montagu makes science the arbiter of the legitimacy or illegitimacy of extermination, Caillois cloaks himself in a version of the self-serving morality that makes the racialized subject into the object of colonial beneficence. Césaire rightly challenges the role Caillois appropriates for himself to speak on behalf of these unnamed Jews, whose uncited objections he ventriloquizes as his own, even as he ignores the Jewish background of several of the statement's authors, including Lévi-Strauss. The "purely moral" terms in which Caillois claims to speak are, for Césaire, no guarantee at all of the recognition of difference, much less adequate grounds for its protection from violent and exterminatory impulses. In sum, whether articulated in UNESCO's reparative and developmental register or in Caillois's unabashed affirmation of European cultural superiority, Césaire questions the postwar reconstitution of the colonized, racialized, and victimized as pupils and grateful recipients of Europe's scientific, developmental, and moral endowments.

At the same time, Césaire is here also demonstrably a pedagogical subject of UNESCO's race project. It is through his engagement with these debates about UNESCO's race project that Césaire developed and sharpened his own thinking, and especially his more direct registration of the specificity of the Jewish genocide, which emerged in his work in the mid-1950s. If, as Caillois proposes, the 1950 Statement on Race sought to respond specifically to Nazi antisemitism and extermination in an educative register, then Césaire's *Dis-*

course on Colonialism demonstrates how such a pedagogy could be put to work in a comparative and counterpedagogical fashion.

In this chapter's second arc, to which I now turn, I examine how a counterpedagogical postcolonial response to the postwar reeducation of race is articulated in Ama Ata Aidoo's *Our Sister Killjoy*. In this work, the registration of the Holocaust and European racism and suspicion of Europe's postwar promises of reparation and development generate a critique of the livability of diasporic life in Europe. To situate Aidoo's text, I first consider how specifically UNESCO conceived the relationship between Europe and the third world in the early postwar period, not least with respect to the role of education.

EQUALIZATION AND EDUCATION

At UNESCO's first general conference, Julian Huxley, who had served as the executive secretary of UNESCO's Preparatory Commission, offered a detailed report of the commission's efforts and articulated his vision for the organization he was about to lead. Among the many spheres of UNESCO's envisioned labors, he stressed that one task—"relief and reconstruction in the war-devastated countries"—had been pressed upon UNESCO by the sheer "grim urgencies of the moment."[117] UNESCO was barred from providing general material necessities (food, medicine, clothing, agricultural tools) that were the responsibility of the United Nations Relief and Rehabilitation Administration (UNRRA).[118] But UNESCO's assistance was imperative, stressed Huxley, in the domains of education, science and culture: "In Greece, there were until recently no blackboards, no pencils, no exercise books, let alone textbooks. In Yugoslavia, the central library now comprises only a few hundred books, and the Germans deliberately burned the new University and its contents. In Poland, there is a terrible shortage of school-houses and of school-teachers," and so on.[119] While in each of these examples, UNESCO envisioned assisting with material and infrastructural needs, these were the means to a greater end that entailed the restoration of moral well-being and the reconstitution of human values. As Huxley remarked, there were countless similar examples to draw on from Denmark, Czechoslovakia, China, France, the Philippines, Holland, Russia, Belgium and Norway, not to mention the urgent extension of "educational reconstruction to ex-enemy countries" that he intended UNESCO to pursue as soon as peace treaties were concluded. Huxley called this entire complex of interventions—which were largely concentrated in Europe—"rehabilitation," or "*bringing back* the level of educational and scientific and cultural opportunity at least to something comparable with the level in similar countries which were spared by the war."[120]

In contrast, a different kind of targeted technical intervention was required in those "more recently settled or more recently industrialized parts of the world" in Asia, South America, and Africa, "where the educational and scientific level is also low, not through their own fault or as a result of war, but through the accidents of history and geography." In such regions, illiteracy was the rule, "indigenous arts and crafts [were] in danger of dying and of being replaced by a shoddy and debased brand of western culture," and science had "scarcely begun to be applied." For these blighted places, rehabilitation was not in question, for there was no prior advanced standard of culture to which they might be restored. Rather, Huxley argued, "the peoples of such regions will judge UNESCO by its success, not in rehabilitation, but in what we may call *habilitation*—the raising of educational and scientific and cultural opportunity at least to a level which enables these countries to participate with more developed nations as partners in the general advance of a world-wide culture."[121] In contrast to rehabilitation, which describes the restoration of a prior capacity, status, or condition, *habilitation*, per the *Oxford English Dictionary*, is "the action of enabling or endowing with ability or fitness; capacitation, qualification." If blackboards, pencils, and schoolhouses were requirements in a Europe that urgently needed education for the purposes of remediating and rehabilitating the miseducation of the prior years, such material necessities and more were required in the third world as an end in themselves, as the very vehicle through which these populations might engage and enter the world. In other words, technical assistance promised equality of opportunity.

The key term Huxley offered to describe this process was *equalization*. Equalization, he argued, was the fundamental UNESCO principle that must guide its overall work in rehabilitation and habilitation. As I noted in chapter 1, equalization echoes the concept of equality that the authors of the 1950 statement abandoned in favor of educability. However, equalization splits the difference; it inhabits the same ideological space as educability and so is not equality but the transit toward equality. Like educability, it demands malleability and a willingness to be the subject or recipient of education or reeducation. And, like educability, it promises improvement: equalization, Huxley notes, is specifically "equalization upwards, to enable the nations that have been less favoured, either in war or peace, to take their places as equals in a single world advance."[122] Equalization is thus a synonym for development.

I want to stress the subtle chiasmus at work in UNESCO's framing of these changing regimes of education and reeducation. While Europe's institutional and infrastructural capacities for culture did exist and must do so again, the worth, much less superiority, of the culture itself has never been more in question. Europe's spiritual fitness for participation in the global constituency of postwar humanity must be anxiously reasserted, even remade from the ground up. The colonized, meanwhile, have shown themselves to be members of cultures "replete with unsuspected humanism," but their righteous anger at decades or centuries of imperial rapaciousness and self-serving racism now threatens to challenge the fragile global order with "nationalism[s] of a hitherto unsuspected vigour," in Ramos's words.[123] Development as a means of incorporation, then, purportedly presumes nothing about the inferiority of the cultures on the receiving end but rather the urgency of their inclusion in a new global humanism, not only for their own benefit but for the world's. In Huxley's report, the technical and infrastructural deficits of the third world are presented dispassionately, as the chance outcomes of what he calls "accidents of history and geography."[124] Correcting these asymmetries or inequalities is a matter of optimizing human resources, both material and spiritual, in order to maximize human peace and prosperity.[125]

As Huxley's remarks imply, education is the hinge between these various modes, bridging habilitation and rehabilitation, development and soul-making. A 1947 publication titled *Introduction to UNESCO: A Summary of the Organisation's Activities during Its First Year* foregrounded both these projects under the heading of "Raising the Standards of Education, Science and Culture." Rehabilitation would help provide those "essentials without which no kind of cultural life can be restored" ("pencils, books, papers" and the like).[126] The report also observed that "the General Conference in 1946 saw that the ideal of one world could not be achieved while half the world was illiterate, as illiterate people cannot play an effective part in the world community.... UNESCO's task in 1947 was immediately concerned with investigation on which to base plans to provide a basic minimum of education for less advanced communities," which in turn would facilitate improvements in fields such as public health, agriculture, and community welfare.[127] UNESCO called this literacy-oriented initiative "fundamental education." The organization pursued this program for about a decade, from UNESCO's inception in 1946 to 1958. During this period, the meaning of fundamental education became increasingly broad, moving beyond literacy to various schemes of community advancement, and the initiative quickly "became an integrated component" of UNESCO's technical assistance program.[128] UNESCO's view of education "as a moral rather than technical objective" eroded with the increasing dominance of technical assistance in the organization's vision. When UNESCO abandoned the fundamental education framework in 1958, then, it was because fundamental education had been effectively subsumed by technical assistance.[129]

Luther Evans's 1956 reflection on the successes and failures of UNESCO's technical assistance program—which Césaire responds to in "Culture and Colonization"—is representative of this narrowed conception of education as an instrument of economic development. He envisions an educated elite in "the so-called underdeveloped countries" that can help optimize the nation's resources, including its human capital. Evans acknowledges that techno-developmental interventions have been introduced, even imposed, without adequate consideration of their cultural reception and integration. His response is to propose a more carefully calibrated and culturally sensitive implementation of these measures, which Césaire ridicules as a wishful and misguided belief in "enlightened colonization." UNESCO must consider much more carefully both the psychological and anthropological coordinates of the communities it seeks to assist: "What makes people work? What kinds of incentives will make them work harder, produce more?" What causes "resistance to technological change," and how does such resistance connect to anthropological insights about "acculturation or cultural contact"?[130] While all of this is "a fertile field for further investigation by social scientists," the most important vehicle for the acceptance of technical improvements and development paradigms is the school.

A major role is played by the school, and by other, related, educational influences. That is why we have always operated on the assumption of a close and intimate relation between UNESCO's programme in the field of education—fundamental education, primary and secondary schools, adult education, etc.—and the whole programme of Technical Assistance. The school has rightly been described as the connecting link between the old and the new culture. It provides new skills and techniques; opens up new horizons of action; adds new values; and modifies preexisting attitudes. Through children it influences the adults and therefore the community as a whole.[131]

The plasticity and educability of the child as a developmental organism is neatly conscripted here as the most effective ideological instrument for social transformation and as the metonym for a community's educability. Evans zeroes in on an even more specific group, declaring that UNESCO is increasingly focused on the education, "whether at home or abroad," of a small group of native elites—"the French refer to them as *évolués*"—whose role it will be to function as "intermediaries between the old culture and the new." So impressed is UNESCO by "the potential importance of this group that our Social Sciences Department is conducting a series of studies of actual and potential leaders in various regions of Africa, and we are now extending the investigation to include the role of feminine leaders. It is quite possible that women in such a position may prepare the way more easily than men for some kinds of technological change." The psychological portrait Evans paints of this elite resembles the familiar description of the colonial go-between or the native informant. Their role as "teachers" will be of profound importance to their communities, and they may well "develop a deep sense of their mission as interpreters of the new way of life." They may also face the particular challenges that confront those tasked with coaxing their peoples into the future: "uprooted and insecure in their position," their lived experience may be one of deracination.[132] This uprootedness was to be literal, not just cultural and spiritual. The urgency of producing "trained personnel" who could prevent the wastage of "raw materials" had prompted UNESCO to "devot[e] a considerable proportion of our fellowships, in the Exchange of Persons programme, to precisely this purpose."[133] Promising students from the third world—themselves raw material of a certain kind—were brought to the first world for the purposes of educational and moral formation.

Initiatives for face-to-face contact and student exchange functioned as a hinge between UNESCO's work in the techno-economic and moral-pedagogical domains. UNESCO's 1947 report on its inaugural priorities stressed this latter dimension and titled this area of activity "Education for International Understanding." In keeping with the intense anxieties expressed in UNESCO's early days about the racism inculcated in classrooms and national educational curricula, education for international understanding entailed initiatives such as teacher trainings and assessments of national textbooks, with an eye to their revision and improvement. But the heart of the program was student exchanges, broadly construed. From its inception, UNESCO was convinced that a new era of direct contact and exchange among peoples was indispensable for the reeducation of humanity. The aim was to "develop within the people of every nation a tolerance and friendliness, based on factual knowledge, towards the people of every other nation, and to co-operate with them in producing citizens conscious of their responsibilities in the world community."[134] In other words, such encounters would provide an important experiential component to the reeducation of race and materially foster the reconstitution of humanity as a political and moral constituency, aware of its universal human solidarity.

These face-to-face encounters took various forms. UNESCO conscripted existing youth groups and student clubs, disseminating ideas for how their members might become "acquainted with the peoples of other countries through exchange visits and correspondence."[135] It also heavily promoted and supported the revival of the formal student exchange. The historian Hilary Perraton has described the first three decades of the postwar era as "glorious years" for student exchange. With important logistical and financial support from UNESCO, "a renewed respect for internationalism was translated both into arguments about the universality of learning and into proposals for student exchanges."[136] Finally, UNESCO, in its own words, sought to collaborate with "youth service camps which aim at building international understanding among the boys and girls of many countries."[137] Precisely such a camp serves as a crucial setting for Ama Ata Aidoo's *Our Sister Killjoy*.

As we will see, Aidoo's portrait of what I term "weak education" is a critical redescription of Evans's vision of education as the medium for development, while her critique of diaspora resists his imperative that African intellectuals accept alienation from their community as the price of education. *Our Sister Killjoy* was published in 1977 but it is set in the late 1960s, as we can surmise from its references to the world's third heart transplant, which took place in early 1968 in apartheid South Africa, when the cardiac surgeon Christiaan

Barnard transplanted the heart of a young Coloured man into a white South African, an event heralded in some quarters as a stunning sign of interracial progress—equalization in a biological register, as it were—and recognized in others as the latest in a long line of medical experiments under conditions of racial inequality and brutality. Indeed, the text connects these events to the Nazi past. Its organizing premise is that European racism and its genocidal consequences have emphatically demonstrated that the colonial distribution of civilization and barbarism has been turned on its head. Like Césaire, Aidoo treats this recent history as evidence of Europe's savagery. While a number of critics have identified *Our Sister Killjoy*'s reversal of the familiar "heart of darkness" trope, my argument here is that Aidoo is more specifically attuned to the pedagogical problem that so preoccupied UNESCO: that of colonial soul-making as a problem that had now come home to roost.[138] In Aidoo's treatment, the postcolonial subject is recruited for this reeducative project. The work narrates the journey of a young Ghanian woman called Sissie to Germany, England, and home again. She is neither an exile nor an economic migrant. Instead, less predictably, she heads off on one of those overseas friendship-and-goodwill programs for youth, this one sponsored by the postwar German government's international largesse. One might describe it as a student exchange program, but the exchange pointedly only goes one way: from Africa to Europe. Sissie's journey is underwritten by European guilt—though for what, exactly, is an open question—and the corresponding requirement to make reparations of some kind. This reparative impulse takes contradictory forms, and her voyage is organized according to the complex dynamics of reeducation and return I have been tracing in this chapter.

Sissie functions as an agent of European racial reeducation by serving as an object lesson. Her Black female body is summoned to European shores as part of a postwar pedagogy that offers the quintessential ordinary German the opportunity to contend bravely with racial difference and tolerantly learn from the cultural other—a gambit Aidoo gleefully ironizes. The text is variously described as a novel, a novella, and a prose poem. While it is mostly written in prose, it breaks at times into poetry. I read this as a formal reflection of its irony, evoking as it does Césaire's aphoristic observation that "poetic knowledge is born in the great silence of scientific knowledge," to which he adds, in lines that he might well have directed at Caillois: "Mankind, once bewildered by sheer facts, finally dominated them through reflection, observation, and experiment. Henceforth mankind . . . knows how to utilize the world. But it is not the lord of the world on that account."[139] European patronage and neocolonial development promise the colonized new capacities to utilize the world, but Aidoo's text ironically counterposes such promises with an attunement to the history of the uses to which such scientific and technical know-how have been put. Indeed, these history lessons are the medium for Sissie's intellectual and political maturation and impel her to reject life in the diaspora and return home.

REPARATION AS WEAK EDUCATION

The first suggestion that Sissie's journey is implicated in some kind of reparative project is the suggestion, in the novel's opening pages, that the German government's sponsorship of her travel "must have had something to do with a people's efforts / 'to make good again.'"[140] This sly literal translation of the postwar West German policy of restitution, *Wiedergutmachung*, implies that Sissie's travels are related to Germany's recent genocidal history. The novel thus indicates that Sissie's journey is related both to Europe's moral exhaustion and its reparative impulse, but what specifically do German guilt and repair have to do with a young Ghanaian woman?[141] How is Sissie to explain the remarkable beneficence she observes in her German sponsors, who "had shown a lot of interest" and "pulled strings for her" and whose ambassador himself "had invited her to his home"?[142] We might look for an answer in *Wiedergutmachung*'s entanglement of material reparation and moral pedagogy. The policy of *Wiedergutmachung* was formalized with the financial reparations treaty of 1953, which West Germany established with Jewish groups in Israel and the diaspora. Anson Rabinbach has observed that if "the symbolic value of the 'Jewish Question' in the history of the Federal Republic of Germany is to hold German sovereignty in escrow," then these reparations were the first step in buying back sovereignty and national legitimacy.[143] *Our Sister Killjoy* suggests how such attempts at restitution go beyond direct reparations to Germany's victims and also take the form of a moral and economic investment in the third world and its development.[144] However, Rabinbach also identifies a shift as early as 1959 from a West German national policy focused on material reparation to one focused on pedagogy and memory: if "reparations substituted policy for pedagogy, the *Vergangenheitsbewältigung* [mastering the past] turned pedagogy into national policy."[145] Aidoo intuits this connection between the material and pedagogical dimensions of this reparative ethos. Or to put it differently, Aidoo discerns that the reparative impulse to invest in history's victims imagines that economic and pedagogical development are of a piece.

This act of reparation cannot but seem to take a developmental form. While Sissie's journey may be nominally driven by the desire to make good, *Our Sister Killjoy* also repeatedly implicates a persistent European cultural vanity that imagines a trip to Europe is, for an "insignificant" young African woman, a declaration of exceptional status and a confirmation that "Our Sister had made it."[146] Sissie's German benefactors understand her journey as a variation on the colonial civilizing mission; it is an educative opportunity for a promising young African woman to enrich her character and prospects through an encounter with European culture. But while the novel will take this presumption to task, *Our Sister Killjoy* is equally a thoroughgoing critique of a class of educated Africans who are all too eager to step into the role Evans outlines for the new "*évolués*," who will emerge from their education "whether at home or abroad" with a zeal to serve as "intermediaries between the old culture and the new."[147] In Aidoo's scathing representation, this exemplary subject of development is in fact a mere functionary: "the interests he is so busy defending are not even his own."[148] The novel's first section, titled "Into a Bad Dream," begins with the narrator's critique of a local educated class that traffics in technocratic calculations and takes as its alibi an enlightened humanism the narrator suspects is nothing more than the regurgitation of received knowledge. The danger of the "the academic-pseudo-intellectual," muses the narrator, is that "in the face of reality that is more tangible than the massive walls of the slave forts standing along our beaches, [the intellectual] still talks of universal truth, universal art, universal literature and the Gross National Product."[149] Mellifluous talk of universalism, charges the narrator, conceals a vulgar economic endgame and denies entirely the pressing weight of historical violence that will not dematerialize merely through the application of developmental or managerial theorems. But this is not all: "the worst of them / these days supply local / statistics for those population studies, and / toy with / genocidal formulations."[150]

The text's opening passages thus establish a negative model of a weak education oriented to bureaucratic rationality. More than an indictment of meager or deluded intellects, Aidoo suggests that the worst tendencies of such an orientation are its readiness to reduce life to a matter of administrative management and, in so doing, to risk inhabiting the role of what Hannah Arendt, describing Adolf Eichmann, terms a "mere functionary"—one whose inability to think critically is "the most reliable of all safeguards against the words and the presence of others, and hence against reality as such."[151] The functionary, or Aidoo's "academic-pseudo-intellectual," understands compliance with such an agenda as only sensible, opining that those who disagree "are too young. You must grow up."[152]

These prefatory passages stake out a position of profound disenchantment. These initial doubts are in no way assuaged once the text moves from this frame to the narrative of Sissie's journey to Europe. The first line of this narrative, "It is a long way from home to Europe," is belied by Sissie's experience there, where she finds another version of the mendacity at home.[153] She finds too that those African students and migrants who have traveled to Europe, the best and brightest, are as misguided as the pseudo-intellectuals at home. Unblocking her view and uncluttering her brain, Sissie discovers, is a task for which she must invent the tools herself. By framing the narrative thus, Aidoo implies that what I am terming weak education is overdetermined. At home in the postcolony, it appears in the guise of a stunted modernity that imitates the worst of received colonial knowledge and bureaucratic forms, whereas in Europe, Sissie encounters a widespread arrogance that refuses to recognize what the recent pasts of fascism and national liberation in the colonies indicate about the limits of Europe's cultural superiority.

In its alertness to the Nazi past and the palliative strategies of forgetfulness, *Our Sister Killjoy* offers a pointed critique of the postwar German project of coming to terms with the past. As Sissie discovers, her sojourn in Germany fulfills another function besides the developmental and reparative ones. She finds herself in decidedly inglorious circumstances at a youth volunteer camp in a quaint-sinister Bavarian village where she plants prospective Christmas trees. There, she is at best a symbolic bit player in attempts to ameliorate the past and at worst, an object of fascination and revulsion to the "natives."[154] In his 1959 lecture "What Does Coming to Terms with the Past Mean?" Theodor

Adorno argues that coming to terms with the past, or *Aufarbeitung der Vergangenheit*, cannot be achieved by learning to know the cultural other in an effort to correct distorted perceptions and recognize their humanity. Not much, he opines, "is accomplished by social gatherings, encounters between young Germans and young Israelis, and other such organized acts of friendship."[155] In this piece and the companion essay of 1966–67, "Education After Auschwitz," he insists instead on what he calls the "turn toward the subject: reinforcement of a person's self-consciousness and, with that, of a sense of self."[156] Sissie's sojourn in the Bavarian village where she helps replant the pine forests is untouched by the disruption of any overt memory work. But the villagers recognize "what the campers could only guess at: that all that to-do was just an excuse to procure the voices of the children of the world to ring carefree through the old forests."[157] Aidoo implies that the dynamic at work in this "organized act of friendship" between German and racial other is the very opposite of what Adorno terms the imperative to "draw near [the horror]" and, in so doing, confront it.[158] Instead, it is the novel's narrator who sees the landscape as a violent palimpsest, decries the attempt to make the earth recover from what it has witnessed, and breaks from prose into poetry to ask "if, should they / Stop cultivating the little pine trees, would / Something else, / Sown there, / Many many years ago, / In / Those Bavarian woods / SPROUT?"[159] Here, figures of development and cultivation reappear but this time explicitly as modes of denial and evasion.

It is against the converging pressure of these multiplying imperatives—in which Sissie is alternatively conscripted as the agent and the object of reeducation—that she must autodidactically marshal the insights gleaned from her journey to formulate a counterpedagogical position. However, the text suggests that the raw experience of this educative journey is not on its own enough to reliably transform Sissie's critical intuitions into articulable positions. Throughout the text, a third-person narrative perspective that critics have sometimes read as a chorus narrates instances in which Sissie formulates but cannot quite enunciate her critique. When the young German woman, Marija, with whom Sissie strikes up a tentative friendship implores Sissie to go visit Munich's treasures, Sissie thinks but does not say—*wants* to say but does not say—that for her, Sissie, Munich is not the crown of Bavaria but is instead "the Original Adolf of the pub-brawls / and mobsters who were looking for / a Führer"; is "Prime

Minister Chamberlain / Hurrying from his island home to / Appease, / While freshly-widowed Yiddisher Mamas wondered / What Kosher pots and pans / Could be saved or not."[160] Similarly, when a German professor earnestly tells her that Germans, the Irish, and Africans are united in their oppression, she is astonished into silence, and "could not ask him whether . . . there are or could have been some other oppressed peoples on the earth, like Afro-Americans or Amerindians or Jews. She forgot to ask / Her Most Learned Guest / If he had heard of / Buchenwald, / or come across / Dachau / even in his reading?"[161] "Could not ask"; "forgot to ask"—these scenes describe missed moments in which her fluency with words and her critical consciousness fail her. In one sense, such apparent failures of speech are a mode of ironizing the lessons that these interlocutors seek to impress upon Sissie, whether on the topic of German cultural grandeur or German historical victimization. Understood thus, we might read her silence as a withdrawal from these supposed "exchanges" and as a critique of the background presumption that such encounters invariably contribute to intercultural understanding and friendship.

Yet the narrative also ironizes Sissie herself, implying that her youthful critical sensibility has not quite achieved full maturation. It is here that *Our Sister Killjoy* demonstrates the connection between irony, education, and temporality that I traced in Arendt and Césaire. Sissie's experiences in Europe with racism and with traces of Nazism and the Holocaust are the unofficial lessons that constitute the true educative substance of her journey to Europe. But while the lessons she gleans from her European sojourn about the impossibility of a diasporic life in Europe impel her to return home, these lessons can only be properly assimilated from a geographical and temporal distance. Only with the completion of the journey's circular itinerary, which in its closing pages has her looking down from her airplane window to Africa "warm and green," will Sissie be able to look back on her experience and better recognize its educative insight.[162] To invoke the text's refrain, the meaning of Sissie's encounter with Europe must be contextualized "by knowledge gained since."[163] While the book ends with Sissie still in flight, this promised maturation would seem to be fulfilled by the fact of the book itself, which looks back at Europe from the perspective of a postcolonial Pan-Africanism unconvinced by postwar assurances of Europe's reeducation and a renovated international order.[164] To understand how the text posits Sissie's journey home as a matter of political and ethical necessity as well as of group survival requires us to attend to the novel's interest in recognition and racial shame.

MISRECOGNITION, MISEDUCATION, AND THE SCENE OF RACIAL SHAME

In his foundational account of the politics of recognition, the philosopher Charles Taylor reflects on the centrality of recognition to democratic polities confronted by difference. Recognition's moral urgency stems from the injuriousness of misrecognition, which denies the cultural other's dignity by refusing to acknowledge their "authenticity" and "distinctness."[165] The principles of liberalism require recognition as a practice of democracy, and such a politics requires two commitments: first, correcting distorted and demeaning perceptions of otherness through the mechanism of what Taylor calls "the world of education" and "the study of the other" and, second, acknowledging that "what the members of distinct societies really aspire to . . . is survival."[166] Taylor's prescriptions for the study of otherness are familiar from the pedagogy of racial reeducation; his specific intervention is to articulate how the problem of recognition is central to this project. As I've suggested, *Our Sister Killjoy* is deeply skeptical of the liberal faith in the earnest study of otherness as a strategy of racial reconciliation. Indeed, it is precisely racial reconciliation that the work resists, identifying in its logic the perpetuation and not rupture of the material conditions of colonial subordination. However, *Our Sister Killjoy* is deeply concerned with group survival, which in this text means a refusal of life in Europe in favor of a politically committed return to one's people. As I argue in what follows, the text stages this commitment to return and against diaspora through a series of racial and historical misrecognitions that for Sissie have an important pedagogical function. Specifically, these scenes are counterpedagogical in their orientation, producing encounters and affects that Sissie must learn to reject or resist in order to achieve her own political maturation.

Aidoo's winking reference to *Wiedergutmachung* in the text's opening pages identifies one discourse that the text reads ironically or rewrites, that of European reparation. However, Aidoo also rewrites the discourse of racial injury, in no small part through her critical engagement with key moments in Frantz Fanon's *Black Skin, White Masks*. Upon her arrival in Frankfurt, the gateway to Germany and thus to her experience of Europe, Sissie has an inaugural experience with the white racial gaze in Europe. As she wanders around the train station, taking in the sights and sounds, she suddenly overhears a woman "telling a young girl who must have been her daughter: 'Ja, das Schwartze Mädchen.'" Sissie understands the meaning of the words—"From the little German that she had been advised to study for the trip, she knew that 'das Schwartze Mädchen' meant 'black girl'"—but only belatedly realizes that the words refer to her: "She was somewhat puzzled. Black girl? Black girl? So she looked around her, really well this time. And it hit her."[167] As other critics have noted, this moment clearly recalls the iconic Fanonian scene of racial interpellation I discussed in chapter 2, when the Black colonial subject's bodily schema is unmade in the encounter with metropolitan racism.[168]

Aidoo's restaging of this Fanonian scene also defiantly rewrites it. Sissie withstands the encounter Fanon experiences as an undoing, demonstrating a certain imperviousness to the wounding of racial interpellation. The blow she experiences is not the painful awareness of her own bodily difference but rather a heightened, disgusted awareness of the foreignness of the bodies all around her: "That crowd of people going and coming in all sorts of directions had the colour of the pickled pig parts that used to come from foreign places to the markets at home.... And she wanted to vomit. / Then she was ashamed of her reaction."[169] "The human sensorium," Paul Gilroy notes, "has had to be educated to the appreciation of racial differences," and, in this scene, Sissie becomes a pupil of precisely this education in the perception of difference.[170] Sissie not only perceives difference but does so in a form that reduces the bodies around her to "pickled pig parts" and, specifically, to the extremities of the animal's body—"trotters, pig-tails, pig-ears"—that least resemble the human form. Aidoo's version of the pedagogical scene as a site for the transmission of race thinking, rather than its undoing, is thus antihumanist in its implications, at odds with that benevolent notion of "the study of the other" that Taylor recommends as the basis for a robust politics of recognition.[171] Instead, this is an instance of miseducation. If this is a moment of enlightenment for Sissie—"and it hit her"—it also represents a sorrowful darkening of her horizons, even a tragic loss of innocence, since "for the rest of her life, she was to regret this moment when she was made to notice differences in human colouring."[172] Like Fanon, Sissie experiences shame. This is not the shame of feeling herself demeaned by misrecognition, however, but shame at the way she is doing the misrecognizing.

In Germany and later in England, shame comes to function as a critical component of Sissie's education, as she increasingly experiences its gendered and racial dimensions and puts shame to work in service of her political commitment to return to Africa. In Germany, she makes the acquaintance of a young German hausfrau named Marija, whose moral implication in Germany's genocidal past is clearly signaled when she announces that "My Mann is called / ADOLF / And zo is our little zon."[173] Nonetheless, she and Sissie strike up a tentative friendship with undercurrents of queer desire. Their friendship and its "inner joys" are disrupted by an encounter with an elderly couple who "stopped dead" at the sight of them, "two pairs of eyes popping out of their sockets," as the man, "breathing heavily and sweating," points to Sissie's body and then his own over and over again.[174] The queerest thing about Sissie and Marija's relationship may be the historical perversity of friendship, much less romance, between "A daughter of mankind's / Self-appointed most royal line, / The House of Aryan" and "A Little / Black / Woman," who, had history unfurled differently, would "Not / Have been / There / Walking / Where the /Führer's feet had trod/."[175] As this passage suggests, Aidoo's text is attuned to the way that National Socialism's genocidal project pursued not only Jews but also Black Germans, among its many victims.[176] Marija is "an heiress to some / Legacy that would make you / Bow / Down / Your head in / Shame and / Cry," yet while Marija is "blushing R-E-D" she is also "smiling, smiling, smiling," seeking to mollify the elderly couple.[177] Is shame for a shameful history appropriately distributed and appropriately acknowledged, Aidoo asks. Have the historical perpetrators of racism absorbed its shameful lessons? And if not, what does it possibly afford to bring together perpetrators and victims in service of reeducation and reparation?

Shame is a racialized affect, as Sissie learns when she experiences the peculiar vulnerability of Marija's white skin to the blush, which Eve Kosofsky Sedgwick calls one of the "blazons" or "semaphores" of shame.[178] When Sissie rejects Marija's tentative erotic overture, she marvels at the consequences on Marija's skin:

It seemed as if according to the motion of her emotions Marija's skin kept switching on and switching off like a two-colour neon sign. So that watching her against the light of the dying summer sun, Sissie could not help thinking that it must be a pretty dangerous matter, being white. It made you awfully exposed, rendered you terribly vulnerable. Like being born without your skin or something. As though the Maker had fashioned the body of a human, stuffed it into a polythene bag instead of the regular protective covering, and turned it loose into the world.[179]

This passage plays with the idea of plasticity, reversing its valences to critical effect. Once again, Sissie speculates about the humanness of other bodies, and concludes that to be white is to be unfinished in one's human form. Marija possesses "the body of a human" but the skin she has is as good as "being born without . . . skin" altogether. Instead, there is a surface of plastic, the body's interface with the world, leaving it "vulnerable" and "exposed" but also impoverished, devoid of skin as a sensory apparatus with which to experience the world in all its tactility.[180] Blackness, meanwhile, becomes protective and powerful in its indecipherability, and the text thus resists the racial melancholia of misrecognition.[181] Despite this self-protectiveness, Sissie experiences what Sedgwick describes as shame's transmissibility, feeling herself "ashamed and unhappy" at the spectacle of Marija's "blushing and blanching."[182] Fanon describes himself as finally freed from the suffocating violence of the scene of racial interpellation when he responds to the objectification of the white woman's gaze with a "'Fuck you,' madame" that "colored [her face] with shame."[183] Sissie in contrast reflects uneasily and ashamedly on the pleasure involved in rejecting Marija's advances and watching her response. While the text thus comments on shame's raced and gendered dimensions, Sissie is also drawn into its circuit of transmission in ways that implicate rather than liberate her. Such experiences suggest that her European education is a negative education; the unofficial lessons she learns there, important as they are, teach her about who she does not want to be.

In England, where Sissie goes after her sojourn in Germany, and where she is confronted by a much larger African migrant population, she puts this insight to work in service of her deep political conviction that Africans abroad should return home. Of all the critiques the text voices—of neocolonial acquiescence at home, of Europe's reparative and historical delusions, and of European racism—perhaps the most trenchant is the novel's portrait of the complicity of the upwardly mobile African migrants who pursue economic and cultural incorporation in Europe, when in fact "for the slave, there is nothing at the centre but worse slavery."[184] For Sissie, Huxley's vision of equalization—in which Europe's shattered spiritual heritage is restored and the third world is allowed to benefit from the gifts of modernity, all facilitated by education and the apparent humanism of intercultural exchange—is in fact a theft, another iteration of an old story in which "for a few pennies now and a / Doctoral degree later / Tell us about / Your people / Your history / Your mind."[185] And if these young would-be African elites consent, then it is not theft but worse: they are "giving away / Not only themselves, but / All of us—."[186] Moreover, contra those who, like Huxley, enthusiastically envision equalization as a eugenic endeavor that will also ensure the biological improvement of populations, not least through their hybridization, the novel offers the object lesson of the first interracial heart transplant in 1968 in South Africa.[187] While some around Sissie embrace this news as a great step forward to "solve the question of apartheid / and rid us, 'African negroes / and all other negroes' of the / Colour Problem"[188] she reflects with horror on the racist experiments on Black and Coloured South African bodies that have undoubtedly made such a medical innovation possible under apartheid. Shame is the medium of Sissie's critique, the tool she now unabashedly deploys to convince the young Africans around her that a life in Europe is both a betrayal and a dead end.

The fear of deracination is at the heart of *Our Sister Killjoy*. Shame is implicated here too, now as a covert fear of being shamed. Sissie's own entreaties to others to return home are echoed as a racist imperative in the mouths of others: "Hot faces in hiding from / Sneering mouths that wonder / When / You are going to / Finish, and go back home."[189] And she is wounded by spectacles of lost dignity as she regards the "wretched" Black population in London, struck by their "pitiful" clothes and the condition of "women who at home would have been dignified matrons" instead "looking ridiculous in a motley of fabrics and colours."[190] In a poignant reversal of the many instances in which the text suggests that Black skin is protective and resilient, the text describes Africans who travel abroad as "migrant birds of the world, / Beginning with such / Few feathers too, which / drop / and / drop / and / drop / and / drop," before concluding, "Until the / Last wing / falls: and / Skins bared to the / Cold winds or / Hot, / Frozen or / Scorched, / We / Die."[191] Here, the text suggests that diasporic life is a threat to group survival. Unlike Taylor, who imagines that the politics of liberal multiculturalism can preserve difference through positive affirmation and tolerance, *Our Sister Killjoy* insists that return is both a political necessity and a means of survival.

KILLJOYS AND PARIAHS

Our Sister Killjoy's perspective on deracination and return may suggest that the work's ethos is unambiguously nativist, yet the killjoy of its title complicates such a characterization. Sissie inhabits the role of killjoy in multiple ways. In the most straightforward sense, she pierces the soothing and gratifying stories that others tell themselves about their own intentions and motives in order to keep doing what they are doing. Sissie addresses her fellow African students from a position of intimacy, "our sister," and appeals to them in the name of their mothers, who wait for them at home, as they endlessly put off their return. By interrogating their contentment to go along with what she understands as the injustice of a neocolonial order that impoverishes her home while luring away its youth, she puts their happiness in question. Yet she also risks her own happiness. As I noted, Sissie cannot always speak. At time she falls silent, "admonish[es] herself to tread / Softly" when in fact she longs to voice her skepticism; at other moments, she speaks up with passionate unrestraint, such as when she confronts a room full of African students, imploring them to go home.[192] The text suggests that this ability to speak up, even when it risks others' pleasures and one's own, is the purpose of education, and the cultivation of this capacity in the face of received knowledge represents the work of maturation.

In Sissie's case, the cultivation of a killjoy's perspective also leads her to challenge the consoling and conciliatory narratives of racial reeducation. As we have seen in this chapter and elsewhere in the book, the project of racial reeducation is in part a project of affective reformation. The bad feelings—hatred, revulsion, shame—that organize racial encounters and even the very reckoning with racism are to be reeducated and managed by training in the reflexes of cultural relativism, liberal recognition, and racial reparation.[193] The work of Aidoo's novel as a whole is to play the role of killjoy, showing how Europe's genocidal history undermines its potential as a schoolroom for projects of soul-making and coming to terms with the past, much less for the instruction of non-Europeans.

In inhabiting both these critical positions, Sissie demonstrates that the role of the killjoy is risky and even alienating. She refuses the palliative pleasures of upward mobility in Europe out of a sense of political loyalty and concern for the survival of her people. At the same time, she cannot be reconciled to the very people whom she takes to be her community because she challenges them, both in Europe and at home, where she refuses the commonsense wisdom of the postcolonial pragmatist. The very question of loyalty is thus complicated, since the killjoy threatens to alienate both friends and enemies.

Aidoo's portrait of the killjoy and her dilemmas bears a striking resemblance to Hannah Arendt's account of the Jewish pariah and the parvenu, which she first developed in her biography of Rahel Varnhagen and then elaborated in her 1944 essay "The Jew as Pariah: A Hidden Tradition." In Arendt's account, the parvenu seeks assimilation at all costs, including the cost of any meaningful community. In her characteristically unsparing way, she describes German Jews of the late eighteenth century as uninterested in being "emancipated as a whole; all they wanted was to escape from Jewishness, as individuals if possible." There was no solidarity among them, she charges, or if there was, it was the "questionable solidarity which survives among people who all want the same thing: to save themselves as individuals."[194] Arendt's critique is not just of the assimilatory impulse as a means of self-advancement and self-preservation, however. For her, the parvenu's most damaging error is that in pursuing assimilation at all costs, he is forced into false reconciliation and, worse, dependence on the very people who oppress and subordinate him. Like Sissie, who despairs most at the way acquiescent Africans at home and abroad strengthen the very forces—economic, political, spiritual—responsible for their historical and contemporary impoverishment, Arendt indicts the parvenu whose efforts are "worth nothing, not because he is poor and begs, but because he begs from those whom he ought to fight, and because he appraises his poverty by the standards of those who have caused it."[195]

To this figure, Arendt contrasts the conscious pariah. While the parvenu seeks to escape Jewish difference at all costs but misapprehends the conditions of oppression and so fails to oppose them, the conscious pariah refuses what Aidoo calls the "general illusion of how well an unfree population think they can do for themselves."[196] Arendt's pariah recognizes the limits, dangers, and implicit conditions of tolerance and assimilation and instead tries "to make of the emancipation of the Jews that which it really should have been—an admission of Jews *as Jews* to the ranks of humanity, rather than a permit to ape the gentiles or an opportunity to play the parvenu."[197] In Arendt's own life, this aspiration for many years directed her to work for Zionist causes and organizations, which she saw as the only movement in Jewish politics that envisioned a specifically political Jewish response to antisemitism and Nazism. While she criticized Zionism in essays of the 1940s and articulated in *The Origins of Totalitarianism* that the formation of a Jewish state as a solution to the European minority problem and statelessness would only reproduce this condition in Palestine, she also continued to believe in Zionism's project of settlement, and her characterizations of Palestinians echo her descriptions of Africans.[198] Yet for Arendt, the critical position of the conscious pariah required that one resist incorporation not just in the forms of assimilation or upward mobility but also false consensus and the demand for uncritical loyalty, even with one's own. As Richard J. Bernstein puts it, to be a "conscious pariah among a pariah people" entails "accepting the challenge and *responsibility* of being an outsider even among one's own people."[199] In Arendt's case, this entailed her willingness to challenge the project of Israeli state-formation and legitimization, despite her limitations on the subject. Even as she critiqued the nation-state form, she continued to believe that "only within the framework of a people can a man live as a man among men, without exhausting himself."[200] Like Aidoo's killjoy, who is committed to the view that difference is to be defended from the blandishments of false universals, Arendt's pariah rebels in service of this position. For both of them, this position of resistance depends on education, in the sense of the cultivation of critical faculties that can see the lessons of the past and anticipate the future that may follow. Or as Arendt puts it, for the pariah, "the contemplative faculty [is] an instrument of self-preservation."[201]

CODA

THE WANING CONSENSUS

Over the long years of writing this book I have had plenty of time to articulate to myself just why I have found UNESCO's reeducation of race so durably fascinating. However, it is still difficult to offer a crisp answer. In large part, this is because the interest of UNESCO's race project is for me overdetermined, touching as it does on the several fields this book tries to bring together. But there is undoubtedly more to my difficulty, and it involves my gradual awareness of the ways in which UNESCO's race project was not only a site of critical engagement for anti- and postcolonial thought but also a resource. Let me briefly give an example to illustrate what I mean, which revisits the reading of Aimé Césaire I offered in chapter 4.

Among the writers this book examines, Césaire offers the most striking example of explicit, direct engagement with UNESCO's race project. One strand of this engagement was his intervention into the controversies the race project occasioned, which I argued was a crucial site for the development of his more acute awareness by the mid-1950s of the specificity of the Jewish genocide. As I worked out my reading of Césaire's furious commentary on Roger Caillois's scathing review of Claude Lévi-Strauss's *Race and History*, it became apparent that I could hardly assert here that Césaire was critiquing UNESCO's race project. He was not precisely defending it either. Rather, what I was arguing was that he was learning from it. In Caillois's telling, the 1950 Statement on Race had presumptuously sought to redefine the meaning of race in the name of murdered Jews. The authors of the statement, such as Ashley Montagu, more or less affirmed this frame for the project (minus of course the accusation of presumption). And Césaire, who perhaps otherwise had little to learn from the statement's reconceptualization of race, emerged from his dustup with

Caillois with a greater attunement to Jewish difference and a more pointed inclusion of antisemitism alongside other forms of racism in the 1955 edition of *Discourse on Colonialism*. At the same time, this episode in which Césaire was meaningfully situated as a pedagogical subject of UNESCO's reeducative efforts in no way diminishes his critique of the reparative developmentalism that unevenly structured its global project of soul-making. This instance crystallized one of the primary claims of this book: that the relationship between postcolonial and Jewish thought was mediated by the concepts and institutions that organized the new moral economy of liberal antiracism. While my reading of Frantz Fanon demonstrates the limitations of the concept of plasticity UNESCO put forth, which despite its supposed universality was still highly racially differentiated, Césaire gives us a glimpse of a moment in which such institutional mediation provoked something important, namely, a recognition of antisemitism as a racism.

But this instance in which I had to reckon with an apparent success, rather than failure, of UNESCO's antiracist pedagogy also had broader implications for how I articulated this book's methodology. UNESCO and the anticolonial discourse I was reading in counterpoint to it were deeply entangled in ways that required me to expand my own sense of this engagement. Yes, UNESCO's antiracism produced concepts wholly insufficient to address the character of colonial racism, stressing the educability of raced subjects and the plasticity of race rather than power, exploitation, and the material interests that motivated racism. Moreover, these concepts were not just insufficient but invidious, since they implicitly demanded that racialized populations submit to plasticity as a racial imperative and settle for interminable educability, rather than equality in the here and now. Certainly, the anticolonial and postcolonial writers I examine in this book register these maneuvers and their implications for the flesh and spirit of the racialized and the colonized, subjecting them to sharp and often quite direct critique. But as I have become convinced over time of the depth and robustness of this engagement, I have accordingly become more aware of what I can only call the intimacy that characterizes the relationship between these writers on the one hand and this reeducative project of postwar world-making on the other. Anticolonial thinkers like Césaire and Fanon discerned the profound significance of these new postwar institutions for cultural and political life even when they were formally excluded from representation there and even when these institutions produced flawed articulations of the humanism to which they were also committed. This book is about two antagonistic but overlapping scenes, as I say in the introduction, but I have also come to see that they are the same scene. Of course, such a recognition of deep entanglement, rather than any simple schematic and predictable critique of this side against that one, is what constitutes a properly contrapuntal reading.

This sense that UNESCO's race project and the anticolonial thinkers I read in opposition to it were part of a shared scene and even, perhaps, a shared project is another reason I have found this midcentury conjuncture so compelling. However, this too is hard to articulate properly, for it can run the risk of seeming ultimately to conclude, after a book's worth of critiques, that everyone was on the same side after all and that UNESCO's liberal antiracism and the more radical antiracist critiques offered by my authors were merely different inflections of the same fundamentally worthy project. This is not the note on which I seek to end, or the circle I am trying to square. And yet I find UNESCO's race project and especially the production of its 1950 statement quite moving, despite everything I have said about its limitations. In part, this is because of the way that the 1950 statement was shaped by some of its authors' own experiences of antisemitism and racial discrimination. However, it is also because from the perspective of our present, this midcentury moment presented possibilities that today seem quite improbable.

The 1950 and 1951 statements are important markers in the periodization of race but they were not a closure of any kind, as their authors aspired and as potted versions of their story sometimes declare. But like the anticolonial energy of the early postwar period, this project speaks to the historical opening of the time, when the tectonic shifts of World War II produced an opportunity to remake the postwar world and potentially even the values that would animate it. There is something historically remarkable in the conviction these scientists had at midcentury that it was possible to produce an authoritative and systematic account of race and the concepts that adjoined it, and so transform the political and moral life of human beings. While the influence of the statement itself has been durable, this belief now reads from our present as a historical artifact, even an oddity, attributable only to its historical moment.

Meanwhile, the durability of the statement's authority is today much diminished. I have always been certain that one reason I have found the midcentury reeducation of race so compelling is that many of the liberal orthodoxies and even more so the contradictions that organize public discourse about race can be traced back to this moment: epidermal difference is meaningless but is also the self-evident meaning of race; race and ethnicity are distinct but also synonymous; race is not a legitimate scientific object but race is also the genetic population, which is only meaningful to scientists, and so on. From this incoherence, certain key claims about race have nonetheless proved remarkably stable. In part, this is because they are true: genetically we are of course vastly more alike than we are different, as the statement asserts. While this explains nothing about how, then, race and racism continue to organize the distribution of life and death, flourishing and impoverishment, truisms such as this continue to organize a liberal consensus that we are, if not properly postracial, at least properly disenchanted with the ruses of scientific racism. Yet the key tenets of apparent consensus about the plasticity of race, the educability of racists and racialized alike, and the maintenance of the line between race and culture are today very much in doubt. There is no reason it should be otherwise, since it is the insufficiency of the concepts to explain, much less ameliorate, the lived realities of racial violence and inequality that make them unpersuasive to both the political left and the right. The midcentury consensus is a waning consensus, as demonstrated by the rise of the global new right and its willingness to dispense completely with its terms.

Today, the attempt at systematization, at a wholesale redefinition of concepts of the kind that UNESCO attempted in 1950 is highly unlikely, or at least unlikely to achieve broad salience and enduring significance. At the same time, definitional debates about racism have not disappeared, nor have they lost their political urgency. Since 2016, a struggle has been unfolding around the International Holocaust Remembrance Alliance's (IHRA) definition of antisemitism. The IHRA is an international organization that aims to advance the goals of Holocaust "education, research and remembrance," coordinating work in these areas among its thirty-five member states. In 2016, amidst "evidence that the scourge of antisemitism is once again on the rise," the IHRA formulated a working definition of antiracism that has been adopted by universities, cultural organizations, and government. As critics of the definition have repeatedly pointed out in letters, public statements, petitions, and an alternative Jerusalem Declaration on Antisemitism issued in 2021, the IHRA working definition effectively delegitimizes and seeks to constrain criticism of Israel and of Zionism by defining as antisemitic the denial of "the Jewish people their right to self-determination, e.g., by claiming that the existence of a State of Israel is a racist definition."[1] In a statement published in *The Guardian*, Palestinian and Arab academics and journalists observed the perilousness of such a definition, not least for the way that it sidelines "the very real threat to Jews coming from rightwing white nationalist movements in Europe and the US," in order to characterize principled support of Palestinian rights and the Boycott, Divestment, and Sanctions movement (BDS) as the avatars of antisemitism in our moment.[2]

Nonetheless, the IHRA definition has continued to be a site of struggle. In November 2022, as I was completing the final revisions of this book, the Israeli ambassador to the United Nations pressed the UN to adopt the working definition. At around the same time, E. Tendayi Achiume, the UN Special Rapporteur on Contemporary Forms of Racism, Racial Discrimination, Xenophobia, and Related Intolerance, submitted a report to the UN General Assembly in which she urged against the adoption of the IHRA definition by UN member states and especially by the UN itself, owing to the "harm done to human rights" by the definition's instrumentalization to stifle dissent in a "period of heightened repression of Palestinians, including escalating, daily gross violations of their human rights."[3] During this same period, vehement ongoing debates in Germany—ignited, among other things, by the 2020 controversy over the Cameroonian political theorist Achille Mbembe's criticisms of Israel—have roiled the public sphere. As A. Dirk Moses has observed, these debates have made clear that in the German discourse of official state-sponsored "anti-antisemitism," the very term *postcolonialism* has come to be seen as constitutively antisemitic.[4]

The risk of these operations on the very meaning of antisemitism is that they threaten to undo precisely the insight Césaire achieved when he situated antisemitism alongside and as racism. By defining antisemitism in such a way as to quell criticism of Israel and delegitimize BDS, the IHRA definition undermines the connections between antisemitism and racism—a connection that is necessary for both intellectual analysis and political solidarity. At the same time, it understates the extent to which antisemitism and racism are fueled by the growth of the far right, even as these extremist discourses shift the wavering liberal center. My point is not that we should produce better definitions of race and racism but that definitions matter, because once they are issued, they shape our concepts and our critiques. "Words rule the lives of men," Ashley Montagu wrote in his wartime effort to disenchant the idea of race, and "a word, a very little word, often means the difference between life and death."[5] About this, at least, I think he was right.

NOTES

Acknowledgments
1. Lucy Holmes, "The Object Within: Childbirth as a Developmental Milestone," *Modern Psychoanalysis* 25, no. 1 (2000), 109–34.

Introduction
1. Ignaz Zollschan, "How to Combat Racial Philosophy," *Man* 43 (1943), 90.
2. Ibid.
3. Elazar Barkan, *The Retreat of Scientific Racism: Changing Concepts of Race in Britain and the United States between the World Wars* (Cambridge: Cambridge UP, 1992), 287, 320.
4. For the fullest consideration of Zollschan's project in the context of these broader transatlantic efforts to mobilize scientists against racism, see the chapter "Confronting Racism: Scientists as Politicians" in Barkan, *The Retreat of Scientific Racism*, 279–340.
5. UNESCO, Constitution of the United Nations Educational, Scientific, and Cultural Organization, in *Basic Texts: 2018 Edition including Texts and Amendments Adopted by the General Conference at Its 39th Session (Paris, 30 October–14 November 2017)* (Paris: UNESCO, 2018), 5. UNESCO's constitution was adopted on November 16, 1945 but the organization was not officially established until the constitution was ratified by the twentieth member state on November 4, 1946.
6. Zollschan, "How to Combat Racial Philosophy," 90.
7. Edward Said, *Culture and Imperialism* (New York: Vintage, 1993), 32, 96.
8. Ibid., 67, 32.
9. Ashley Montagu, *Statement on Race: An Extended Discussion in Plain Language of the UNESCO Statement by Experts on Race Problems* (New York: Henry Schuman, 1951), ix, 6.
10. Sebastián Gil-Riaño, "Relocating Anti-Racist Science: The 1950 UNESCO Statement on Race and Economic Development in the Global South," *The British Journal for the History of Science* 51, no. 2 (June 2018), 281–303.
11. Claude Lévi-Strauss, *Tristes Tropiques*, trans. John Weightman and Doreen Weightman (New York: Penguin, 2012), 24.
12. Emmanuelle Loyer's recent biography describes his upbringing in "a large, warm and close-knit extended family, perfectly coherent in its secular and patriotic Judaism," which had "enjoyed the classic French experience of upward mobility, from Alsace to Paris." Loyer, *Lévi-Strauss: A Biography* (Cambridge: Polity Press, 2018), 3.
13. Lévi-Strauss, *Tristes Tropiques*, 231.
14. David Damrosch, "The Ethnic Ethnographer: Judaism in *Tristes Tropiques*," *Representations* 50 (1995), 1. Damrosch goes on to offer a fascinating reading of the suppression

of Judaism in *Tristes Tropiques*' concluding reflections on religion and poses the question of what links might exist between Lévi-Strauss's Jewishness and his formation as an ethnographer; he asks, for instance, how we might understand the relation between his sympathetic accounts of Brazilian ethnic minorities ravaged by historical violence and mistreatment and his apparent lack of interest in the role that antisemitism would have played in rendering his grandfather's Versailles synagogue "empty" and "desolate," in his own words. Damrosch, "The Ethnic Ethnographer," 5; Lévi-Strauss, *Tristes Tropiques*, 231.

15. Lévi-Strauss's invitation to join the New School for Social Research as a means of securing refuge in the United States was facilitated by Métraux, who would later serve as the director of UNESCO's Department of Social Sciences at the time of the 1950 statement's publication. Lévi-Strauss, *Tristes Tropiques*, 23. On Métraux's role in the postwar creation of a transatlantic network of scholars studying race and antiracism, see Alice Conklin, "'Nothing Is Less Universal Than the Idea of Race': Alfred Métraux, American Social Science and UNESCO's Anti-Racist Campaign in 1950s Paris," *Durkheimian Studies* 25 (2021), 107–32; on Boas's interwar role, see Barkan, *The Retreat of Scientific Racism*. Lévi-Strauss acknowledged his singular debt to Boas (who famously died beside him at a Columbia University luncheon) on questions of race and racism; see Kamala Visweswaran, *Un/common Cultures: Racism and the Rearticulation of Cultural Difference* (Durham, NC: Duke UP, 2010), 76.

16. Werner J. Cahnman, "Ginsberg, Morris," in *Encyclopedia Judaica*, 2nd ed., vol. 7, ed. Michael Berenbaum and Fred Skolnik (Detroit: Macmillan Reference, 2007), 610.

17. Morris Ginsberg, *The Unity of Mankind* (Oxford: Oxford UP, 1935), 4.

18. Julian Huxley and A. C. Haddon, *We Europeans: A Survey of "Racial" Problems* (New York: Harper and Brothers, 1936).

19. Morris Ginsberg, "Anti-Semitism," *The Sociological Review* 35, nos. 1–2 (1943); Pierre Birnbaum, "The Absence of an Encounter: Sociology and Jewish Studies," in *Modern Judaism and Historical Consciousness: Identities, Encounters, Perspectives*, ed. Christian Wiese and Andreas Gotzmann (Leiden: Brill, 2007), 266n129. Ginsberg also authored a wartime report reflecting on the ongoing catastrophe—whose "magnitude [was] unparalleled" in Jewish history, since "never before have the Jews been threatened with destruction or disintegration in so many different parts of the world at the same time"—and assessing various political solutions to the Jewish question, including assimilatiom, Zionism, and ethnic rights. Ginsberg, *The Jewish Problem* (London: British Section of the World Jewish Congress, 1943), 1.

20. UNESCO, Statement on Race, in *Four Statements on the Race Question* (Paris: UNESCO, 1969), 35. On Montagu's leading but controversial role, see Elazar Barkan, "The Politics of the Science of Race: Ashley Montagu and UNESCO's Anti-racist Declarations," in *Race and Other Misadventures: Essays in Honor of Ashley Montagu in His Ninetieth Year*, ed. Larry T. Reynolds and Leonard Lieberman (Dix Hills, NY: General Hall, 1996), 96–105.

21. Anthony Q. Hazard, *Boasians at War: Anthropology, Race, and World War II* (Cham, Switzerland: Palgrave Macmillan, 2020), 62–63; on Montagu and McCarthyism, see Susan Sperling, "Ashley's Ghost: McCarthyism, Science, and Human Nature," in *Anthropology at the Dawn of the Cold War: The Influence of Foundations, McCarthyism and the CIA*, ed. Dustin Wax (London: Pluto Press, 2008), 17–36.

22. Sperling's published biography of Montagu is no longer available, but see Susan Sperling, "Ashley Montagu (1905–1999)," *American Anthropologist* 102, no. 3 (September 2000), 584.

23. Mitchell Hart, *Social Science and the Politics of Modern Jewish Identity* (Stanford, CA: Stanford UP, 2000), 222.

24. On Boas's early experiences with antisemitism and his family's relationship to Judaism, see Julia E. Liss, "German Culture and German Science in the *Bildung* of Franz Boas,"

in *Volksgeist as Method and Ethic: Essays on Boasian Ethnography and the German Anthropological Tradition*, ed. George W. Stocking (Madison: University of Wisconsin Press, 1996), 155–84. On Boas as a theorist of Jewish assimilation, see Amos Morris-Reich, *The Quest for Jewish Assimilation in Modern Social Science* (New York: Routledge, 2007). On the significance of Boas's Jewishness for the character of American anthropology, see Gelya Frank, "Jews, Multiculturalism, and Boasian Anthropology," *American Anthropologist* 99, no. 4 (1997), 731–45. Lee D. Baker has traced how Boas has been an object of conspiracy theories on the antisemitic far right; see Baker, "The Cult of Franz Boas and His 'Conspiracy' to Destroy the White Race," in *Anthropology and the Racial Politics of Culture* (Durham, NC: Duke UP, 2010), 156–219.

25. Ruth Benedict and Gene Weltfish, *The Races of Mankind*, Public Affairs Pamphlet no. 85 (New York: Public Affairs Committee, 1943), 25. This booklet caused considerable controversy in the United States among conservative and mainstream politicians and institutions, such as the United Service Organizations, which thought its conclusions went too far in the direction of egalitarianism. For an account of its reception, see Hazard, *Boasians at War*, 198–211.

26. UNESCO, Constitution, 5.

27. The following studies offer especially insightful and critical analysis of UNESCO's race projects and the statement. These titles are cited again at various points throughout the book but it is useful to name them here collectively: Barkan, "The Politics of the Science of Race," 96–105; Michelle Brattain, "Race, Racism, and Antiracism: UNESCO and the Politics of Presenting Science to the Postwar Public," in *The American Historical Review* 112, no. 5 (Dec 2007), 1386–413; Sebastián Gil-Riaño, "Historicizing Anti-Racism: UNESCO's Campaigns against Race Prejudice in the 1950s" (PhD diss., University of Toronto, 2014); Gil-Riaño, "Relocating Anti-Racist Science," 281–303; Donna Haraway, "Race: Universal Donors in a Vampire Culture," in *Modest_Witness@Second_Millennium. FemaleMan_Meets_Onco-Mouse: Feminism and Technoscience* (New York: Routledge, 1997), 213–65; Anthony Q. Hazard, *Postwar Anti-Racism: The United States, UNESCO, and "Race," 1945–1968* (New York: Palgrave Macmillan, 2012); Iain Morland, "Gender, Genitals, and the Meaning of Being Human," in *Fuckologies: Critical Essays on John Money's Diagnostic Concepts*, ed. Lisa Downing, Iain Morland, and Nikki Sullivan (Chicago: University of Chicago Press, 2015), 69–98; Staffan Müller-Wille, "Claude Lévi-Strauss on Race, History, and Genetics," *BioSocieties* 5, no. 3 (2010), 330–47; Robert N. Proctor, "Three Roots of Human Recency: Molecular Anthropology, the Refigured Acheulean, and the UNESCO Response to Auschwitz," *Current Anthropology* 44, no. 2 (2003), 213–39; Jenny Reardon, "Decoding Race and Human Difference in a Genomic Age," *differences: A Journal of Feminist Cultural Studies* 15, no. 3 (Fall 2004), 38–65; Perrin Selcer, "Beyond the Cephalic Index: Negotiating Politics to Produce UNESCO's Scientific Statements on Race," *Current Anthropology* 53, no. S5 (April 2012), S173–84.

28. In his account of the changing relationship between race and imperialism in the thought and practice of American and British international relations, Frank Füredi describes this as a "shift from racial confidence to racial fear." This shift, he shows, began in the interwar period when "Anglo-American foreign policy elites regarded racial thinking as having the potential to disrupt the world system"; after World War II, "racism was so discredited that Western diplomats were forced to devote considerable resources to eliminating it from international affairs altogether." Füredi, *The Silent War: Imperialism and the Changing Perception of Race* (New Brunswick, NJ: Rutgers UP, 1998), 2, 1. On race and the discipline of international relations in the early twentieth century, see also Robert Vitalis, *White World Order, Black Power Politics: The Birth of American International Relations* (Ithaca, NY: Cornell

UP, 2017). Vitalis demonstrates both that race was long unabashedly understood to constitute the "international" in "international relations" among mainstream American international relations theorists and that the Howard School of International Relations gave rise to a rich, understudied critical tradition produced by scholars of color.

Füredi's account of political anxiety in the '20s and '30s that comes to crisis in the postwar period is synchronous with what historians of science have argued about revisions to the race concept in the Anglo-American scientific and especially anthropological establishment: an "interwar period of doubt" (Stepan, *The Idea of Race in Science*) that culminates in the postwar crisis I am describing—a dual crisis, that is. On the interwar status of the race concept in Anglo-American sciences, particularly anthropology, see especially Barkan, *The Retreat of Scientific Racism*; and Nancy Stepan, *The Idea of Race in Science: Great Britain 1800–1960* (London: Palgrave Macmillan, 1982), 140–69.

29. Adom Getachew, *Worldmaking after Empire: The Rise and Fall of Self-Determination* (Princeton, NJ: Princeton UP, 2019), 2.

30. W. E. B. Du Bois, "Color and Democracy: Colonies and Peace," in *The World and Africa and Color and Democracy* (Oxford: Oxford UP, 2014), 246.

31. Du Bois, *The World and Africa*, 27.

32. This was true too of India's complaint to the UN General Assembly against South Africa for its discriminatory Asiatic Land Tenure and Indian Representation Act, which Mark Mazower describes as "the first act of assertion [at the UN] by the colonial world against the principles of racial hierarchy and European rule"; see Mazower, *No Enchanted Palace: The End of Empire and the Ideological Origins of the United Nations* (Princeton, NJ: Princeton UP, 2009), 26. For a full account of this episode, see Mazower, "Jawaharlal Nehru and the Emergence of the Global United Nations," in *No Enchanted Palace*, 149–89. For an account that centers the UN as the key site of postwar anticolonial and antiracist activism, see Vijay Prashad, *The Darker Nations: A People's History of the Third World* (New York: The New Press, 2007).

33. A number of studies have reflected on this Cold War racial (and antiracist) history, such as Penny M. Von Eschen, *Race against Empire: Black Americans and Anticolonialism, 1937–1957* (Ithaca, NY: Cornell UP, 1997). For a recent analysis that also incorporates thoughtful consideration of the role of Europe's recent fascist history in these dynamics, see Vaughn Rasberry, "Our Totalitarian Critics: Desegregation, Decolonization, and the Cold War," in *Race and the Totalitarian Century: Geopolitics in the Black Literary Imagination* (Cambridge, MA: Harvard UP, 2016), 63–106. For a seminal expression of liberal antiracism as a bulwark against communism, see Gunnar Myrdal, *An American Dilemma: The Negro Problem and Modern Democracy* (New York: Routledge, 2017). Myrdal was peripherally involved with UNESCO's race statements, and his frequent collaborator and spouse, Alva Reimer Myrdal, led UNESCO's Department of Social Sciences—which housed its race project—in the early 1950s.

34. A. James Arnold, *Modernism and Négritude: The Poetry and Poetics of Aimé Césaire* (Cambridge, MA: Harvard UP, 1981), 177.

35. The historian Fabian Klose has shown that the extreme violence of British counterinsurgency in Kenya and French counterinsurgency in Algeria in the 1950s not only claimed what historian Frederick Cooper terms a "colonial exemption" from human rights norms but in fact drew on human rights language for legitimization. However, in a critical review, Cooper argues that Klose underestimates the role that public repugnance and political opposition in international venues such as the UN played in forcing an end to these conflicts and an acknowledgment of postcolonial independence. Klose, *Human Rights in the Shadow*

of Colonial Violence: The Wars of Independence in Kenya and Algeria, trans. Dona Geyer (Philadelphia: University of Pennsylvania Press, 2013); Cooper, "Review: *Human Rights in the Shadow of Colonial Violence,*" *American Historical Review* 119, no. 2 (April 2014), 650–51.

36. The experience of racial hypocrisy shaped the biographies of figures central to anticolonial and postcolonial thought, including Frantz Fanon, who has an important place in this book. Fanon's biographer David Macey describes his experience in the Free French Forces, which he joined at great personal risk and where he encountered unvarnished French racism, as the great disillusionment of his life. Macey, *Frantz Fanon: A Biography* (London: Verso, 2012), 91–109. It is also represented in canonical works of postcolonial cultural production as well as recent postcolonial theory. For instance, Ousmane Sembène and Thierno Faty Sow's 1988 film *Camp de Thiaroye* depicts both the brutalities and the hypocrisies of the French treatment of Senegalese soldiers. Sembène and Sow, *Camp de Thiaroye* (Enaproc, 1988). And Leela Gandhi has recently elaborated an account of anticolonial practices of inconsequence and imperfection, in part through a reading of Indian naval mutinies around 1946, when Indian naval enlistees, animated by antifascist commitments and indignation at imperial Britain's blatant contradictions, rebelled against both imperial domination and anticolonial nationalism's foregone conclusions. Gandhi, "Inconsequence: Some Little Known Mutinies around 1946," in *The Common Cause: Postcolonial Ethics and the Practice of Democracy, 1900-1950* (Chicago: University of Chicago Press, 2014), 116-48.

37. Reeducation, Fisher notes, was "probably the Allies' most resonant postwar policy." Jaimey Fisher, *Disciplining Germany: Youth, Reeducation, and Reconstruction after the Second World War* (Detroit: Wayne State UP, 2007), 15.

38. James Tent, *Mission on the Rhine: Reeducation and Denazification in American-Occupied Germany* (Chicago: University of Chicago Press, 1982), 1.

39. James P. Sewell, *UNESCO and World Politics: Engaging in International Relations* (Princeton, NJ: Princeton UP, 1975), 33–70.

40. Ibid., 38. While CAME considered from its early days the extent to which any new postwar international educational organization should take on the responsibility of denazification in Germany (UNESCO would continue to ponder this question in its early years, as well as that of its possible role in Japan), this was not its focus.

41. Ibid., 63–65.

42. For a useful study that considers the philosophical background to UNESCO's work in the field of global development and the influence of scientific humanism on the organization's ideology, see Vincenzo Pavone, *From the Labyrinth of the World to the Paradise of the Heart: Science and Humanism in UNESCO's Approach to Globalization* (Lanham, MD: Lexington Books, 2008). On the entangled and mutually reinforcing relationship of the developmental and the moral-spiritual dimensions of UNESCO's work, see Sarah Brouillette, *UNESCO and the Fate of the Literary* (Stanford, CA: Stanford UP, 2019). Brouillette shows how UNESCO's decades-long commitment to humanist education as a matter of not just literacy but also of the literary as an expression of human values tracks with three distinct phases in the global political economy of literary production, from liberal cosmopolitanism through decolonizing left-liberalism to neoliberalism. On soul-making, see Gayatri Chakravorty Spivak, *A Critique of Postcolonial Reason: Toward a History of the Vanishing Present* (Cambridge, MA: Harvard UP, 1999), 112–40.

43. I draw this short definition of population genetics from the useful introductory primer for nonspecialists in Luigi Luca Cavalli-Sforza, Paolo Menozzi, and Alberto Piazza, *The History and Geography of Human Genes* (Princeton, NJ: Princeton UP, 2018), 3–22.

44. Thus, Cavalli-Sforza, perhaps the best-known population geneticist of the last quarter century, and his co-authors affirm in 2018 the same central planks of the scientific antiracist thesis that population genetics elaborated at midcentury: "the classification of races has proved to be a futile exercise for reasons that were already clear to Darwin. Human races are still extremely unstable entities in the hands of modern taxonomists.... All populations or population clusters overlap when single genes are considered, and in almost all populations, all alleles are present but in different frequencies.... There is great genetic variation in all populations, even in small ones.... The difference between groups is therefore small when compared with that within the major groups, or even within a single population." Cavalli-Sforza, Menozzi, and Piazza, *The History and Geography of Human Genes*, 19. On the political ambiguities and implications of Cavalli-Sforza's and others' work on the Human Genome Diversity Project, see Jenny Reardon *Race to the Finish: Identity and Governance in an Age of Genomics* (Princeton, NJ: Princeton UP, 2005).

45. See for instance Lisa Gannett, "Racism and Human Genome Diversity Research: The Ethical Limits of 'Population Thinking,'" *Philosophy of Science* 68, no. 3 (2001): S479–92; Donna Haraway, "Remodeling the Human Way of Life: Sherwood Washburn and the New Physical Anthropology, 1950–1980," in *Bones, Bodies, Behavior: Essays on Biological Anthropology*, ed. George W. Stocking (Madison: University of Wisconsin Press, 1988), 206–59; Veronika Lipphardt, "Isolates and Crosses in Human Population Genetics; or, a Contextualization of German Race Science," *Current Anthropology* 53, supp. 5 (April 2012), S69–82; and Reardon, "Decoding Race and Human Difference in a Genomic Age." Lipphardt nicely characterizes such revisionist accounts challenging the narrative of a clean midcentury break in racial epistemologies as "powerful critiques directed at the boundary work done to distinguish old from new race science" (S71).

46. The discourse of genetic populations continues to play a role in the design and interpretation of projects dedicated to tracing human genetic sameness and variation; it has helped give meaning both to the Human Genome Project and its assertion of the negligible genetic manifestation of perceived racial differences, as well as to the Human Genome Diversity Project, controversial precisely for its pursuit of the genetic differences among cultural, linguistic, and ethnic groups. See Reardon, *Race to the Finish*.

47. See Gannett, "Racism and Human Genome Diversity Research"; Lipphardt, "Isolates and Crosses in Human Population Genetics."

48. Gil-Riaño, "Relocating Anti-Racist Science," 283.

49. Ibid.

50. As I discuss in the next section, Franz Boas's seminal argument about the plasticity of race emerged directly from his studies of environmental influence on racial form. Equally, genetic and now postgenomic developments have laid privileged claim to the biosocial terrain of the plastic; epigenetics, for instance, is now deemed "the science of plasticity." See Becky Mansfield and Julie Guthman, "Epigenetic Life: Biological Plasticity, Abnormality, and New Configurations of Race and Reproduction," *Cultural Geographies* 22, no. 1 (2013), 4.

51. UNESCO, Statement on Race, 32.

52. Influential accounts of plasticity include Catherine Malabou's varied works on this topic, especially *What Should We Do with Our Brain?*, trans. Sebastian Rand (New York: Fordham UP, 2008); and *Plasticity at the Dusk of Writing: Dialectic, Destruction, Deconstruction*, trans. Carolyn Shread (New York: Columbia UP, 2010); and Elizabeth Grosz, *Volatile Bodies: Toward a Corporeal Feminism* (Bloomington: Indiana UP, 1994). See also Jane Bennett, *Vibrant Matter: A Political Ecology of Things* (Durham, NC: Duke UP, 2010), for a

closely related analysis not focused on the plasticity of the human but similarly attuned to the agency of matter.

53. Spivak, *A Critique of Postcolonial Reason*, 110.

54. S. Pearl Brilmyer, "Plasticity, Form, and the Matter of Character in *Middlemarch*," *Representations* 130, no. 1 (Spring 2015), 64.

55. Malabou, *What Should We Do with Our Brain?*, 5.

56. Ibid., 17.

57. Ibid., 77.

58. Scholars have recognized this entanglement, and there is a growing body of critical work that examines plasticity's racialized history and so also challenges its apparently emancipatory politics. My project builds on and hopes to contribute to this body of critical scholarship. I take up key works in what follows, but see Sianne Ngai, *Ugly Feelings* (Cambridge, MA: Harvard UP, 2005), especially on "animatedness"; Donna V. Jones, *The Racial Discourses of Life Philosophy: Négritude, Vitalism, and Modernity* (New York: Columbia UP, 2010); Mel Y. Chen, *Animacies: Biopolitics, Racial Mattering, and Queer Affect* (Durham, NC: Duke UP, 2012); Monique Allewaert, *Ariel's Ecology: Plantations, Personhood, and Colonialism in the American Tropics* (Minneapolis: University of Minnesota Press, 2013); Jayna Brown, "Being Cellular: Race, the Inhuman, and the Plasticity of Life," *GLQ* 21, nos. 2–3 (2015), 321–41; Zakiyyah Iman Jackson, "Losing Manhood: Animality and Plasticity in the (Neo)Slave Narrative," *Qui Parle: Critical Humanities and Social Sciences* 25, nos. 1–2 (2016), 95–136; Michelle N. Huang, "Ecologies of Entanglement in the Great Pacific Garbage Patch," *Journal of Asian American Studies* 20, no. 1 (2017), 95–117; Deepika Bahri, *Postcolonial Biology: Psyche and Flesh after Empire* (Minneapolis: University of Minnesota Press, 2017); Kyla Schuller, *The Biopolitics of Feeling: Race, Sex, and Science in the Nineteenth Century* (Durham, NC: Duke UP, 2018); Kyla Schuller and Jules Gill-Peterson, "Introduction: Race, the State, and the Malleable Body," *Social Text* 38, no. 2 (2020), 1–17; Neel Ahuja, "Reversible Human: Rectal Feeding, Gut Plasticity, and Racial Control in US Carceral Warfare," *Social Text* 38, no. 2 (2020), 19–47; Kadji Amin, "Trans* Plasticity and the Ontology of Race and Species," *Social Text* 38, no. 2 (2020), 49–71.

59. Franz Boas, "Changes in the Bodily Form of Descendants of Immigrants," *American Anthropologist* 14, no. 3 (July 1912), 556.

60. Ibid., 557. For an overview of Boas's study and its historical context and significance in light of prevailing views about race in physical anthropology, see, for instance, George W. Stocking Jr., "The Critique of Racial Formalism," in *Race, Culture, and Evolution: Essays in the History of Anthropology* (New York: The Free Press, 1968), 161–94.

61. As Stocking notes, "Boas, like the eugenicists of the same period, was inclined to look for biological solutions to what we would today regard as *social* problems." Stocking, "The Critique of Racial Formalism," 179.

62. Quoted in Leonard B. Glick, "Types Distinct from Our Own: Franz Boas on Jewish Identity and Assimilation," *American Anthropologist* 84, no. 3 (September 1982), 557. Many thanks to Itamar Francez for directing me to this piece.

63. Boas, "Changes in the Bodily Form of Descendants of Immigrants," 555.

64. As Stocking notes, Boas was interested in the question of child development and the influence of childhood environment before he turned to questions of race. This was thanks to his training under the German anthropologist Rudolf Virchow as well as due to the influence of colleagues at Clark University, where he held his first position at a US institution starting in 1889 and conducted empirical studies on schoolchildren. Stocking, "The Critique of Racial Formalism," 165–71.

65. Bahri, *Postcolonial Biology*, 3.

66. Ibid. This book has many questions in common with Bahri's *Postcolonial Biology*. Like Robert J. C. Young, who, in *Colonial Desire: Hybridity in Theory, Culture and Race* (London: Routledge, 1995), insists on postcolonial cultural hybridity's entanglement with the concept's racial history, Bahri takes up hybridity at the switch point of race/culture. Hybridity is "*hybridity in the flesh*," she argues, operating on the body in its "*retail* particulars at the level of muscle, tongue, glottis, viscera, and myriad administrations of the sensorium and bodily expression" (18–19). It is in service of this argument about hybridity (her key term, in keeping with its centrality for postcolonial theory) that she invokes the plastic being of both the colonial subject and the contemporary subject (or consumer) of commodity culture. In *The Reeducation of Race*, in contrast, *plasticity* is the organizing term, owing to its centrality for both historical experiments in the modification of racial form as well as for liberal antiracism. However, *plasticity/educability* maps closely to the paired terms *hybridity/mimicry* as they are articulated in postcolonial theory.

67. Franz Boas, "The Problem of the American Negro," *Yale Review* 10 (1921), 384.

68. Ibid., 394.

69. Ibid., 392.

70. Ibid., 393.

71. Chen, *Animacies*.

72. Jackson, "Losing Manhood," 119, 118.

73. Jayna Brown has identified an association of Blackness with both "hypo- and hyper plasticity" in the fiction of the influential biologist Julian Huxley, who served as UNESCO's first director-general and had a hand in UNESCO's race project and who will be encountered in more detail in chapters 1 and 4. Brown, "Being Cellular."

74. Jackson, "Losing Manhood," 119.

75. Albert Memmi, *Racism*, trans. Steve Martinot (Minneapolis: University of Minnesota Press, 2000), 55.

76. See, for instance, Kamala Visweswaran on Boas's (and Lévi-Strauss's) roles in what she nicely calls "the internationalization of the race concept" in *Un/common Cultures*, 52–102, 149.

77. Glick has noted that the US Immigration Commission had been charged with collecting data on social and economic questions, and it was Boas who insisted on conducting a study of physical types. Glick, "Types Distinct from Our Own," 557.

78. Eric Porter, "*The Problem of the Future World: W. E. B. Du Bois and the Race Concept at Midcentury* (Durham, NC: Duke UP, 2010), 3.

79. Schuller and Gill-Peterson, "Introduction: Race, the State, and the Malleable Body," 2.

80. Huang, "Ecologies of Entanglement in the Great Pacific Garbage Patch," 105.

81. Ibid., 109.

82. Ibid., 110–11.

83. Gary Wilder, *Freedom Time: Negritude, Decolonization, and the Future of the World* (Durham, NC: Duke UP, 2015), 3–4. In Adom Getachew's important analysis of this terrain, she demonstrates that twentieth-century anticolonial nationalists pursued their goals in a synoptic fashion: recognizing that the assertion of national sovereignty would afford new nations little in a stubbornly racially hierarchical international order, they "turned to projects of worldmaking that would secure the conditions of international nondomination." Getachew, *Worldmaking after Empire*, 9–10.

84. Getachew, *Worldmaking After Empire*, 73.

85. Roland Burke, *Decolonization and the Evolution of Human Rights* (Philadelphia: University of Pennsylvania Press, 2013), 2.

86. For instance, Steven L. B. Jensen argues that it was developments of the 1960s driven by the decolonizing world, including the 1960 establishment of the right to self-determination, that reinvigorated human rights discourse at a time when it otherwise had little broad significance. Jensen, *The Making of International Human Rights: The 1960s, Decolonization, and the Reconstruction of Global Values* (New York: Cambridge UP, 2016), 18–68.

87. Joseph R. Slaughter, "Hijacking Human Rights: Neoliberalism, the New Historiography, and the End of the Third World," *Human Rights Quarterly* 40, no. 4 (2018), 739. Important, non-mythologizing accounts of such influence do also exist; see, for instance, Lydia H. Liu, "Shadows of Universalism: The Untold Story of Human Rights around 1948," *Critical Inquiry*, 40, no. 4 (2014), 385–417.

88. Indeed, authors in this book have featured in such analyses; Anne W. Gulick has recently shown how Césaire's long poem *Cahier d'un retour au pays natal* formally and conceptually engages the Universal Declaration of Human Rights. Gulick, *Literature, Law, and Rhetorical Performance in the Anticolonial Atlantic* (Columbus: Ohio State UP, 2016), 77–120.

89. On personhood and human personality, see Joseph R. Slaughter, *Human Rights, Inc.: The World Novel, Narrative Form, and International Law* (New York: Columbia UP, 2007). On dignity, see Elizabeth S. Anker, *Fictions of Dignity: Embodying Human Rights in World Literature* (Ithaca, NY: Cornell UP, 2012). On the cultural influence of multiple human rights documents, see Crystal Parikh, *Writing Human Rights: The Political Imaginaries of Writers of Color* (Minneapolis: University of Minnesota Press, 2017).

90. Brouillette, *UNESCO and the Fate of the Literary*. Similarly, Joseph R. Slaughter has discussed UNESCO's role in policing intellectual property laws in the global literary sphere. Slaughter, "World Literature as Property," *Alif: Journal of Comparative Poetics*, 34 (2014), 39–73.

91. For key works on this question, see Gayatri Chakravorty Spivak, "Three Women's Texts and a Critique of Imperialism," *Critical Inquiry* 12, no. 1 (Autumn 1985), 243–61; Gauri Viswanathan, *Masks of Conquest: Literary Study and British Rule in India* (New York: Columbia UP, 1989); Ann Laura Stoler, *Carnal Knowledge and Imperial Power: Race and the Intimate in Colonial Rule* (Berkeley: University of California Press, 2002); Ashis Nandy, *The Intimate Enemy: Loss and Recovery of Self Under Colonialism* (New Delhi: Oxford UP, 2009); Slaughter, *Human Rights, Inc.*; Ben Conisbee Baer, *Indigenous Vanguards: Education, National Liberation, and the Limits of Modernism* (New York: Columbia UP, 2019).

92. For analyses of this shift, see Visweswaran, *Un/common Cultures*, 52–73; and Haraway, "Remodeling the Human Way of Life," 206–59.

93. For an important study of racial periodization and liberal antiracism focused on the US context, see Jodi Melamed, *Represent and Destroy: Rationalizing Violence in the New Racial Capitalism* (Minneapolis: University of Minnesota Press, 2011). On liberal antiracism, see Joseph Darda, *The Strange Career of Racial Liberalism* (Stanford, CA: Stanford UP, 2022). For important recent studies that examine US racial formation in international perspective, see Keith P. Feldman, *A Shadow over Palestine: The Imperial Life of Race in America* (Minneapolis: University of Minnesota Press, 2015); Erica R. Edwards, *The Other Side of Terror: Black Women and the Culture of US Empire* (New York: NYU Press, 2021). Robert Stam and Ella Shohat offer a robustly comparative account of race and racism in an Atlantic context in *Race in Translation: Culture Wars around the Postcolonial Atlantic* (New York: NYU Press, 2012). Howard Winant emphasizes the global importance of what he calls the global rupture of race at midcentury but pays little attention to the international institutions that mediated it. See Winant, *The World Is a Ghetto: Race and Democracy since World War II* (New York: Basic Books, 2001).

94. On relational racism, see David Theo Goldberg, "Racial Comparisons, Relational Racisms: Some Thoughts on Method," *Ethnic and Racial Studies* 32, no. 7 (2009), 1271–82. For an analysis of antisemitism in an imperial frame that draws on relational methods, see Dorian Bell, *Globalizing Race: Antisemitism and Empire in French and European Culture* (Chicago: Northwestern UP, 2018). While Goldberg makes the case for the relational over the comparative, I am less convinced of the utility of one term over the other. For an analysis of comparative racialization as a method attuned both to the global (rather than nation-state centered) frame of reference and to the significance of past racial formations for the present, see for instance Shu-Mei Shih, "Comparative Racialization: An Introduction," *PMLA* 123, no. 5 (2008), 1347–62.

95. This is a large and growing field, but see especially Volker Langbehn and Mohammad Salama, eds., *German Colonialism: Race, the Holocaust and Postwar Germany* (New York: Columbia UP, 2011); A. Dirk Moses, "Conceptual Blockages and Definitional Dilemmas in the 'Racial Century': Genocides of Indigenous Peoples and the Holocaust," *Patterns of Prejudice* 36, no. 4 (2002), 7–36; Richard H. King and Dan Stone, eds., *Hannah Arendt and the Uses of History: Imperialism, Nation, Race, and Genocide* (New York: Berghahn, 2007), which builds on Arendt's status as an early (though ambiguous) theorist of these connections, to name just a few. In very recent German public discourse, these scholarly approaches to comparative genocide have been invoked in heated debates about the legitimacy of such comparisons. The historian Jürgen Zimmerer and the cultural critic Michael Rothberg, whose work has been central to these debates, explain the contours of the controversy and assess the limitations of the anti-comparative critique. Jürgen Zimmerer and Michael Rothberg, "Enttabuisiert den Vergleich!," *Die Zeit* (April 4, 2021), https://www.zeit.de/2021/14/erinnerungskultur-gedenken-pluralisieren-holocaust-vergleich-globalisierung-geschichte; Michael Rothberg, "We Need to Re-center the New *Historikerstreit*," *Die Zeit* (July 24, 2021), https://www.zeit.de/kultur/2021-07/dealing-with-the-holocaust-historikerstreit-controversy-genocide-english.

96. Michael Rothberg, *Multidirectional Memory: Remembering the Holocaust in the Age of Decolonization* (Stanford, CA: Stanford UP, 2009), 7.

97. Andreas Huyssen, *Present Pasts: Urban Palimpsests and the Politics of Memory* (Stanford, CA: Stanford UP, 2003); Michael Rothberg, Debarati Sanyal, and Max Silverman, eds. "*Nœuds de mémoire*: Multidirectional Memory in Postwar French and Francophone Culture," *Yale French Studies*, 118–19 (2010); François Lionnet, "'*Dire exactement*': Remembering the Interwoven Lives of Jewish Deportees and Coolie Descendants in 1940s Mauritius," *Yale French Studies*, 118– 119 (2010), 111–35; Marianne Hirsch, *The Generation of Postmemory* (New York: Columbia UP, 2012); Max Silverman, *Palimpsestic Memory: The Holocaust and Colonialism in French and Francophone Fiction and Film* (New York: Berghahn, 2013); Debarati Sanyal, *Memory and Complicity: Migrations of Holocaust Remembrance* (New York: Fordham UP, 2015). In some cases, the kinds of comparative or multidirectional borrowings at work in these engagements are metaphorical and analogical, so that not just the history but also the subsequent figuration and representation of the Holocaust seem prismatically to illuminate other geopolitically distant national or transnational experiences or be concerned with the transit of particular concepts, such as trauma. On such a prismatic status for Holocaust memory in late twentieth-century global cultural memory, see especially Huyssen, *Present Pasts*, 14 and passim. Somewhat similarly, Daniel Levy and Natan Sznaider have argued for a cosmopolitan Holocaust memory. However, while Huyssen suggests that the metaphorical and analogical uses of the Holocaust depend on its status as a "universal trope" while necessarily also "decentering" it (14), Levy and Sznaider treat the Holocaust as a kind of master discourse through which other histories become legible. Levy and Sznaider, *The Holocaust*

and Memory in the Global Age, trans. Assenka Oksiloff (Philadelphia: Temple UP, 2006). For valuable studies that take up key concepts prominently theorized in Holocaust memory studies, such as the categories of "trauma" and "testimony," and assess the status of Holocaust as lens and limit, treating it alongside other histories and genealogies, see, for instance, Stef Craps, *Postcolonial Witnessing: Trauma Out of Bounds* (London: Palgrave, 2013); and Jill Jarvis, *Decolonizing Memory: Algeria and the Politics of Testimony* (Durham, NC: Duke UP, 2021). The final chapter of Paul Gilroy, *The Black Atlantic: Modernity and Double Consciousness* (Cambridge, MA: Harvard UP, 1993), 187–204, is an enduringly important intervention in this vein, attuned to overlapping questions about suffering and the limits of representation in Black diasporic and Jewish writing.

98. Other recent works not comfortably housed under the category of memory studies have also contributed to this broader comparative intellectual project. For instance, Aamir Mufti and Bryan Cheyette have demonstrated that the history of particular concepts—minority and diaspora, respectively—necessarily draw together postcolonial and Jewish thought and histories. Mufti, *Enlightenment in the Colony: The Jewish Question and the Crisis of Postcolonial Culture* (Princeton, NJ: Princeton UP, 2007); Cheyette, *Diasporas of the Mind: Jewish and Postcolonial Writing and the Nightmare of History* (New Haven, CT: Yale UP, 2014). Sarah Phillips Casteel has shown that such connections are especially profoundly registered in Caribbean literature and has traced the historical and cultural conditions that have generated these engagements. Casteel, *Calypso Jews: Jewishness in the Caribbean Literary Imagination* (New York: Columbia UP, 2016). Paul Gilroy and Dorian Bell have traced the conjoined histories of antisemitism, anti-Blackness, and colonial racism in a global context. Gilroy, *Against Race: Imagining Political Culture Beyond the Color Line* (Cambridge, MA: Harvard UP, 2000); Bell, *Globalizing Race*.

99. Stuart Hall, "Race, the Floating Signifier: What More Is There to Say about Race?", in Stuart Hall, *Selected Writings on Race and Difference*, ed. Paul Gilroy and Ruth Wilson Gilmore (Durham, NC: Duke UP, 2021), 362. This semantic and ideological changeability speaks to the highly variable ways in which racial meaning is made and racial value assigned in specific conflicts of power and exploitation or in relation to other socially differentiating concepts such as caste, for instance, which put pressure on the meaning of race. Lisa Lowe maps the variability of race in the context of "the 'coloniality' of modern world history," demonstrating the "precisely spatialized and temporalized processes of both differentiation and connection." Lowe, *The Intimacies of Four Continents* (Durham, NC: Duke UP), 8.

100. These arguments have often been elaborated in one or another national historical context. See, inter alia, Henry Rousso, *The Vichy Syndrome: History and Memory in France since 1944*, trans. Arthur Goldhammer (Cambridge, MA: Harvard UP, 1994); Annette Wieviorka, *The Era of the Witness*, trans. Jared Stark, (Ithaca, NY: Cornell UP, 2006); Samuel Moyn, *A Holocaust Controversy: The Treblinka Affair in Postwar France*; (Waltham, MA: Brandeis UP, 2005); Peter Novick, *The Holocaust in American Life* (Boston: Mariner Books, 2000); Tom Segev, *The Seventh Million: The Israelis and the Holocaust*, trans. Haim Watzman (New York: Henry Holt, 2000). Of the widespread notion that the UDHR was a direct response to the Holocaust, Samuel Moyn observes that while this may be "the most universally repeated myth about their origins," in fact "there was no widespread Holocaust consciousness in the postwar era, so human rights could not have been a response to it." Moyn, *The Last Utopia: Human Rights in History* (Cambridge, MA: Belknap, 2010), 6–7; see also Marco Duranti, "The Holocaust, the Legacy of 1789 and the Birth of International Human Rights Law: Revisiting the Foundation Myth," *Journal of Genocide Research* 14, no. 2 (June 2012): 159–86; Stephen Hopgood, *The Endtimes of Human Rights* (Ithaca, NY: Cornell UP, 2013), 53. Scholars have

made a similar case for the relative minimization of the specificity of Jewish suffering at the Nuremberg trials, for instance in the form of witness testimony. See Lawrence Douglas, *The Memory of Judgment: Making Law and History in the Trials of the Holocaust* (New Haven, CT: Yale UP, 2001), 11–94; Donald Bloxham, *Genocide on Trial: War Crimes Trials and the Formation of Holocaust History and Memory* (Oxford: Oxford UP, 2001).

101. This work has variously challenged the assertions of early postwar silence, offered new accounts of the relationship between the formation of postwar human rights institutions and Jewish politics, and complicated the timeline and sphere in which we conceive of Holocaust memory. See for instance David Cesarani and Eric J. Sundquist, eds., *After the Holocaust: Challenging the Myth of Silence* (London: Routledge, 2012); Laura Jockusch, "Justice at Nuremberg?: Jewish Responses to Nazi War-Crime Trials in Allied-Occupied Germany," *Jewish Social Studies* 19, no. 1 (2012): 107–47; James Loeffler, *Rooted Cosmopolitans: Jews and Human Rights in the Twentieth Century* (New Haven, CT: Yale UP, 2018); Johannes Morsink, *The Universal Declaration of Human Rights and the Holocaust: An Endangered Connection* (Washington, DC: Georgetown UP, 2019). As Moyn has acknowledged in a review-essay of some of this work, the categorical assertion of postwar silence does not hold. While still holding to a timeline weighted toward the late 1960s, he nuances his own earlier position and suggests that we relinquish the view that "the Holocaust was either entirely absent or integrally present from the start" and focus instead on "the changing forms of Holocaust memory" and the work they do, including for "international politics as a whole." Samuel Moyn, "Silence and the Shoah," *Times Literary Supplement*, August 7, 2013. I'm grateful to Lauren Berlant for sending me this essay.

102. For a different view, see Shirli Gilbert's and Avril Alba's introduction to their edited collection on Holocaust memory and racism, which "challenges the notion that there is an unproblematic connection between Holocaust memory and the discourse of anti-racism." Gilbert and Alba observe that the scholarship on UNESCO's race statements demonstrates that postwar science struggled to find consensus on the status of race, indicating that "the presumed anti-racist lessons of the Holocaust have been written back to the postwar years themselves." This glosses over how significantly the statement was shaped by the context of Nazi antisemitism. UNESCO's race project did not succeed in solving the race question (and in fact perpetuated it in new forms), but this only makes its historical connection to the Holocaust more complex and not less meaningful. Gilbert and Alba, "Introduction," in *Holocaust Memory and Racism in the Postwar World* (Detroit: Wayne State UP, 2019), 1, 3–4.

103. Said's own work gestured to these engagements—for instance, his 1979 essay "Zionism from the Standpoint of Its Victims," in *The Selected Works of Edward Said, 1966-2006*, ed. Moustafa Bayoumi and Andrew Rubin (New York: Vintage, 2019), 115–69; and Said, *Freud and the Non-European* (London: Verso, 2003).

104. On the role of the UN and the institutions of international justice in the perpetuation of Palestinian dispossession, see Noura Erakat, *Justice for Some: Law and the Question of Palestine* (Stanford, CA: Stanford UP, 2019).

105. Hart, *Social Science and the Politics of Modern Jewish Identity*, 140.

106. Ibid., 139–68; Amos Morris-Reich, "Circumventions and Confrontations: Georg Simmel, Franz Boas and Arthur Ruppin and Their Responses to Antisemitism," *Patterns of Prejudice* 44, no. 2 (2010), 195–215; Nadia Abu El-Haj, *The Genealogical Science: The Search for Jewish Origins and the Politics of Epistemology* (Chicago: University of Chicago Press, 2012), 63–108.

107. For a sense of Zollschan's views on Jewish racial purity and superiority, see Ignaz Zollschan, "The Significance of the Mixed Marriage," in *Jews and Race: Writings on Identity*

and Difference, 1880-1940, ed. Mitchell B. Hart (Waltham, MA: Brandeis UP, 2011), 175–84. See also Hart, *Social Science and the Politics of Modern Jewish Identity*, 64–66, 77–78 and 74–95. For a fuller though less critical account of Zollschan's thought, see John M. Efron, *Defenders of the Race: Jewish Doctors and Race Science in Fin-de-Siècle Europe* (New Haven, CT: Yale UP, 1994), 123–74.

108. Elazar Barkan, "Review—*Defenders of the Race: Jewish Doctors and Race Science in Fin-de-Siècle Europe*," *The American Historical Review* 101, no. 3 (1996), 839; see also Barkan, *The Retreat of Scientific Racism*, 284, 319.

109. Alfred Métraux, "UNESCO and the Racial Problem," *International Social Science Bulletin* 2, no. 3 (1950), 385.

110. Leslie C. Dunn and Stephen P. Dunn, "The Jewish Community of Rome," *Scientific American* 196, no. 3 (March 1957), 118–32.

111. Abu El-Haj, *The Genealogical Science*, 63–108.

112. Mufti, *Enlightenment in the Colony*.

113. Samuel Moyn, *The Last Utopia*; for an important rejoinder, see Slaughter, "Hijacking Human Rights." For a fascinating recent contribution to the historiography of human rights that centers UNESCO, see *Letters to the Contrary: A Curated History of the UNESCO Human Rights Survey*, ed. Mark Goodale (Stanford, CA: Stanford UP, 2018).

114. The Tunisian-Jewish novelist and anticolonial critic Albert Memmi theorizes racism in a way that exemplifies this naturalization of the properly racial body. Racism, he writes, is "strictly speaking," "a theory of *biological differences*" that organizes hierarchies among groups. But biology is both metaphor and metonymy: nonbiological differences can be biologized and the debased values ascribed to biological difference are transmitted "from biology to ethics, from ethics to politics, from politics to metaphysics," as racism's object is saturated with negative meaning. Memmi, "An Attempt at a Definition," in *Racism*, trans. Steve Martinot (Minneapolis: University of Minnesota Press, 2000), 170, 174. Sylvia Wynter calls this process the "transumption of the principle of Sameness/Difference to a new bio-ontological form." Wynter, "The Ceremony Must Be Found: After Humanism," *boundary 2* 12, no. 3 (1984), 36. And yet, biological difference in Memmi's account is not just metaphor but matter. The dreadful success of biological racism is attributable in part to the undeniable materiality of the original referent in this chain of negative signification: the body and its "substratum," "the flesh, the blood, and the genes of the victim" (174). In Memmi's analysis, any difference can be biologized but some are more biological than others: "The Black is irremediably black, the woman is irremediably a woman. Thus, we encounter the undying efforts to biologically characterize the Jew and the colonized, even though biology is irrelevant." The epidermal differences of Blackness and the sexual difference of women, Memmi suggests, threaten to obscure the tactical character of their negative valuation because they are properly biological, in contrast to Jews and the colonized, for whom a biology must be invented. Memmi's characterization of Blackness as irremediable and inescapable treats epidermal difference as a self-evident truth of the racial body. Memmi, *Racism*, 55.

115. Abu El-Haj, *The Genealogical Science*, 45–46.

116. Visweswaran, "Race and the Culture of Anthropology," in *Un/Common Cultures*, 52–73, demonstrates how the ascendence and internationalization of a Boasian race concept that treated race and culture as antonyms in turn facilitated the naturalization of culture characteristic of contemporary cultural racism. Such an attempted disaggregation began much earlier in Boas's work, though it was only at midcentury that these efforts were formalized at international institutions such as UNESCO. George Stocking shows how Boas's thought

was indebted to Romantic and Herderian views about the organic forms that expressed the national or ethnic group's character. But whereas some versions of this tradition tacked toward the racial taxonomies Boas seemed to throw into question, Boas sought to "define 'the genius of a people' in other terms than racial heredity. His answer, ultimately, was the anthropological idea of culture." On Boas's centrality for the development of the culture concept in twentieth-century anthropology and his role in the shift from the idea of culture as a single evolutionist category to a plural notion of culture necessary for a properly anthropological perspective, see George W. Stocking Jr., "Franz Boas and the Culture Concept," in *Race, Culture, and Evolution: Essays in the History of Anthropology* (New York: The Free Press, 1968), 214.

Chapter 1

1. Ashley Montagu, *Statement on Race: An Extended Discussion in Plain Language of the UNESCO Statement by Experts on Race Problems* (New York: Schuman, 1951), ix.

2. Donna Haraway, "Race: Universal Donors in a Vampire Culture," in *Modest_Witness@Second_Millenium. FemaleMan_Meets_OncoMouse: Feminism and Technoscience* (New York: Routledge, 1997), 239; Elazar Barkan, *The Retreat of Scientific Racism: Changing Concepts of Race in Britain and the United States between the World Wars* (Cambridge: Cambridge UP, 1992), 341.

3. Perrin Selcer, "Beyond the Cephalic Index: Negotiating Politics to Produce UNESCO's Scientific Statements on Race," *Current Anthropology* 53, no. S5 (April 1, 2012), S174.

4. Jenny Reardon explains this retrospective consecration of the statements by observing that "if one adopts the position that scientific claims are the product of a set of methods that progressively reveal truth and oppose ideology, then it is understandable that historians and social scientists would later identify the UNESCO Statements on Race as the watershed moment when the truth that race is biologically meaningless escaped the grip of ideology." Reardon, "Decoding Race and Human Difference in a Genomic Age," *differences: A Journal of Feminist Cultural Studies* 15, no. 3 (Fall 2003), 52.

5. Ibid., 38–65; Anthony Q. Hazard, *Postwar Anti-Racism: The United States, UNESCO, and "Race," 1945–1968* (New York: Palgrave Macmillan, 2012).

6. Michelle Brattain, "Race, Racism, and Antiracism: UNESCO and the Politics of Presenting Science to the Postwar Public," *The American Historical Review* 112, no. 5 (December 1, 2007), 1413. See also Sebastián Gil-Riaño, "Historicizing Anti-Racism: UNESCO's Campaigns against Race Prejudice in the 1950s" (PhD diss., University of Toronto, 2014), which examines the UNESCO statements as a study in what Gil-Riaño usefully describes (following Ian Hacking) as the historical ontology of race; Haraway, *Modest_Witness*, 213–48, theorizes the biological frameworks according to which we might periodize race's scientific imaginaries as they shift from blood to population (with the UNESCO statements and after) and now to the genome. Robert N. Proctor, "Three Roots of Human Recency: Molecular Anthropology, the Refigured Acheulean, and the UNESCO Response to Auschwitz," *Current Anthropology* 44, no. 2 (April 1, 2003): 213–39.

7. UNESCO, Statement on Race, in *Four Statements on the Race Question* (Paris: UNESCO, 1969), 32.

8. My reading thus resonates with Elazar Barkan's *The Retreat of Scientific Racism*, which argues that when Anglo-American scientists began to challenge scientific racism in the 1920s and '30s, scientific developments of the 1920s cleared the way but did not incite or produce a shift that he argues was fundamentally political. Or, as he puts it elsewhere, "though the shift may seem almost irreversible, nothing in 'science' had determined such a development." Elazar Barkan, "The Politics of the Science of Race: Ashley Montagu and UNESCO's Anti-Racist Declarations," in *Race and Other Misadventures: Essays in Honor of Ashley Montagu in*

His Ninetieth Year, ed. Larry T. Reynolds and Leonard Lieberman (Dix Hills, NY: General Hall, 1996), 104. But for a contrasting view, see Nancy Stepan, *The Idea of Race in Science: Great Britain, 1800–1960* (London: Palgrave Macmillan, 1982).

9. Julian Huxley, "On Living in a Revolution," *Harper's Magazine* 185, no. 1108 (1942), 337.

10. Ibid., 346.

11. Ibid., 343.

12. Ibid., 339.

13. Ibid., 340.

14. UNESCO, Constitution of the United Nations Educational, Scientific, and Cultural Organization, in *Basic Texts: 2018 Edition including Texts and Amendments Adopted by the General Conference at its 39th Session (Paris, 30 October–14 November, 2017)* (Paris: UNESCO, 2018), 5.

15. UNESCO, *General Conference—First Session, UNESCO House, Paris, November 20–December 10, 1946.* UNESCO/C/30 (Paris: UNESCO, 1947), 18.

16. The early postwar period saw the development of many of the legal instruments crucial to what Ruti Teitel has called "humanity law"—a legal regime whose "orientation or telos is the preservation of humanity." UNESCO's work underscores that the work of constituting humanity as "both the subject and object of [legal] action" also depends on the cultivation of an ethicopolitical subjectivity that allows individuals to understand themselves as belonging to humanity. Teitel, *Humanity's Law* (New York: Oxford UP, 2011), 19. On humanity, law, and subjectivity, see also Joseph R. Slaughter's account of the human person and Samera Esmeir's analysis of colonial law as a project of humanization. Slaughter, *Human Rights, Inc.: The World Novel, Narrative Form, and International Law* (New York: Fordham UP, 2007); Esmeir, *Juridical Humanity: A Colonial History* (Stanford, CA: Stanford UP, 2012).

17. UNESCO, *General Conference—First Session*, 47, 27, 49, 37.

18. Ibid., 18, 59, 28, 27.

19. Ibid., 59.

20. Ibid.

21. The cultural critic and Germanist Jaimey Fisher argues that in Germany in the early postwar period, particularly the years of Allied occupation (1945–1949), the discourse of reeducation revolved especially around the problem of German youth and the trope of German youth in crisis. In his examination of texts, debates, and films from the German public sphere, the dominant figuration of young Germans is as especially convinced Nazis, driven by immature zeal and yet redeemable, even victimized, because they have been indoctrinated and miseducated: "They could be perpetrator and victim simultaneously," he observes. Moreover, he writes, the occupied Allied forces also accepted this characterization. The Nicaraguan delegate's remarks suggest that this was not just a dynamic visible in postwar Germany but a problem with global implications, requiring international intervention. The tension that characterizes the delegate's remarks, which cast the young German Nazi as both the perpetrator of abominable violence and also as the victim of a grotesque miseducation, echoes precisely the duality that Fisher identifies at work in the German public sphere during the early postwar period. See Fisher, *Disciplining Germany: Youth, Reeducation, and Reconstruction after the Second World War* (Detroit: Wayne State UP 2007), 14, 66.

22. UNESCO, *General Conference—First Session*, 47, 27.

23. Ibid., 51, 59.

24. Rebekah Sheldon, *The Child to Come: Life after the Human Catastrophe* (Minneapolis: University of Minnesota Press, 2008), 2.

25. UNESCO, *General Conference—First Session*, 59.

26. Claudia Castañeda, *Figurations: Child, Bodies, Worlds* (Durham, NC: Duke UP, 2002), 3.

27. UNESCO, *General Conference—First Session*, 43.

28. In a fascinating article that also considers the significance of the child's plastic character, Iain Morland argues that UNESCO's focus on racial plasticity and educability significantly influenced theories of gender plasticity in the 1960s and the treatment of intersex children, whose psychological and biological plasticity was thought to make them educable into either gender. Morland, "Gender, Genitals, and the Meaning of Being Human," in *Fuckologies: Critical Essays on John Money's Diagnostic Concepts,* ed. Lisa Downing, Iain Morland, and Nikki Sullivan (Chicago: University of Chicago Press, 2015), 69–98. My thanks to Kyla Schuller for the reference.

29. Natasha Levinson, "The Paradox of Natality: Teaching in the Midst of Belatedness," in *Hannah Arendt and Education: Renewing Our Common World*, ed. Mordechai Gordon (Boulder, CO: Westview Press, 2001), 11–36.

30. Hannah Arendt, *The Origins of Totalitarianism*, rev ed. (New York: Harcourt Brace Jovanovich, 1973), 478–79.

31. Ibid., 479. For a careful reconstruction of the emergence of both the idea of natality and the term itself in Arendt's work, see Miguel Vatter, "Natality and Biopolitics in Hannah Arendt," *Revista de Ciencia Política* 26, no. 2 (2006): 137–59.

32. Hannah Arendt, *The Human Condition*, 2nd ed. (Chicago: University of Chicago Press, 1998), 9.

33. See Arendt, *The Human Condition*, especially 9, 178, and 247, on natality as birth. On natality's inextricable relation to the event of biological birth, contra some accounts that insist Arendt is describing a second birth into political life, see Vatter, "Natality and Biopolitics in Hannah Arendt"; and Rosalyn Diprose and Ewa Plonowska Ziarek, "Time for Beginners: Natality, Biopolitics, and Political Theology," *philoSOPHIA* 3, no. 2 (2013): 107–20. For an overview of this debate, see Anne O'Byrne, *Natality and Finitude* (Bloomington: Indiana UP, 2010), 90–101.

34. Levinson, "The Paradox of Natality," 13.

35. Hannah Arendt, "What Is Freedom?" in *Between Past and Future: Eight Exercises in Political Thought* (New York: Penguin Books, 2006), 169; see also Levinson, "The Paradox of Natality," 14. Or as Arendt puts it in *The Human Condition*, "The new always happens against the overwhelming odds of statistical laws and their probability.... The new therefore always appears in the guise of a miracle" (178).

36. Levinson, "The Paradox of Natality," 17.

37. Hannah Arendt, "The Crisis in Education," in *Between Past and Future: Eight Exercises in Political Thought* (New York: Penguin Books, 2006), 171, 174.

38. See also Levinson, "The Paradox of Natality," who frames the paradox of natality as something confronted most vividly in the context of teaching, which she observes always takes place in "the midst of belatedness."

39. UNESCO, *General Conference—First Session*, 55, 43.

40. Gayatri Chakravorty Spivak, *A Critique of Postcolonial Reason: Toward a History of the Vanishing Present* (Cambridge, MA: Harvard UP, 1999), 112–40.

41. UNESCO, *General Conference—First Session*, 50, 80.

42. Mark Mazower, *No Enchanted Palace: The End of Empire and the Ideological Origins of the United Nations* (Princeton, NJ: Princeton UP, 2009), 17.

43. Walter H. C. Laves and Charles A. Thomson, *UNESCO: Purpose, Progress, Prospects* (Bloomington: Indiana UP, 1957), 63, 370n38.

44. For an account of this episode, see Mazower, *No Enchanted Palace*, 149–51.

45. These tensions were also felt at UNESCO. In 1951, Alva Myrdal, then director of UNESCO's Department of Social Sciences, would report to the anthropologist Alfred Métraux, who ran the race project, the "sad news" that UNESCO's director-general had nixed their attempts for a resolution related to race in UNESCO's 1953–54 program on the grounds that "we would not be able to steer a middle course between metropolitan interests and those of the freedom-seeking populations, and rather than have the resolution torn to pieces . . . he prefers to present one which has a greater chance of success, and set in a wider framework, namely, one on discrimination as a whole." Letter from Alva Myrdal to Alfred Métraux, October 22, 1951, SS/262.215, folder 323.12 A 102, box 147, UNESCO Archives, Paris.

46. See Carol Anderson, *Eyes Off the Prize: The United Nations and the African American Struggle for Human Rights, 1944–1955* (Cambridge: Cambridge UP, 2003), especially 58–112.

47. UN Economic and Social Council, Commission on Human Rights, Sub-commission on the Prevention of Discrimination and the Protection of Minorities, first session, November 24–December 6, 1947, *Report Submitted to the Commission on Human Rights, December 6, 1947*, 17, E/CN.4/52, undocs.org/en/E/CN.4/52; UN Economic and Social Council, "Resolution 116 (VI) B, Report of the Second Session of the Commission on Human Rights, March 1-2, 1948," in *Resolutions Adopted by the Economic and Social Council During its Sixth Session from 2 February to 11 March, 1948* (Lake Success, NY: United Nations, 1948), 17, E/777, undocs.org/en/E/777.

48. UNESCO, *General Conference—First Session*, 18.

49. UNESCO, *Introduction to UNESCO: A Summary of the Organisation's Activities during its First Year With Selected List of Documents* (Paris: UNESCO, 1947), 14, 15, 24.

50. UNESCO, *General Conference—First Session*, 23.

51. Ibid.

52. UNESCO, Statement on Race, 32.

53. UNESCO, *Meeting of Experts on Race Problems—Summary Report of Six Meetings*, December 12–14, 1949, UNESCO/SS/Conf.1/SR.1, 2. The minutes of the six meetings share the document code UNESCO/SS/Conf.1/SR, with a final number between 1 and 6 designating the specific meeting.

54. UNESCO, *Meeting of Experts on Race Problems*, mtg. 1, p. 5; mtg. 3, p. 9.

55. Ibid., mtg. 1, p. 7.

56. Ibid., mtg. 2, p. 9; mtg. 1, pp. 11–12; mtg. 2, p. 7; mtg. 2, p. 3.

57. Ibid., mtg. 3, p. 8.

58. Ibid., mtg. 6, p. 1.

59. UNESCO, Statement on Race, 34.

60. UNESCO, *Meeting of Experts on Race Problems*, mtg. 2, p. 7.

61. Ibid., mtg. 2, p. 7; mtg. 1, p. 6. That such a proposal should come from Lévi-Strauss may be surprising, since he would not seem an obvious candidate to fall back on a biological or genetic explanation for human difference. But as Staffan Müller-Wille has shown, "cultural and genetic diversity appeared to Lévi-Strauss from very early on as analogous phenomena, exhibiting similar patterns and being subject to the same type of historical processes." Müller-Wille, "Claude Lévi-Strauss on Race, History, and Genetics," *BioSocieties* 5, no. 3 (2010), 332. This analogical relationship is not premised on the evolutionary paradigm of history that Lévi-Strauss wrote against, in which the primitive might achieve (or fail to achieve) the status of modernity through development. Rather, the consonance here is between a nonteleological history and a definition of biological race—which Lévi-Strauss was casting after and found in the notion of genetic populations—that placed its emphasis on change,

contingency, and flux rather than on the fixity or even stability of racial form over time. On Lévi-Strauss's conception of race, see also Kamala Visweswaran, *Un/common Cultures: Racism and the Rearticulation of Cultural Difference* (Durham, NC: Duke UP, 2010), 74–102.

62. UNESCO, Statement on Race, 30–31.

63. UNESCO, *Meeting of Experts on Race Problems*, mtg. 1, p. 12.

64. On the race project's delimited notion of equality as simply equality of opportunity, see Brattain, "Race, Racism, and Antiracism," 1386–413.

65. UNESCO, Statement on Race, 30.

66. Donna Haraway, "Remodeling the Human Way of Life: Sherwood Washburn and the New Physical Anthropology, 1950–80," in *Bones, Bodies, Behavior: Essays on Biological Anthropology*, ed. George W. Stocking (Madison: University of Wisconsin Press, 1988), 211.

67. This attempt to reconcile the terms *mankind* and *Homo sapiens* is particularly interesting in light of Foucault's observation that "the dimension in which the population is immersed amongst the other living beings appears and is sanctioned when, for the first time, men are no longer called 'mankind" (*le genre humaine*) and begin to be called 'the human species' (*l'espèce humaine*)." Michel Foucault, *Security, Territory, Population: Lectures at the Collège de France, 1977–1978* (New York: Picador, 2007), 75.

68. Proctor, in "Three Roots of Human Recency," has excavated the remarkable political and epistemological consequences of these tensions. He suggests that debates about the timing of the origins of the first humans were so fundamentally shaped by the political rather than strictly scientific consensus that emerged from the 1950 race statement that the acknowledgment of the recency of human origins was effectively delayed one or two decades, because of the concern that making the case for recency would be tantamount to expelling certain forms of humanoid life from "the human."

69. UNESCO, *Meeting of Experts on Race Problems*, mtg. 2, p. 8.

70. UNESCO, Statement on Race, 31. "Race was the result of culture and not vice-versa," Lévi-Strauss observed. UNESCO, *Meeting of Experts on Race Problems*, mtg. 3, p. 9.

71. UNESCO, Statement on Race, 30.

72. As Lisa Gannett has argued, genetic populations are not "mind-independent objects whose properties and relations scientists discover." They are not found but made: "Genes become bounded in space and time in ways that fulfill aims, interests, and values associated with particular explanatory contexts." Gannett, "Making Populations: Bounding Genes in Space and Time," *Philosophy of Science* 70, no. 5 (2003), 990.

73. UNESCO, Statement on Race, 31.

74. Ibid.

Chapter 2

1. Frantz Fanon, *Black Skin, White Masks*, trans. Richard Philcox (New York: Grove Press, 2008), 101; and Fanon, *Peau noire, masques blancs* (Paris: Éditions du seuil, 1952), 98.

2. Fanon, *Black Skin*, 101, 69.

3. Paul Gilroy, *Against Race: Imagining Political Culture beyond the Color Line* (Cambridge, MA: Harvard UP, 2000).

4. For a sustained discussion of Gilroy's reading of Fanon in *Against Race*, see Anthony C. Alessandrini, *Frantz Fanon and the Future of Cultural Politics: Finding Something Different* (Lexington Books, 2014), 135–62.

5. Fanon, *Black Skin*, 95, 143; Fanon, *Peau noire*, 93.

6. See, for instance, Jared Sexton, "The Curtain of the Sky: An Introduction," *Critical Sociology* 36, no. 1 (2010), 11–24; and Frank B. Wilderson, *Red, White and Black: Cinema*

and the Structure of U.S. Antagonisms (Duke, 2010). Sexton encapsulates Fanon's significance to this discourse: Fanon theorizes Black non-existence (rather than simply articulating the feeling of Black inferiority) and he reframes racism as anti-Blackness, rather than white supremacy. Notably, to advance these arguments, both Sexton and Wilderson take up Fanon's remarks on antisemitism and Jewishness, only to dismiss or understate their complexity and significance, as I will show. For a different methodological perspective that challenges the facticity of racial and especially epidermal difference by historicizing the conditions of racial visibility and the meaning of skin as surface in midcentury aesthetics, see Anne Anlin Cheng, *Second Skin: Josephine Baker and the Modern Surface* (New York: Oxford UP, 2011). Cheng notes that while Fanon is the exemplary thinker of race "as something ineluctably tied to the modality of the visible," his account of the overweening visibility of race is put in question by other paradigms of skin and corporeality (7).

7. Henry Louis Gates Jr., "Critical Fanonism," *Critical Inquiry* 17, no. 3 (1991), 457–58.

8. For instance, Jay Garcia has shown how Fanon's discussion of the 1944 American film *Home of the Brave* in *Black Skin, White Masks* critically engages the midcentury liberal antiracism of the early Cold War era, when Hollywood produced a series of films challenging anti-Black racism and antisemitism. Garcia, "*Home of the Brave*, Frantz Fanon and Cultural Pluralism," *Comparative American Studies: An International Journal* 4, no. 1 (2006): 49–65.

9. Alastair Bonnett, *Anti-Racism* (London: Routledge, 2000), 1–2. See also Alana Lentin, *Racism and Anti-Racism in Europe* (London: Pluto Press, 2004), who underscores this tendency in the social sciences "to mobilise a commonsense depiction of anti-racism as simply the inverse of racism" and who offers a historically nuanced account of competing and overlapping antiracist discourses in postwar Western Europe (1).

10. UNESCO, Statement on Race, in *Four Statements on the Race Question* (Paris: UNESCO, 1969), 31.

11. UNESCO, Statement on Race, 31–32.

12. UNESCO, Statement on the Nature of Race and Race Differences, in *Four Statements on the Race Question* (Paris: UNESCO, 1969), 37.

13. Irene Tucker, *The Moment of Racial Sight: A History* (Chicago: University of Chicago Press, 2012), 7.

14. Nicole R. Fleetwood, *Troubling Vision: Performance, Visuality, and Blackness* (Chicago: University of Chicago Press, 2011), 22–23.

15. Fanon, *Black Skin*, 89; Fanon, *Peau noire*, 88.

16. Fanon, *Black Skin*, 92.

17. Fanon, *Black Skin*, 95; Fanon, *Peau noire*, 93.

18. Levinson, who theorizes this paradox in her reading of Arendt, also turns to Fanon to illustrate its racial dimension. For her related reading of Fanon, see Natasha Levinson, "The Paradox of Natality: Teaching in the Midst of Belatedness," in *Hannah Arendt and Education: Renewing Our Common World*, ed. Mordechai Gordon (Boulder, CO: Westview Press, 2001), 15, 22–23.

19. UNESCO, Statement on Race, 30.

20. Fanon, *Black Skin*, 91, 29.

21. Fanon, *Black Skin*, 95; Fanon, *Peau noire*, 93.

22. I take up some of the most important readings of this passage later in the chapter, but see Daniel Boyarin, "Homophobia and the Postcoloniality of the 'Jewish Science,'" in *Queer Theory and the Jewish Question*, ed. Daniel Boyarin, Daniel Itzkovitz, and Ann Pellegrini (New York: Columbia UP, 2003), 166–98; Sander Gilman, *The Jew's Body* (New York: Routledge, 1991), 198–209; Bryan Cheyette, "Frantz Fanon and the Black-Jewish Imaginary," in *Frantz Fanon's* Black Skin, White Masks: *New Interdisciplinary Essays*, ed. Max Silverman

(Manchester: Manchester UP, 2005), 74–99; and Ella Shohat, "Post-Fanon and the Colonial: A Situational Diagnosis," in *Taboo Memories, Diasporic Voices* (Durham, NC: Duke UP, 2006), 250–89.

23. UNESCO, Statement on Race, 31.

24. Daniel Boyarin, *Judaism: The Genealogy of a Modern Notion* (New Brunswick, NJ: Rutgers UP, 2019), 107.

25. For an account of this historical transformation, see Leora Batnitzky, *How Judaism Became a Religion: An Introduction to Modern Jewish Thought* (Princeton, NJ: Princeton UP, 2011). For an assessment of the role of these developments in the creation of the concept of the religious minority in secular thought, see Aamir Mufti, *Enlightenment in the Colony: The Jewish Question and the Crisis of Postcolonial Culture* (Princeton, NJ: Princeton UP, 2007).

26. Gil Anidjar, *Semites: Race, Religion, Literature* (Stanford, CA: Stanford UP, 2008), 19. This operation has not been successful, for Jewishness continues to name a cultural and ethnic identity and for some (Jews as well as non-Jews), a racial one. On this question, see Steven Kaplan, "If There Are No Races, How Can Jews Be a 'Race'?," *Journal of Modern Jewish Studies* 2, no. 1 (2003), 79–96. On the overdetermination of Jewishness, see Cynthia M. Baker, *Jew* (New Brunswick, NJ: Rutgers UP, 2017). Anidjar argues that Nazism's differential treatment of Jew and Arab gave rise to a framework that remains operative today: Islam "became fully established as the paradigm of religiosity," while Jews "never quite recovered their privileged religious identity" (19). These are questions the next chapter takes up.

27. On the itinerary of the idea of the Semites, see Anidjar, *Semites*; Gil Hochberg, "'Re-Membering Semitism' or 'On the Prospect of Re-Membering the Semites,'" *Re-Orient* 1, no. 2 (Spring 2016), 192–223; and Maurice Olender, *The Languages of Paradise: Race, Religion, and Philology in the Nineteenth Century* (Cambridge, MA: Harvard UP, 1992).

28. Olender, *The Languages of Paradise*, 13.

29. Julian S. Huxley and A. C. Haddon, *We Europeans: A Survey of "Racial" Problems* (New York: Harper and Brothers, 1936), 18.

30. Ibid., 121.

31. Ibid., 140.

32. Amos Morris-Reich, "Photography in Economies of Demonstration: The Idea of the Jews as a Mixed-Race People," *Jewish Social Studies* 20, no. 1 (Fall 2013), 150–83.

33. Mitchell Hart, *Social Science and the Politics of Modern Jewish Identity* (Stanford, CA: Stanford UP, 2000), 140.

34. Morris-Reich, "Photography in Economies of Demonstration," 170.

35. Hart, *Social Science and the Politics of Modern Jewish Identity*, 139–68; Amos Morris-Reich, "Circumventions and Confrontations: Georg Simmel, Franz Boas and Arthur Ruppin and Their Responses to Antisemitism," *Patterns of Prejudice* 44, no. 2 (2010), 195–215; Nadia Abu El-Haj, *The Genealogical Science: The Search for Jewish Origins and the Politics of Epistemology* (Chicago: University of Chicago Press, 2012), 63–108.

36. Juan Comas, *Racial Myths* (Paris: UNESCO, 1951), 30.

37. Ibid., 31.

38. Harry L. Shapiro, *The Jewish People: A Biological History* (Paris: UNESCO, 1960), 30.

39. Ibid., 32.

40. Comas, *Racial Myths*, 12.

41. Maurice Fishberg, "Aryan and Semite, With Particular Reference to the Aryan," in *Aryan and Semite: With Particular Reference to Nazi Racial Dogmas—Addresses Delivered Before the Judaeans and the Jewish Academy of Arts and Sciences, March 4th, 1934, in New York City* (Cincinnati: B'nai B'rith, 1934), 18.

42. Ibid., 19.

43. Maurice Fishberg, *Jews, Race, and Environment* (New Brunswick, NJ: Transaction, 2006), 90.

44. Ibid., 515.

45. Ibid.

46. At times, however, the argument for the mixed-race descent of Jews was employed precisely to lay claim to whiteness, or at least to refute the ascription of Africanness. Eric Goldstein has shown how, in the American context, some Jews were attached to the idea of their Semitic origins but began to deemphasize this connection at a moment when, in the work of scholars such as Daniel G. Brinton and William Z. Ripley, the Semites were being ascribed an African origin. See Goldstein, *The Price of Whiteness: Jews, Race, and American Identity* (Princeton, NJ: Princeton UP, 2006), 108–10. Goldstein reads Fishberg as complicit with this practice, though this seems to me to understate the complexity of Fishberg's argument.

47. As Boas notes in his final report, the study had begun in 1908 with "the east European Hebrew." "When the essential points to be investigated became clearer by the results of this inquiry, the investigation was extended over Italians, . . .Bohemians, and Hungarians." Franz Boas, *Changes in Bodily Form of Descendants of Immigrants*, Final Report, Immigration Commission (Washington, DC: Government Printing Office, 1911), 1.

48. Ibid., 76.

49. Quoted in Bernice A. Kaplan, "Environment and Human Plasticity," *American Anthropologist* 56, no. 5 (October 1954), 780. Writing at midcentury, Kaplan reviewed two generations' worth of anthropological work that had built on Boas's study, which she described as the turning point for physical anthropology's interest in the "dynamic aspects of racial development." Before Boas, she remarked, "racial classification was virtually the raison d'etre of physical anthropology of the living," but "interest in the plasticity of the human organism has grown since 1911" (780–81).

50. This is an especially striking choice because, according to Leonard B. Glick, the Immigration Commission had been mandated with collecting data on social and economic questions, yet Boas insisted on conducting a study of physical types. Glick, "Types Distinct from Our Own: Franz Boas on Jewish Identity and Assimilation," *American Anthropologist* 84, no. 3 (September 1982), 557.

51. Franz Boas, "Are the Jews a Race?," reprinted as "The Jews," in *Race and Democratic Society* (New York: J. J. Augustin, 1945), 38–39.

52. Ibid., 40–41.

53. Franz Boas, *Aryans and Non-Aryans* (New York: Information and Service Associates, 1934). Melville J. Herskovits, *Franz Boas: The Science of Man in the Making* (New York: Scribner, 1953), cited in Gelya Frank, "Jews, Multiculturalism, and Boasian Anthropology," *American Anthropologist* 99, no. 4 (December 1997), 734.

54. Amos Morris-Reich, "Project, Method, and the Racial Characteristics of Jews: A Comparison of Franz Boas and Hans F.K. Günther," in *Jewish Social Studies* 13, no. 1 (2006), 146. See also Amos Morris-Reich, *The Quest for Jewish Assimilation in Modern Social Science* (New York: Routledge, 2008), 39, for another formulation of this argument.

55. Ashley Montagu, *Man's Most Dangerous Myth: The Fallacy of Race*, 6th ed. (Walnut Creek, CA: Altamira, 1997), 418.

56. Shapiro, *The Jewish People*, 80–81.

57. Franz Boas, "Changes in the Bodily Form of Descendants of Immigrants," *American Anthropologist* 14, no. 3 (July 1912), 555.

58. Ibid., 557.

59. Quoted in Glick, "Types Distinct from Our Own," 557.

60. Boas, *Changes in Bodily Form of Descendants of Immigrants*, 76.
61. Ibid., 2.
62. UNESCO, Statement on Race, 32.
63. That Boas understands the problem of racial form and its transformation as a problem of educability is also apparent in his focus on the child and its development. While Boas did not adjudicate which aspects of the American environment were most responsible for these changes, it is notable that he focused his investigations on children and that the thousands of children examined for the study were observed in their schools. This in itself is not singular. Boas's mentor, Rudolf Virchow, had undertaken racial and physiological studies of schoolchildren in Germany, but Boas's argument lends itself to the supposition that not only aspects of the American physical environment but also its social and institutional life were responsible for these changes. Indeed, Boas's study would in turn play a role in American school desegregation, appearing in the Supreme Court decision *Brown v. Board of Education*. See Lee D. Baker, "Unraveling the Boasian Discourse: The Racial Politics of 'Culture' in School Desegregation, 1944–1954," in *Transforming Anthropology* 7, no. 1 (1998), 15–32.
64. Franz Boas, *The Mind of Primitive Man* (New York: MacMillan, 1911), 261–62.
65. Boas, "The Jews," in *Race and Democratic Society*, 41.
66. Ibid., 40.
67. Franz Boas, "The Problem of the American Negro," *Yale Review* 10 (1921), 392.
68. Franz Boas, "Commencement Address at Atlanta University, May 31, 1906," available at Robert W. Williams's online Du Bois Archive, http://www.webdubois.org/BoasAtlantaCommencement.html. Williams points out Du Bois's reference to this speech in his 1939 *Black Folk Then and Now*. For another account of the (decidedly mixed) response to Boas's multiple addresses at Atlanta University during that visit, see Anthony Q. Hazard, *Boasians at War: Anthropology, Race, and World War II* (Cham, Switzerland: Palgrave Macmillan, 2020), 15.
69. Boas, "The Problem of the American Negro," 394–95.
70. Jared Sexton, *Amalgamation Schemes: Antiblackness and the Critique of Multiracialism* (Minneapolis: University of Minnesota Press, 2008). On hybridity's redemption of the mongrel and mongrelization, see Tavia Nyong'o, *The Amalgamation Waltz: Race, Performance, and the Ruses of Memory* (Minneapolis: Minnesota UP, 2009).
71. "By cleavage is meant the manner in which minerals separate or split off with regularity. The difference between a break or fracture and a 'cleave,' is that the former may be anywhere throughout the substance of the broken body, with an extremely remote chance of another fracture being identical in form, whereas in the latter, when a body is 'cleaved,' the fractured part is more readily severed, and usually takes a similar if not an actually identical form in the divided surface of each piece severed. Thus we find a piece of wood may be 'broken' or 'chopped' when fractured across the grain, no two fractured edges being alike; but, strictly speaking, we only 'cleave' wood when we 'split' it with the grain, or, in scientific language, along the line of cleavage." John Mastin, *The Chemistry, Properties and Tests of Precious Stones* (New York: Spon and Chamberlain, 1911), 19.
72. This anti-Blackness is explicit in Boas's assurance in *The Mind of Primitive Man* that Southern anxieties about protecting "the white race against the infusion of negro blood" are unfounded, since racial amalgamation proceeds by way of "unions between . . . white men and negro women." "If a considerable number of their children are those of white fathers, the race as a whole must necessarily lose its pure negro type," he observes. "At the same time no such infusion of negro blood into the white race through the maternal line occurs, so that the process is actually one of lightening the negro race without corresponding admixture in the white race." Boas, *The Mind of Primitive Man*, 277.

73. The idea of population (as opposed to type) also appears in Boas's work and undergirds some of his ideas about racial mixture, which are premised on the transmission of traits rather than the continuity of types; see Amos Morris-Reich, *The Quest for Jewish Assimilation in Modern Social Science*, 37–41. For a discussion of Boas's conceptual critique of racial type (a concept he nonetheless continued to use) and for the parallels between his approach and later developments in population genetics, see George W. Stocking Jr., "The Critique of Racial Formalism," in *Race, Culture, and Evolution: Essays in the History of Anthropology* (New York: The Free Press, 1968), 181–83, 186–89, 192–94.

74. Nyong'o, *The Amalgamation Waltz*, 174. See also Robert J. C. Young, *Colonial Desire: Hybridity in Theory, Culture and Race* (London: Routledge, 1995), which shows how the centrality of the idea of hybridity to some versions of postcolonial theory reveals the continuities between colonial-era race thinking and contemporary concepts of culture.

75. Fanon, *Black Skin*, 138–43; Fanon, *Peau noire*, 130–34.

76. Cheyette, "Frantz Fanon and the Black-Jewish Imaginary," 89.

77. Ibid., 88, 83.

78. Jean-Paul Sartre, *Anti-Semite and Jew*, trans. George J. Becker (New York: Schocken 1976), 69. See, for instance, the essays in the special issue of *October* on "Jean-Paul Sartre's 'Anti-Semite and Jew'" 87 (Winter 1999), many of which review and reiterate this critique even as several of the essays offer generous or revisionist readings of Sartre's intentions. For a comprehensive study of Sartre's writings on Jewishness, see Jonathan Judaken, *Jean-Paul Sartre and the Jewish Question: Anti-antisemitism and the Politics of the French Intellectual* (Lincoln: University of Nebraska Press, 2006).

79. Sartre, *Anti-Semite and Jew*, 54.

80. Frantz Fanon, "West Indians and Africans," in *Toward the African Revolution*, trans. Haakon Chevalier (New York: Monthly Review Press, 1967), 17–18; Fanon, "Antillais et Africains," *Esprit* 223, no. 2 (février 1955), 261.

81. Fanon, "West Indians and Africans," 18; Fanon, "Antillais et Africains," 262.

82. Fanon, "West Indians and Africans," 18; Fanon, "Antillais et Africains," 262.

83. Fanon, "West Indians and Africans," 18; Fanon, "Antillais et Africains," 261–62.

84. Boyarin, "Homophobia and the Postcoloniality of the 'Jewish Science,'" 176.

85. Sigmund Freud, "Analysis of a Phobia in a Five-Year-Old Boy," in *The Standard Edition of the Complete Psychological Works of Sigmund Freud*, vol. 10, trans. James Strachey (London: Vintage Books, 2001), 36.

86. Boyarin, "Homophobia and the 'Postcoloniality' of the Jewish Science," 170, see also 173.

87. Eliza Slavet, *Racial Fever: Freud and the Jewish Question* (New York: Fordham, 2009), 115.

88. Boyarin, "Homophobia and the 'Postcoloniality' of the Jewish Science," 166.

89. Ibid., 176.

90. Ibid., 179.

91. Hortense J. Spillers, "Mama's Baby, Papa's Maybe: An American Grammar Book," *Diacritics* 17, no. 2 (Summer 1987), 67.

92. My reading of this passage thus corrects Sander Gilman's, which culminates in the claim that "the Jew becomes a symbolic collective for Fanon; the black—his own body—remains that of an individual." While Gilman is right to note that Fanon theorizes Jewishness as a collective identity, this collectivity is not "symbolic," if *symbolic* is here understood as a pallid abstraction in contrast to the robust embodiment of the individual. More importantly, I am contesting Gilman's suggestion that for Fanon, the Black body gets to attain (or retain) the status of individuality, or individual difference. What Gilman misses is Fanon's insistence that the Black body is made a thing, "an object among other objects," incapable

of individuation (*Black Skin, White Masks*, 89). Gilman, "The Jewish Essence: Anti-Semitism and the Body in Psychoanalysis," in *The Jew's Body*, 198.

93. See, for instance, Gilman, *The Jew's Body*; and for a more recent study, Jay Geller's deeply erudite *The Other Jewish Question: Identifying the Jew and Making Sense of Modernity* (New York: Fordham, 2011).

94. Daniel Boyarin, *A Radical Jew: Paul and the Politics of Identity* (Berkeley: University of California Press, 1994), 231.

95. Geller, *The Other Jewish Question*, 10–11.

96. For a discussion of this doubled meaning, see for instance Julia Reinhard Lupton, "*Ethnos* and Circumcision in the Pauline Tradition: A Psychoanalytic Exegesis," in *The Psychoanalysis of Race*, ed. Christopher Lane (New York: Columbia UP, 1998), 193–210.

97. Sigmund Freud, "Moses and Monotheism," in *The Standard Edition of the Complete Psychological Works of Sigmund Freud*, vol. 23, trans. James Strachey (London: Vintage, 2001), see especially 98–102.

98. Ibid., 91, 98.

99. Sartre not only offers up a portrait of the negative Jew but also characterizes antisemitic violence in the nineteenth-century terms of social discrimination and pogroms, even in the immediate aftermath of the Holocaust. As Enzo Traverso notes, "Not only does Sartre never place the genocide at the center of his reflections, he elaborates his arguments as if it had never taken place. Many passages in his book indicate quite clearly that, although he knew what had happened, he was absolutely incapable of conceiving it, let alone of grasping its significance. His phenomenology of anti-Semitism stops at the pogrom, perceived as the extreme form of hatred of the Jews." Traverso, "The Blindness of the Intellectuals: Historicizing Sartre's *Anti-Semite and Jew*," trans. Stuart Liebman, *October* 87 (Winter 1999), 73.

100. Slaughter writes that "the synecdochal, identitarian logic that configures the individual person as an embodiment of group personality and of the vulnerability of a social texture is the very basis of the Genocide Convention, which aspires to punish and prevent not only the killing of individuals as representatives of ethnic, racial, religious, and national groups but also acts of violence that target the modes and mechanics of group identity reproduction. . . . To die as a victim of genocide is, precisely, not to die as an individual but as an instance of a racialized, ethnicized, nationalized, or sectionalized group." Joseph R. Slaughter, *Human Rights, Inc.: The World Novel, Narrative Form, and International Law* (New York: Fordham UP, 2007), 161.

101. Orlando Patterson, *Slavery and Social Death: A Comparative Study* (Cambridge, MA: Harvard UP, 1982), 7.

102. Sexton, "The Curtain of the Sky," 17.

103. Wilderson, *Red, White and Black*, 31, 35, 38.

104. Laurence Mordekhai Thomas, *Vessels of Evil: American Slavery and the Holocaust* (Philadelphia: Temple UP, 1993), 125.

105. Ibid., 160.

106. Ibid., 162.

107. Ibid., 153.

108. Claudia Card, "Genocide and Social Death," *Hypatia* 18, no 1 (Winter 2003), 77.

109. Ibid.

110. Frantz Fanon, *The Wretched of the Earth*, trans. Richard Philcox (New York: Grove Press, 2004), 219–20.

111. Frantz Fanon, "Racism and Culture," in *Toward the African Revolution*, trans. Haakon Chevalier (New York: Grove, 1967), 33, 37.

Chapter 3

1. Juan Comas, *Racial Myths* (Paris: UNESCO, 1951), 7.
2. In 1956, UNESCO collected the booklets published thus far into one volume, *The Race Question in Modern Science* (Paris: UNESCO, 1956).
3. Michel Leiris, *Race and Culture* (Paris: UNESCO, 1951), 41, 40.
4. Ibid., 41.
5. Comas, *Racial Myths*, 7.
6. As Ania Loomba has argued, ideas about what race has meant at particular historical junctures are integral to the production of periodization and periodizing terms. Loomba, "Race and the Possibilities of Comparative Critique," *New Literary History* 40, no. 3 (2009): 501–22.
7. I discuss some of these debates in what follows, but for an overview that situates these issues in light of new efforts in medieval and early modern studies to expand the study of race, see Urvashi Chakravarty and Ayanna Thompson, "Race and Periodization: Introduction," *New Literary History* 52, no. 3–4 (2021), v–xvi; and Margo Hendricks, "Coloring the Past, Considerations on Our Future: RaceB4Race," *New Literary History* 52, no. 3–4 (2021), 365–84, as well as other articles in this special issue.
8. Frantz Fanon, "Racism and Culture," in *Toward the African Revolution*, trans. Haakon Chevalier (New York: Grove, 1967), 32.
9. Ibid., 33.
10. Ibid., 32; Frantz Fanon, "Racisme et culture," *Présence Africaine*, no. 8/10 (1956), 122.
11. Fanon, "Racism and Culture," 32.
12. Ibid., 32–33, translation modified; Fanon, "Racisme et culture," 123.
13. Fanon, "Racism and Culture," 37.
14. Christopher Bonner, "Alioune Diop and the Cultural Politics of Negritude: Reading the First Congress of Black Writers and Artists, 1956," *Research in African Literatures* 50, no. 2 (Summer 2019), 13. Eileen Julien also offers an analysis of the different conceptions of culture circulating in the presentations at the congress. Julien, "Terrains de Rencontre: Césaire, Fanon, and Wright on Culture and Decolonization," *Yale French Studies* 98 (2000), 149–66.
15. Julien observes that it is "difficult to miss the reference here to Senghorian 'négritude,'" even if Fanon does not say so explicitly. Julien, "Terrains de Rencontre," 158.
16. Fanon, "Racism and Culture," 31; Fanon, "Racisme et culture," 122.
17. Lévi-Strauss's message can be found in the collection of messages of support sent to the congress. Joséphine Bouillon et al., "Messages," *Présence Africaine*, no. 8/10 (1956): 385–87.
18. Fanon, "Racism and Culture," 32.
19. The anthropologist Kamala Visweswaran has importantly traced some of these developments, arguing that culture comes to substitute for race. Visweswaran, *Un/common Cultures: Racism and the Rearticulation of Cultural Difference* (Durham, NC: Duke UP, 2010), especially 1–17, 52–73. In my reading, this is less a substitution than an inversion of race's and culture's relative relationship to plasticity.
20. Étienne Balibar, "Is There a Neo-Racism?," ch. 1 in Balibar and Immanuel Wallerstein, *Race, Nation, Class: Ambiguous Identities*, trans. Chris Turner (London: Verso, 1991), 21.
21. UNESCO, Statement on Race, in *Four Statements on the Race Question* (Paris: UNESCO, 1969), 31.
22. The term *ethnic group* decisively enters the scientific discourse on race and common circulation at midcentury, thanks to Julian Huxley and A. C. Haddon, *We Europeans: A Survey of 'Racial' Problems* (New York: Harper and Brothers, 1936). For Huxley and Haddon, the advantage of the term *ethnic group* was its flexibility. It could describe many kinds

and scales of groups—"at times a tribe, at times a political unit"—"marked off from other groups by complex factors of which kinship is one, but that at least as important are language, religion, culture or tradition" (17–18). The ethnic group thus named types of differences that could not properly be described via "biological terms and the ideas that are at the back of them" (115). In other words, these were differences that were not reducible to race and could not rightly be described in this idiom, even as their faithful transmission over generations demonstrated the singular human "capacity for transmitting experience by what we may broadly call tradition, without recourse to physical inheritance."

23. Alana Lentin, "Europe and the Silence about Race," *European Journal of Social Theory* 11, no. 4 (2008), 497. See also David Theo Goldberg, "Racial Europeanization," *Ethnic and Racial Studies* 29, no. 2 (2006), 331–64.

24. Goldberg, "Racial Europeanization," 359; Lentin, "Europe and the Silence about Race," 497.

25. There is a growing scholarly literature on what Michael Rothberg and Yasemin Yildiz term "the unavoidable conjunction in contemporary Europe of Holocaust remembrance and migrant history." Rothberg and Yildiz, "Memory Citizenship: Migrant Archives of Holocaust Remembrance in Contemporary Germany," *Parallax* 17, no. 4 (2010), 34. While this conjunction can be politically and aesthetically generative for migrant subjects who mobilize Holocaust memory to critique racial exclusion and lay claim to citizenship, it also has a disciplinary dimension, demonstrated by the way that some European nation-states deploy official Holocaust memory to mark the boundaries of the nation. On these dynamics, see for instance Sa'ed Atshan and Katharina Galor, *The Moral Triangle: Germans, Israelis, Palestinians* (Durham, NC: Duke UP, 2020).

26. UNESCO, Statement on Race and Racial Prejudice, in *Four Statements on the Race Question* (Paris: UNESCO, 1969), 50. As Michael Banton notes, the statement characterizes racism "as a social force possessing the autonomy of a social and political actor." Banton, *The International Politics of Race* (London: Polity Press, 2002), 35.

27. UNESCO, Statement on Race and Racial Prejudice, 51.

28. Ibid., 52.

29. Balibar, "Is There a Neo-Racism?," 23.

30. Ibid., 24.

31. Ibid., 23–24.

32. Claude Lévi-Strauss, *Race and History* (Paris: UNESCO, 1952), 6–7.

33. In his introduction to the 1951 UNESCO Statement on the Nature of Race and Race Differences, Dunn (who served as the committee's rapporteur) wrote that "the physical anthropologists and the man in the street both know that races exist; the former, from the scientifically recognizable and measurable congeries of traits which he uses in classifying the varieties of man; the latter from the immediate evidence of his senses when he sees an African, a European, an Asiatic and an American Indian together." UNESCO, Statement on the Nature of Race and Race Differences, in *Four Statements on the Race Question* (Paris: UNESCO, 1969), 37. For my discussion of Dunn's remarks as indicative of the production of a racial residuum, see chapter 2.

34. Lévi-Strauss, *Race and History*, 25–26.

35. Ibid., 25.

36. Ibid., 11, translation modified. The English translation offers the phrase "instinctive antipathy," but Lévi-Strauss does not go quite so far in the original French, which instead invokes a "*frisson*." See Lévi-Strauss, *Race et histoire* (Paris: Denoël, 1987 [1952]), 19.

37. Lévi-Strauss, *Race and History*, 11.

38. Claude Lévi-Strauss, "Race and Culture," *International Social Science Journal* 23, no. 4 (1971), 617–18. For an important analysis of the influential role population genetics played in Lévi-Strauss's concept of culture, see Staffan Müller-Wille, "Claude Lévi-Strauss on Race, History and Genetics," *BioSocieties* 5, no. 3 (2010), 330–47. For a fuller gloss of the argument of *Race and History*, as well as a careful reconstruction of Lévi-Strauss's changing views on race in the twenty years between *Race and History* and "Race and Culture," see Visweswaran, "The Interventions of Culture: Claude Lévi-Strauss and the Internationalization of the Modern Concept of Race," in *Un/common Cultures*, 74–102.

39. Lévi-Strauss, "Race and Culture," 623.

40. Visweswaran, *Un/common Cultures*, 83.

41. Lévi-Strauss, "Race and Culture," 624–25.

42. Martin Barker, *The New Racism: Conservatives and the Ideology of the Tribe* (London: Junction Books, 1981).

43. Paul Gilroy, *There Ain't No Black in the Union Jack: The Cultural Politics of Race and Nation* (Oxfordshire: Routledge, 2002), 4.

44. Balibar, "Is There a Neo-Racism?," 22.

45. Caryl Phillips, *The European Tribe* (New York: 2000), 9.

46. Ibid., 53–54.

47. On Phillips's foregrounding of his childhood perspective, see for instance Michael Rothberg, *Multidirectional Memory: Remembering the Holocaust in the Age of Decolonization* (Stanford, CA: Stanford UP, 2009), 154–57; and Sarah Phillips Casteel, *Calypso Jews: Jewishness in the Caribbean Literary Imagination* (New York: Columbia UP, 2016), 235–70. Thanks to its autobiographical voice and nonfictional genre, *The European Tribe* in some respects set the scene for subsequent critical responses to the politics and ethics of Phillips's identification with Jews and the Holocaust, best represented by a highly disapproving review of *The Nature of Blood* by Hilary Mantel, "Black Is Not Jewish," *Literary Review* (February 1997), 40. For thoughtful engagements with questions of identification and appropriation in Phillips's writing, see Wendy Zierler, "'My Holocaust Is Not Your Holocaust': 'Facing' Black and Jewish Experience in *The Pawnbreaker, Higher Ground,* and *The Nature of Blood*," *Holocaust and Genocide Studies* 18, no. 1 (Spring 2004), 46–67; Stef Craps, "Linking Legacies of Loss: Traumatic Histories and Cross-Cultural Empathy in Caryl Phillips's *Higher Ground* and *The Nature of Blood*," *Studies in the Novel* 40, no. 1–2 (Spring–Summer 2008), 191–202; Rothberg, *Multidirectional Memory*, 135–72.

48. As Graham Huggan has noted, the itinerary of Phillips's journey harkens back to the "gentleman's educative circuit" of the European Grand Tour. Huggan, "Counter-Travel Writing and Postcoloniality," in *Being/s in Transit*, ed. Liselotte Glage (Leiden: Brill, 2000), 40.

49. Phillips, *The European Tribe*, 1–2.

50. Ibid.

51. Ibid., 1.

52. Ibid., 66.

53. Ibid., 66–67.

54. Ibid., 67. Casteel traces Phillips's enduring intertextual engagement with Anne Frank's *The Diary of a Young Girl* and deems the work an origin scene for Phillips's preoccupation with the Holocaust, affording him a "permission to write" that he retrospectively implies stretches back even to this youthful effort at representation (246). See Casteel, *Calypso Jews*, 235–70.

55. Gilroy, *Against Race: Imagining Political Culture beyond the Color Line* (Cambridge, MA: Harvard UP, 2000), 4.

56. Phillips, *The European Tribe*, 52.

57. James Baldwin, "Negroes Are Anti-Semitic Because They're Anti-White," in *Collected Essays*, ed. Toni Morrison (New York: Library of America, 1998), 741.

58. Ibid., 744.

59. Jonathan Boyarin, *The Unconverted Self: Jews, Indians, and the Identity of Christian Europe* (Chicago: University of Chicago Press, 2009), 15, see also 54–69.

60. Phillips, *The European Tribe*, 53.

61. On the ideological operations and ruses of the Judeo-Christian as a promise of pluralism, see Tomoko Masuzawa, *The Invention of World Religions: Or, How European Universalism Was Preserved in the Language of Pluralism* (Chicago: University of Chicago Press, 2005), 301–3.

62. In its contemporary form, this project involves mobilizing the concept of the Judeo-Christian as an element of Islamophobic discourse. This dynamic will be important to the chapter's argument. For illuminating reflections on this question, see for instance Gil Anidjar, *The Jew, the Arab: A History of the Enemy* (Stanford, CA: Stanford UP, 2003), 59–60, 93–98.

63. Phillips, *The European Tribe*, ix.

64. Caryl Phillips, *The Nature of Blood* (New York: Vintage, 1997).

65. Bart Moore-Gilbert observes that Phillips's practice is contrapuntal but contrapuntality of the kind that Edward Said calls "atonal ensemble." Rothberg notes that Phillips eschews "metaphoric substitution" in favor of metonymic connections, while Stephen Clingman observes the "displacement back and forth between the metonymic and metaphoric." Casteel deems Phillips's method "a rhizomatic approach to intertextuality and identification." Moore-Gilbert, "Postcolonialism and 'the Figure of the Jew': Caryl Phillips and Zadie Smith," in *The Contemporary British Novel since 1980*, ed. J. Acheson et al. (London: Palgrave Macmillan, 2006), 107; Rothberg, *Multidirectional Memory*, 156; Stephen Clingman, "Forms of History and Identity in *The Nature of Blood*," *Salmagundi*, no. 143 (2004), 160; Casteel, *Calypso Jews*, 258.

66. Dawson, "To Remember Too Much is Indeed a Form of Madness: Caryl Phillips's *The Nature of Blood* and the Modalities of European Racism," *Postcolonial Studies*, 7, no. 1 (2004), 83–101. In a recent reading, Yogita Goyal has argued that the novel's mobilization of a transnational and potentially anachronistic history of race challenges the sufficiency of familiar frameworks for locating race in space and time, such as the Black Atlantic, Black Britain, or African American. Goyal, *Runaway Genres: The Global Afterlives of Slavery* (New York: NYU Press, 2019), 151–60.

67. Phillips, *The Nature of Blood*, 50.

68. David Nirenberg observes of scholarship on anti-Jewish violence in France and the Crown of Aragon in 1348 that "the aggression itself is usually explained sparely, by allusion to psychosocial phenomena: 'irrational,' 'fantasy,' 'unconscious,' 'projection.' These are important concepts, but they could acquire explanatory sense only in the context of a medieval psychology that is never provided." His work takes on the task of refuting such a perspective, which argues (or assumes) that modern attitudes toward minorities derive from "collective beliefs, beliefs formed in the Middle Ages and transmitted to the present day." Nirenberg, *Communities of Violence: Persecution of Minorities in the Middle Ages* (Princeton: Princeton UP, 1996), 232, 4.

69. Phillips, *The Nature of Blood*, 50–51.

70. Ibid., 59.

71. Zygmunt Bauman, *Modernity and the Holocaust* (Ithaca, NY: Cornell UP, 1989), 1.

72. Nirenberg, *Communities of Violence*, 4–5.

73. Michael André Bernstein, *Foregone Conclusions: Against Apocalyptic History* (Berkeley: University of California Press, 1994), 10.

74. Ibid., 29.
75. Ibid., 23.
76. Nirenberg, *Communities of Violence*, 229.
77. Phillips, *The Nature of Blood*, 55, 53.
78. Dawson, "To Remember Too Much Is Indeed a Form of Madness," 87–88; Clingman, "Forms of History and Identity in *The Nature of Blood*," 152–54. Nirenberg, *Communities of Violence*, 127, describes such historical alternations of intolerance and tolerance as the joint role of "stereotype and strategy." R. Po-Chia Hsia's historical study of the 1475 blood libel in Trent, which Phillips singles out in the novel's acknowledgments as one of two scholarly works to which he is especially indebted, documents the political and judicial machinations that involved the interests of Trent's prince-bishop, the emperor, the archduke, and the pope. Hsia, *Trent 1475: Stories of a Ritual Murder Trial* (New Haven, CT: Yale UP, 1992). Critics have also observed Phillips's attunement here and in the Othello narrative to Venice's prototypical imperial and capitalist history. See Rothberg, *Multidirectional Memory*, 157. On Venice in Phillips's work, see also Bryan Cheyette, "Venetian Spaces: Old-New Literatures and the Ambivalent Uses of Jewish History," in *Reading the "New" Literatures in a Postcolonial Era*, ed. Susheila Nasta (Cambridge: D. S. Brewer, 2000), 53–72.
79. Hannah Arendt, *The Origins of Totalitarianism*, rev. ed. (New York: Harcourt Brace Jovanovich, 1973); Michel Foucault, *"Society Must Be Defended": Lectures at the Collège de France, 1975–1976*, ed. Mauro Bertani and Alessandro Fontana, trans. David Macey (New York: Picador, 2003); George L. Mosse, *Toward the Final Solution: A History of European Racism* (Madison: University of Wisconsin Press, 1985); Gilroy, *Against Race*.
80. Boyarin, *The Unconverted Self*, 14.
81. Irene Silverblatt, *Modern Inquisitions: Peru and the Colonial Origins of the Civilized World* (Durham, NC: Duke UP, 2004), 217. While Silverblatt does not say so, I think her argument consequently challenges Arendt's conception of the boomerang effect. The strict geographical distinction Arendt preserves between Europe and the colonies as discrete geographies and the logic of preparation and refinement of violence abroad as a separate stage from its return home are complicated by Silverblatt's description of Jews' and Muslims' conscription to race-making in the metropole and colony. Arendt suggests that imperial violence (with no relation to Jews or Jewishness) subsequently rebounded on Europe's Jews. But in Silverblatt's account, Jews' and Muslims' literal and cultural presence in the Americas—with all the questions of blood, conversion, and assimilability that are imposed on them—produce the very categories of imperial racial bureaucracy and governance. In other words, Arendt provincializes antisemitism as a narrowly European question, and her account of the boomerang effect is insufficiently relational. I discuss Arendt's boomerang thesis in the next chapter.
82. Ibid., 226, 6.
83. Ibid., 219.
84. Ibid., 25; María Elena Martínez, *Genealogical Fictions: Limpieza de Sangre, Religion, and Gender in Colonial Mexico* (Stanford, CA: Stanford UP, 2008).
85. Silverblatt, *Modern Inquisitions*, 32.
86. For instance, James Shapiro's examination of Jewishness in the very different cultural and political context of early modern England emphasizes nation, not race as the operative term and notes that "in theological terms the Jews were understood not only to be inveterate opponents of Christians but also imminent coreligionists whose conversion would confirm the rightness of the Christians' faith." Nonetheless, he notes there was widespread concern in England about "counterfeit Christians" (that is, insincere New Christians) on the grounds that "faith was disguisable, religious identity a role one could assume or discard if one had

sufficient improvisational skill." Shapiro, *Shakespeare and the Jews* (New York: Columbia UP, 1996), 34, 17; on race and nation, see 175, 199–224.

87. On the centrality of the figure of the converso for the broader Caribbean cultural context in which she situates Phillips, see Casteel, *Calypso Jews*; on the converso as a figure in contemporary fiction, see Daliya Kandiyoti, *The Converso's Return: Conversion and Sephardi History in Contemporary Literature and Culture* (Stanford, CA: Stanford UP, 2020).

88. Phillips, *The European Tribe*, 55.

89. Janet Adelman, *Blood Relations: Christian and Jew in The Merchant of Venice* (Chicago: University of Chicago Press, 2008). The play should be contextualized by anxieties about conversos circulating in England and elsewhere at the time, Adelman explains: "The conversos were Jews who had become Catholics who had become [in England] Protestants who were—maybe—still Jews after all" (11). Similarly, Brian Pullan observes of the Venetian Inquisition of 1547 onward that it seldom concerned itself with Venice's long-standing communities of Jews, focusing instead on conversos, especially Sephardic conversos who had converted back to Judaism: "Such notions of faithlessness and unreliability developed . . . into fears of treachery towards Christian countries and of alliance with the Turk." Pullan, *The Jews of Europe and the Inquisition of Venice* (Totowa, NJ: Barnes and Noble Books, 1983), 13, 19.

90. Adelman, *Blood Relations*, 75.

91. Phillips, *The Nature of Blood*, 154.

92. Ibid., 155.

93. Ibid., 168.

94. Rothberg, *Multidirectional Memory*, 158.

95. Qtd. in Bernstein, *Foregone Conclusions*, 10.

96. Ashley Montagu, "The Myth of Blood," reprinted as "'Race' and 'Blood,'" in *Man's Most Dangerous Myth: The Fallacy of Race*, 2nd ed. (New York: Columbia UP, 1945), 181.

97. Ibid.

98. Ibid., 186, 181.

99. Ibid., 186–88.

100. Ibid., 189.

101. Ibid., 187, 189.

102. Ibid., 189. In fact, as Jenny Bangham has shown, blood transfusion as an emergency medical technology during World War II was a crucial site for knowledge production about human genetics in Britain, and the American practice of racially segregating the blood of African American soldiers prompted British scientists to experiment with various ways of categorizing and studying the blood of their own population. Bangham, *Blood Relations: Transfusion and the Making of Human Genetics* (Chicago: University of Chicago Press, 2020).

103. Montagu, *Man's Most Dangerous Myth*, 191.

104. Ibid., 188.

105. Ibid., 182, 181.

106. Staffan Müller-Wille and Hans-Jörg Rheinberger, *A Cultural History of Heredity* (Chicago: University of Chicago Press, 2012), 2, 5.

107. David Biale, *Blood And Belief: The Circulation of a Symbol Between Jews and Christians* (Berkeley: University of California Press, 2007), 44–80.

108. Ibid., 68.

109. As Biale puts it, this "meaning of 'blood community' is very far from what it was to become in the age of modern nationalism, namely, a nation based on common racial origins." Ibid., 42–43.

110. Ibid., 43.

111. Nadia Abu El-Haj, *The Genealogical Science: The Search for Jewish Origins and the Politics of Epistemology* (Chicago: University of Chicago Press, 2012), 3.
112. Phillips, *The Nature of Blood*, 52.
113. Biale, *Blood and Belief*, 82.
114. Miri Rubin, *Gentile Tales: The Narrative Assault on Late Medieval Jews* (New Haven: Yale UP, 1999).
115. Phillips, *The Nature of Blood*, 57.
116. Ibid.
117. Ibid., 58. For a discussion of cliché as a formal fixture in Phillips's writing, see Timothy Bewes, "Shame, Ventriloquy, and the Problem of the Cliché: Caryl Phillips," in *The Event of Postcolonial Shame* (Princeton, NJ: Princeton UP, 2011), 48–72.
118. Phillips, *The Nature of Blood*, 58.
119. Ibid., 51.
120. Ibid.
121. Ibid., 52.
122. Lévi-Strauss, "Race and Culture," 617–21.
123. Abu El-Haj, *The Genealogical Science*, 22.
124. Ibid., 22, 12.
125. Ibid., 22.
126. Ibid., 119.
127. Ibid., 106, 128. Alondra Nelson, whose work is closely related to Abu El-Haj's, has similarly argued that the results of ancestry testing demand imaginative labor and narrative meaning-making in order for them to signify or feel "true" to those who undergo testing. See Nelson, "The Factness of Diaspora: The Social Sources of Genetic Genealogy," in *Rites of Return: Diaspora Poetics and the Politics of Memory*, ed. Marianne Hirsch and Nancy K. Miller (New York: Columbia UP, 2011), 23–39.
128. Biale is also attuned to these questions, which he considers in his epilogue in *Blood and Belief*, 207–13.
129. Phillips, *The Nature of Blood*, 208.
130. Ibid., 201.
131. Caryl Phillips, "Blood," in *Color Me English: Reflections on Migration and Belonging* (New York: The New Press, 2011), 168.
132. Caryl Phillips, "Belonging to Israel," in *Color Me English*, 194.
133. Ibid., 195–96.
134. Phillips, *The Nature of Blood*, 107.
135. Ibid., 116.
136. Ibid., 115.
137. Ibid., 120.
138. Ibid., 144.
139. Ibid., 120.
140. Ibid., 130.
141. Elizabeth Povinelli, *The Empire of Love: Toward a Theory of Intimacy, Genealogy, and Carnality* (Durham, NC: Duke UP, 2006), 4.
142. Daniel Vitkus, *Turning Turk: English Theater and the Multicultural Mediterranean, 1570–1630* (New York: Palgrave, 2003), 90.
143. Jonathan Burton, *Traffic and Turning: Islam and English Drama 1579–1624* (Newark: University of Delaware Press, 2005), 253.
144. Phillips, *The European Tribe*, 46.

145. Daniel Boyarin, "Othello's Penis: Or, Islam in the Closet," in *Shakesqueer: A Queer Companion to the Complete Works of Shakespeare*, ed. Madhavi Menon (Durham, NC: Duke UP, 2011), 254.

146. Julia Reinhard Lupton argues that "whereas for the modern reader or viewer a black Othello is more subversive, 'other,' or dangerous, in the Renaissance scene a paler Othello more closely resembling the Turks whom he fights might actually challenge more deeply the integrity of the Christian paradigms set up in the play as the measure of humanity." In contrast, Emily C. Bartels notes that an Arab Moorish figure often connotated nobility as opposed to the more villainous Black Moor. Efraim Sicher and Linda Weinhouse are similarly interested in the implications of Othello's Moorishness in Phillips's novel, and note the differing valuations and associations of the term established in some of this critical scholarship. However, they do not consider what I am arguing is a symptomatic avoidance on Phillips's part of Othello's relationship to Islam. Lupton, "*Othello* Circumcised: Shakespeare and the Pauline Discourse of Nations," *Representations* 57, no. 1 (1997), 74; Emily C. Bartels, *Speaking of the Moor: from Alcazar to Othello* (Philadelphia: University of Pennsylvania Press, 2008), 9; Sicher and Weinhouse, "The Color of Shylock: Caryl Phillips," in *Under Postcolonial Eyes: Figuring "the jew" in Contemporary British Writing* (Lincoln: University of Nebraska Press, 2013), 122–43.

147. Phillips, *Color Me English*, 4.

148. Ibid., 6–7.

149. Phillips, *The European Tribe*, 67.

150. Phillips, *Color Me English*, 11, 14.

151. Ibid., 6, 15.

152. Ibid., 15.

153. Bartels also offers an account of the development of scholarship on *Othello* and race from its inception in the mid-1960s, when, during the civil rights era, scholars began to contest the assumed whiteness of the early modern world and reclaimed the Moor as African and Black. Bartels, *Speaking of the Moor*, 3–4, 10–13.

154. Fanon, "Racism and Culture," 32–33, translation modified.

155. Phillips, *Color Me English*, 11.

156. Ibid., 16.

157. Gil Anidjar, *The Jew, the Arab*, 102, 111.

158. Moore-Gilbert, "Postcolonialism and 'the Figure of the Jew,'" 114–15; Ana Miller, "The Silence of Palestinians in Caryl Phillips's *The Nature of Blood*," *Journal of Postcolonial Writing* 50, no. 5 (2014), 509–21; Ahlam Masri and Tahrir Hamdi, "Where Is Palestine in Caryl Phillips's *The Nature of Blood*?," *International Journal of Arabic-English Studies* 18 (2018), 7–22. More often, the literary criticism on *The Nature of Blood* has reproduced this silence, as Miller carefully traces.

159. Moore-Gilbert, "Postcolonialism and 'the Figure of the Jew,'" 115; Rothberg, *Multidirectional Memory*, 168; Miller, "The Silence of Palestinians." Miller, who has offered the most sustained reading of this question, nonetheless concludes that "the fact that Phillips's engagement with Palestine is so hidden that most readers overlook it perhaps indicates a reluctance to be explicit on Phillips's part that implicates him in the larger historical and political context of an unwillingness to criticize Israel in many western countries" (518–19).

160. Masri and Hamdi, "Where Is Palestine in Caryl Phillips's *The Nature of Blood*?"

161. Ibid., 12.

162. Ibid., 19–20.

Chapter 4

1. Arthur Ramos, "The Question of Race and the Democratic World," *UNESCO Courier* 11, no. 10 (November 1949), 14.

2. Observers of this purportedly quintessential Brazilian racial ethos argued that tolerance of cultural and religious differences had produced both rich cultural variety as well as racial and cultural syncretism. In a social context of unforced and unhampered racial mixture, racism was supposedly socially irrelevant. On Ramos's early use of the term and his debt to Gilberto Freyre, see Antonio Sérgio Alfredo Guimarães, "Racial Democracy," in *Imagining Brazil*, ed. Jessé Souza and Valter Sinder (Lanham, MD: Lexington 2005), 119. Guimarães notes that UNESCO was a crucial venue for the term's uptake and popularization; Ramos and others "emphasized [racial democracy's] universalism as a 'Brazilian contribution to humanity'... appropriate to the antifascist and antiracist coalition of the time" (133). In other words, racial democracy was characterized as intrinsically antiracist and even postracial, which resonated at UNESCO. For a fascinating account of the reception of the lusotropical racial solutions of Ramos's close associate the sociologist Gilberto Freyre in postwar France during decolonization, see Ian Merkel, "Brazilian Race Relations, French Social Scientists, and African Decolonization: A Transatlantic History of the Idea of Miscegenation," *Modern Intellectual History* 17, no 3 (2020), 801–32.

3. On Ramos's trajectory from self-taught ethnologist to his wartime and postwar reorientation to applied anthropology, see Antonio Sérgio Alfredo Guimarães, "Africanism and Racial Democracy: The Correspondence between Herskovits and Arthur Ramos (1935–1949)," *Estudios Interdisciplinarios de América Latina y el Caribe* 19, no. 1 (2008), 53–79. On the institutionalization of applied anthropology during the interwar period, see George W. Stocking Jr., "Introduction: Thoughts toward a History of the Interwar Years," in *American Anthropology 1921–1945: Papers from the American Anthropologist*, ed. George W. Stocking Jr. (Lincoln: University of Nebraska Press, 2002), 44–54. Of early applied anthropology in the United States, Stocking observes that interventions into "problems of 'native administration' along lines similar to the experience of British 'indirect rule'" occurred during the same years in which "anthropologists began to respond to the racialist and anti-democratic threat posed by Hitler's ascension to power in Germany" (49–50). This suggestion of a historical and political consonance between anthropology's "application" to midcentury antiracist activism on the one hand and to problems of colonial (and eventually postcolonial) management on the other goes beyond the US context and is important to this chapter's argument, as will become clear.

4. Sebastián Gil-Riaño has paid sustained attention to Ramos's work at UNESCO and has shown how Ramos's intellectual formation—which drew on Brazilian race relations, psychoanalysis, and developments in American social science in pursuit of advancement for culturally backward peoples—materially shaped the character of UNESCO's antiracist interventions. Indeed, Gil-Riaño has shown how Ramos's orientation to issues of modernization exemplifies UNESCO's approach to the intersection of antiracism and third world development. Gil-Riaño's argument that UNESCO's race project and the race statements in particular demand to be situated within colonial genealogies as well as Cold War and postcolonial ideologies of development and modernization in the Global South is very resonant with the arguments of this book and is especially relevant to this chapter. See Gil-Riaño, "Relocating Anti-Racist Science," with Sebastián Gil-Riaño, "Relocating Anti-Racist Science: The 1950 UNESCO Statement on Race and Economic Development in the Global South," *The British Journal for the History of Science* 51, no. 2 (June 2018), 281–303, for an illuminating analysis of how thoroughly enmeshed the scientists Ramos assembled to draft the 1950 Statement on Race were in various colonial and neocolonial projects of cultural salvage and third world development in

sites across the globe. For Gil-Riaño's discussion of Ramos's "The Question of Race and the Democratic World," see Gil-Riaño, "Historicizing Anti-Racism," (PhD diss., University of Toronto, 2014), 1–10. Although he highlights some of the same ideological currents in Ramos's essay, our arguments pursue very different subsequent directions.

5. For this point and other reflections on the *Courier*'s history, see Alan Tormaid Campbell, "The UNESCO Courier Is 70! An Inspiring Read," *UNESCO Courier*, no. 1 (January–March 2018), 60.

6. Ramos, "The Question of Race and the Democratic World," *UNESCO Courier*, 14.

7. Ibid.

8. Ibid.

9. Ibid.

10. Aimé Césaire, *Discourse on Colonialism*, trans. Joan Pinkham (New York: Monthly Review Press, 2000), 32; Césaire, "Discours sur le colonialisme," in *Discours sur le colonialisme suivi du Discours sur la négritude* (Paris: Présence Africaine, 1955, repr. 2004), 8.

11. Ramos, "The Question of Race and the Democratic World," *UNESCO Courier*, 14.

12. Leela Gandhi, *The Common Cause: Postcolonial Ethics and the Practice of Democracy, 1900–1955* (Chicago: University of Chicago Press, 2014), 3.

13. Ibid., 4.

14. Gayatri Chakravorty Spivak, *A Critique of Postcolonial Reason: Toward a History of the Vanishing Present* (Cambridge, MA: Harvard UP, 1999), 112–40. This section of the "Literature" chapter of *A Critique of Postcolonial Reason* is a revision of Spivak's essay "Three Women's Texts and a Critique of Imperialism," *Critical Inquiry* 12, no. 1 (1985), 243–61. Sangeeta Ray observes that this essay marks the centrality of "a critique of pedagogy" to Spivak's intellectual project. Ray, *Gayatari Chakravorty Spivak: In Other Words* (Chichester: Wiley and Sons, 2009), 28.

15. Spivak, *Critique of Postcolonial Reason*, 116, 123.

16. Ben Conisbee Baer, *Indigenous Vanguards: Education, National Liberation, and the Limits of Modernism* (New York: Columbia UP, 2019), 8–9.

17. Spivak, *Critique of Postcolonial Reason*, 134.

18. On the birth of UNESCO's technical assistance program and its historically variable relationship to UNESCO's humanist initiatives, see Vincenzo Pavone, *From the Labyrinth of the World to the Paradise of the Heart: Science and Humanism in UNESCO's Approach to Globalization* (Lanham, MD: Lexington, 2008), 77–89.

19. The sense in which I use reparative morality in this chapter is quite different from its elaboration in the work of the political theorist C. Fred Alford, who has discussed reparative morality in dialogue with the writings of the psychoanalyst Melanie Klein. For Alford, reparative morality is a position to which we ought to aspire; it is a morality "based upon *caritas*, a love and concern for the object for its own sake." As will become clear, the reparative morality that animated UNESCO's project of racial reeducation is both more instrumental and more complex in its relationship to the object of repair. Alford, *Melanie Klein and Critical Social Theory: An Account of Politics, Art, and Reason Based on Her Psychoanalytic Theory* (New Haven, CT: Yale UP, 1989), 83.

20. Baer, *Indigenous Vanguards*, 8, 295n17.

21. Ramos, "The Question of Race and the Democratic World," *UNESCO Courier*, 14.

22. On genres of rule, see Ann Laura Stoler, *Duress: Imperial Durabilities in Our Time* (Durham, NC: Duke UP, 2016), especially her observation that "blurred genres of rule are not empires in distress but imperial polities in active realignment and reformation" (194). My interest in Stoler's term was sparked by Jini Kim Watson's discussion of the new "politi-

cal economic grammar[s]" of the "Cold War-decolonizing matrix" in *Cold War Reckonings: Authoritarianism and the Genres of Decolonization* (New York: Fordham UP, 2021), 17.

23. On "arrested decolonization" as a historical-conceptual frame for *Our Sister Killjoy*, see Yogita Goyal, "From Revolution to Arrested Decolonization: Ama Ata Aidoo and the Long View of History," in *Romance, Diaspora, and Black Atlantic Literature* (Cambridge: Cambridge UP, 2010), 181–204. "Compulsory development" is Joseph R. Slaughter's formulation for the critical representation of third world development in postcolonial fiction, which he argues connects the developmental imperative, increasingly institutionalized in human rights during the 1960s and 1970s, to the genre of the bildungsroman. While Slaughter does not discuss *Our Sister Killjoy* or consider UNESCO's significant role in development work, his analysis of development's educative dimension and its critical reception and rewriting in postcolonial literature is highly relevant to my reading here. See Slaughter, "Compulsory Development: Narrative Self-Sponsorship and the Right to Self-Determination," in *Human Rights, Inc.: The World Novel, Narrative Form, and International Law* (New York: Fordham UP, 2007), 205–69.

24. Arthur Ramos, "The Question of Race and the Democratic World," *International Social Science Bulletin* 1, nos. 3-4 (1949), 9.

25. Ibid., 10–11.

26. A. Dirk Moses offers a brief genealogy, identifying Rosa Luxemburg as the source of the related and "now well-known trope that Europe's criminal exploitation of the non-European world would be dialectically imported in heightened form into Europe itself." He notes that this insight was developed in the work of Francophone intellectuals who saw its pertinence for Nazism specifically, as well as in the thought of Anglophone theorists of slavery and Black internationalism, such as W. E. B. Du Bois. Moses too puts particular emphasis on Césaire's and Arendt's accounts and their resemblance. Moses, "Empire, Colony, Genocide: Keywords and the Philosophy of History," in *Empire, Colony, Genocide: Conquest, Occupation and Subaltern Resistance in World History*, ed. A. Dirk Moses (New York: Berghahn, 2008), 34–35. For additional reflections on Luxemburg's formulations and those of the Marxist thinker Karl Korsch and their subsequent influence on Césaire's identification of the *choc en retour*, see Michael Rothberg, *Multidirectional Memory: Remembering the Holocaust in the Age of Decolonization* (Stanford, CA: Stanford UP, 2009), 96–107. As Robin D. G. Kelley notes, such an analysis was already familiar in Black radical thought before Césaire published *Discourse on Colonialism* and appeared in the work of W. E. B. Du Bois, C. L. R. James, George Padmore, Oliver Cox, Ralph Bunche, and others. See Kelley, "A Poetics of Anticolonialism," in Aimé Césaire, *Discourse on Colonialism*, 20–21. Du Bois in particular offers sustained reflections on this question alongside his powerful commentary on the limitations of the United Nations as a democratic institution capable of challenging colonial rule. See Du Bois, *The World and Africa* (Oxford: Oxford UP, 2007), especially 11–27.

27. The scholarship on Arendt's racial politics is considerable and growing, but for specific consideration of Arendt's reliance on racial tropes in her analysis of Africa and Africans in *The Origins of Totalitarianism*, see Shiraz Dossa, "Human Status and Politics: Hannah Arendt on the Holocaust," *Canadian Journal of Political Science* 13, no. 2 (1980), 309–23; Anne Norton, "Heart of Darkness: Africa and African Americans in the Writings of Hannah Arendt," in *Feminist Interpretations of Hannah Arendt*, ed. Bonnie Honig (University Park: Pennsylvania State UP, 1995), 247–61; Kathryn T. Gines, "Race Thinking and Racism in Hannah Arendt's *The Origins of Totalitarianism*," in *Hannah Arendt and the Uses of History: Imperialism, Nation, Race, and Genocide*, ed. Richard H. King and Dan Stone (New York:

Berghahn, 2007), 38–53; Kathryn T. Gines, *Hannah Arendt and the Negro Question* (Bloomington: Indiana UP, 2014), 77–111; Rothberg, *Multidirectional Memory*, 54–65.

28. Rothberg has offered the most sustained comparative assessment of Arendt's and Césaire's accounts in *Multidirectional Memory*, 33–107. For methodological reflections on both the ambiguities of Arendt's analysis and its simultaneous generativity for contemporary scholarship in genocide studies and history, see King and Stone, "Introduction," in *Hannah Arendt and the Uses of History*, 1–17; and Dan Stone, "Defending the Plural: Hannah Arendt and Genocide Studies," *New Formations* 71 (2011), 46–57. One key ambiguity in Arendt's account concerns the precise causal and historical relationship she is positing between the imperial developments she examines in Africa in the late nineteenth and early twentieth centuries and the eventual return to Europe of some of these tendencies that she identifies as the "boomerang effect." As Richard King notes, "It is not clear whether, for instance, Arendt is claiming a causal connection between the enslavement and mass murder of Africans by Europeans... and the emergence of the concentration/extermination camp system in Europe; or whether she intends the African experience to serve as a foreshadowing of the Holocaust, a hint of what was to come, but without strong causal links to it." King, *Race, Culture, and the Intellectuals, 1940–1970* (Washington, DC: Woodrow Wilson Center Press, 2004), 100.

29. The current, widely read English translation of *Discourse on Colonialism* renders *choc en retour* as "boomerang effect" and this has no doubt also spurred the comparative assessments. For particular attention to translation and its bearing on our comparative understanding of Césaire's and Arendt's figures, see Ben Ratskoff, "Splattering the Object: Césaire, Nazi Racism, and the Colonial," in *Caribbean Jewish Crossings: Literary History and Creative Practice*, ed. Sarah Phillips Casteel and Heidi Kaufman (Charlottesville: University of Virginia Press, 2019), 177–97.

30. Sianne Ngai, *Ugly Feelings* (Cambridge, MA: Harvard UP, 2005), 46.

31. Rothberg, *Multidirectional Memory*, 101.

32. On Arendt's evolving ideas and her revisions to this work, see, for instance, Margaret Canovan, *Hannah Arendt: A Reinterpretation of Her Political Thought* (Cambridge: Cambridge UP, 1992), especially 17–98.

33. Aimé Césaire, "Discours sur le colonialisme," genetic ed., in Aimé Césaire, *Poésie, Théâtre, Essais et Discours: Édition Critique*, ed. Albert James Arnold (Paris: CNRS Éditions and Présence Africaine, 2013), 1448–76; Daniel Delas, "Discours sur le colonialisme: Présentation," in Césaire, *Poésie, Théâtre, Essais et Discours: Édition Critique*, 1444.

34. On the revisions to *Cahier d'un retour au pays natal*, see A. James Arnold's forceful arguments about the 1939 edition's authoritative status, as well as reflections by Christopher Miller and Natalie Melas that offer a more nuanced reading of the revisions. Arnold, "Beyond Postcolonial Césaire: Reading *Cahier d'un retour au pays natal* Historically," *Modern Language Studies* 44, no. 3 (2008), 258–75; Arnold, "Introduction," in *The Original 1939 Notebook of a Return to the Native Land*, trans. and ed. A. James Arnold and Clayton Eshleman (Middletown, CT: Wesleyan UP, 2013), xi–xxii; Miller, "Editing and Editorializing: The New Genetic *Cahier* of Aimé Césaire," *The South Atlantic Quarterly* 115, no. 3 (July 2016), 441–55; Melas, "Poetry's Circumstance and Racial Time: Aimé Césaire 1935–1945," *The South Atlantic Quarterly* 115, no. 3 (July 2016), 469–93.

35. Hannah Arendt, *The Origins of Totalitarianism*, rev. ed. (New York: Harcourt Brace Jovanovich, 1973), 22.

36. Ibid., 155.

37. Karuna Mantena, "Genealogies of Catastrophe: Arendt on the Logic and Legacy of Imperialism," in *Politics in Dark Times: Encounters with Hannah Arendt*, ed. Seyla Benhabib (New York: Cambridge UP, 2010), 93. Accordingly, Mantena remarks, "the histori-

cally consequential boomerang effects, then, have less to do with the undoing of a specific mother country's liberal institutions than the step-by-step degeneration and disruption of the underlying principles of Western politics tout court" (92).

38. Arendt, *The Origins of Totalitarianism*, 205–6.
39. Ibid., 206.
40. Ibid.
41. Ibid., xvii.
42. Ibid., xix.
43. Ibid., xxi.
44. Ibid., xviii.
45. Ibid., xxii.
46. Lyndsey Stonebridge, "Refugee Style: Hannah Arendt and the Perplexities of Rights," *Textual Practice* 25, no. 1 (2011), 75. Arendt's irony has been widely remarked and has received sustained scholarly scrutiny as well as occasional public odium, in the case of what Deborah Nelson has called the "scandal of tone" in *Eichmann in Jerusalem*. Nelson, *Tough Enough: Arbus, Arendt, Didion, McCarthy, Sontag, Weil* (Chicago: University of Chicago Press, 2017), 45. Both Stonebridge and Nelson stress that Arendt's irony should be understood not just as an expression of the losses she suffered as a German Jew and a refugee but more specifically as an integral aspect of the political philosophy she formulated in response to those experiences.
47. Césaire, *Discourse on Colonialism*, 36; Césaire, "Discours sur le colonialisme," in *Discours sur le colonialismse suivi du Discours sur la négritude*, 12–13.
48. Brent Hayes Edwards, "Aimé Césaire and the Syntax of Influence," *Research in African Literatures* 36, no. 2 (Summer 2005), 8.
49. Rothberg, *Multidirectional Memory*, 73–91, has proposed that the *choc en retour* shares the traumatic temporal structure of the return of the repressed.
50. Césaire, *Discourse on Colonialism*, 36.
51. See Césaire, "Discours sur le colonialisme," genetic ed., 1149–50.
52. Césaire, *Discourse on Colonialism*, 41; Césaire, "Discours sur le colonialisme," in *Discours sur le colonialismse suivi du Discours sur la négritude*, 21.
53. A. James Arnold, *Modernism and Négritude: The Poetry and Poetics of Aimé Césaire* (Cambridge, MA: Harvard UP, 1981), 177.
54. Césaire, *Discourse on Colonialism*, 76.
55. Rothberg, *Multidirectional Memory*, 73.
56. On the political dynamics that shaped this position, see Gary Wilder, *Freedom Time: Negritude, Decolonization, and the Future of the World* (Durham, NC: Duke UP, 2015), 127–30.
57. Monica Popescu singles out Césaire for his early recognition of Cold War conflicts: "Written a few years after the end of the war, [*Discourse on Colonialism*] shows Césaire at a moment when he was beginning to discern the contours of a new global configuration of power, yet without having a full grasp of its pitfalls." Popescu, *At Penpoint: African Literatures, Postcolonial Studies, and the Cold War* (Durham, NC: Duke UP, 2020), 9. Here too, we find attributed to Césaire and specifically this essay, especial perspicacity in recognizing historical patterns that were not yet widely recognized.
58. Ramos, "The Question of Race and the Democratic World," *International Social Science Bulletin*, 9–10.
59. See for instance Jacob W. Gruber, "Ethnographic Salvage and the Shaping of Anthropology," *American Anthropology* 72, no. 6 (December 1970), 1289–99, which sketches the pervasiveness of this orientation across various anthropological traditions on both sides of the Atlantic and which notes the appearance of similar concerns about the disappearance of

native culture in British imperial policy, such as the 1837 parliamentary report of the British Select Committee on Aborigines.

60. Ramos, "The Question of Race and the Democratic World," *International Social Science Bulletin*, 11–12.

61. Ibid., 9.

62. Ibid., 12.

63. "Members of the United Nations which have or assume responsibilities for the administration of territories whose peoples have not yet attained a full measure of self-government recognize the principle that the interests of the inhabitants of these territories are paramount, and accept as a sacred trust the obligation . . . to ensure, with due respect for the culture of the peoples concerned, their political, economic, social, and educational advancement . . . ; to develop self-government, to take due account of the political aspirations of the peoples, and to assist them in the progressive development of their free political institutions, according to the particular circumstances of each territory and its peoples and their varying stages of advancement." United Nations, Charter of the United Nations and Statute of the International Court of Justice (San Francisco: UN, 1945), 14.

64. Ramos, "The Question of Race and the Democratic World," *International Social Science Bulletin*, 13.

65. Ibid., 10.

66. As Wilder has demonstrated about Césaire in particular, the notion that anticolonial self-determination inevitably entailed national independence and state sovereignty was by no means settled or inevitable in the early postwar period. Wilder, *Freedom Time*.

67. Arturo Escobar, *Encountering Development: The Making and Unmaking of the Third World* (Princeton, NJ: Princeton UP, 2012), 30, 3–4. Escobar stresses the novelty of the postwar development paradigm, despite important precedents in the colonial period, and demonstrates how crucial the early 1950s were for the consolidation of this discourse and its institutionalization. See Escobar, *Encountering Development*, 21–54. Harry S. Truman, "Inaugural Address, Thursday, January 20, 1949," in *Inaugural Addresses of the Presidents of the United States: From George Washington 1789 to George Bush 1989* (Washington, DC: United States Government Printing Office, 1989), 289.

68. Aimé Césaire, "Culture and Colonization," trans. Brent Hayes Edwards, *Social Text* 28, no. 2 (Summer 2010), 128.

69. Césaire, "Culture and Colonization," 130.

70. Ibid., 129.

71. Ibid., 129–30, 127.

72. Ibid., 130.

73. Ibid., 131; Aimé Césaire, "Culture et colonisation," *Présence Africaine*, no. 8/10 (1956), 194.

74. Ramos, "The Question of Race and the Democratic World," *Internatonial Social Science Bulletin*, 12.

75. Ibid.

76. Césaire, "Culture and Colonization," 135, 140.

77. Ibid., 137, 135.

78. Ibid., 133; Césaire, "Culture et colonisation," 196. There is some confusion regarding the publication date of Evans's essay. Césaire attributes Evans's essay to the February 1956 issue of the *Courier*. In his 2010 translation of "Culture and Colonization," Edwards calls this an error and indicates that the essay appeared in the April 1956 issue. In fact, Césaire's original February 1956 citation is correct. The other work Césaire cites in this paragraph, by the anthropologist Margaret Mead, is also a UNESCO publication; a 1953 manual on

technical assistance and its cultural impact that Mead prepared and edited, titled *Cultural Patterns and Technical Change* (Paris: UNESCO, 1953).

79. Luther Evans, "The Human Side of Progress," *UNESCO Courier* (February 1956), 12.

80. Ibid., 14.

81. Césaire, "Culture and Colonization," 133.

82. Aimé Césaire, *Resolutely Black: Conversations with Françoise Vergès*, trans. Matthew B. Smith (Cambridge: Polity Press, 2020), 16–17.

83. Ibid., 17; Aimé Césaire, *Nègre je suis, nègre je resterai: Entretiens avec Françoise Vergès* (Paris: Albin Michel, 2005), 39.

84. See, for instance, Susan Slymovics, *How to Accept German Reparations* (Philadelphia: University of Pennsylvania Press, 2014); Stephen Best and Saidiya Hartman, "Fugitive Justice," *Representations* 92, no. 1 (2005), 1–15.

85. Césaire, *Resolutely Black*, 17; Césaire, *Nègre je suis*, 39.

86. Césaire, *Resolutely Black*, 19.

87. Ibid., 17. Translation modified; Césaire, *Nègre je suis*, 39.

88. Césaire, *Resolutely Black*, 19; Césaire, *Nègre je suis*, 41.

89. A. James Arnold, "Césaire Is Dead: Long Live Césaire!: Recuperations and Reparations," *French Politics, Culture and Society* 27, no. 3 (Winter 2009), 15–16. Arnold suggests that the impasse implicit in such a position largely describes Martinique's contemporary status in its politically unequal and economically dependent relations with France.

90. David L. Eng, "Colonial Object Relations," *Social Text* 126, vol. 34, no. 1 (2016), 1–19.

91. Notably, Eng also suggests a connection between the logic of reparation and the structure of the boomerang effect, proposing that Freud's theory of the death drive formulated in the wake of World War I is "the psychoanalytic corollary of Sartre's 'boomerang,' a detailed exegesis of the damaging effects that war, violence, and colonialism exacted on the European psyche." In other words, the European subject's reckoning with psychic violence and the necessity of repair is historically impelled only by the experience of colonial violence brought home to Europe. Ibid., 2. For Klein's account of reparation, see especially Melanie Klein, "Love, Guilt and Reparation," in *Love, Guilt and Reparation and Other Works, 1921–1954*, vol. 1 (New York: Free Press, 1975), 306–43.

92. Eng, "Colonial Object Relations," 9.

93. Ibid., 3.

94. Ibid., 13.

95. Ibid., 5.

96. Ibid., 1, 11; Césaire, *Discourse on Colonialism*, 42. On Césaire as a theorist of "dehumanization" and the limits of this concept, see Samera Esmeir, *Juridical Humanity: A Colonial History* (Stanford, CA: Stanford UP, 2012), 1–17.

97. Such incorporation is of course an educative project. On the logic of incorporation and its relationship to both education and human rights, see Slaughter, *Human Rights, Inc.*, especially 20–24, 249–54. On Césaire's extended reflections on pedagogy and education in the context of *négritude* and cultural formation, see Baer, *Indigenous Vanguards*, 139–88.

98. On the intellectual and political shifts that characterize Césaire's writing from this year, chiefly concerning his growing skepticism about Martinican assimilation and departmentalization, see Brent Hayes Edwards, "Introduction: Césaire in 1956," *Social Text* 103, vol. 28, no. 2 (2010), 115–25; and Wilder, *Freedom Time*, 167–76.

99. Delas, "Discours sur le colonialisme: Présentation," 1445.

100. Ibid., 1446.

101. Ibid., 1445.

102. Ama Ata Aidoo, *Our Sister Killjoy* (White Plains, NY: Longman 2004), 36.

103. Rothberg, *Multidirectional Memory*, 99.

104. Ibid., 100.

105. Roger Caillois, "Illusions à rebours," part 1, *La nouvelle nouvelle revue française*, no. 24 (December 1954), 1010–24; and Caillois, "Illusions à rebours," part 2, *La nouvelle nouvelle revue française*, no. 25 (January 1955), 58–70. All translations are my own.

106. The controversy occasioned by Caillois's denunciatory review and Lévi-Strauss's withering response are well discussed in biographies and secondary literature; my focus here is on those elements of Caillois's essay that have the most resonance for the themes of this chapter and are most relevant to Césaire's remarks. For fuller discussion of the controversy and its context, see Emanuelle Loyer, *Lévi-Strauss: A Biography* (Cambridge: Polity Press, 2018); Denis Hollier, "Surrealism and Its Discontents," *Papers of Surrealism* 7 (2007), 1–16; François Dosse, *History of Structuralism: The Rising Sign 1945–1966*, trans. Deborah Glassman (Minneapolis: University of Minnesota Press, 1997), 126–30.

107. Caillois, "Illusions à rebours," part 1, 1013–14. Caillois settles on surrealism as an especially potent incubator of this attitude—a position that Hollier argues makes little historical sense in Lévi-Strauss's case but which Césaire may have found irksome. Hollier, "Surrealism and its Discontents," 1–16.

108. Caillois, "Illusions à rebours," part 1, 1017–24.

109. Ibid., 1024; and Caillois, "Illusions à rebours," part 2, 61–64.

110. Caillois, "Illusions à rebours," part 2, 65.

111. Ibid., 61–62.

112. Aimé Césaire, *Discourse on Colonialism*, 72.

113. Ibid., 73. For clarity and ease of comparison, I reproduce here Pinkham's translation of these lines from Caillois's essay as they appear in *Discourse on Colonialism*, which also includes Césaire's own parenthetical observation.

114. Ibid.

115. Caillois, "Illusions à rebours," part 1, 1018.

116. Ashley Montagu, *Statement on Race: An Extended Discussion in Plain Language of the UNESCO Statement by Experts on Race Problems* (New York: Schuman, 1951), ix.

117. UNESCO, *General Conference—First Session, UNESCO House, Paris, November 20–December 10, 1946*, UNESCO/C/30 (Paris: UNESCO, 1947), 23.

118. As Miriam Intrator notes, following Chloé Maurel, "Reconstruction constituted the main justification and source of momentum for UNESCO at its founding. In fact, UNESCO was briefly to be called the United Nations Organization for Educational and Cultural Reconstruction, a name that was subsequently rejected as it risked creating confusion with the United Nations Relief and Rehabilitation Administration (UNRAA) and, moreover, did not reflect the long-term, global mission of the organization as it ultimately was formed." Intrator, *Books across Borders: UNESCO and the Politics of Postwar Cultural Reconstruction, 1945–1951* (Cham, Switzerland: Palgrave 2019), 5.

119. UNESCO systematically set about documenting these material and spiritual deficits in UNESCO, *The Book of Needs of Fifteen War-Devastated Countries in Education, Science and Culture*, vol. 1 (Paris: UNESCO, 1947), to which Huxley contributed the foreword. The first volume of the *Book of Needs* covered Austria, Belgium, Burma, China, Czechoslovakia, Ethiopia, France, Greece, Iran, Italy, Luxembourg, Netherlands, Philippines, Poland, and Yugoslavia. See too the American educator Leonard S. Kenworthy's documentary report for UNESCO and the US Commission for International Educational Reconstruction, *Going*

to School in War-Devastated Countries (Washington, D.C.: Commission for International Education Reconstruction, 1947).

120. UNESCO, General Conference—First Session 1946, 23. Emphasis added. As Intrator notes, "despite the vastness of the problem, reconstruction efforts were, especially initially, concentrated in Europe." Intrator, Books across Borders, 29.

121. UNESCO, General Conference—First Session 1946, 23.

122. Ibid.

123. Ramos, "The Question of Race and the Democratic World," International Social Science Bulletin, 10.

124. UNESCO, General Conference—First Session 1946, 23. I hasten to add that Huxley's politics were considerably more invested in traditional defenses of British imperialism than this studied neutrality might suggest. On his colonial apologetics, see Glenda Sluga, "UNESCO and the (One) World of Julian Huxley," Journal of World History 21, no. 3 (September 2010), 393–418; and Sarah Brouillette, UNESCO and the Fate of the Literary (Stanford, CA: Stanford UP, 2019), 26–36.

125. On UNESCO's interlacing of techno-economic development and affective, humanist, and spiritual aspirations about human progress and the formation of new human subjectivities, see Pavone, "The Humanism of Development," in From the Labyrinth of the World to the Paradise of the Heart, 97–124.

126. UNESCO, Introduction to UNESCO: A Summary of the Organisation's Activities during Its First Year—With Selected List of Documents (Paris: UNESCO, 1947), 12.

127. Ibid., 14–15.

128. Jens Boel, "UNESCO's Fundamental Education Program, 1946–1958: Vision, Actions and Impact," in A History of UNESCO: Global Actions and Impacts, ed. Poul Duedahl (Houndmills, UK: Palgrave Macmillan, 2016), 158.

129. Ibid., 163. Boel is not especially critical of this outcome, arguing that UNESCO "succeeded in mainstreaming, within the UN system, the idea of education as an essential and indispensable tool for development" (164).

130. Evans, "The Human Side of Progress," 12.

131. Ibid., 13.

132. Ibid.

133. Ibid.

134. UNESCO, Introduction to UNESCO, 28.

135. Ibid.

136. Hilary Perraton, International Students 1860–2010: Policy and Practice Round the World (New York: Palgrave Macmillan, 2020), 82–83.

137. UNESCO, Introduction to UNESCO, 29.

138. For readings that address Aidoo's reversal of Conrad's "heart of darkness" trope, see Hildegard Hoeller, "Ama Ata Aidoo's Heart of Darkness," Research in African Literatures 35, no. 1 (Spring 2004); Goyal, Romance, Diaspora, and Black Atlantic Literature, 181–204; and Elizabeth Baer, "Ama Ata Aidoo's Our Sister Killjoy: The African Gaze of Resistance Today," in The Genocidal Gaze: From German Southwest Africa to the Third Reich" (Detroit, Wayne State UP, 2017), 115–30. Baer in particular notes that Sissie's apprehension of the Holocaust is central to her characterization of Germany as the heart of darkness. She argues that Sissie's experience of racialization in Europe attunes her to the existence of what Baer calls the "genocidal gaze," allowing her to grasp the connections between genocidal histories in Europe and in Africa, such as the Herero and Nama genocide in German Southwest Africa that is the focus of Baer's book.

139. Aimé Césaire, "Poetry and Knowledge," in *Lyric and Dramatic Poetry, 1946-82*, trans. Clayton Eshleman and Annette Smith (Charlottesville: UP of Virginia, 1990), xlii.

140. Aidoo, *Our Sister Killjoy*, 8.

141. Barbara Mennel has observed how Germany's presence in the text displaces the familiar colony/metropole narrative, while also presenting a provocation to German studies, as "neither German nor migrant literature." Mennel, "'Germany Is Full of Germans Now': Germanness in Ama Ata Aidoo's *Our Sister Killjoy* and Chantal Akerman's *Meetings with Anna*," in *Gender and Germanness: Cultural Productions of Nation*, ed. Patricia Herminghouse and Magda Mueller (Providence, RI: Berghahn Books, 1997), 245, 238.

142. Aidoo, *Our Sister Killjoy*, 8.

143. Anson Rabinbach, "The Jewish Question in the German Question," *New German Critique* 44 (Spring–Summer 1998), 159.

144. For an examination of how such (material and imaginative) investments in the third world on the German left in the 1960s represented the "dream of the German liberated from his fascist past," see Arlene Teraoka, *East, West and Others: The Third World in Postwar German Literature* (Lincoln: University of Nebraska Press, 1996), 169. Quinn Slobodian has argued that the third world was not just the passive object or beneficiary of this German activism and investment but that students from Africa, Latin America, and Asia who traveled to Germany played an active role in these cultural and political developments. Slobodian, *Foreign Front: Third World Politics in Sixties West Germany* (Durham, NC: Duke UP, 2012).

145. Rabinbach, "The Jewish Question in the German Question," 171.

146. Aidoo, *Our Sister Killjoy*, 9.

147. Evans, "The Human Side of Progress," 13.

148. Aidoo, *Our Sister Killjoy*, 6.

149. Ibid.

150. Ibid., 7.

151. Hannah Arendt, *Eichmann in Jerusalem: A Report on the Banality of Evil*, rev. ed. (New York: Penguin, 1992), 289, 49.

152. Aidoo, *Our Sister Killjoy*, 6.

153. Ibid., 8.

154. Ibid., 43.

155. Theodor W. Adorno, "What Does Coming to Terms with the Past Mean?," in *Bitburg in Moral and Political Perspective*, ed. Geoffrey Hartman (Indianapolis: Indiana UP, 2000), 127.

156. Ibid., 128. Theodor W. Adorno, "Education after Auschwitz," in *Critical Models: Interventions and Catchwords*, trans. Henry W. Pickford (New York: Columbia UP, 2005), 192–93.

157. Aidoo, *Our Sister Killjoy*, 36.

158. Adorno, "Education after Auschwitz," 195.

159. Aidoo, *Our Sister Killjoy*, 37.

160. Ibid., 81.

161. Ibid., 93–94.

162. Ibid., 132.

163. Ibid., 36.

164. As Caroline Rooney observes of this formal dimension of the text, it is "written from the place [it is] heading towards. Among the lessons that can be drawn from this is that the event of the story is a writing up. . . . This process of writing up is one that validates the textually originating conclusions." Rooney, "'Dangerous Knowledge' and the Poetics of Survival: A Reading of *Our Sister Killjoy* and *A Question of Power*," in *Motherlands: Black Women's Writing from Africa, the Caribbean and South Asia*, ed. Susheila Nasta (New Bruns-

wick, NJ: Rutgers UP), 123. On Aidoo's Pan-Africanism, see Ranu Samantrai, "Caught at the Confluence of History: Ama Ata Aidoo's Necessary Nationalism," *Research in African Literatures* 26, no. 2 (1995), 140–57; Delia Kumavie, "Ama Ata Aidoo's Woman Centered Pan-Africanism," *Feminist Africa* 20, no. 1 (2015), 57–68.

165. Charles Taylor, "The Politics of Recognition," in *Multiculturalism: Examining the Politics of Recognition*, ed. Amy Gutmann (Princeton, NJ: Princeton UP, 1992), 31, 38.

166. Ibid., 65, 72, 61. As Patchen Markell notes, this version of recognition assumes the transparency and stability of identity, "demanding that others recognize us as who we *already* really are," which would seem to leave little room for an educative or transformation encounter. Markell, *Bound by Recognition*, (Princeton, NJ: Princeton UP, 2003), 14.

167. Aidoo, *Our Sister Killjoy*, 12.

168. See, for instance, Goyal, *Romance, Diaspora, and Black Atlantic Literature*, 192–93, for a reading of this moment, and 181–88 for her discussion of Fanon's influence on Aidoo. But as I suggest here and further elaborate in the pages that follow, Aidoo significantly and critically rewrites the dynamics of racial shame at the Fanonian scene of racial (mis)recognition.

169. Aidoo, *Our Sister Killjoy*, 12.

170. Paul Gilroy, *Against Race: Imagining Political Culture Beyond the Color Line* (Cambridge, MA: Harvard UP, 2000), 42.

171. As such, the text challenges what Elizabeth Povinelli describes as the "moral sensibility" of recognition that makes it an affective regime, in which recognition requires the disciplining of repugnance or disgust at the other's difference, even as the apparent affective truth of one's disgust or repugnance comes to mark the limits of what is recognizable and tolerable. Povinelli, *The Cunning of Recognition: Indigenous Alterities and the Making of Australian Multiculturalism* (Durham, NC: Duke UP, 2002), 3–17.

172. Aidoo, *Our Sister Killjoy*, 12–13.

173. Ibid., 23.

174. Ibid., 48, 47.

175. Ibid., 48.

176. On the status of Black Germans under National Socialism, see Tina Campt, *Other Germans: Black Germans and the Politics of Race, Gender, and Memory in the Third Reich* (Ann Arbor: University of Michigan Press, 2005).

177. Aidoo, *Our Sister Killjoy*, 48, 47.

178. Eve Kosofsky Sedgwick, *Touching Feeling: Affect, Pedagogy, Performativity* (Durham, NC: Duke UP, 2003), 36.

179. Aidoo, *Our Sister Killjoy*, 76. There is a rich body of commentary on this scene. While Gay Wilentz cursorily concludes that Aidoo depicts homosexuality as a European pathology, Chris Dunton argues that Aidoo disrupts such a stigmatized representation. Jarrod Hayes observes that Dunton overlooks Aidoo's references to the repression of homosexuality in Africa by European missionaries, arguing that Aidoo does not just disrupt the stigmatization of homosexuality in Africa but historically contextualizes it. Michelle M. Wright offers a reading along these lines, arguing that queer desire in the text confounds "the linear spacetime that marks precolonial, colonial, and now postcolonial Ghana." Wilentz, "The Politics of Exile: Ama Ata Aidoo's *Our Sister Killjoy*," *Studies in 20th Century Literature* 15, no. 1 (1991), 6; Dunton, "'Wheyting be Dat?': The Treatment of Homosexuality in African Literature," *Research in African Literatures* 20, no 3 (Autumn 1989), 431–34; Hayes, *Queer Roots for the Diaspora: Ghosts in the Family Tree* (Ann Arbor: University of Michigan Press, 2016), 95–97; Wright, *Physics of Blackness: Beyond the Middle Passage Epistemology* (Minneapolis: University of Minnesota Press, 2015), 140.

180. Aidoo, *Our Sister Killjoy*, 76.

181. On recognition and racial melancholia, see Anne Anlin Cheng, *The Melancholy of Race: Psychoanalysis, Assimilation, and Hidden Grief* (Oxford: Oxford UP, 2001).

182. Aidoo, *Our Sister Killjoy*, 72.

183. Frantz Fanon, *Black Skin, White Masks*, trans. Richard Philcox (New York: Grove, 2008), 94.

184. Aidoo, *Our Sister Killjoy*, 88. For an early and sustained reading focused especially on this dimension of the text, see Wilentz, "The Politics of Exile," 159–73.

185. Aidoo, *Our Sister Killjoy*, 86.

186. Ibid., 87. Baer offers a reading of Césaire on the politics of education and the role of the educated, "partly assimilated [youth] that, subject to the laws of assimilation, must constitute the vanguard against assimilation" that illuminates *Our Sister Killjoy*'s perspective on assimilation and return. Baer, *Indigenous Vanguards*, 145.

187. For Huxley's opinions on the biological and eugenic dimensions of equalization, see the reflections on UNESCO's prospects that he wrote in his capacity as future director general of the organization. There, he forthrightly advocated that UNESCO should play a role in ensuring at an international level one of the "primary aims of eugenics": "the raising of the mean level of all desirable [biological] qualities." Julian Huxley, *UNESCO: Its Purpose and Its Philosophy* (London: Preparatory Commission of UNESCO, 1946), 21.

188. Aidoo, *Our Sister Killjoy*, 96.

189. Ibid., 104.

190. Ibid., 87–88.

191. Ibid., 20, 23.

192. Ibid., 96, 122–31. Inspired in part by Aidoo's text, Sara Ahmed has argued that a killjoy is the person who "refuse[s] to go along. . . . To refuse the place in which you are placed, is to be seen as trouble, as causing discomfort for others." She aligns the killjoy with a feminist critique that assesses how women are often required to ensure the smooth operation of social happiness and the costs to them of such a role. Ahmed, *The Promise of Happiness* (Durham, NC: Duke UP, 2010), 69.

193. The killjoy's work, Ahmed argues, is about political affect: "There is a political struggle about how we attribute good and bad feelings, which hesitates around the apparently simple question of who introduces what feelings to whom" (69). On "killjoy politics" and their connection to repair as a site of feminist debate, see Rachel Stuelke, *The Ruse of Repair: US Neoliberal Empire and the Turn From Critique* (Durham, NC: Duke UP, 2021), 31–69.

194. Hannah Arendt, *Rahel Varnhagen: The Life of a Jewish Woman*, rev. ed., trans. Richard Winston and Clara Winston (New York: Harcourt Brace Jovanovich, 1974), 7, 6.

195. Hannah Arendt, "The Jew as Pariah: A Hidden Tradition," in *The Jewish Writings*, ed. Jerome Kohn and Ron H. Feldman (New York: Schocken, 2007), 285.

196. Aidoo, *Our Sister Killjoy*, 89.

197. Arendt, "The Jew as Pariah," 275.

198. On Arendt's involvement in Zionist organizations and organizing, see Elizabeth Young-Bruehl, *Hannah Arendt: For Love of the World*, 2nd ed. (New Haven, CT: Yale UP, 2004); Richard J. Bernstein, *Hannah Arendt and the Jewish Question* (Cambridge, MA: MIT Press, 1996). For Arendt's critiques of Zionist politics, see the collected essays in Hannah Arendt, *The Jewish Writings*, ed. Jerome Kohn and Ron H. Feldman (New York: Schocken, 2007); Arendt, *The Origins of Totalitarianism*, 290. There is a substantial scholarly literature on Arendt's ambivalent relationship to Zionism. See, for instance, Judith Butler, *Parting Ways: Jewishness and the Critique of Zionism* (New York: Columbia UP, 2012), 114–50; Amnon

Raz-Krakotzkin, "Jewish Peoplehood, 'Jewish Politics,' and Political Responsibility: Arendt on Zionism and Partitions," *College Literature* 38, no. 1 (Winter 2011), 57–74. On Arendt's depiction of Palestinians, see Shmuel Lederman, "Making the Desert Bloom: Hannah Arendt and Zionist Discourse," *The European Legacy* 21, no. 4 (2016), 393–407.

199. Bernstein, *Hannah Arendt and the Jewish Question*, 18.

200. Arendt, "The Jew as Pariah," 297.

201. Ibid., 290.

Coda

1. International Holocaust Remembrance Association, "The Working Definition of Antisemitism," https://www.holocaustremembrance.com/resources/working-definitions-charters/working-definition-antisemitism. The alternative Jerusalem Declaration on Antisemitism is available at https://jerusalemdeclaration.org/. For criticisms of this supposedly improved definition, see Samer Abdelnour, "The Jerusalem Declaration's Fatal Flaw," *Jewish Currents*, April 21, 2021, https://jewishcurrents.org/the-jerusalem-declarations-fatal-flaw; and Barry Trachtenberg, "Why I Signed the Jerusalem Declaration on Antisemitism," *Jewish Currents*, March 26, 2021, https://jewishcurrents.org/why-i-signed-the-jerusalem-declaration-on-antisemitism.

2. "Palestinian Rights and the IHRA Definition of Antisemitism," *The Guardian*, November 29, 2020, https://www.theguardian.com/news/2020/nov/29/palestinian-rights-and-the-ihra-definition-of-antisemitism.

3. United Nations, Report of the Special Rapporteur on Contemporary Forms of Racism, Racial Discrimination, Xenophobia and Related Intolerance, E. Tendayi Achiume, October 7, 2022, 14, 16, A/77/512, https://documents-dds-ny.un.org/doc/UNDOC/GEN/N22/618/67/PDF/N2261867.pdf?OpenElement.

4. For an overview of the so-called Mbembe affair and ongoing German debates about anti-antisemitism that have stifled criticism of Israel and designated even Jewish critics of Zionism as antisemites, see A. Dirk Moses, "The German Catechism," *Geschichte der Gegenwart*, May, 23, 2021, https://geschichtedergegenwart.ch/the-german-catechism/; and the dossier of responses published collectively under the title "The Catechism Debate" on *The New Fascism Syllabus* in summer 2021, https://newfascismsyllabus.com/category/opinions/the-catechism-debate/. For Moses's observation about the supposedly constitutively antisemitic status of "the postcolonial" in these debates, see his contribution to the dossier, "Dialectic of *Vergangenheitsbewältigung*," *The New Fascism Syllabus*, June 15, 2021, https://newfascismsyllabus.com/opinions/the-catechism-debate/dialectic-of-vergangenheitsbewaltigung/. Michael Rothberg, whose work has been another flashpoint in these controversies, has reconstructed the German debate and reflected on its import. See Rothberg, "Lived Multidirectionality: '*Historikerstreit* 2.0' and the Politics of Holocaust Memory," *Memory Studies* 15, no. 6 (2022), 1316-1329.

5. Ashley Montagu, *Man's Most Dangerous Myth: The Fallacy of Race*, 2nd ed. (New York: Columbia UP, 1945), 180–81.

BIBLIOGRAPHY

Abdallag, Samir, et al. "Palestinian Rights and the IHRA Definition of Antisemitism." Letters. *The Guardian*, November 29, 2020. https://www.theguardian.com/news/2020/nov/29/palestinian-rights-and-the-ihra-definition-of-antisemitism.
Abdelnour, Samer. "The Jerusalem Declaration's Fatal Flaw." *Jewish Currents*, April 21, 2021. https://jewishcurrents.org/the-jerusalem-declarations-fatal-flaw.
Abu El-Haj, Nadia. *The Genealogical Science: The Search for Jewish Origins and the Politics of Epistemology*. Chicago: University of Chicago Press, 2012.
Adelman, Janet. *Blood Relations: Christian and Jew in* The Merchant of Venice. Chicago: University of Chicago Press, 2008.
Adorno, Theodor W., "Education after Auschwitz." In *Critical Models: Interventions and Catchwords*, translated by Henry W. Pickford, 191–204. New York: Columbia University Press, 2005.
———. "What Does Coming to Terms with the Past Mean?" In *Bitburg in Moral and Political Perspective*, edited by Geoffrey Hartman, 114–29. Indianapolis: Indiana University Press, 2000.
Ahmed, Sara. *The Promise of Happiness*. Durham, NC: Duke University Press, 2010.
Ahuja, Neel. "Reversible Human: Rectal Feeding, Gut Plasticity, and Racial Control in US Carceral Warfare." *Social Text* 38, no. 2 (2020): 19–47.
Aidoo, Ama Ata. *Our Sister Killjoy*. White Plains, NY: Longman, 2004.
Alessandrini, Anthony C. *Frantz Fanon and the Future of Cultural Politics: Finding Something Different*. Lanham, MD: Lexington, 2014.
Alford, C. Fred. *Melanie Klein and Critical Social Theory: An Account of Politics, Art, and Reason Based on Her Psychoanalytic Theory*. New Haven, CT: Yale University Press, 1989.
Allewaert, Monique. *Ariel's Ecology: Plantations, Personhood, and Colonialism in the American Tropics*. Minneapolis: University of Minnesota Press, 2013.
Amin, Kadji. "Trans* Plasticity and the Ontology of Race and Species." *Social Text* 38, no. 2 (2020): 49–71.
Anderson, Carol. *Eyes Off the Prize: The United Nations and the African American Struggle for Human Rights, 1944–1955*. Cambridge: Cambridge University Press, 2003.
Anidjar, Gil. *The Jew, the Arab: A History of the Enemy*. Stanford, CA: Stanford University Press, 2003.
———. *Semites: Race, Religion, Literature*. Stanford, CA: Stanford University Press, 2008.
Anker, Elizabeth S. *Fictions of Dignity: Embodying Human Rights in World Literature*. Ithaca, NY: Cornell University Press, 2012.

Arendt, Hannah. "The Crisis in Education." In *Between Past and Future: Eight Exercises in Political Thought*, 170–93. New York: Penguin Books, 2006.
———. *Eichmann in Jerusalem: A Report on the Banality of Evil*. Rev. ed. New York: Penguin, 1992.
———. *The Human Condition*. 2nd ed. Chicago: University of Chicago Press, 1998.
———. "The Jew as Pariah: A Hidden Tradition." In *The Jewish Writings*, edited by Jerome Kohn and Ron H. Feldman, 275–97. New York: Schocken, 2007.
———. *The Jewish Writings*. Edited by Jerome Kohn and Ron H. Feldman. New York: Schocken, 2007.
———. *The Origins of Totalitarianism*. Rev. ed. New York: Harcourt Brace Jovanovich, 1973.
———. *Rahel Varnhagen: The Life of a Jewish Woman*. Rev. ed. Translated by Richard Winston and Clara Winston. New York: Harcourt Brace Jovanovich, 1974.
———. "What Is Freedom?" In *Between Past and Future: Eight Exercises in Political Thought*, 142–69. New York: Penguin Books, 2006.
Arnold, A. James. "Beyond Postcolonial Césaire: Reading *Cahier d'un retour au pays natal* Historically." *Modern Language Studies* 44, no. 3 (2008): 258–75.
———. "Césaire Is Dead: Long Live Césaire!: Recuperations and Reparations." *French Politics, Culture and Society* 27, no. 3 (Winter 2009): 9–18.
———. "Introduction." In *The Original 1939 Notebook of a Return to the Native Land*, translated and edited by A. James Arnold and Clayton Eshleman, xi–ii. Middletown, CT: Wesleyan University Press, 2013.
———. *Modernism and Negritude: The Poetry and Poetics of Aimé Césaire*. Cambridge, MA: Harvard University Press, 1981.
Atshan, Sa'ed and Katharina Galor. *The Moral Triangle: Germans, Israelis, Palestinians*. Durham, NC: Duke University Press, 2020.
Baer, Ben Conisbee. *Indigenous Vanguards: Education, National Liberation, and the Limits of Modernism*. New York: Columbia University Press, 2019.
Baer, Elizabeth. "Ama Ata Aidoo's *Our Sister Killjoy*: The African Gaze of Resistance Today." In *The Genocidal Gaze: From German Southwest Africa to the Third Reich*, 115–30. Detroit: Wayne State University Press, 2017.
Bahri, Deepika. *Postcolonial Biology: Psyche and Flesh after Empire*. Minneapolis: University of Minnesota Press, 2017.
Bakara, Hadji. "Poetry in the Shadow of Human Rights." *American Literary History* 28, no. 3 (2016): 512–41.
Baker, Cynthia M. *Jew*. New Brunswick, NJ: Rutgers University Press, 2017.
Baker, Lee D. *Anthropology and the Racial Politics of Culture*. Durham, NC: Duke University Press, 2010.
———. "Unraveling the Boasian Discourse: The Racial Politics of 'Culture' in School Desegregation, 1944–1954." *Transforming Anthropology* 7, no. 1 (1998): 15–32.
Baldwin, James. "Negroes Are Anti-Semitic Because They're Anti-White." In *James Baldwin: Collected Essays*, edited by Toni Morrison, 739–48. New York: Library of America, 1998.
Balibar, Étienne. "Is There a Neo-Racism?" In *Race, Nation, Class: Ambiguous Identities*, 17–28. London: Verso, 1991.
Bangham, Jenny. *Blood Relations: Transfusion and the Making of Human Genetics*. Chicago: University of Chicago Press, 2020.
Banton, Michael. *The International Politics of Race*. London: Polity Press, 2002.
Barkan, Elazar. "The Politics of the Science of Race: Ashley Montagu and UNESCO's Anti-racist Declarations." In *Race and Other Misadventures: Essays in Honor of Ashley*

Montagu in His Ninetieth Year, edited by Larry T. Reynolds and Leonard Lieberman, 96–105. Dix Hills, NY: General Hall, 1996.

———. *The Retreat of Scientific Racism: Changing Concepts of Race in Britain and the United States between the World Wars*. Cambridge: Cambridge University Press, 1992.

———. "Review—*Defenders of the Race: Jewish Doctors and Race Science in Fin-de-Siècle Europe*." *The American Historical Review* 101, no. 3 (1996): 838–39.

Barker, Martin. *The New Racism: Conservatives and the Ideology of the Tribe*. London: Junction Books, 1981.

Bartels, Emily C. *Speaking of the Moor: from* Alcazar *to* Othello. Philadelphia: University of Pennsylvania Press, 2008.

Batnitzky, Leora. *How Judaism Became a Religion: An Introduction to Modern Jewish Thought*. Princeton, NJ: Princeton University Press, 2011.

Bauman, Zygmunt. *Modernity and the Holocaust*. Ithaca, NY: Cornell University Press, 1989.

Bell, Dorian. *Globalizing Race: Antisemitism and Empire in French and European Culture*. Chicago: Northwestern University Press, 2018.

Benedict, Ruth, and Gene Weltfish. *The Races of Mankind*, Public Affairs Pamphlet no. 85. New York: Public Affairs Committee, 1946.

Bennett, Jane. *Vibrant Matter: A Political Ecology of Things*. Durham, NC: Duke University Press, 2010.

Bernstein, Michael André. *Foregone Conclusions: Against Apocalyptic History*. Berkeley: University of California Press, 1994.

Bernstein, Richard J. *Hannah Arendt and the Jewish Question*. Cambridge, MA: MIT Press, 1996.

Best, Stephen, and Saidiya Hartman. "Fugitive Justice." *Representations* 92, no. 1 (2005): 1–15.

Bewes, Timothy. "Shame, Ventriloquy, and the Problem of the Cliché: Caryl Phillips." In *The Event of Postcolonial Shame*, 48–72. Princeton, NJ: Princeton University Press, 2011.

Birnbaum, Pierre. "The Absence of an Encounter: Sociology and Jewish Studies." In *Modern Judaism and Historical Consciousness: Identities, Encounters, Perspectives*, edited by Christian Wiese and Andreas Gotzmann, 224–73. Leiden, NL: Brill, 2007.

Bloxham, Donald. *Genocide on Trial: War Crimes Trials and the Formation of Holocaust History and Memory*. Oxford: Oxford University Press, 2001.

Boas, Franz. "Are the Jews a Race?" Reprinted as "The Jews" in *Race and Democratic Society*, 38–42. New York: J. J. Augustin, 1945.

———. *Aryans and Non-Aryans*. New York: Information and Service Associates, 1934.

———. "Changes in the Bodily Form of Descendants of Immigrants." *American Anthropologist* 14, no. 3 (July 1912): 530–62.

———. *Changes in Bodily Form of Descendants of Immigrants*, Final Report, Immigration Commission. Washington, DC: Government Printing Office, 1911.

———. "Commencement Address at Atlanta University, May 31, 1906." Atlanta University Leaflet, no. 19. http://www.webdubois.org/BoasAtlantaCommencement.html

———. *The Mind of Primitive Man*. New York: MacMillan, 1911.

———. "The Problem of the American Negro." *Yale Review* 10 (1921): 384–95.

Boel, Jens. "UNESCO's Fundamental Education Program, 1946–1958: Vision, Actions and Impact." In *A History of UNESCO: Global Actions and Impacts*, edited by Poul Duedahl, 153–67. Basingstoke, UK: Palgrave Macmillan, 2016.

Bonner, Christopher. "Alioune Diop and the Cultural Politics of Negritude: Reading the First Congress of Black Writers and Artists, 1956." *Research in African Literatures* 50, no. 2 (Summer 2019): 1–18.

Bonnett, Alastair. *Anti-Racism*. London: Routledge, 2000.

Boyarin, Daniel. "Homophobia and the Postcoloniality of the 'Jewish Science.'" In *Queer*

Theory and the Jewish Question, edited by Daniel Boyarin, Daniel Itzkowitz, and Ann Pellegrini, 166–98. New York: Columbia University Press, 2003.

———. *Judaism: The Genealogy of a Modern Notion*. New Brunswick, NJ: Rutgers University Press, 2019.

———. "Othello's Penis: Or, Islam in the Closet." In *Shakesqueer: A Queer Companion to the Complete Works of Shakespeare*, edited by Madhavi Menon, 254–62. Durham, NC: Duke University Press, 2011.

———. *A Radical Jew: Paul and the Politics of Identity*. Berkeley: University of California Press, 1994.

Boyarin, Jonathan. *The Unconverted Self: Jews, Indians, and the Identity of Christian Europe*. Chicago: University of Chicago Press, 2009.

Brattain, Michelle. "Race, Racism, and Antiracism: UNESCO and the Politics of Presenting Science to the Postwar Public." *The American Historical Review* 112, no. 5 (December 2007): 1386–413.

Brilmyer, S. Pearl. "Plasticity, Form, and the Matter of Character in *Middlemarch*." *Representations* 130, no. 1 (Spring 2015): 60–83.

Brouillette, Sarah. *UNESCO and the Fate of the Literary*. Stanford, CA: Stanford University Press, 2019.

Brown, Jayna. "Being Cellular: Race, the Inhuman, and the Plasticity of Life." *GLQ* 21, nos. 2–3 (2015): 321–41.

Burke, Roland. *Decolonization and the Evolution of International Human Rights*. Philadelphia: University of Pennsylvania Press, 2013.

Burton, Jonathan. *Traffic and Turning: Islam and English Drama, 1579–1624*. Newark: University of Delaware Press, 2005.

Butler, Judith. *Parting Ways: Jewishness and the Critique of Zionism*. New York: Columbia University Press, 2012.

Cahnman, Werner J. "Ginsberg, Morris." In *Encyclopedia Judaica*. 2nd ed. Vol. 7. Edited by Michael Berenbaum and Fred Skolnik, 610. Detroit: Macmillan Reference, 2007.

Caillois, Roger. "Illusions à rebours," part 1. *La nouvelle nouvelle revue française* no. 24 (December 1954): 1010–24.

———. "Illusions à rebours," part 2. *La nouvelle nouvelle revue française* no. 25 (January 1955): 58–70.

Campbell, Alan Tormaid. "The UNESCO Courier Is 70!: An Inspiring Read." *UNESCO Courier* no. 1 (January–March 2018).

Campt, Tina M. *Other Germans: Black Germans and the Politics of Race, Gender, and Memory in the Third Reich*. Ann Arbor: University of Michigan Press, 2005.

Canovan, Margaret. *Hannah Arendt: A Reinterpretation of Her Political Thought*. Cambridge: Cambridge University Press, 1994.

Card, Claudia. "Genocide and Social Death." *Hypatia* 18, no. 1 (Winter 2003), 63–79.

Castañeda, Claudia. *Figurations: Child, Bodies, Worlds*. Durham, NC: Duke University Press, 2002.

Casteel, Sarah Phillips. *Calypso Jews: Jewishness in the Caribbean Literary Imagination*. New York: Columbia University Press, 2016.

"Catechism Debate," edited by Jennifer Evans and Brian J. Griffith. *The New Fascism Syllabus*, Summer 2021. https://newfascismsyllabus.com/category/opinions/the-catechism-debate/.

Cavalli-Sforza, Luigi Luca, Paolo Menozzi, and Alberto Piazza. *The History and Geography of Human Genes*. Princeton, NJ: Princeton University Press, 2018.

Césaire, Aimé. "Culture and Colonization." Translated by Brent Hayes Edwards. *Social Text* 103, vol. 28, no. 2 (Summer 2010): 127–44.
———. "Culture et Colonisation." *Présence Africaine*, no. 8/10 (1956): 190–205.
———. *Discourse on Colonialism*. Translated by Joan Pinkham. New York: Monthly Review Press, 2000.
———. "Discours sur le colonialisme." In *Discours sur le colonialisme suivi du Discours sur la négritude*. Paris: Présence Africaine, 2004.
———. "Discours sur le colonialisme." Genetic ed. In Aimé Césaire, *Poésie, théatre, essais et discours: Édition critique*, edited by Albert James Arnold, 1448–76. Paris: CNRS Éditions and Présence Africaine, 2013.
———. *Nègre je suis, nègre je resterai: Entretiens avec Françoise Vergès*. Paris: Albin Michel, 2005.
———. "Poetry and Knowledge." In *Lyric and Dramatic Poetry*, translated by Clayton Eshleman and Annette Smith, xlii–lvi. Charlottesville: University Press of Virginia, 1990.
———. *Resolutely Black: Conversations with Françoise Vergès*. Translated by Matthew B. Smith. Cambridge: Polity Press, 2020.
Cesarani, David, and Eric J. Sundquist, eds. *After the Holocaust: Challenging the Myth of Silence*. London: Routledge, 2012.
Chen, Mel Y. *Animacies: Biopolitics, Racial Mattering, and Queer Affect*. Durham, NC: Duke University Press, 2012.
Cheng, Anne Anlin. *The Melancholy of Race: Psychoanalysis, Assimilation, and Hidden Grief*. Oxford: Oxford University Press, 2001.
———. *Second Skin: Josephine Baker and the Modern Surface*. Oxford: Oxford University Press, 2010.
Cheyette, Bryan. *Diasporas of the Mind: Jewish and Postcolonial Writing and the Nightmare of History*. New Haven, CT: Yale University Press, 2014.
———. "Frantz Fanon and the Black–Jewish Imaginary." In *Frantz Fanon's Black Skin, White Masks: New Interdisciplinary Essays*, edited by Max Silverman, 74–99. Manchester: Manchester University Press, 2005.
———. "Venetian Spaces: Old-New Literatures and the Ambivalent Uses of Jewish History." In *Reading the "New" Literatures in a Postcolonial Era*, edited by Susheila Nasta, 53–73. Cambridge: D. S. Brewer, 2000.
Clingman, Stephen. "Forms of History and Identity in *The Nature of Blood*." *Salmagundi* no 143 (Summer 2004): 141–66.
Comas, Juan. *Racial Myths*. Paris: UNESCO, 1951.
Conklin, Alice. "'Nothing Is Less Universal Than the Idea of Race': Alfred Métraux, American Social Science and UNESCO's Anti-Racist Campaign in 1950s Paris." *Durkheimian Studies* 25 (2021): 107–32.
Cooper, Frederick. "Review: *Human Rights in the Shadow of Colonial Violence*." *American Historical Review* 119, no. 2 (April 2014): 650–1.
Craps, Stef. "Linking Legacies of Loss: Traumatic Histories and Cross-Cultural Empathy in Caryl Phillips's *Higher Ground* and *The Nature of Blood*." *Studies in the Novel* 40, nos. 1–2 (Spring–Summer 2008): 191–202.
———. *Postcolonial Witnessing: Trauma Out of Bounds*. London: Palgrave, 2013.
Damrosch, David. "The Ethnic Ethnographer: Judaism in *Tristes Tropiques*." *Representations* 50 (Spring 1995): 1–13.
Darda, Joseph. *The Strange Career of Racial Liberalism*. Stanford, CA: Stanford University Press, 2002.

Dawson, Ashley. "'To Remember Too Much Is Indeed a Form of Madness': Caryl Phillips's *The Nature of Blood* and the Modalities of European Racism." *Postcolonial Studies* 7, no. 1 (2004): 83–101.

Delas, Daniel. "Discours sur le colonialisme: Présentation." In Aimé Césaire, *Poésie, théâtre, essais et discours: Édition critique*, edited by Albert James Arnold, 1443–47. Paris: CNRS Éditions and Présence Africaine, 2013.

Diprose, Rosalyn, and Ewa Plonowska Ziarek. "Time for Beginners: Natality, Biopolitics, and Political Theology." *philoSOPHIA* 3, no. 2 (2013): 107–20.

Dossa, Shiraz. "Human Status and Politics: Hannah Arendt on the Holocaust." *Canadian Journal of Political Science* 13, no. 2 (1980): 309–23.

Dosse, François. *History of Structuralism: The Rising Sign, 1945–1966*. Translated by Deborah Glassman. Minneapolis: University of Minnesota Press, 1997.

Douglas, Lawrence. *The Memory of Judgment: Making Law and History in the Trials of the Holocaust*. New Haven, CT: Yale University Press, 2001.

Du Bois, W. E. B. *The World and Africa and Color and Democracy*. Oxford: Oxford University Press, 2014.

Dunn, Leslie C., and Stephen P. Dunn. "The Jewish Community of Rome." *Scientific American* 196, no. 3 (March 1957): 118–32.

Dunton, Chris. "Wheyting be Dat?: The Treatment of Homosexuality in African Literature." *Research in African Literatures* 20, no 3 (Autumn 1989): 431–34.

Duranti, Marco. "The Holocaust, the Legacy of 1789 and the Birth of International Human Rights Law: Revisiting the Foundation Myth." *Journal of Genocide Research* 14, no. 2 (June 2012): 159–86.

Edwards, Brent Hayes. "Aimé Césaire and the Syntax of Influence." *Research in African Literatures* 36, no. 2 (Summer 2005): 1–18.

———. "Introduction: Césaire in 1956." *Social Text* 28, no. 2 (2010): 115–25.

Edwards, Erica R. *The Other Side of Terror: Black Women and the Culture of US Empire*. New York: New York University Press, 2021.

Efron, John M. *Defenders of the Race: Jewish Doctors and Race Science in Fin-de-Siècle Europe*. New Haven, CT: Yale University Press, 1994.

Eng, David L. "Colonial Object Relations." *Social Text* 126, vol. 34, no. 1 (March 2016): 1–19.

Erakat, Noura. *Justice for Some: Law and the Question of Palestine*. Stanford, CA: Stanford University Press, 2019.

Escobar, Arturo. *Encountering Development: The Making and Unmaking of the Third World*. Princeton, NJ: Princeton University Press, 2012.

Esmeir, Samera. *Juridical Humanity: A Colonial History*. Stanford, CA: Stanford University Press, 2012.

Evans, Luther. "The Human Side of Progress." *UNESCO Courier*, February 1956, 12–14.

Fanon, Frantz. "Antillais et Africains." *Esprit* 223, no. 2 (February 1955): 261–9.

———. *Black Skin, White Masks*. Translated by Richard Philcox. New York: Grove Press, 2008.

———. *Peau noire, masques blancs*. Paris: Éditions du Seuil, 1952.

———. "Racism and Culture." In *Toward the African Revolution*, translated by Haakon Chevalier, 31–44. New York: Grove Press, 1967.

———. "Racisme et culture." *Présence Africaine*, no. 8/10 (1956): 122–31.

———. "West Indians and Africans." In *Toward the African Revolution*, translated by Haakon Chevalier, 17–27. New York: Monthly Review Press, 1967.

———. *The Wretched of the Earth*. Translated by Richard Philcox. New York: Grove Press, 2004.
Feldman, Keith P. *A Shadow over Palestine: The Imperial Life of Race in America*. Minneapolis: University of Minnesota Press, 2015.
Fishberg, Maurice. "Aryan and Semite, With Particular Reference to the Aryan." In *Aryan and Semite: With Particular Reference to Nazi Racial Dogmas—Addresses Delivered Before the Judaeans and the Jewish Academy of Arts and Sciences, March 4th, 1934, in New York City*. Cincinnati, OH: B'nai B'rith, 1934.
———. *Jews, Race, and Environment*. New Brunswick, NJ: Transaction, 2006.
Fisher, Jaimey. *Disciplining Germany: Youth, Reeducation, and Reconstruction after the Second World War*. Detroit: Wayne State University Press, 2007.
Fleetwood, Nicole R. *Troubling Vision: Performance, Visuality, and Blackness*. Chicago: University of Chicago Press, 2011.
Foucault, Michel. *Security, Territory, Population: Lectures at the Collège de France, 1977–1978*. Edited by Michel Senellart. Translated by Graham Burchell. New York: Picador, 2007.
———. *"Society Must Be Defended": Lectures at the Collège de France, 1975–1976*. Edited by Mauro Bertani and Alessandro Fontana. Translated by David Macey. New York: Picador, 2003.
Frank, Gelya. "Jews, Multiculturalism, and Boasian Anthropology." *American Anthropologist* 99, no. 4 (1997), 731–45.
Freud, Sigmund. "Analysis of a Phobia in a Five-Year-Old Boy." In *The Standard Edition of the Complete Psychological Works of Sigmund Freud*. Vol. 10, translated by James Strachey. London: Vintage, 2001.
———. "Moses and Monotheism." In *The Standard Edition of the Complete Psychological Works of Sigmund Freud*. Vol. 23, translated by James Strachey. London: Vintage, 2001.
Füredi, Frank. *The Silent War: Imperialism and the Changing Perception of Race*. New Brunswick, NJ: Rutgers University Press, 1998.
Gandhi, Leela. *The Common Cause: Postcolonial Ethics and the Practice of Democracy, 1900–1950*. Chicago: University of Chicago Press, 2014.
Gannett, Lisa. "Making Populations: Bounding Genes in Space and Time." *Philosophy of Science* 70, no. 5 (2003): 989–1001.
———. "Racism and Human Genome Diversity Research: The Ethical Limits of 'Population Thinking.'" *Philosophy of Science* 68, no. 3 (2001): S479–92.
Garcia, Jay. "*Home of the Brave*, Frantz Fanon and Cultural Pluralism." *Comparative American Studies: An International Journal* 4, no. 1 (2006), 49–65.
Gates, Henry Louis. "Critical Fanonism." *Critical Inquiry* 17, no. 3 (1991): 457–70.
Geller, Jay. *The Other Jewish Question: Identifying the Jew and Making Sense of Modernity*. New York: Fordham University Press, 2011.
Getachew, Adom. *Worldmaking after Empire: The Rise and Fall of Self-Determination*. Princeton, NJ: Princeton University Press, 2019.
Gilbert, Shirli, and Avril Alba. "Introduction." In *Holocaust Memory and Racism in the Postwar World*, edited by Shirli Gilbert and Avril Alba, 1–12. Detroit, MI: Wayne State University Press, 2019.
Gilman, Sander. *The Jew's Body*. New York: Routledge, 1991.
Gil-Riaño, Sebastián. "Historicizing Anti-Racism: UNESCO's Campaigns against Race Prejudice in the 1950s." PhD diss., University of Toronto, 2014.
———. "Relocating Anti-Racist Science: The 1950 UNESCO Statement on Race and

Economic Development in the Global South." *The British Journal for the History of Science* 51, no. 2 (June 2018): 281–303.

Gilroy, Paul. *Against Race: Imagining Political Culture beyond the Color Line*. Cambridge, MA: Harvard University Press, 2000.

———. *The Black Atlantic: Modernity and Double Consciousness*. Cambridge, MA: Harvard University Press, 1993.

———. *There Ain't No Black in the Union Jack: The Cultural Politics of Race and Nation*. Oxford: Routledge, 2002.

Gines, Kathryn T. *Hannah Arendt and the Negro Question*. Bloomington: Indiana University Press, 2014.

———. "Race Thinking and Racism in Hannah Arendt's *The Origins of Totalitarianism*." In *Hannah Arendt and the Uses of History: Imperialism, Nation, Race, and Genocide*, edited by Richard H. King and Dan Stone, 38–53. New York: Berghahn, 2007.

Ginsberg, Morris. "Anti-Semitism." *The Sociological Review* 35, no. 1–2 (1943): 1–11.

———. *The Jewish Problem*. London: British Section of the World Jewish Congress, 1943.

———. *The Unity of Mankind*. Oxford: Oxford University Press, 1935.

Glick, Leonard B. "Types Distinct from Our Own: Franz Boas on Jewish Identity and Assimilation." *American Anthropologist* 84, no. 3 (September 1982): 545–65.

Goldberg, David Theo. "Racial Comparisons, Relational Racisms: Some Thoughts on Method." *Ethnic and Racial Studies* 32, no. 7 (2009): 1271–82.

———. "Racial Europeanization." *Ethnic and Racial Studies* 29, no. 2 (2006): 331–64.

Goldstein, Eric L. *The Price of Whiteness: Jews, Race, and American Identity*. Princeton, NJ: Princeton University Press, 2006.

Goodale, Mark, ed. *Letters to the Contrary: A Curated History of the UNESCO Human Rights Survey*. Stanford, CA: Stanford University Press, 2018.

Goyal, Yogita. *Romance, Diaspora, and Black Atlantic Literature*. Cambridge: Cambridge University Press, 2010.

———. *Runaway Genres: The Global Afterlives of Slavery*. New York: New York University Press, 2019.

Grosz, Elizabeth. *Volatile Bodies: Toward a Corporeal Feminism*. Bloomington: Indiana University Press, 1994.

Gruber, Jacob W. "Ethnographic Salvage and the Shaping of Anthropology." *American Anthropology* 72, no. 6 (December 1970): 1289–99.

Guimarães, Antonio Sérgio Alfredo. "Africanism and Racial Democracy: The Correspondence between Herskovits and Arthur Ramos (1935–1949)." *Estudios Interdisciplinarios de América Latina y el Caribe* 19, no. 1 (2008): 53–79.

———. "Racial Democracy." In *Imagining Brazil*, edited by Jessé Souza and Valter Sinder, 119–40. Lanham, MD: Lexington, 2005.

Gulick, Anne W. *Literature, Law, and Rhetorical Performance in the Anticolonial Atlantic*. Columbus: Ohio State University Press, 2016.

Hall, Stuart. "Race, the Floating Signifier: What More Is There to Say about Race?" In Stuart Hall, *Selected Writings On Race and Difference*, edited by Paul Gilroy and Ruth Wilson Gilmore, 359–73. Durham, NC: Duke University Press, 2021.

Haraway, Donna. *Modest_Witness@Second_Millenium. FemaleMan_Meets_OncoMouse: Feminism and Technoscience*. New York: Routledge, 1997.

———. "Remodeling the Human Way of Life: Sherwood Washburn and the New Physical Anthropology, 1950–1980." In *Bones, Bodies, Behavior: Essays in Behavioral Anthro-*

pology, edited by George W. Stocking Jr., 206–59. Madison: University of Wisconsin Press, 1988.

Hart, Mitchell. *Social Science and the Politics of Modern Jewish Identity*. Stanford, CA: Stanford University Press, 2000.

Hazard, Anthony Q. *Boasians at War: Anthropology, Race, and World War II*. Cham, Switzerland: Palgrave Macmillan, 2020.

———. *Postwar Anti-Racism: The United States, UNESCO, and "Race," 1945–1968*. New York: Palgrave Macmillan, 2012.

Hayes, Jarrod. *Queer Roots for the Diaspora: Ghosts in the Family Tree*. Ann Arbor: University of Michigan Press, 2016.

Herskovits, Melville J. *Franz Boas: The Science of Man in the Making*. New York: Scribner, 1953.

Hirsch, Marianne. *The Generation of Postmemory*. New York: Columbia University Press, 2012.

Hochberg, Gil. "'Re-Membering Semitism' or 'On the Prospect of Re-Membering the Semites.'" *Re-Orient* 1, no. 2 (Spring 2016): 192–223.

Hoeller, Hildegard. "Ama Ata Aidoo's *Heart of Darkness*." *Research in African Literatures* 35, no. 1 (Spring 2004): 130–47.

Hollier, Denis. "Surrealism and Its Discontents." *Papers of Surrealism* 7 (2007): 1–16.

Hopgood, Stephen. *The Endtimes of Human Rights*. Ithaca, NY: Cornell University Press, 2013.

Hsia, R. Po-Chia. *Trent 1475: Stories of a Ritual Murder Trial*. New Haven, CT: Yale University Press, 1992.

Huang, Michelle N. "Ecologies of Entanglement in the Great Pacific Garbage Patch." *Journal of Asian American Studies* 20, no. 1 (2017): 95–117.

Huggan, Graham. "Counter-Travel Writing and Postcoloniality." In *Being/s in Transit*, edited by Liselotte Glage, 37–59. Leiden, NL: Brill, 2000.

Huxley, Julian. "On Living in a Revolution." *Harper's Magazine* 185, no. 1108 (1942): 337–47.

———. *UNESCO: Its Purpose and Its Philosophy*. London: Preparatory Commission of the United Nations Educational, Scientific and Cultural Organization, 1946.

Huxley, Julian, and A. C. Haddon. *We Europeans: A Survey of "Racial" Problems*. New York: Harper and Brothers, 1936.

Huyssen, Andreas. *Present Pasts: Urban Palimpsests and the Politics of Memory*. Stanford, CA: Stanford University Press, 2003.

Intrator, Miriam. *Books across Borders: UNESCO and the Politics of Postwar Cultural Reconstruction, 1945–1951*. Cham, Switzerland: Palgrave Macmillan, 2019.

Jackson, Zakiyyah Iman. "Losing Manhood: Animality and Plasticity in the (Neo)Slave Narrative." *Qui Parle: Critical Humanities and Social Sciences* 25, nos. 1–2 (2016): 95–136.

Jarvis, Jill. *Decolonizing Memory: Algeria and the Politics of Testimony*. Durham, NC: Duke University Press, 2021.

Jensen, Steven L. B. *The Making of International Human Rights: The 1960s, Decolonization, and the Reconstruction of Global Values*. New York: Cambridge University Press, 2016.

Jockusch, Laura. "Justice at Nuremberg?: Jewish Responses to Nazi War-Crime Trials in Allied-Occupied Germany." *Jewish Social Studies* 19, no. 1 (2012): 107–47.

Jones, Donna V. *The Racial Discourses of Life Philosophy: Négritude, Vitalism, and Modernity*. New York: Columbia University Press, 2010.

———. "Rethinking Anti-Semitism: Introduction." *American Historical Review* 123, no. 4 (October 2018): 1123–38.

Julien, Eileen. "Terrains de Rencontre: Césaire, Fanon, and Wright on Culture and Decolonization." *Yale French Studies* 98 (2000): 149–66.

Kaplan, Bernice A. "Environment and Human Plasticity." *American Anthropologist* 56, no. 5 (October 1954): 780–800.
Kaplan, Steven. "If There Are No Races, How Can Jews Be a 'Race'?" *Journal of Modern Jewish Studies* 2, no. 1 (2003): 79–96.
Kelley, Robin D. G. "A Poetics of Anticolonialism." In Aimé Césaire, *Discourse on Colonialism,* translated by Joan Pinkham. New York: Monthly Review Press, 2000.
Kenworthy, Leonard S. *Going to School in War-Devastated Countries.* Washington, DC: Commission for International Education Reconstruction, 1947.
King, Richard H. *Race, Culture, and the Intellectuals, 1940–1970.* Washington, DC: Woodrow Wilson Center Press, 2004.
King, Richard H., and Dan Stone, eds. *Hannah Arendt and the Uses of History: Imperialism, Nation, Race, and Genocide.* New York: Berghahn, 2007.
Klein, Melanie. "Love, Guilt and Reparation." In *Love, Guilt and Reparation and Other Works, 1921–1954,* 306–43. Vol. 2. New York: Free Press, 1975.
Klose, Fabian. *Human Rights in the Shadow of Colonial Violence: The Wars of Independence in Kenya and Algeria.* Translated by Dona Geyer. Philadelphia: University of Pennsylvania Press, 2013.
Kumavie, Delia. "Ama Ata Aidoo's Woman Centered Pan-Africanism." *Feminist Africa* 20, no. 1 (2015): 57–68.
Langbehn, Volker, and Mohammad Salama, eds. *German Colonialism: Race, the Holocaust and Postwar Germany.* New York: Columbia University Press, 2011.
Laves, Walter H. C., and Charles A. Thomson. *UNESCO: Purpose, Progress, Prospects.* Bloomington: Indiana University Press, 1957.
Lederman, Shmuel. "Making the Desert Bloom: Hannah Arendt and Zionist Discourse." *The European Legacy*, 21, no. 4 (2016): 393–407.
Leiris, Michel. *Race and Culture.* Paris: UNESCO, 1951.
Lentin, Alana. "Europe and the Silence about Race." *European Journal of Social Theory* 11, no. 4 (2008): 487–503.
———. *Racism and Anti-Racism in Europe.* London: Pluto Press, 2004.
Lévi-Strauss, Claude. "Race and Culture." *International Social Science Journal* 23, no. 4 (1971): 617–18.
———. *Race and History.* Paris: UNESCO, 1952.
———. *Race et histoire.* Paris: Denoël, 1987.
———. *Tristes Tropiques.* Translated by John Weightman and Doreen Weightman. New York: Penguin, 2012.
Levinson, Natasha. "The Paradox of Natality: Teaching in the Midst of Belatedness." In *Hannah Arendt and Education: Renewing our Common World*, edited by Mordechai Gordon, 11–36. Boulder, CO: Westview Press, 2001.
Levy, Daniel and Natan Sznaider. *The Holocaust and Memory in the Global Age.* Translated by Assenka Oksiloff. Philadelphia: Temple UP, 2006.
Lionnet, François. "'*Dire exactement*': Remembering the Interwoven Lives of Jewish Deportees and Coolie Descendants in 1940s Mauritius." *Yale French Studies* 118–119 (2010): 111–35.
Lipphardt, Veronika. "Isolates and Crosses in Human Population Genetics; or, a Contextualization of German Race Science." *Current Anthropology* 53, supp. 5 (April 2012): S69–82.
Liss, Julia E. "German Culture and German Science in the *Bildung* of Franz Boas." In *Volksgeist as Method and Ethic: Essays on Boasian Ethnography and the German*

Anthropological Tradition, edited by George W. Stocking, 155–84. Madison: University of Wisconsin Press, 1996.

Liu, Lydia H. "Shadows of Universalism: The Untold Story of Human Rights around 1948." *Critical Inquiry* 40, no. 4 (2014): 385–417.

Loeffler, James. *Rooted Cosmopolitans: Jews and Human Rights in the Twentieth Century*. New Haven, CT: Yale University Press, 2018.

Loomba, Ania. "Race and the Possibilities of Comparative Critique." *New Literary History* 40, no. 3 (Summer 2009): 501–22.

Lowe, Lisa. *The Intimacies of Four Continents*. Durham, NC: Duke University Press, 2015.

Loyer, Emanuelle. *Lévi-Strauss: A Biography*. Cambridge: Polity Press, 2018.

Lupton, Julia Reinhard. "*Ethnos* and Circumcision in the Pauline Tradition: A Psychoanalytic Exegesis." In *The Psychoanalysis of Race*, edited by Christopher Lane, 193–210. New York: Columbia University Press, 1998.

———. "*Othello* Circumcised: Shakespeare and the Pauline Discourse of Nations." *Representations* 57, no. 1 (1997): 73–89.

Macey, David. *Frantz Fanon: A Biography*. London: Verso, 2012.

Malabou, Catherine. *Plasticity at the Dusk of Writing: Dialectic, Destruction, Deconstruction*. Translated by Carolyn Shread. New York: Columbia University Press, 2010.

———. *What Should We Do with Our Brain?* Translated by Sebastian Rand. New York: Fordham University Press, 2008.

Mansfield, Becky, and Julie Guthman. "Epigenetic Life: Biological Plasticity, Abnormality, and New Configurations of Race and Reproduction." *Cultural Geographies* 22, no. 1 (2015): 3–20.

Mantel, Hilary. "Black Is Not Jewish." *Literary Review*, February 1997, 40.

Mantena, Karuna. "Genealogies of Catastrophe: Arendt on the Logic and Legacy of Imperialism." In *Politics in Dark Times: Encounters with Hannah Arendt*, edited by Seyla Benhabib, 83–112. New York: Cambridge University Press, 2010.

Markell, Patchen. *Bound by Recognition*. Princeton, NJ: Princeton University Press, 2003.

Martínez, María Elena. *Genealogical Fictions: Limpieza de Sangre, Religion, and Gender in Colonial Mexico*. Stanford, CA: Stanford University Press, 2008.

Masri, Ahlam, and Tahrir Hamdi. "Where Is Palestine in Caryl Phillips's *The Nature of Blood*?" *International Journal of Arabic-English Studies* 18 (2018): 7–22.

Mastin, John. *The Chemistry, Properties, and Tests of Precious Stones*. New York: Spon and Chamberlain, 1911.

Masuzawa, Tomoko. *The Invention of World Religions: Or, How European Universalism Was Preserved in the Language of Pluralism*. Chicago: University of Chicago Press, 2005.

Mazower, Mark. *No Enchanted Palace: The End of Empire and the Ideological Origins of the United Nations*. Princeton, NJ: Princeton University Press, 2009.

Mead, Margaret, ed. *Cultural Patterns and Technical Change*. Paris: UNESCO, 1953.

Melamed, Jodi. *Represent and Destroy: Rationalizing Violence in the New Racial Capitalism*. Minneapolis: University of Minnesota Press, 2011.

Melas, Natalie. "Poetry's Circumstance and Racial Time: Aimé Césaire, 1935–1945." *The South Atlantic Quarterly* 115, no. 3 (July 2016): 469–93.

Memmi, Albert. *Racism*. Translated by Steve Martinot. Minneapolis: University of Minnesota Press, 2000.

Mennel, Barbara. "'Germany Is Full of Germans Now': Germanness in Ama Ata Aidoo's *Our Sister Killjoy* and Chantal Akerman's *Meetings with Anna*." In *Gender and Germanness: *Cultural Productions of Nation*, edited by Patricia Herminghouse and Magda Mueller, 235–47. Providence: Berghahn Books, 1997.

Merkel, Ian. "Brazilian Race Relations, French Social Scientists, and African Decolonization: A Transatlantic History of the Idea of Miscegenation." *Modern Intellectual History* 17, no. 3 (2020): 801–32.

Métraux, Alfred. "UNESCO and the Racial Problem." *International Social Science Bulletin* 2, no. 3 (1950): 384–90.

Miller, Ana. "The Silence of Palestinians in Caryl Phillips's *The Nature of Blood*." *Journal of Postcolonial Writing* 50, no. 5 (2014): 509–21.

Miller, Christopher. "Editing and Editorializing: The New Genetic *Cahier* of Aimé Césaire." *The South Atlantic Quarterly* 115, no. 3 (July 2016): 441–55.

Montagu, Ashley. *Man's Most Dangerous Myth: The Fallacy of Race*. 2nd ed. New York: Columbia University Press, 1945.

———. *Man's Most Dangerous Myth: The Fallacy of Race*. 6th ed. Walnut Creek, CA: Altamira, 1997.

———. *Statement on Race: An Extended Discussion in Plain Language of the UNESCO Statement by Experts on Race Problems*. New York: Schuman, 1951.

Moore-Gilbert, Bart. "Postcolonialism and 'the Figure of the Jew': Caryl Phillips and Zadie Smith." In *The Contemporary British Novel since 1980*, edited by J. Acheson et al., 106–16. London: Palgrave Macmillan, 2006.

Morland, Iain. "Gender, Genitals, and the Meaning of Being Human." In *Fuckologies: Critical Essays on John Money's Diagnostic Concepts*, edited by Lisa Downing, Iain Morland, and Nikki Sullivan, 69–98. Chicago: University of Chicago Press, 2015.

Morris-Reich, Amos. "Circumventions and Confrontations: Georg Simmel, Franz Boas and Arthur Ruppin and their Responses to Antisemitism." *Patterns of Prejudice* 44, no. 2 (2010): 195–215.

———. "Photography in Economies of Demonstration: The Idea of the Jews as a Mixed-Race People." *Jewish Social Studies* 20, no. 1 (Fall 2013): 150–83.

———. "Project, Method, and the Racial Characteristics of Jews: A Comparison of Franz Boas and Hans F. K. Günther." *Jewish Social Studies* 13, no. 1 (2006): 136–69.

———. *The Quest for Jewish Assimilation in Modern Social Science*. New York: Routledge, 2008.

Morsink, Johannes. *The Universal Declaration of Human Rights and the Holocaust: An Endangered Connection*. Washington, DC: Georgetown University Press, 2018.

Moses, A. Dirk. "Conceptual Blockages and Definitional Dilemmas in the 'Racial Century': Genocides of Indigenous Peoples and the Holocaust." *Patterns of Prejudice* 36, no. 4 (2002): 7–36.

———. "Dialectic of *Vergangenheitsbewältigung*." *The New Fascism Syllabus*, June 15, 2021. https://newfascismsyllabus.com/opinions/the-catechism-debate/dialectic-of-vergangenheitsbewaltigung/.

———. "Empire, Colony, Genocide: Keywords and the Philosophy of History." In *Empire, Colony, Genocide: Conquest, Occupation and Subaltern Resistance in World History*, edited by A. Dirk Moses, 3–54. New York: Berghahn, 2008.

———. "The German Catechism." *Geschichte der Gegenwart*, May 23, 2021. https://geschichtedergegenwart.ch/the-german-catechism.

Mosse, George. *Toward the Final Solution: A History of European Racism*. Madison: University of Wisconsin Press, 1985.

Moyn, Samuel. *A Holocaust Controversy: The Treblinka Affair in Postwar France*. Waltham, MA: Brandeis University Press, 2005.
———. *The Last Utopia: Human Rights in History*. Cambridge, MA: Belknap, 2010.
———. "Silence and the Shoah." *Times Literary Supplement*. August 7, 2013.
Mufti, Aamir. *Enlightenment in the Colony: The Jewish Question and the Crisis of Postcolonial Culture*. Princeton, NJ: Princeton University Press, 2007.
Müller-Wille, Staffan. "Claude Lévi-Strauss on Race, History and Genetics." *BioSocieties* 5, no. 3 (2010): 330–47.
Müller-Wille, Staffan, and Hans-Jörg Rheinberger. *A Cultural History of Heredity*. Chicago: University of Chicago Press, 2012.
Myrdal, Gunnar. *An American Dilemma: The Negro Problem and Modern Democracy*. New York: Routledge, 2017.
Nandy, Ashis. *The Intimate Enemy: Loss and Recovery of Self Under Colonialism*. New Delhi, NCR: Oxford University Press, 2009.
Nelson, Alondra. "The Factness of Diaspora: The Social Sources of Genetic Genealogy." In *Rites of Return: Diaspora Poetics and the Politics of Memory*, edited by Marianne Hirsch and Nancy K. Miller, 23–39. New York: Columbia University Press, 2011.
Nelson, Deborah. *Tough Enough: Arbus, Arendt, Didion, McCarthy, Sontag, Weil*. Chicago: University of Chicago Press, 2017.
Ngai, Sianne. *Ugly Feelings*. Cambridge, MA: Harvard University Press, 2005.
Nirenberg, David. *Communities of Violence: Persecution of Minorities in the Middle Ages*. Princeton, NJ: Princeton University Press, 1996.
Norton, Anne. "Heart of Darkness: Africa and African Americans in the Writings of Hannah Arendt." In *Feminist Interpretations of Hannah Arendt*, edited by Bonnie Honig, 247–61. University Park: Pennsylvania State University Press, 1995.
Novick, Peter. *The Holocaust in American Life*. Boston: Mariner Books, 2000.
Nyong'o, Tavia. *The Amalgamation Waltz: Race, Performance, and the Ruses of Memory*. Minneapolis: Minnesota University Press, 2009.
O'Byrne, Anne. *Natality and Finitude*. Bloomington, IN: Indiana University Press, 2010.
Olender, Maurice. *The Languages of Paradise: Race, Religion, and Philology in the Nineteenth Century*. Cambridge, MA: Harvard University Press, 1992.
Parikh, Crystal. *Writing Human Rights: The Political Imaginaries of Writers of Color*. Minneapolis: Minnesota University Press, 2017.
Patterson, Orlando. *Slavery and Social Death: A Comparative Study*. Cambridge, MA: Harvard University Press, 1982.
Pavone, Vincenzo. *From the Labyrinth of the World to the Paradise of the Heart: Science and Humanism in UNESCO's Approach to Globalization*. Lanham, MD: Lexington, 2008.
Perraton, Hilary. *International Students 1860–2010: Policy and Practice round the World*. New York: Palgrave Macmillan, 2020.
Phillips, Caryl. *Color Me English: Migration and Belonging before and after 9/11*. New York: The New Press, 2011.
———. *The European Tribe*. New York: Vintage, 2000.
———. *The Nature of Blood*. New York: Vintage, 1997.
Popescu, Monica. *At Penpoint: African Literatures, Postcolonial Studies, and the Cold War*. Durham, NC: Duke University Press, 2020.
Porter, Eric. *The Problem of the Future World: W. E. B. Du Bois and the Race Concept at Midcentury*. Durham, NC: Duke University Press, 2010.

Povinelli, Elizabeth A. *The Cunning of Recognition: Indigenous Alterities and the Making of Australian Multiculturalism*. Durham, NC: Duke University Press, 2002.

——. *The Empire of Love: Toward a Theory of Intimacy, Genealogy and Carnality*. Durham, NC: Duke University Press, 2006.

Prashad, Vijay. *The Darker Nations: A People's History of the Third World*. New York: The New Press, 2007.

Proctor, Robert N. "Three Roots of Human Recency: Molecular Anthropology, the Refigured Acheulean, and the UNESCO Response to Auschwitz." *Current Anthropology* 44, no. 2 (2003): 213–39.

Pullan, Brian S. *The Jews of Europe and the Inquisition of Venice, 1550–1670*. Totowa, NJ: Barnes and Noble Books, 1983.

Rabinbach, Anson. "The Jewish Question in the German Question." *New German Critique* 44 (Spring–Summer 1998): 159–92.

Ramos, Arthur. "The Question of Race and the Democratic World." *UNESCO Courier* 11, no. 10 (November 1949): 14.

——. "The Question of Race and the Democratic World." *International Social Science Bulletin* 1, nos. 3–4 (1949): 14.

Rasberry, Vaughn. "Our Totalitarian Critics: Desegregation, Decolonization, and the Cold War." In *Race and the Totalitarian Century: Geopolitics in the Black Literary Imagination*, 63–106. Cambridge, MA: Harvard University Press, 2016.

Ratskoff, Ben. "Splattering the Object: Césaire, Nazi Racism, and the Colonial." In *Caribbean Jewish Crossings: Literary History and Creative Practice*, edited by Sarah Phillips Casteel and Heidi Kaufman, 177–97. Charlottesville: University of Virginia Press, 2019.

Ray, Sangeeta. *Gayatri Chakravorty Spivak: In Other Words*. New York: Wiley-Blackwell, 2009.

Raz-Krakotzkin, Amnon. "Jewish Peoplehood, 'Jewish Politics,' and Political Responsibility: Arendt on Zionism and Partitions." *College Literature* 38, no. 1 (2011): 57–74.

Reardon, Jenny. "Decoding Race and Human Difference in a Genomic Age." *differences: A Journal of Feminist Cultural Studies* 15, no. 3 (Fall 2004): 38–65.

——. *Race to the Finish: Identity and Governance in an Age of Genomics*. Princeton, NJ: Princeton University Press, 2005.

Rooney, Caroline. "'Dangerous Knowledge' and the Poetics of Survival: A Reading of *Our Sister Killjoy* and *A Question of Power*." In *Motherlands: Black Women's Writing from Africa, the Caribbean and South Asia*, edited by Susheila Nasta, 99–126. New Brunswick, NJ: Rutgers University Press.

Rothberg, Michael. "Lived Multidirectionality: '*Historikerstreit* 2.0' and the Politics of Holocaust Memory." *Memory Studies* 15, no. 6 (2022): 1316–29.

——. *Multidirectional Memory: Remembering the Holocaust in the Age of Decolonization*. Stanford, CA: Stanford University Press, 2009.

——. "We Need to Re-Center the New *Historikerstreit*." *Die Zeit*, July 24, 2021, zeit.de/kultur/2021-07/dealing-with-the-holocaust-historikerstreit-controversy-genocide-english.

Rothberg, Michael, Debarati Sanyal, and Max Silverman, eds. "Nœuds de mémoire: Multidirectional Memory in Postwar French and Francophone Culture." *Yale French Studies*, 118–19 (2010).

Rothberg, Michael, and Yasemin Yildiz. "Memory Citizenship: Migrant Archives of Holocaust Remembrance in Contemporary Germany." *Parallax* 17, no. 4 (2010): 32–48.

Rousso, Henry. *The Vichy Syndrome: History and Memory in France since 1944*. Translated by Arthur Goldhammer. Cambridge, MA: Harvard University Press, 1994.

Rubin, Miri. *Gentile Tales: The Narrative Assault on Late Medieval Jews.* New Haven, CT: Yale University Press, 1999.
Said, Edward. *Culture and Imperialism.* New York: Vintage, 1993.
———. *Freud and the Non-European.* London: Verso Books, 2003.
———. "Zionism from the Standpoint of Its Victims." In *The Selected Works of Edward Said, 1966–2006,* edited by Moustafa Bayoumi and Andrew Rubin, 115–69. New York: Vintage, 2019.
Samantrai, Ranu. "Caught at the Confluence of History: Ama Ata Aidoo's Necessary Nationalism." *Research in African Literatures* 26, no. 2 (1995): 140–57.
Sanyal, Debarati. *Memory and Complicity: Migrations of Holocaust Remembrance.* New York: Fordham University Press, 2015.
Sartre, Jean-Paul. *Anti-Semite and Jew.* Translated by George J. Becker. New York: Schocken, 1976. First published as *Réflexions sur la Question Juive* by Éditions Morihien (Paris) in 1946.
Schuller, Kyla. *The Biopolitics of Feeling: Race, Sex, and Science in the Nineteenth Century.* Durham, NC: Duke University Press, 2018.
Schuller, Kyla, and Jules Gill-Peterson. "Introduction: Race, the State, and the Malleable Body." *Social Text* 38, no. 2 (2020): 1–17.
Sedgwick, Eve Kosofsky. *Touching Feeling: Affect, Pedagogy, Performativity.* Durham, NC: Duke University Press, 2003.
Segev, Tom. *The Seventh Million: The Israelis and the Holocaust.* Translated by Haim Watzman. New York: Henry Holt, 2000.
Selcer, Perrin. "Beyond the Cephalic Index: Negotiating Politics to Produce UNESCO's Scientific Statements on Race." *Current Anthropology* 53, no. S5 (April 2012): S173–84.
Sewell, James Patrick. *UNESCO and World Politics: Engaging in International Relations.* Princeton, NJ: Princeton University Press, 1975.
Sexton, Jared. *Amalgamation Schemes: Antiblackness and the Critique of Multiracialism.* Minneapolis: University of Minnesota Press, 2008.
———. "The Curtain of the Sky: An Introduction." *Critical Sociology* 36, no. 1 (2010): 11–24.
Shapiro, Harry L. *The Jewish People: A Biological History.* Paris: UNESCO, 1960.
Shapiro, James. *Shakespeare and the Jews.* New York: Columbia University Press, 1996.
Sheldon, Rebekah. *The Child to Come: Life after the Human Catastrophe.* Minneapolis: University of Minnesota Press, 2008.
Shih, Shu-Mei. "Comparative Racialization: An Introduction." *PMLA* 123, no. 5 (2008): 1347–62.
Shohat, Ella. "Post-Fanon and the Colonial: A Situational Diagnosis." In *Taboo Memories, Diasporic Voices,* 250–89. Durham, NC: Duke University Press, 2006.
Sicher, Efraim, and Linda Weinhouse. "The Color of Shylock: Caryl Phillips." In *Under Postcolonial Eyes: Figuring "the jew" in Contemporary British Writing,* 122–43. Lincoln: University of Nebraska Press, 2013.
Silverblatt, Irene. *Modern Inquisitions: Peru and the Colonial Origins of the Civilized World.* Durham, NC: Duke University Press, 2004.
Silverman, Max. *Palimpsestic Memory: The Holocaust and Colonialism in French and Francophone Fiction and Film.* New York: Berghahn, 2013.
Slaughter, Joseph R. "Hijacking Human Rights: Neoliberalism, the New Historiography, and the End of the Third World." *Human Rights Quarterly* 40, no. 4 (2018): 739.
———. *Human Rights, Inc.: The World Novel, Narrative Form, and International Law.* New York: Fordham University Press, 2007.

---. "World Literature as Property." *Alif: Journal of Comparative Poetics*, no. 34 (2014): 39–73.
Slavet, Eliza. *Racial Fever: Freud and the Jewish Question*. New York: Fordham, 2009.
Slobodian, Quinn. *Foreign Front: Third World Politics in Sixties West Germany*. Durham, NC: Duke University Press, 2012.
Sluga, Glenda. "UNESCO and the (One) World of Julian Huxley." *Journal of World History* 21, no. 3 (September 2010): 393–418.
Slymovics, Susan. *How To Accept German Reparations*. Philadelphia: University of Pennsylvania Press, 2014.
Sperling, Susan. "Ashley Montagu (1905–1999)." *American Anthropologist* 102, no. 3 (September 2000): 583–88.
---. "Ashley's Ghost: McCarthyism, Science, and Human Nature." In *Anthropology at the Dawn of the Cold War: The Influence of Foundations, McCarthyism and the CIA*, edited by Dustin M. Wax, 17–36. London: Pluto Press, 2008.
Spillers, Hortense J. "Mama's Baby, Papa's Maybe: An American Grammar Book." *Diacritics* 17, no. 2 (Summer 1987): 64–81.
Spivak, Gayatri Chakravorty. *A Critique of Postcolonial Reason: Toward a History of the Vanishing Present*. Cambridge, MA: Harvard University Press, 1999.
---. "Three Women's Texts and a Critique of Imperialism." *Critical Inquiry* 12, no. 1 (1985): 243–46.
Stam, Robert, and Ella Shohat. *Race in Translation: Culture Wars around the Postcolonial Atlantic*. New York: New York University Press, 2012.
Stepan, Nancy. *The Idea of Race in Science: Great Britain, 1800–1960*. London: Palgrave Macmillan, 1982.
Stocking, George W., Jr. "The Critique of Racial Formalism." In *Race, Culture, and Evolution: Essays in the History of Anthropology*, 161–94. New York: The Free Press, 1968.
---. "Franz Boas and the Culture Concept." In *Race, Culture, and Evolution: Essays in the History of Anthropology*. New York: The Free Press, 1968.
---. "Introduction: Thoughts Toward a History of the Interwar Years." In *American Anthropology, 1921–1945: Papers from the American Anthropologist*, edited by George W. Stocking, Jr., 44–54. Lincoln: University of Nebraska Press, 2002.
Stoler, Ann Laura. *Carnal Knowledge and Imperial Power: Race and the Intimate in Colonial Rule*. Berkeley: University of California Press, 2002.
---. *Duress: Imperial Durabilities in Our Time*. Durham, NC: Duke University Press, 2016.
Stone, Dan. "Defending the Plural: Hannah Arendt and Genocide Studies." *New Formations* 71 (2011): 46–57.
Stonebridge, Lyndsey. "Refugee Style: Hannah Arendt and the Perplexities of Rights." *Textual Practice* 25, no. 1 (2011): 71–85.
Stuelke, Rachel. *The Ruse of Repair: US Neoliberal Empire and the Turn from Critique*. Durham, NC: Duke University Press, 2021.
Taylor, Charles. "The Politics of Recognition," In *Multiculturalism: Examining the Politics of Recognition*, edited by Amy Gutmann. Princeton, NJ: Princeton University Press, 1992.
Teitel, Ruti G. *Humanity's Law*. New York: Oxford University Press, 2011.
Tent, James. *Mission on the Rhine: Reeducation and Denazification in American-Occupied Germany*. Chicago: University of Chicago Press, 1982.
Teraoka, Arlene. *East, West and Others: The Third World in Postwar German Literature*. Lincoln: University of Nebraska Press, 1996.

Thomas, Laurence Mordekhai. *Vessels of Evil: American Slavery and the Holocaust*. Philadelphia: Temple University Press, 1993.
Trachtenberg, Barry. "Why I Signed the Jerusalem Declaration on Antisemitism." *Jewish Currents*, March 26, 2021. https://jewishcurrents.org/why-i-signed-the-jerusalem-declaration-on-antisemitism.
Traverso, Enzo. "The Blindness of the Intellectuals: Historicizing Sartre's *Anti-Semite and Jew*." Translated by Stuart Liebman. *October* 87 (Winter 1999): 73–88.
Truman, Harry S. "Inaugural Address, Thursday, January 20, 1949." In *Inaugural Addresses of the Presidents of the United States: From George Washington 1789 to George Bush 1989*, 285–91. Washington, DC: United States Government Printing Office, 1989.
Tucker, Irene. *The Moment of Racial Sight: A History*. Chicago: University of Chicago Press, 2012.
UN Economic and Social Council. "Resolution 116 (VI) B, Report of the Second Session of the Commission on Human Rights, March 1-2, 1948." In *Resolutions Adopted by the Economic and Social Council during Its Sixth Session from 2 February to 11 March 1948*. Lake Success, NY: United Nations, 1948. E/777. https://undocs.org/en/E/777.
UN Economic and Social Council, Commission on Human Rights, Sub-commission on the Prevention of Discrimination and the Protection of Minorities, first session, November 24–December 6, 1947. *Report Submitted to the Commission on Human Rights, December 6, 1947*. E/CN.4/52. undocs.org/en/E/CN.4/52.
UNESCO. Constitution of the United Nations Educational, Scientific, and Cultural Organization. In *Basic Texts: 2018 Edition including Texts and Amendments Adopted by the General Conference at its 39th Session (Paris, 30 October–14 November 2017)*. Paris: UNESCO, 2018.
———. *General Conference—First Session, UNESCO House, Paris, November 20–December 10, 1946*. UNESCO/C/30. Paris: UNESCO, 1947.
———. *Introduction to UNESCO: A Summary of the Organisation's Activities during Its First Year—With Selected List of Documents*. Paris: UNESCO, 1947.
———. *Meeting of Experts on Race Problems—Summary Report of Six Meetings*. December 12–14, 1949. UNESCO/SS/Conf.1/SR.
———. *The Race Question in Modern Science*. Paris: UNESCO, 1956.
———. Statement on the Nature of Race and Race Differences. In *Four Statements on the Race Question*, 36–43. Paris: UNESCO, 1969.
———. Statement on Race. In *Four Statements on the Race Question*, 30–5. Paris: UNESCO, 1969.
———. Statement on Race and Racial Prejudice. In *Four Statements on the Race Question*, 50–6. Paris: UNESCO, 1969.
———. *The Book of Needs of Fifteen War-Devastated Countries in Education, Science and Culture*. Vol. 1. Paris: UNESCO, 1947.
United Nations. Charter of the United Nations and Statute of the International Court of Justice. San Francisco: UN, 1945.
United Nations, Office of the High Commissioner for Human Rights. Report of the Special Rapporteur on Contemporary Forms of Racism, Racial Discrimination, Xenophobia and Related Intolerance. October 7, 2022, A/77/512. https://documents-dds-ny.un.org/doc/UNDOC/GEN/N22/618/67/PDF/N2261867.pdf?OpenElement.
Vatter, Miguel. "Natality and Biopolitics in Hannah Arendt." *Revista de Ciencia Política* 26, no. 2 (2006): 137–59.
Viswanathan, Gauri. *Masks of Conquest: Literary Study and British Rule in India*. New York: Columbia University Press, 1989.

Visweswaran, Kamala. *Un/common Cultures: Racism and the Rearticulation of Cultural Difference*. Durham, NC: Duke University Press, 2010.

Vitalis, Robert. *White World Order, Black Power Politics: The Birth of American International Relations*. Ithaca, NY: Cornell University Press, 2017.

Vitkus, Daniel. *Turning Turk: English Theater and the Multicultural Mediterranean, 1570–1630*. New York: Palgrave, 2003.

Von Eschen, Penny M. *Race against Empire: Black Americans and Anticolonialism, 1937–1957*. Ithaca, NY: Cornell University Press, 1997.

Watson, Jini Kim. *Cold War Reckonings: Authoritarianism and the Genres of Decolonization*. New York: Fordham University Press, 2021.

Wieviorka, Annette. *The Era of the Witness*. Translated by Jared Stark. Ithaca, NY: Cornell University Press, 2006.

Wilder, Gary. *Freedom Time: Negritude, Decolonization, and the Future of the World*. Durham, NC: Duke University Press, 2015.

Wilderson, Frank B. *Red, White and Black: Cinema and the Structure of U.S. Antagonisms*. Durham, NC: Duke University Press, 2010.

Wilentz, Gay. "The Politics of Exile: Ama Ata Aidoo's *Our Sister Killjoy*." *Studies in 20th Century Literature* 15, no. 1 (1991): 159–73.

Winant, Howard. *The World Is a Ghetto: Race and Democracy since World War II*. New York: Basic Books, 2001.

Wright, Michelle M. *Physics of Blackness: Beyond the Middle Passage Epistemology*. Minneapolis: University of Minnesota Press, 2015.

Wynter, Sylvia. "The Ceremony Must Be Found: After Humanism." *boundary 2* 12, no. 3 (Spring–Autumn 1984): 19–70.

Young, Robert J. C. *Colonial Desire: Hybridity in Theory, Culture and Race*. London: Routledge, 1995.

Young-Bruehl, Elisabeth. *Hannah Arendt: For Love of the World*. New Haven, CT: Yale University Press, 2004.

Zierler, Wendy. "'My Holocaust Is Not Your Holocaust': 'Facing' Black and Jewish Experience in *The Pawnbreaker*, *Higher Ground*, and *The Nature of Blood*." *Holocaust and Genocide Studies* 18, no. 1 (Spring 2004): 46–67.

Zimmerer, Jürgen, and Michael Rothberg. "Enttabuisiert den Vergleich!." *Die Zeit*, April 4, 2021. zeit.de/2021/14/erinnerungskultur-gedenken-pluralisieren-holocaust-vergleich-globalisierung-geschichte.

Zollschan, Ignaz. "How to Combat Racial Philosophy." *Man* 43 (1943): 90.

———. "The Significance of Mixed Marriage." In *Jews and Race: Writings on Identity and Difference, 1880–1940*, ed. Mitchell B. Hart, 175–84. Waltham, MA: Brandeis University Press.

INDEX

Abu El-Haj, Nadia: on genetic history and culture, 124, 127–28; on 1950s population genetics studies, 34; on racial-cultural distinctions, 37. *See also* genetic population; genetics
Achiume, E. Tendayi: and the IHRA definition of antisemitism, 195. *See also* antisemitism
activism, 6, 12, 16, 229n3; of Boas, 9, 66, 73, 79; of Huxley, 45; of Montagu, 8; Palestinian, 40
adaptability, 18–19, 24, 80, 82, 98, 134. *See also* assimilation; plasticity
Adelman, Janet: on conversos, 226n89; on *The Merchant of Venice*, 119–20. *See also* conversion; *Merchant of Venice, The* (Shakespeare)
Adorno, Theodor W.: on coming to terms with the past, 179–80
Ahmed, Sara: on the killjoy, 240nn192–93. *See also Our Sister Killjoy* (Aidoo)
Aidoo, Ama Ata: and irony, 176–77, 181–82; on the killjoy, 144; on "knowledge gained since," 163; *Our Sister Killjoy*, 3, 39, 111, 141, 143–44, 170, 175–87, 238n141, 238n164, 239n179
Alba, Avril: on Holocaust memory and racism, 208n102. *See also* Holocaust, the
Alford, C. Fred: on reparative morality, 230n19. *See also* morality: reparative
alienation: and deracination, 93; and genocide, 68, 93–94; and the killjoy, 188; and race, 69, 86, 93
Angell, Robert: on UNESCO's 1950 statement, 56. *See also* UNESCO (United Nations Educational, Scientific and Cultural Organization)
Anidjar, Gil: on community/fellowship in *Othello* and *The Merchant of Venice*, 135; on Nazi racialization and detheologization of the Jew, 74; on Nazi treatment of Jew vs. Arab, 216n26. *See also Othello* (Shakespeare); *Merchant of Venice, The* (Shakespeare)

anthropology: and genetics, 127; and imperialism, 29; and (anti)racism, 1–2, 37, 137–38, 154–55
antiessentialism, 33–34
antisemitism, 5–6, 8–9, 64, 79, 85–87; anti-, 195; and anti-Blackness, 162–64; and the blood myth, 122; Black American, 113; and the castration complex / circumcision, 89–92; defining of, 194–95; Fanon on, 64, 86–88; Freud on, 89–91; and identity, 8–9; and imperialism, 31; and Islamophobia, 106; "modern," 105; periodization of, 32; as political weapon, 149; Sartre on, 85–87; and UNESCO's race project, 5, 32, 191–92, 208n102; right-wing, 40. *See also* blood libel; Holocaust, the
apartheid, 12, 53, 175–76, 186
Arendt, Hannah, 31; and the boomerang effect, 39, 140–41, 146–51, 225n78, 232n28, 232n37; and education, 51, 141, 144, 148, 150–51, 189; on Eichmann, 179; *The Human Condition*, 51, 212n35; on imperialism and race thinking, 118, 149; and irony, 147–48, 151, 233n46; and the Jewish pariah, 39, 144, 188–89; on natality/newness, 50–51, 70, 212n35; *The Origins of Totalitarianism*, 50, 140, 147–51, 189; racism of, 146, 149–50; and Zionism, 189. *See also* boomerang effect; natality; newness
Arnold, A. James: on Césaire's denunciation of racism, 13; on Césaire's *Discourse on Colonialism*, 147–48; on Césaire's style, 153. *See also* Césaire, Aimé
Asiatic Land Tenure and Indian Representation Act, 53, 200n32
assimilation: and Blackness, 71, 83–84; and conversion, 119; fatigue, 134; Jewish, 5, 9, 34, 73–76, 78–82, 92, 135; and plasticity, 9, 21–22, 26–27, 34, 81–82; political, 21, 78; and race, 16, 24, 82, 85, 133; as

resisted, 39, 126–27, 188–89, 240n186; vs. xenophobia, 109. *See also* adaptability; plasticity
autodidacticism, 111, 179–80. *See also* education/reeducation; *Our Sister Killjoy* (Aidoo)

Baer, Ben Conisbee, 140, 142, 240n186. *See also* soul-making
Baer, Elizabeth: on Aidoo's *Our Sister Killjoy*, 237n138. *See also Our Sister Killjoy* (Aidoo)
Bahri, Deepika: on hybridity, 204n66; on plasticity and colonialism, 22. *See also* plasticity
Baker, Lee D.: on Boas, 199n24. *See also* Boas, Franz
Baldwin, James: "Negroes Are Anti-Semitic Because They're Anti-White," 112–13, 133. *See also* antisemitism
Balibar, Etienne: on culture, 110; on "neo-racism," 101–2, 105. *See also* culture; racism
Bangham, Jenny: on blood transfusion during WWII, 226n102. *See also* blood
Banton, Michael: on UNESCO's 1967 statement on race, 222n26. *See also* UNESCO (United Nations Educational, Scientific and Cultural Organization)
Barkan, Elazar: on scientific racism, 210n8; on Zollschan, 1. *See also* Zollschan, Ignaz
Barker, Martin, 109–10; on the new racism, 109. *See also* racism
Bartels, Emily: on Moorishness, 134, 228n146, 228n153. *See also* Moorishness
Bauman, Zygmunt: on the Holocaust's modern character, 116. *See also* Holocaust, the
belonging: and "humanity law," 211n16; and race, 128–33; and suicide bombing, 134. *See also* assimilation
Benedict, Ruth, 8; on the horrors of racism, 10–11. *See also* racism
Bernstein, Michael André: on "backshadowing," 117, 120
Bernstein, Richard J.: on the conscious pariah, 189. *See also* Arendt, Hannah: and the Jewish pariah
betrayal, 129–36
Biale, David: on (Jewish and Christian) "blood communities," 123–24, 126, 226n109. *See also* blood
Birnbaum, Pierre: on Ginsberg, 8. *See also* Ginsberg, Morris
Black Skin, White Masks (Fanon), 3–4, 64–65, 68–69, 86–89, 95, 182–83, 215n8. *See also* Fanon, Frantz
Blackness: and assimilation, 71, 83–84; and the body, 71, 86–91, 183, 219n92; and collectivity, 88–89, 91, 93; and fixity, 10, 36–37, 63, 67–68, 70, 72–73, 85, 104, 112; indecipherability of, 185; ontology of, 65–66; and *Othello*, 228n146, 228n153 and plasticity, 24, 71, 204n73; as protection, 185–86
blood: and conversion, 118–20; and culture, 123–24, 226n109; vs. genetics, 121–23, 126; and identity, 121–25; and race, 105, 120–29, 226n109; and ritual, 123–25; segregation of, 122, 129, 226n102; "stained," 118
blood libel, 105, 114–16, 119–20, 124–25, 225n78. *See also* antisemitism; blood
Blum, Léon: on UNESCO, 46, 53. *See also* UNESCO (United Nations Educational, Scientific and Cultural Organization)
Boas, Franz, 1, 7–8, 66, 77, 199n24, 203n61, 204n77, 217n47, 217n50, 219n73; activism of, 66, 73, 79; "Are the Jews a Race?," 79; *Aryans and Non-Aryans*, 79; and assimilation, 9, 27, 76; on Blackness, 23–24, 73, 83–85, 218n72; *Changes in Bodily Form of Descendants of Immigrants*, 78–79; children in the work of, 20, 78, 203n64, 218n63; "Commencement Address at Atlanta University," 83–84; Jewishness of, 9, 76, 79; and Lévi-Strauss, 7; *The Mind of Primitive Man*, 82, 218n72; "The Problem of the American Negro," 23–24, 83; on race and culture, 209n116; on racial plasticity, 9–10, 20–26, 30, 34, 63, 68, 73, 78–85, 202n50, 217nn49–50, 218n63; on Zollschan, 33–34
Boel, Jens: on UNESCO and education, 237n129. *See also* UNESCO (United Nations Educational, Scientific and Cultural Organization)
Bonner, Christopher: on Fanon's "Racism and Culture" speech, 99. *See also* Fanon, Frantz
Bonnett, Alastair: on scholarly treatment of antiracism, 66
boomerang effect, 39, 99, 140–42, 146–59, 167, 231n26, 232nn28–29, 232n37, 235n91. *See also* Arendt, Hannah; Césaire, Aimé
Boyarin, Daniel, 89–92; on circumcision, 92; on Fanon's work, 89, 91; on Freud's view of the antisemite, 90; on Judaism, 74; on *Othello*'s Moorishness, 131. *See also* Jewishness
Boyarin, Jonathan, 135; on "Christendom," 113; on modernity (and colonization), 118
Brattain, Michelle: on UNESCO's race statements, 43. *See also* UNESCO (United Nations Educational, Scientific and Cultural Organization)
Brouillette, Sarah: on UNESCO and literary value, 29, 201n42. *See also* UNESCO

INDEX   263

(United Nations Educational, Scientific
   and Cultural Organization)
Brown, Jayna: on Blackness and plasticity,
   204n73. *See also* Blackness; plasticity
Burton, Jonathan, 133; on Othello's
   Moorishness, 131. *See also* Moorishness;
   Othello (Shakespeare)

Caillois, Roger, 176, 236n107; review of Lévi-
   Strauss's *Race and History*, 100, 142, 162–
   70, 191–92
Card, Claudia: on genocide and alienation, 94.
   See also alienation; genocide; social death
Castañeda, Claudia: on the malleability of
   children, 50. *See also* children; plasticity
Casteel, Sarah Phillips, 207n98; on Phillips's
   method, 223n54, 224n65. *See also* Phillips,
   Caryl
Cavalli-Sforza, Luigi Luca: on population
   genetics, 202n44. *See also* genetic
   population; genetics
Césaire, Aimé, 29, 31, 191–94, 205n88,
   234n66; *choc en retour*, 39, 99, 140–42,
   146–47, 151–57, 159, 167, 232n29,
   233n49; "Culture and Colonization," 157–
   63, 173; *Discourse on Colonialism*, 3–4, 13,
   99–100, 139–40, 151–57, 162–64, 192,
   232n29, 233n57; on Europe (as
   indefensible), 139, 176; and irony, 147–
   48, 152–53, 163; *Letter to Maurice Thorez*,
   164; on Lévi-Strauss's *Race and History*,
   142; *Resolutely Black: Conversations with
   Françoise Vergès*, 159–61; on UNESCO
   and repair, 158–62, 169, 191–92
Chen, Mel, 24
Cheng, Anne Anlin, 215n6
Cheyette, Bryan: on Fanon and the antithesis
   between Jews and Blacks, 86; on Jewish
   and postcolonial diaspora, 207n98. *See also*
   Fanon, Frantz
children: in Boas's work, 20, 78, 203n64,
   218n63; and (re)education, 44–45, 173–
   74; and plasticity, 22, 29, 44, 70, 78, 174,
   212n28; natives as, 52, 140; as savior, 49–
   50; in UNESCO's discourse, 49–50
choc en retour. *See* boomerang effect; Césaire,
   Aimé
circumcision, 89–92, 123. *See also* Jewishness
civilization: as genocidal idea, 154; and
   humanity, 52; as responsible for barbarism,
   48, 138, 152; reverse, 139–42
class consciousness: and racism, 23–24, 83. *See
   also* racism
cleavage, lines of, 83–84, 218n71
Clingman, Stephen: on Phillips's method,
   224n65. *See also* Phillips, Caryl
colonialism, 98, 137–89; continental (vs.
   overseas), 148; and culture, 157–58; and

dependency, 154, 161, 235n89; indirect
   rule, 141, 155–56, 158, 229n3; and
   inhumanity, 138–40, 153, 162; vs. law,
   149; and modernity, 118; and plasticity,
   22; and race, 12–13, 145, 169, 207n99;
   and racism, 52–56, 98; and social death,
   95; and solidarity, 157. *See also*
   Europeanization
Comas, Juan: and antiracism, 73; on the Jews as
   a mixed people, 76; on race and culture,
   96–98, 101, 104–5; and UNESCO's 1950
   Statement on Race, 41
common life, 58–59, 61. *See also* equality
common sense: and race, 39–40, 42–43, 67–70,
   77, 99, 102–3, 106–7, 215n9, 222n33; as
   refused, 188. *See also* epistemology
Conference of Allied Ministers of Education
   (CAME), 14, 201n40. *See also* education/
   reeducation
continuity, 48; cultural, 37, 68, 86–87, 91–95,
   99, 108, 125–27. *See also* fidelity, cultural/
   religious; Jewishness
conversion, 38; 226n89; and assimilation, 119;
   and blood, 118–20; and culture, 96–136;
   and educability, 119; figural (Jews into
   Christians), 113–14; forced, 120; freedom
   of, 131; and race-making, 118–19;
   resistance to, 105, 119–20; superficial,
   118, 130–31, 225n86
Cooper, Frederick: on colonial violence and
   human rights, 200n35. *See also* human
   rights
cultural death, 93–95. *See also* genocide; social
   death
cultural racism/prejudice, 37–38, 101, 103–5,
   108–9, 115, 119, 132–36, 209n116. *See
   also* culture; racism
cultural relativism, 100–101, 106–9, 164–65,
   187. *See also* culture
culture: vs. alienation, 94; vs. biology, 80; and
   brutality, 47; and clothing, 126, 186; and
   colonialism, 157–58; and conversion, 96–
   136; fluidity of, 96–97; and genetics, 123;
   vs. genetics, 17, 126–28; and mediation,
   107; and plasticity, 101, 119, 135–36;
   porosity of, 96; vs. race, 37–38, 60, 74–75,
   123; and race, 96–136, 209n116, 214n70,
   221n19; and repetition, 125–27

Dahlberg, Gunnar: and UNESCO's 1950
   Statement on Race, 41
Damrosch, David: on Judaism and Lévi-
   Strauss's *Tristes Tropiques*, 7, 197n14. *See
   also* Lévi-Strauss, Claude
Dawson, Ashley: on cultural racism in *The
   Nature of Blood*, 115. *See also* cultural
   racism/prejudice; *Nature of Blood, The*
   (Phillips)

Delas, Daniel: on Césaire's *Discourse on Colonialism*, 147–48, 163. *See also Discourse on Colonialism* (Césaire)
democracy: and race, 137–41, 229n2; as spiritual project, 14
denazification, 14, 201n40
deracination, 39, 174; and alienation, 93; Black, 93–95; fear of, 186–87
development, 234n67; compulsory, 143, 231n23; vs. decolonization, 156–59; and education, 3, 15, 17, 173–75, 178, 186, 231n23, 237n129; as reparations, 140–41; vs. reparations, 160–61, 177–78; and UNESCO, 3, 15, 17, 39, 54, 140–46, 148, 154–59, 167, 171, 173–75. *See also* equalization; repair
difference: and blood, 129; class, 113; and clothing, 112, 126; cultural, 100–101, 104, 119; epidermal, 36, 38, 72, 85, 110–14, 129, 132–33, 183, 209n114; Jewish, 5, 9–10, 27, 30, 34, 37, 73, 87–88, 91–92, 125–27, 192; and multiculturalism, 186–87; population-level, 62–63; racial, 16, 58, 183, 209n114; and recognition, 182; religious, 104–5; sexual, 209n114; and temporality, 62
Diop, Alioune: on culture, 99. *See also* culture
Discourse on Colonialism (Césaire), 3–4, 13, 99–100, 139–40, 151–57, 162–64, 192, 232n29, 233n57. *See also* Césaire, Aimé
disgust: at foreign bodies, 183
Dobzhansky, Theodosius: and population genetics, 16; and UNESCO's 1950 Statement on Race, 41
Du Bois, W. E. B., 231n26; *Appeal to the World*, 12, 36, 53; on Boas's influence, 83; on the UN and imperialism, 12
Dunn, L. C.: and population genetics, 16, 34; and UNESCO's 1950 statement on race, 41; and UNESCO's 1951 statement on race, 68–69; on racial common sense, 106–7, 222n33. *See also* UNESCO (United Nations Educational, Scientific and Cultural Organization)
Dunton, Chris: on Aidoo's *Our Sister Killjoy*, 239n179. *See also Our Sister Killjoy* (Aidoo)

educability, 42–49; colonial, 142–43; and conversion, 119; crisis of, 110–11; and cultural memory, 32; and cultural prejudice, 108; vs. equality (in the 1950 UNESCO statement), 36, 56–63; vs. equalization, 171–72; and plasticity, 21–26, 43–45, 51, 55–59, 82–83, 85, 174, 212n28; and race, 14–18, 63, 69, 194, 218n63; in UNESCO's discourse, 10, 17–18, 29, 35–36, 42–45, 52, 55–56, 82, 138,

171–75, 192, 212n28. *See also* education/reeducation
education/reeducation, 46–49, 109, 148, 178, 211n21; and anticolonialism, 151; as bound to fail, 23–24; and brutality, 47; and children, 44–45, 173–74; counterpedagogy, 162–70, 180; and development, 3, 15, 17, 173–75, 178, 186, 231n23, 237n129; and equalization, 170–77, 186; and exchange, 143–44, 174–76, 181, 186; fundamental, 172–73; and humanity, 140, 183; and ideology, 48–49; and imperialism, 15; and natality, 44–45, 50–52; and recognition, 182; and repair, 39, 47–48, 137–89; and speaking up, 187; as spiritual project, 14–15, 46, 54; and temporality, 163; weak education, 142, 175, 177–82. *See also* autodidacticism; educability; miseducation
Edwards, Brent Hayes: on Césaire's style, 152. *See also* Césaire, Aimé
Eng, David: on reparation and colonial morality, 161–62, 235n91. *See also* reparation
epistemology: and the midcentury racial crisis, 10; racial, 69. *See also* common sense
equality: vs. educability (in the 1950 UNESCO statement), 36, 56–63; and ethics, 58–59. *See also* common life; equalization; inequality
equalization, 54–55; and contingency, 55; and education, 170–77, 186. *See also* development; equality
Escobar, Arturo, 234n67; on the "invention of development," 156. *See also* development
ethnic group: vs. race, 9, 37, 60, 102, 221n22, 234n67. *See also* race
ethnography, 6–7, 165–66
eugenics, 24, 45, 83, 186, 203n61, 240n187
Europeanization, 138, 144–46, 158–59; of Europe, 145. *See also* colonialism
euthanasia, 166
Evans, Luther, 234n78; on (the limits of) development, 159, 167, 173–75, 178. *See also* development
evolutionary theory, 15, 60, 68; and imperial discourse, 55
exchange: student/cultural, 143–44, 174–76, 181, 186. *See also* education/reeducation

Fanon, Frantz, 29, 31, 63–95, 103, 185, 192–93, 201n36, 215n18; on antisemitism, 64, 86–88; appropriation of, 64–66; on Blackness, 24, 36–37, 69–70, 85–95, 104, 219n92; *Black Skin, White Masks*, 3–4, 64–65, 68–69, 86–89, 95, 182–83, 215n8; on cultural relativism, 100; on the Holocaust, 36–37, 65, 72, 85, 93; on Jewishness, 36–

37, 65, 67, 71–72, 85–95, 104–5, 219n92; on racial plasticity, 82, 192; on racism, 95, 97–99, 103–4, 134, 214n6; "Racism and Culture," 95, 97–103, 134, 221n15; and UNESCO's race project, 66; "West Indians and Africans," 88–89, 95; *The Wretched of the Earth*, 95

fidelity, cultural/religious, 38, 105, 119–20, 125–31, 133, 136. *See also* continuity

First Congress of Negro Writers and Artists, 97, 99–100, 103, 142, 157, 221nn14–15

Fishberg, Maurice: on Jewishness, 9, 77–78. *See also* Jewishness

Fisher, Jaimey: on the discourse of reeducation in postwar Germany, 14, 211n21. *See also* education/reeducation; miseducation

fixity: and Blackness, 10, 36–37, 63, 67–68, 70, 72–73, 85, 104, 112; and culture, 136; of race, 96; of racial classification, 67–68. *See also* Blackness

Fleetwood, Nicole: on "the Fanonian moment," 69. *See also* Fanon, Frantz

foreign aid: as instrument of domination, 151, 154

Foucault, Michel: on "mankind" vs. "the human species," 214n67

Frazier, E. Franklin: on racial prejudice, 56; and UNESCO's 1950 Statement on Race, 3, 6, 41. *See also* UNESCO (United Nations Educational, Scientific and Cultural Organization)

Freud, Sigmund, 89–92; on antisemitism, 89–91; death drive, 235n91; "Moses and Monotheism," 92; on reparation, 161. *See also* antisemitism; psychoanalysis

Füredi, Frank: on the shift from racial confidence to racial fear, 199n28

Gandhi, Leela: on anticolonialism, 139, 201n36

Gannett, Lisa: on genetic populations, 214n72. *See also* genetic population; genetics

Garcia, Jay: on Fanon's discussion of *Home of the Brave*, 215n8. *See also* Fanon, Frantz

Gates Jr., Henry Louis: on appropriations of Fanon, 65. *See also* Fanon, Frantz

gaze: genocidal, 237n138; molecular, 71, 127; white, 69–70, 183, 185. *See also* visual, the

Geller, Jay: on circumcision, 92. *See also* circumcision

genetic population, 214n72; and plasticity, 108; vs. race, 15–16, 34, 55, 60–61, 63, 67, 71, 84, 102, 127–28, 194, 202n44, 202n46, 213n46. *See also* genetics

genetics: vs. blood, 121–23, 126; and blood, 226n102; and culture, 123; vs. culture, 17, 126–28; and liberation, 62; and narrative, 227n127; and nationalism, 128; and plasticity, 19, 202n50; and race, 11, 15–16, 60, 105. *See also* genetic population

genocide: the Genocide Convention, 220n100; as natal alienation, 68, 93–94; vs. slavery, 94; as social death, 93–95. *See also* cultural death; Holocaust, the

Getachew, Adom, 12; on twentieth-century anticolonial nationalists, 204n77. *See also* nationalism

Gil-Riaño, Sebastián: on UNESCO's statements and development discourse, 16–17, 229n4; on UNESCO's statements and the ontology of race, 210n6. *See also* development; race; UNESCO (United Nations Educational, Scientific and Cultural Organization)

Gilbert, Shirli: on Holocaust memory and racism, 208n102. *See also* Holocaust, the

Gill-Peterson, Jules: on racial plasticity, 26. *See also* plasticity

Gilman, Sander: on the Jew for Fanon, 219n92. *See also* Fanon, Frantz; Jewishness

Gilroy, Paul: on antisemitism vs. other racisms, 207n98; on appreciation of racial differences, 183; on culture, 109–10; and Fanon, 65; on Jewish persecution (and race), 112; on representation in Black and Jewish writing, 207n97

Ginsberg, Morris, 6–8; on defining race, 56; and Jewish studies, 8; and UNESCO's 1950 Statement on Race, 6–7, 41, 57–58; on WWII, 198n19

Glick, Leonard B.: on Boas's study of racial form, 204n77, 217n50. *See also* Boas, Franz

Goldberg, David Theo: on relational analysis of racism, 206n94; on the silencing of race, 102, 111. *See also* race; racism; silence

Goldstein, Eric: on Jewish attachment to Semitic origins, 217n46. *See also* Semite

Goyal, Yogita: on arrested decolonization, 143; on Fanon's significance in *Our Sister Killjoy*, 239n168; on Phillips's *The Nature of Blood*, 224n66. *See also Nature of Blood, The* (Phillips); *Our Sister Killjoy* (Aidoo)

Gulick, Anne W.: on Césaire's *Cahier d'un retour au pays natal*, 205n88. *See also* Césaire, Aimé

Günther, Hans F. K.: Nazi race theories of, 76. *See also* racism

habilitation, 171

Haddon, A. C., 8; and antiracism, 73, 75; and the term "ethnic group," 221n22; on Jews, 34

Hall, Stuart: on race, 31. *See also* race

Hamdi, Tahrir: on Phillips's engagement with

Palestine, 135–36. *See also* Palestine; Phillips, Caryl
Haraway, Donna: on racial periodization, 210n6; on scientific authority, 61. *See also* science
Hart, Mitchell, 9; on "Diasporist" Jewish social scientific thought, 33, 76
Hayes, Jarrod: on Aidoo's *Our Sister Killjoy*, 239n179. *See also Our Sister Killjoy* (Aidoo)
Herskovits, Melville, 79
Hobhouse, L. T., 7
Holocaust, the, 36–37, 41–42, 93–94, 148, 206n07; and Black Germans, 184; as inevitable, 117; and memory, 30–32, 102–4, 110–11, 194–95, 206n97, 208nn101–2, 222n25; as modern, 116; as not without precedent, 30, 36, 65, 72, 93; and pedagogy, 103–4; and Phillips, 110, 223n67; silence regarding, 208n101, 220n99; as singular, 117; and UNESCO's race project, 5, 32, 73, 167, 191, 207n100. *See also* antisemitism; genocide
Howe, Irving: on death in concentration camps (and ideas of Jewish fidelity/fixity), 120. *See also* Holocaust, the; Jewishness
Huang, Michelle N.: on plasticity as "an Asian American 'racial form,'" 26–27. *See also* plasticity
Huggan, Graham: on Phillips's *The European Tribe*, 223n48. *See also* Phillips, Caryl
human rights: and colonial violence, 200n35; law, 28; and self-determination, 205n86; and the UN, 12, 33, 35–36, 41–42, 53, 56–57, 60–61, 137–38, 195, 207n100; Universal Declaration of Human Rights, 32, 137–38, 205n88
humanism, 4, 46, 53–54, 64, 99, 111, 128, 138–39, 144, 147, 154–55, 167, 172, 178, 186, 193, 201n42; new humanism, 35, 139, 161
Huxley, Julian, 8–9; and Blackness, 204n73; and antiracism, 73, 75; on development, 167; and the term "ethnic group," 221n22; on equalization and UNESCO's work, 54–55, 142, 170–74, 186, 240n187; on Jews, 34; on living in a revolution, 45–46; and population genetics, 16; and UNESCO's *Book of Needs*, 236n119; and UNESCO's 1950 Statement on Race, 41
Huyssen, Andreas: on transnational Holocaust memory, 206n97. *See also* Holocaust, the; memory
hybridity/hybridization, 22, 60, 204n66, 219n74; and the body, 204n66; and equalization, 186; as "redemption," 83–84. *See also* mixing
hypocrisy, 12–13, 53
hysteria, 116–17

identity: and antisemitism, 8–9; and blood, 121–25; and recognition, 239n166; and ritual/culture, 121–28
immigration: and cultural racism, 101; and kinship, 132; and plasticity/assimilation, 21–22, 78–82, 134, 204n77, 217n50
indirect rule, 141, 155–56, 158, 229n3. *See also* colonialism
inequality, 11, 34, 103–4, 145, 167–68, 176, 194; and contingency, 55, 171–72. *See also* equality
Intrator, Miriam: on UNESCO and reconstruction, 236n118, 237n120. *See also* UNESCO (United Nations Educational, Scientific and Cultural Organization)
irony, 53, 141; in the work of Aidoo, 176–77, 181–82; in the work of Arendt, 147–48, 151, 233n46; in the work of Caillois, 167; in the work of Césaire, 139, 147–48, 152–53, 163; in the work of Ramos, 141
Islamophobia, 38, 132, 134–36; and antisemitism, 106
isolation, cultural, 60, 62, 127–28, 130. *See also* culture
Israel, 33–34, 104, 115, 128–29, 135–36, 177, 189, 195, 228n159. *See also* Zionism

Jackson, Zakiyyah Iman: on plasticity in American chattel slavery, 24. *See also* plasticity; slavery
Jensen, Steven L. B.: on human rights, 205n86. *See also* human rights
Jewishness, 63–65, 71–72; and assimilation, 5, 9, 34, 73–76, 78–82, 92, 135; and blood, 123–24; and continuity, 37, 68, 86–87, 91–95; vs. Judaism, 74, 78; and memory, 10, 86–87, 92; particularism of, 32, 34, 37–38, 86–87, 105, 126, 130; and plasticity, 9–10, 26–27, 32–34, 36, 38, 63, 67–85, 87, 92, 105; and psychoanalysis, 86–87, 89–90; and specificity, 9, 27, 49, 68, 86, 88, 113, 164; as a race, 33, 88, 106, 192; as not a race, 9, 73–75, 77–80, 88–89, 91, 95, 219n92, 225n86; and whiteness, 26, 36–37, 65, 71–72, 77–80, 85, 90–91, 104–5, 110–14, 133, 217n46
Judaism: vs. Jewishness, 74, 78. *See also* Jewishness
Judeo-Christian, 113–14, 135–36
Julien, Eileen, 221nn14–15. *See also* First Congress of Negro Writers and Artists

Kabir, Humayun: on UNESCO and the defining of race, 57. *See also* race
Kaplan, Bernice A.: on Boas's inflence on anthropology, 217n49. *See also* Boas, Franz

INDEX

Kelley, Robin D. G., 231n26. *See also* boomerang effect
King, Richard: on Arendt's "boomerang effect," 232n28. *See also* Arendt, Hannah; boomerang effect
Klein, Melanie, 230n19; on reparation, 161. *See also* psychoanalysis; reparation
Klose, Fabian: on counterinsurgencies and human rights, 200n35. *See also* human rights

language: and race, 74–75, 102; and trust, 132–34
Lawson, Edward: on UNESCO and the defining of race, 56–57, 60–61. *See also* race
League of Nations: International Institute of Intellectual Cooperation, 2, 33; as a product of empire, 53
Leiris, Michel: on race and culture, 96–99, 101, 104. *See also* culture; race
Lentin, Alana, 215n9; on the making unspeakable of race, 102–3, 111. *See also* race; silence
Lévi-Strauss, Claude, 197n12; on culture and race, 100–101, 106–9, 127–28; on defining race, 60, 213n61; and Judaism, 7, 197n14, 198n15; *Race and History*, 100, 106, 142, 164–65, 191; on racial plasticity, 62; *Tristes Tropiques*, 7, 197n14; and UNESCO's 1950 Statement on Race, 3, 6–7, 41, 57, 59–60
Levinson, Natasha: on the paradox of natality, 50–51, 70, 212n38, 215n18. *See also* natality
Levy, Daniel: on transnational Holocaust memory, 206n97. *See also* Holocaust, the; memory
Lie, Trygve: on UNESCO's mission, 47–48. *See also* UNESCO (United Nations Educational, Scientific and Cultural Organization)
Lipphardt, Veronika, 202n45
literacy, 54–55, 171, 173, 201n42. *See also* education/reeducation
Loomba, Ania: on race and periodization, 221n6. *See also* race
Lowe, Lisa, 207n99
Loyer, Emmanuelle: on Lévi-Strauss, 197n12. *See also* Lévi-Strauss, Claude
Lupton, Julia Reinhard: on *Othello* and Blackness, 228n146. *See also* Blackness; *Othello* (Shakespeare)
Luxemburg, Rosa, 231n26

Macey, David: on Fanon, 201n36. *See also* Fanon, Frantz

Malabou, Catherine: on neuroplasticity, 19–20. *See also* plasticity
Mantena, Karuna: on Arendt's *The Origins of Totalitarianism*, 149–50; on the boomerang effect, 232n37. *See also* Arendt, Hannah
Markell, Patchen: on recognition and identity, 239n166. *See also* recognition
Martínez, María Elena: on the categories of mulatto and mestizo, 118. *See also* mixing
Masri, Ahlam: on Phillips's engagement with Palestine, 135–36. *See also* Palestine; Phillips, Caryl
materiality: and biology, 98; and plasticity, 20; and racism, 209n114
Mazower, Mark, 200n32; on internationalism and imperial thought, 53
Mbembe, Achille, 195
melancholy: and Europeanization, 138, 155, 164–65; and misrecognition, 185. *See also* Europeanization
Memmi, Albert: on colonialism and racial taxonomy, 24–25; on racism, 209n114. *See also* race; racism
memory: and the body, 92; cultural, 32; forgetfulness, 179; and the Holocaust, 30–32, 102–4, 110–11, 194–95, 206n97, 208nn101–2, 222n25; and Jewishness, 10, 86–87, 92; "multidirectional" (Rothberg), 31
Mennel, Barbara: on Aidoo's *Our Sister Killjoy*, 238n141. *See also Our Sister Killjoy* (Aidoo)
Merchant of Venice, The (Shakespeare), 113, 119–20, 226n89. *See also* Phillips, Caryl
metaphor: biology as, 24–35, 209n114; blood as, 122–24, 129; the Holocaust as, 206n97
Métraux, Alfred, 33, 213n45; and Lévi-Strauss, 7, 198n15; on UNESCO's Statement on Race, 33
Miller, Ana: on Phillips's engagement with Palestine, 135–36, 228n159. *See also* Palestine; Phillips, Caryl
miseducation, 18, 35, 48–49, 115–16, 171, 182–87; avoiding, 57; of Nazis, 48, 211n21. *See also* education/reeducation
mixing: racial, 11, 24, 71, 73, 75–84, 218n72, 229n2; as corrective/solution, 24, 82–83, 229n2. *See also* hybridity/hybridization
Montagu, Ashley: and antiracism, 73; on blood and race, 121–24, 126–27, 129; on Jewish heterogeneity, 80; and Jewish identity, 8–9; on the importance of words, 196; *Man's Most Dangerous Myth: The Fallacy of Race*, 8–9, 73, 121–23; and UNESCO's 1950 Statement on Race, 3, 6–9, 32, 41–42, 169, 191
Moore-Gilbert, Bart: on Phillips's engagement with Palestine, 135–36, 228n159; on

Phillips's contrapuntal practice, 224n65. *See also* Palestine; Phillips, Caryl
Moorishness, 131–32, 134, 228n146, 228n153. *See also* Blackness; *Othello* (Shakespeare)
morality: colonial, 161–62, 168; and recognition, 182, 239n171; reparative, 141–42, 160–61, 163, 230n19; and science, 166–69; and the technical, 146
Morland, Iain: on gender plasticity, 212n28. *See also* plasticity
Morris-Reich, Amos: on Boas's refutation of antisemitism, 79; on the origin of the Jews, 75–76. *See also* antisemitism; Boas, Franz; Jewishness
Moses, A. Dirk: on the boomerang effect, 231n26; on the term "postcolonialism," 195. *See also* boomerang effect
Moyn, Samuel: on the origins of the UDHR, 207n100; on silence and the Holocaust, 208n101. *See also* Holocaust, the; United Nations: and human rights
Mufti, Aamir: on the figure of the minority, 35, 207n98
Müller, F. Max: on "Aryans," 75
Müller-Wille, Staffan: on heredity, 123; on Lévi-Strauss and cultural/genetic diversity, 213n61
multiculturalism, 111, 134–35; and difference, 186–87; and human rights law, 28
Myrdal, Alva: and UNESCO, 200n33, 213n45. *See also* UNESCO (United Nations Educational, Scientific and Cultural Organization)
Myrdal, Gunnar: and UNESCO's 1950 Statement on Race, 41, 200n33. *See also* UNESCO (United Nations Educational, Scientific and Cultural Organization)

NAACP: *Appeal to the World*, 12, 53, 53. *See also* Du Bois, W. E. B.
natality: for the Black subject, 69–70; and education, 44–45, 50–52; and the figure of the child, 44, 49; paradox of, 50–51, 70, 212n38, 215n18; and plasticity, 49–52, 70; and temporality, 70, 212n38. *See also* newness
nationalism: anticolonial, 204n83; and blood, 226n109; among the colonized, 156; and genetics, 128; Jewish, 33; methodological, 28; vigorous, 172
Nature of Blood, The (Phillips), 3, 38, 104–5, 114–36, 224n66, 225n78. *See also* Phillips, Caryl
Nelson, Alondra: on ancestry testing and narrative, 227n127. *See also* genetics
Nelson, Deborah: on Arendt's irony, 233n46. *See also* Arendt, Hannah
newness, 46–49, 69–70, 212n35; New Christians, 118, 225n86; and racism, 98, 101–2, 105. *See also* natality
Ngai, Sianne: on ideological communication and tone, 147
Nirenberg, David: on dubious practices of certain historians, 116, 224n68
Nyong'o, Tavia: on racial mixing and hybridity, 84. *See also* hybridity/hybridization; mixing

Olender, Maurice: on the use of the terms "Aryan" and "Semite," 75. *See also* Semite
Othello (Shakespeare): as evoked in Phillips's *The Nature of Blood*, 105–6, 114, 119, 129–36, 228n146. *See also* *Nature of Blood, The* (Phillips); Phillips, Caryl
Our Sister Killjoy (Aidoo), 3, 39, 111, 141, 143–44, 170, 175–87, 238n141, 238n164, 239n179. *See also* Aidoo, Ama Ata

Palestine, 32–34, 40, 195; absence of (in Phillips's writing), 106, 135–36, 228n159. *See also* Zionism
passing, racial, 112, 126. *See also* race
Patterson, Orlando: on natal alienation, 93. *See also* social death
Perraton, Hilary: on student exchange, 175. *See also* exchange: student/cultural
Philcox, Richard, 91
Phillips, Caryl, 103, 224n65, 228n159; "Color Me English," 132–34; *The European Tribe*, 104, 110–14, 119, 132–35, 223nn47–48; on Halkin's *Across the Sabbath River*, 129; *The Higher Ground*, 114; *The Nature of Blood*, 3, 38, 104–5, 114–36, 224n66, 225n78; and Palestine, 106, 135–36, 228n159
plasticity: and agency, 19; and antiracism, 22, 204n66; and assimilation, 9, 21–22, 26–27, 34, 81–82; and biopolitics, 4, 18, 22, 26, 45, 54–55, 62; and Blackness, 24, 71, 204n73; and children, 22, 29, 44, 70, 78, 174, 212n28; and colonialism, 22; and culture, 101, 119, 135–36; and educability, 1–26, 43–45, 51, 55–59, 82–83, 85, 174, 212n28; and gender, 212n28; and genetics, 19, 202n50; and inclusion, 21; and Jewishness, 9–10, 26–27, 32–34, 36, 38, 63, 67–85, 87, 92, 105; and materiality, 20; mental, 82; and natality, 49–52, 70; neuroplasticity, 19–20; periodization of, 114–20; of plasticity, 25, 81; of populations, 15–16; of race, 4, 9–10, 15–27, 35–38, 43–44, 61–63, 67–85, 96, 98, 101, 108, 135–36, 192, 194, 202n50, 217nn49–50, 218n63; of racism, 23–24, 70, 98; of religion, 135; and repair, 19–20; and the social, 19–21; and temporality,

67–69; as threat, 33; and UNESCO's discourse 9, 15, 16–18, 25–26, 67–71, 80–81, 192; universality of, 10, 25, 30; and whiteness, 26. *See also* adaptability; assimilation

Popescu, Monica: on Césaire's *Discourse on Colonialism*, 233n57. *See also Discourse on Colonialism* (Césaire)

population genetics. *See* genetic population

Porter, Eric: on "the first post-racial moment," 25

Povinelli, Elizabeth: on the "autological subject," 130–31; on recognition, 239n171. *See also* recognition

Powell, Enoch, 103, 109, 111. *See also* racism

Proctor, Robert: on human recency, 214n68

psychoanalysis: and Jewishness, 86–87, 89–90; and reparation, 161–62, 235n91. *See also* Jewishness; reparation

Pullan, Brian: on the Venetian Inquisition and conversos, 226n89. *See also* conversion

purity: cultural, 99; racial, 76–77, 218n72; religious, 104

Rabinbach, Anson: on German reparations, 177–78. *See also* reparation

race: and belonging, 128–33; and blood, 105, 120–29, 226n109; and colonialism, 12–13, 145, 169, 207n99; and common sense, 39–40, 42–43, 67–70, 77, 99, 102–3, 106–7, 215n9, 222n33; and conversion, 118–19; and culture, 96–136, 209n116, 214n70, 221n19; vs. culture, 37–38, 60, 74–75, 123; defining of, 4–6, 11–15, 31, 41–43, 56–63, 67, 73–74, 102, 213n61; and democracy, 137–41, 229n2; and educability, 14–18, 63, 69, 194, 218n63; and emotion, 121; vs. ethnic group, 9, 37, 60, 102, 221n22, 234n67; vs. genetic population, 15–16, 34, 55, 60–61, 63, 67, 71, 84, 102, 127–28, 194, 202n44, 202n46, 213n46; and genetics, 11, 15–16, 60, 105; and international relations, 199n28; and knowledge production, 38, 42–43, 69; and language, 74–75, 102; meaning of, 207n99; meaninglessness of, 61; mixing, 11, 24, 71, 73, 75–84, 218n72, 229n2; and modernity, 97, 117–18; and passing, 112, 126; periodization of, 29–30, 38, 42, 97–98, 105, 127, 221n6; and plasticity, 9–10, 15–27, 35–38, 43–44, 61–63, 67–85, 96, 98, 101, 108, 135–36, 192, 194, 202n50, 217nn49–50, 218n63; and politics, 11–13, 42, 44, 57, 61–62; principle (and Asians), 149–50; and purity, 76–77, 218n72; vs. religion, 97; science, 1–3, 11, 16, 41–43, 45, 52–54, 76, 127, 186, 202n44; silencing of, 102–4, 110–11; taxonomy of, 11, 25, 63, 71, 77–78, 85; and the visual, 69–72, 95, 103, 112, 126. *See also* racial residuum; racism

racial residuum, 37, 63–95, 110–14. *See also* race; racism

racism: and anthropology, 1–2, 37, 137–38, 154–55; and anti-Blackness (vs. white supremacy), 93, 214n6; and class consciousness, 23–24, 83; and colonialism, 52–56, 98; cultural, 37–38, 101, 103–5, 108–9, 115, 119, 132–36, 209n116; defining, 209n114, 222n26; Fanon on, 95, 97–99, 103–4, 134, 214n6; inherited, 51–52; and materiality, 209n114; "new," 101–2, 105, 109; and plasticity, 23–24, 70, 98; and science, 1–3, 8, 16, 72–73, 75, 166, 210n8; as technique, 144–46; and temporality, 98. *See also* race; racial residuum

Radhakrishnan, Sir Sarvepalli: on the UNESCO's mission, 46, 49. *See also* UNESCO (United Nations Educational, Scientific and Cultural Organization)

Ramos, Arthur, 56, 229n4; on the boomerang effect, 154; on race and the democratic world, 137–41, 143–48, 150, 153–57, 159, 164–67, 172, 229n2. *See also* boomerang effect; repair

Reardon, Jenny: on UNESCO's statements on race, 210n4. *See also* UNESCO (United Nations Educational, Scientific and Cultural Organization)

recognition: and education, 182; and identity, 239n166; and morality of, 182, 239n171; misrecognition, 69–70, 182–87

Red Summer, 23

relativism: cultural, 100–101, 106–9, 164–65, 187; moral, 152

repair: and (re)education, 39, 47–48, 137–89; and plasticity, 19–20; racial, 29; resisting, 157–62; and temporality, 49–50. *See also* reparation

reparation, 138, 140–41, 144, 160–63, 168, 170, 176–78, 182, 184, 187, 235n91; vs. development, 160–61, 177–78. *See also* repair

repetition: anaphoric (in Césaire), 152–53; of colonial relations, 141, 144; of the past, 50–51, 150–51; and ritual, 125–27; and safety/happiness, 126

return: in Aidoo's *Our Sister Killjoy*, 177, 181–82, 185–87; as rebound, 144–57. *See also Our Sister Killjoy* (Aidoo)

revision: of Arendt's *The Origins of Totalitarianism*, 147–48; of Césaire's *Discourse on Colonialism*, 3, 147–48, 163; of educational materials, 175; of

UNESCO's 1950 Statement on Race, 3, 8–9, 68, 16–17, 34, 42, 44, 68–69, 84, 96, 103–4, 193, 208n102, 222n33
Rheinberger, Hans-Jörg: on heredity, 123
Rooney, Caroline on Aidoo's *Our Sister Killjoy*, 238n164. *See also Our Sister Killjoy* (Aidoo)
Rosenberg, Alfred: and the weaponization of the blood myth, 122. *See also* blood
Rothberg, Michael: on Arendt and Césaire, 147, 232n28; on Césaire's *Discourse on Colonialism*, 147, 154, 163–64, 167, 233n49; on contemporary German memory debates, 206n95, 241n4; on Holocaust memory and migration, 222n25; on multidirectional memory, 30–31; on Phillips's work, 120, 135, 224n65. *See also* Arendt, Hannah; Césaire, Aimé; Holocaust, the; memory; Phillips, Caryl

Said, Edward: on contrapuntal reading, 5, 224n65; and Palestine, 32, 208n103
Sartre, Jean-Paul, 66, 93, 235n91; on antisemitism, 85–87, 220n99; *Black Orpheus*, 72; *Reflections on the Jewish Question*, 65, 72
Schuller, Kyla: on racial plasticity, 26. *See also* plasticity
science: and authority, 61, 75; and brutality, 47; race, 1–3, 11, 16, 41–43, 45, 52–54, 76, 127, 186, 202n44; and (anti)racism, 1–3, 8, 16, 72–73, 75, 166, 210n8. *See also* scientific method
scientific method, 164–65. *See also* science
Sedgwick, Eve Kosofsky: on blushing/shame, 184–85. *See also* shame
self-determination, 5, 12, 28, 195, 205n86; and creative power, 157–58; vs. sovereignty, 234n66
self-reckoning: of Europe, 138–39, 145–46, 154, 164–66
Semite, 75, 77, 217n46. *See also* Jewishness
Sexton, Jared, 83; on Fanon, 214n6. *See also* Fanon, Frantz
shame: and color, 184–85; at feeling disgust, 183; and gender, 184–85; and misrecognition, 183–84; political, 12–13; and progress, 139; racial, 39, 182–87; and resistance, 144
Shapiro, Harry L.: on the Jews as a mixed people, 76–77, 80. *See also* Jewishness; mixing
Shapiro, James: on Jewishness in early modern England, 225n86. *See also* Jewishness
Sheldon, Rebekah: on the post-catastrophic logic of the child who saves, 49. *See also* children
Sicher, Efraim: on Othello's Moorishness in Phillips's *The Nature of Blood*, 228n146. *See also Nature of Blood, The* (Phillips); *Othello* (Shakespeare)
silence: as critique, 181, 187; myth of, 32; regarding the Holocaust, 208n101, 220n99; regarding Palestine (for Phillips), 106, 135–36, 228n159; regarding race, 102–4, 110–11
Silverblatt, Irene, 135; on imperialism and race thinking, 118–20, 225n81
Slaughter, Joseph: on "compulsory development," 143, 231n23; on human rights law, 28; on the synecdochal logic of genocide, 93, 220n100; on UNESCO and intellectual property law, 205n90. *See also* development; genocide
slavery, 31, 185–86; vs. genocide, 94; and natal alienation, 93; and plasticity, 24
Slavet, Eliza: on Freud's view of the antisemite, 90. *See also* antisemitism; Freud, Sigmund
Smuts, Jan: "twisted contradiction" of (Du Bois), 12
social death, 93–95. *See also* Card, Claudia; cultural death; genocide; Patterson, Orlando
solidarity, 18, 39, 46, 144, 151, 175; between Blacks and Jews, 64–66, 83; limits of, 31; Palestinian, 40; political, 195; questionable, 188; vertical/horizontal, 157
soul-making, 39; and imperialism, 139–42, 144, 176; and (re)education, 15, 55, 142, 144, 187
specificity: Jewish, 9, 27, 49, 68, 86, 88, 113, 164; of the Jewish genocide, 169, 191, 207n100. *See also* Jewishness
Sperling, Susan: on Montagu and Jewish identity, 8. *See also* Montagu, Ashley
Spillers, Hortense: on body vs. flesh, 91. *See also* Blackness
Spivak, Gayatri Chakravorty, 19; on soul-making, 15, 52, 139–40. *See also* soul-making
sterilization, 86, 88–89, 91
Stocking, George: on applied anthropology in the US, 229n3; on Boas, 203n61, 203n64, 209n116. *See also* anthropology; Boas, Franz
Stoler, Ann Laura: on genres of rule, 230n22
Stonebridge, Lyndsey: on Arendt's irony, 151, 233n46. *See also* Arendt, Hannah
Sznaider, Natan: on transnational Holocaust memory, 206n97. *See also* Holocaust, the; memory

Taylor, Charles: on the politics of recognition, 182–83, 186–87. *See also* recognition
Teitel, Ruti: on "humanity law," 211n16
temporality: and difference, 62; and education, 163; and natality, 70, 212n38; and

plasticity, 67–69; and racism, 98; and repair, 49–50; and repetition, 50–51, 150–51; and the work of Arendt and Césaire, 147–48
Tent, James: on American reeducation efforts in Germany, 14. *See also* education/reeducation
Thomas, Laurence Mordekhai: on slavery vs. genocide, 94. *See also* genocide; slavery
tolerance, 229n2; and distance, 109
Traverso, Enzo: on Sartre's silence regarding the Holocaust, 220n99. *See also* Holocaust, the; Sartre, Jean-Paul
Truman, Harry: and the development era, 156–57. *See also* development
truth: as corrective, 11; and narrative, 227n127
Tucker, Irene: on "the moment of racial sight," 69. *See also* race; visual, the

UNESCO (United Nations Educational, Scientific and Cultural Organization), 2–6, 32, 96–97, 101, 137–96, 197n5, 208n102, 213n45, 229n2, 230n19; *Book of Needs*, 236n119; and (anti)colonialism, 27, 52–56; and educability, 10, 17–18, 29, 35–36, 42–45, 52, 55–56, 82, 138, 171–75, 192, 212n28; and (re)education, 2–4, 14–18, 42–47, 50–63, 142–44, 169, 172–74, 212n28, 237n129; and humanism, 46, 53, 155, 201n42; and intellectual property law, 205n90; and Jewish plasticity, 33, 85; and literary value, 29; mission of, 11, 14, 46–47, 49–50, 170–74, 236n118; and plasticity, 9, 15, 16–18, 25–26, 67–71, 80–81, 192; The Race Question in Modern Science (book series), 96, 100, 106–7; 1950 Statement on Race, 2–12, 15–18, 25–26, 33–36, 41–45, 53, 55–63, 67–68, 70–75, 80–81, 84, 96, 102–3, 137, 162, 167–69, 191, 193–94, 208n102, 210n4, 222n26, 229n4; 1951 Statement on the Nature of Race and Race Differences, 3, 8–9, 16–17, 34, 42, 44, 68–69, 84, 96, 103, 193, 208n102, 222n33; 1967 Statement on Race and Racial Prejudice, 103–4, 222n26. *See also* United Nations
United Nations: and (anti)colonialism, 12–13, 28–29, 45, 52–56, 138–98, 155–56, 234n63; and human rights, 12, 33, 35–36, 41–42, 53, 56–57, 60–61, 137–38, 195, 207n100; and Palestine, 33. *See also* UNESCO (United Nations Educational, Scientific and Cultural Organization)
universality: of antiracism (as goal for UNESCO), 6, 70–71; of blood, 122; Christian, 122, 126; Marxist, 164; of plasticity, 10, 25, 30

Virchow, Rudolf: and the study of children, 203n64, 218n63. *See also* Boas, Franz
visual, the: and race; 69–72, 95, 103, 112, 126; and self-loathing, 90. *See also* gaze
Visweswaran, Kamala, 109; on the Boasian race concept 209n116; on race and culture, 221n19. *See also* Boas, Franz; culture; race
Vitalis, Robert: on race and international relations, 199n28. *See also* race
Vitkus, Daniel: on the term "Moor," 131. *See also* Moorishness
von Luschan, Felix: on the origin of the Jews, 76. *See also* Jewishness

Watson, Jini Kim: on Cold War decolonization, 230n22
weak: education, 142, 175, 177–82; ethnicity, 26–27
Weinhouse, Linda: on Othello's Moorishness in Phillips's *The Nature of Blood*, 228n146. *See also* Moorishness; *Nature of Blood, The* (Phillips)
Weininger, Otto, 90
Weltfish, Gene: on the horrors of racism, 10–11. *See also* racism
White, Leslie: on Western Values, 166
Wiedergutmachung, 177, 182. *See also* reparation
Wilder, Gary: on the postwar history of decolonization, 27–28; on self-determination vs. sovereignty, 234n66
Wilderson, Frank: on Fanon, 93, 214n6. *See also* Fanon, Frantz
Wilentz, Gay: on Aidoo's *Our Sister Killjoy*, 239n179. *See also Our Sister Killjoy* (Aidoo)
Winant, Howard, 205n93
Wright, Michelle M.: on Aidoo's *Our Sister Killjoy*, 239n179. *See also Our Sister Killjoy* (Aidoo)
Wynter, Sylvia: on race, 209n114

Yildiz, Yasemin: on Holocaust memory and migration, 222n25. *See also* Holocaust, the; memory
Young, Robert J. C.: on hybridity, 204n66. *See also* hybridity/hybridization

Zimmerer, Jürgen: on contemporary German memory debates, 206n95. *See also* memory
Zionism, 32–33, 135–36, 189, 195. *See also* Israel; Palestine
Zollschan, Ignaz: vs. Boas, 33–34; on the combating of racial philosophy, 1–2; and Zionism, 33

Stanford Studies in
COMPARATIVE RACE AND ETHNICITY

Published in collaboration with the Center for Comparative Studies in Race and Ethnicity, Stanford University

Giving Form to an Asian and Latinx America
Long Le-Khac
2020

Arab Routes: Pathways to Syrian California
Sarah M. A. Gualtieri
2019

South Central Is Home: Race and the Power of Community Investment in Los Angeles
Abigail Rosas
2019

The Border and the Line: Race, Literature, and Los Angeles
Dean J. Franco
2019

Black Power and Palestine: Transnational Countries of Color
Michael R. Fischbach
2018

Race and Upward Mobility: Seeking, Gatekeeping, and Other Class Strategies in Postwar America
Elda María Román
2017

The Emotional Politics of Racism: How Feelings Trump Facts in an Era of Colorblindness
Paula Ioanide
2015

Beneath the Surface of White Supremacy: Denaturalizing U.S. Racisms Past and Present
Moon-Kie Jung
2015

Race on the Move: Brazilian Migrants and the Global Reconstruction of Race
Tiffany D. Joseph
2015

The Ethnic Project: Transforming Racial Fiction into Racial Factions
Vilna Bashi Treitler
2013

On Making Sense: Queer Race Narratives of Intelligibility
Ernesto Javier Martínez
2012